# THE HARMONY GUIDE TO
# CROCHETING

# THE HARMONY GUIDE TO

# CROCHETING

## *Techniques and Stitches*

### Edited by Debra Mountford

Lyric Books Limited

Originally published in two separate volumes as:
The Harmony Guide to Crochet Stitches and
The Harmony Guide to 100's More Crochet Stitches

ISBN 0 7111 0034 9

Printed in Spain

# CONTENTS

# Introduction

## About Crochet

Traditionally crochet was worked almost exclusively in very fine cotton yarn to create or embellish household items such as curtains, table cloths or place mats. Crochet was often added as decoration or trimming on collars and fine lawn handkerchiefs. The frill on the front of a man's shirt was often crochet work.

With the increase in the availability of yarn in a wide variety of textures and colours we are no longer limited to just these articles when we consider ways to use the craft of crochet. The samples in this book were worked in a fine mercerised cotton, but may take on a totally different appearance if different yarns are used. The lacier stitches probably look their best in these smooth threads, but some of the all-over stitches and many of the Tunisian stitches can be more interesting when worked in tweedy or textured yarns.

## Equipment

### Crochet Hooks

Crochet hooks are usually made from steel, aluminium or plastic in a range of sizes according to their diameter. As each crochet stitch is worked separately until only one loop remains on the hook, space is not needed to hold stitches and the hooks are made to a standard convenient length.

## Holding the Hook and Yarn

There are no hard and fast rules as to the best way to hold the hook and yarn. The diagrams below show just one method, but choose whichever way you find the most comfortable.

Due to the restrictions of space it is not possible to show diagrams for both right and left handed people. Left handers may find it easier to trace the diagrams and then turn the tracing paper over, thus reversing the image, alternatively reflect the diagrams in a mirror. Read left for right and right for left where applicable.

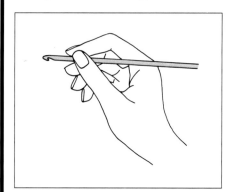

The hook is held in the right hand as if holding a pencil.

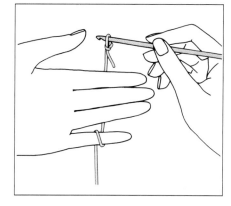

To maintain the slight tension in the yarn necessary for easy, even working, it can help to arrange the yarn around the fingers of the left hand in this way.

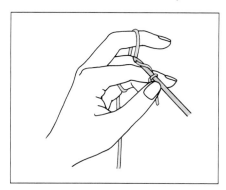

The left hand holds the work and at the same time controls the yarn supply. The left hand middle finger is used to manipulate the yarn, while the index finger and thumb hold on to the work.

## To Start

Almost all crochet begins with a base or starting chain, which is a series of chain stitches, beginning with a slip knot.

## Slip Knot

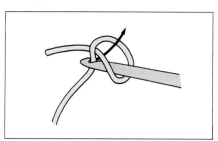

Make a loop then hook another loop through it. Tighten gently and slide the knot up to the hook.

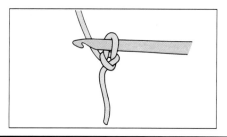

## Yarn Over (yo)

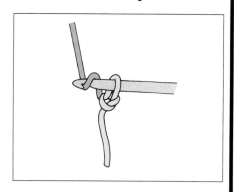

Wrap the yarn from back to front over the hook (or hold the yarn still and manoeuvre the hook). This movement of the yarn over the hook is used over and over again in crochet and is usually called 'yarn over', abbreviated as 'yo'.

## Chain Stitch (ch ○ )

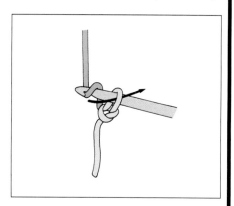

Yarn over and draw the yarn through to form a new loop without tightening up the previous one.

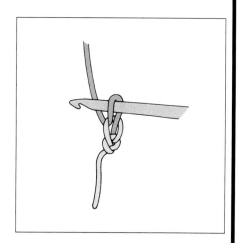

Repeat to form as many chains as required. Do not count the slip knot as a stitch.

**Note:** Unless otherwise stated, when working into the starting chain always work under two strands of chain loops as shown in the diagram.

# Basic Stitches

All the crochet patterns in this book are produced using combinations of the following basic stitches. They are shown in the diagrams worked into a starting chain but the method is the same whatever part of the work the stitch is worked into.

## Slip Stitch (sl st ●)

This is the shortest of crochet stitches and unlike other stitches is not used on its own to produce a fabric. It is used for joining, shaping and where necessary carrying the yarn to another part of the fabric for the next stage.

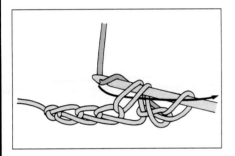

Insert the hook into the work (second chain from hook in diagram), yarn over and draw the yarn through both the work and loop on the hook in one movement.

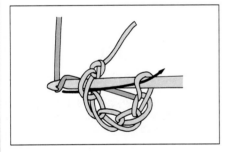

To join a chain ring with a slip stitch, then insert hook into first chain, yarn over and draw through the work and the yarn on the hook.

## Double Crochet (dc +)

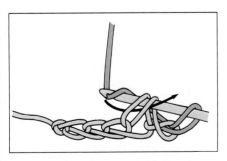

1. Insert the hook into the work (second chain from hook on starting chain), *yarn over and draw yarn through the work only.

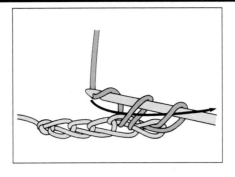

2. Yarn over again and draw the yarn through both loops on the hook.

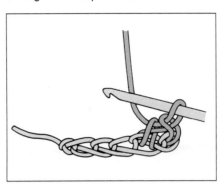

3. 1 dc made. Insert hook into next stitch; repeat from * in step 1.

## Half Treble (htr ⊤)

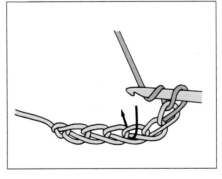

1. Yarn over and insert the hook into the work (third chain from hook on starting chain).

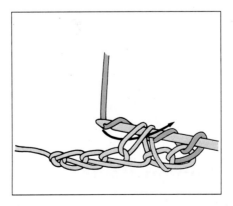

2. *Yarn over and draw through the work only.

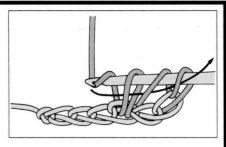

3. Yarn over again and draw through all three loops on the hook.

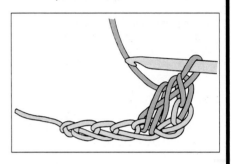

4. 1 htr made. Yarn over, insert hook into next stitch; repeat from * in step 2.

## Treble (tr ⊤)

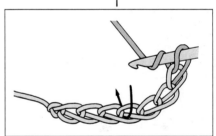

1. Yarn over and insert the hook into the work (fourth chain from hook on starting chain).

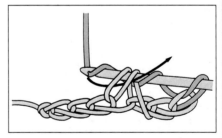

2. *Yarn over and draw through the work only.

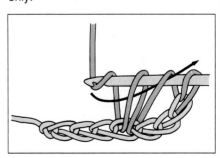

3. Yarn over and draw through the first two loops only.

# Making Crochet Fabric

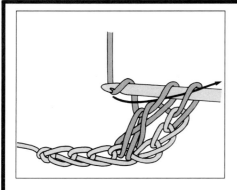

4. Yarn over and draw through the last two loops on the hook.

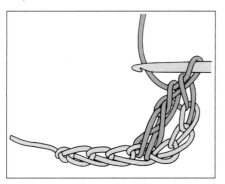

5. 1 tr made. Yarn over, insert hook into next stitch; repeat from * in step 2.

## Double Treble (dtr⊤ )

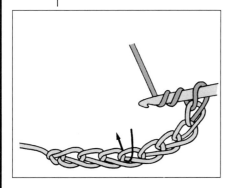

1. Yarn over twice, insert the hook into the work (fifth chain from hook on starting chain).

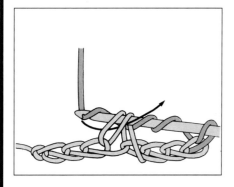

2. *Yarn over and draw through the work only.

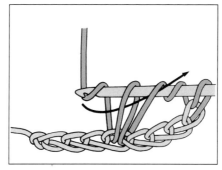

3. Yarn over again and draw through the first two loops only.

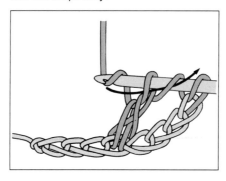

4. Yarn over again and draw through the next two loops only.

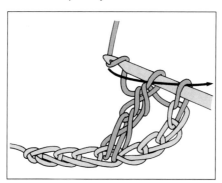

5. Yarn over again and draw through the last two loops on the hook.

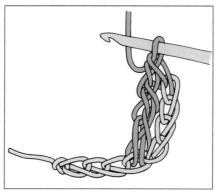

6. 1 dtr made. Yarn over twice, insert hook into next stitch; repeat from * in step 2.

## Longer Basic Stitches

Triple treble (ttr), quadruple treble (quadtr), quintuple treble (quintr) etc. are made by wrapping the yarn over three, four, five times etc. at the beginning and finishing as for a double treble, repeating step 4 until two loops remain on hook, finish with step 5.

# Making Crochet Fabric

These are the basic procedures for making crochet fabrics.

## Starting Chain

To make a flat fabric worked in rows you must begin with a starting chain. The length of the starting chain is the number of stitches needed for the first row of fabric plus the number of chain needed to get to the correct height of the stitches to be used in the first row. All the patterns in this book indicate the length of starting chain required to work one repeat of the design. See 'Starting Chains and Pattern Repeats' on page 11.

> ### TIP
> When working a large piece it is sensible to start with more chain than necessary as it is simple to undo the extra chain if you have miscounted.

## Working in Rows

A flat fabric can be produced by turning the work at the end of each row. Right handers work from right to left and left handers from left to right. One or more chain must be worked at the beginning of each row to bring the hook up to the height of the first stitch in the row. The number of chain used for turning depends upon the height of the stitch they are to match as follows:

**double crochet** = 1 chain
**half treble** = 2 chain
**treble** = 3 chain
**double treble** = 4 chain

When working half trebles or longer stitches the turning chain takes the place of the first stitch. Where one chain is worked at the beginning of a row starting with double crochet it is usually for height only and is in addition to the first stitch.

## Basic Treble Fabric

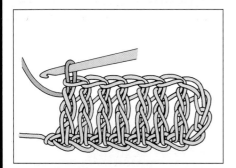

Make a starting chain of the required length plus two chain. Work one treble into fourth chain from hook. The three chain at the beginning of the row form the first treble. Work one treble into the next and every chain to the end of the row.

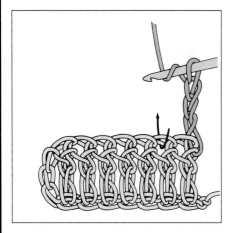

At the end of each row turn the work so that another row can be worked across the top of the previous one. It does not matter which way the work is turned but be consistent. Make three chain for turning. These turning chain will count as the first treble.

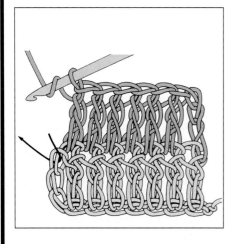

Miss the first treble in the previous row, work a treble into the top of the next and every treble including the last treble in row, then work a treble into third of three chain at the beginning of the previous row.

**Note:** Unless otherwise stated when working into the top of a stitch, always work under two strands as shown in diagram.

## Fastening Off

To fasten off the yarn permanently break off the yarn about 5cm (2 ins) away from the work (longer if you need to sew pieces together). Draw the end through the loop on hook and tighten gently.

## Joining in New Yarn and Changing Colour

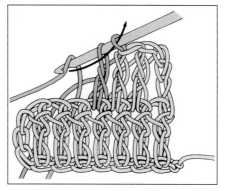

When joining in new yarn or changing colour, work in the old yarn until two loops of the last stitch remain in the old yarn or colour. Use the new colour or yarn to complete the stitch.

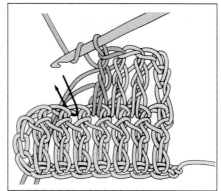

Continue to work the following stitches in the new colour or yarn, as before.

If you are working whole rows in different colours, make the change during the last stitch in the previous row, so the new colour for the next row is ready to work the turning chain.

Do not cut off any yarns which will be needed again later at the same edge, but continue to use them as required, leaving an unbroken 'float' thread up the side of the fabric.

If, at the end of a row, the pattern requires you to return to the beginning of the same row without turning and to work another row in a different colour in the same direction, complete the first row in the old colour and fasten off by lengthening the final loop on the hook, passing the whole ball through it and gently tighten again. That yarn is now available if you need to rejoin it later at this edge (if not, cut it).

# Stitch Variations

Most crochet stitch patterns, however elaborate, are made using combinations of basic stitches. Different effects can be created by small variations in the stitch making procedure or by varying the position and manner of inserting the hook into the fabric. The following techniques are used frequently to build up crochet fabric.

**Note:** Terms such as 'group', 'cluster', 'picot', 'shell', 'fan', 'flower', 'petal', 'leaf' and 'bobble' do not denote a fixed arrangement of stitches. Exactly what they mean may be different for each pattern. The procedure is therefore always given at the beginning of each set of instructions as a Special Abbreviation.

## Groups or Shells

These consist of several complete stitches worked into the same place. They can be worked as part of a pattern or as a method of increasing.

### Five Treble Group

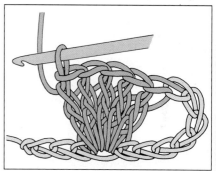

Work five trebles into one stitch.

## Summary of Common Groups or Shells

On diagrams the point at the base of the group will be positioned above the space or stitch where the hook is to be inserted.

**2, 3 and 4 half treble group**

Work 2(3,4) half treble into same place.

**2, 3, 4 and 5 treble group**

Work 2(3,4,5) treble into same place.

**2, 3, 4 and 5 double treble group**

Work 2(3,4,5) double treble into same place.

# Stitch Variations

## Clusters

Any combination of stitches may be joined into a cluster by leaving the last loop of each temporarily on the hook until they are worked off together at the end. Working stitches together in this way can also be a method of decreasing.

It is important to be sure exactly how and where the hook is to be inserted for each 'leg' of the cluster. The 'legs' may be worked over adjacent stitches, or stitches may be missed between 'legs'.

### Three Treble Cluster

(Worked over adjacent stitches).

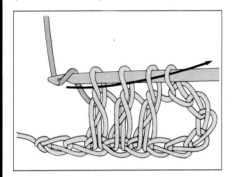

Work a treble into each of the next three stitches leaving the last loop of each treble on the hook.

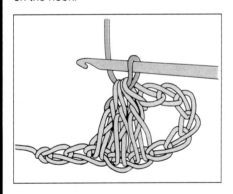

Yarn over and draw through all four loops on the hook.

### Summary of Common Clusters

(Worked over adjacent stitches).

On diagrams each 'leg' of the cluster will be positioned above the stitch where the hook is to be inserted.

**3, 4 and 5 treble cluster**

Work a treble into each of the next 3(4,5) stitches leaving the last loop of each on the hook. Yarn over and draw through all loops on hook.

**3, 4 and 5 double treble cluster**

Work a double treble into each of the next 3(4,5) stitches leaving the last loop of each on the hook. Yarn over and draw through all loops on hook.

## Bobbles

When a cluster is worked into one stitch it forms a bobble.

### Five Treble Bobble

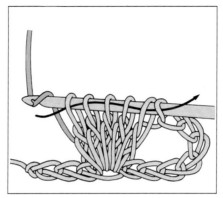

1. Work five trebles into one stitch leaving the last loop of each on the hook.

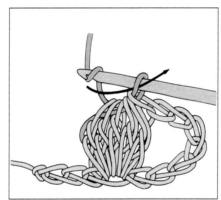

2. Yarn over and draw through all the loops on the hook.

More bulky bobbles can be secured with an extra chain stitch. If this is necessary it would be indicated within the pattern.

### Summary of Common Bobbles

Follow instructions as if working a cluster but for each 'leg' insert the hook into the same stitch or space.

**3, 4 and 5 treble bobble**

**4, 5, 6 and 7 double treble bobble**

## Popcorns

Popcorns are groups of complete stitches usually worked into the same place, folded and closed at the top. An extra chain can be worked to secure the popcorn.

## Five Treble Popcorn

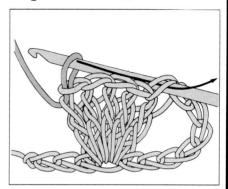

1. Work five trebles into one stitch. Take the hook out of the working loop and insert it into the top of the first treble made, from front to back.

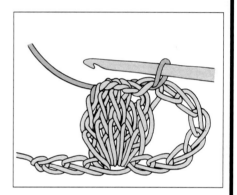

2. Pick up the working loop and draw this through to close the popcorn. If required work one chain to secure the popcorn.

### Summary of Common Popcorns

On diagrams the point at the base of the popcorn will be positioned above the space or stitch where it is to be worked.

**3 and 4 half treble popcorn**

Work 3(4) half treble into the same place, drop loop off hook, insert hook into first htr, pick up dropped loop and draw through.

**3, 4 and 5 treble popcorn**

Work 3(4,5) treble into the same place, drop loop off hook, insert hook into first treble, pick up dropped loop and draw through.

**3, 4 and 5 double treble popcorn**

Work 3(4,5) double treble into the same place, drop loop off hook, insert hook into first double treble, pick up dropped loop and draw through.

## Puff Stitches

These are similar to bobbles but worked using half trebles, into the same stitch or space. However because half trebles cannot be worked until one loop remains on the hook, the stitches are not closed until the required number have been worked.

### Three Half Treble Puff Stitch

(Worked into one stitch).

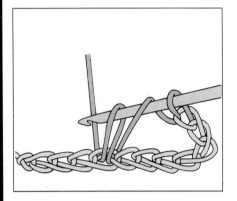

1. Yarn over, insert the hook, yarn over again and draw a loop through (three loops on the hook).

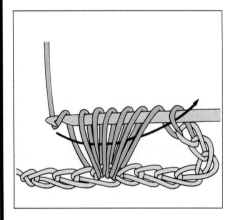

2. Repeat this step twice more, inserting the hook into the same stitch (seven loops on the hook); yarn over and draw through all the loops on the hook.

3. As with popcorns and bulky bobbles an extra chain stitch is often used to secure the puff stitch firmly. This will be indicated within the pattern if necessary.

A **cluster** of half treble stitches is worked in the same way as a puff stitch but each 'leg' is worked where indicated.

## Picots

A picot is normally a chain loop formed into a closed ring by a slip stitch or double crochet. The number of chains in a picot can vary.

### Four Chain Picot

(Closed with a slip stitch).

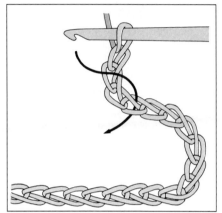

1. Work four chain.

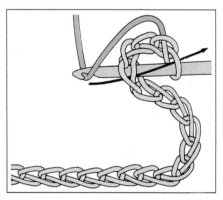

2. Into fourth chain from hook work a slip stitch to close.

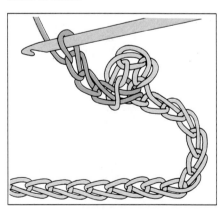

3. Continue working chain or required stitch.

**Note:** When working a picot closed with a slip stitch at the top of a chain arch, the picot will not appear central unless an extra chain is worked after the slip stitch.

## Crossed Stitches

This method produces stitches that are not entangled with each other and so maintain a clear 'X' shape.

### Crossed Double Treble

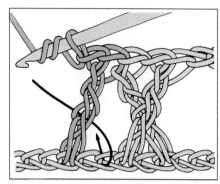

Miss two stitches and work the first double treble into next stitch. Work one chain then work second double treble into first of missed stitches taking the hook behind the first double treble before inserting.

See individual pattern instructions for variations on crossed stitch.

## 'X', 'λ' and 'Y' Shapes

In lacy stitch patterns long stitches are sometimes made into 'X' and 'Y' shapes without crossing them.

### Double Treble 'λ' and 'X' shapes

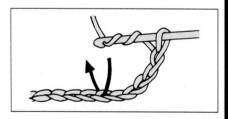

1. Wrap the yarn round the hook twice, insert the hook as required to make the lower part of the first 'leg'.

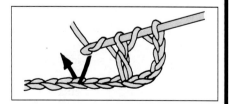

2. Wrap the yarn, draw a loop through, wrap the yarn and draw through 2 loops (3 loops on the hook); wrap the yarn once more and insert the hook again as required to make the lower part of the second 'leg'.

# Stitch Variations

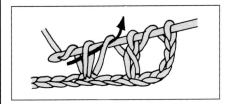

3. Wrap the yarn, draw a loop through, wrap the yarn and draw through 2 loops to complete both lower 'legs'.

4. Wrap the yarn and draw through 2 loops: repeat this last step twice more to complete the first 'arm' - note that at this stage you have completed a 'λ' shape.

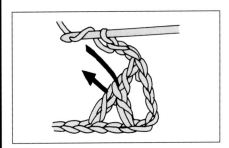

5. Make chains as required to take the hook to the top of the second 'arm', wrap the yarn once, insert the hook into the centre of the cluster just completed, picking up two threads at the left-hand side, and draw a loop through.

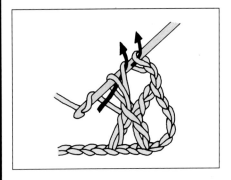

6. Wrap the yarn and draw through 2 loops.

7. Repeat this last step to complete the second 'arm' and the whole 'X' shape.

## Triple Treble 'Y' Shape

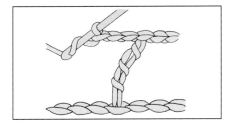

1. Work one complete triple treble stitch for the lower 'leg' and first 'arm'.

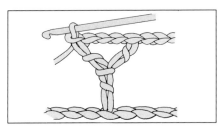

2. Make some chains as required to take the hook to the top of second 'arm' and work 1 double crochet into the centre of the triple treble to complete the second 'arm' and whole 'Y' shape in the same way as for the 'X' shape above.

## Loop (Fur) Stitch

Loop stitch is a variation of double crochet and is usually worked on 'wrong side' rows because the loops form at the back of the fabric.

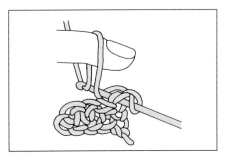

1. Using the left-hand finger to control the loop size insert the hook, pick up both threads of the loop and draw these through; wrap the supply yarn over the hook.

2. Draw through all the loops on the hook to complete.

**Note:** When each loop is cut afterwards the texture of the fabric resembles fur.

## Bullion Stitch

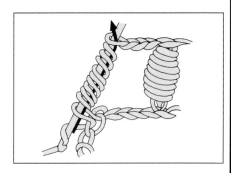

Wrap the yarn over the hook as many times as specified (usually 7 to 10 times); insert the hook as required; wrap the yarn once again and draw a loop through; wrap the yarn again and draw through loops on the hook, picking them off one at a time, if necessary; work a chain to complete the bullion stitch.

## Lace Loops

Lace loops are most often used either as a decorative edging or for the kind of fabric making sometimes called 'broomstick' crochet.

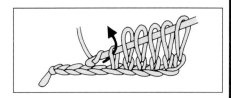

1. Insert the hook, wrap the yarn over the hook and draw a loop through; wrap the yarn again, draw another loop through the first and lengthen his as required; repeat this procedure, keeping each loop on the hook.

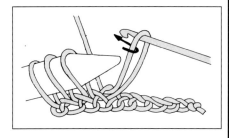

2. To help keep larger loops even in size, work from left to right and transfer each loop to a large size knitting needle (or 'broomstick').

3. 2 or more lace loops can be made into clusters in various ways as an alternative to basic stitches.

## Solomon's Knot

A Solomon's knot is a lengthened chain stitch locked with a double crochet stitch worked into its back loop.

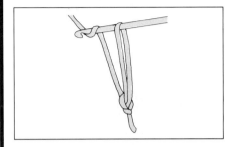

1. Make 1 chain and lengthen the loop as required; wrap the yarn over the hook.

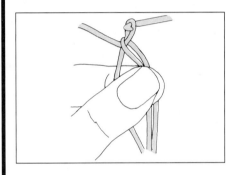

2. Draw through the loop on the hook, keeping the single back thread of this long chain separate from the 2 front threads.

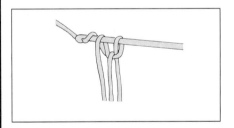

3. Insert the hook under this single back thread and wrap the yarn again.

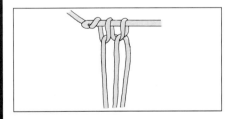

4. Draw a loop through and wrap again.

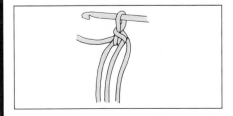

5. Draw through both loops on the hook to complete.

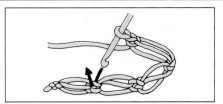

6. It is necessary to work back into the 'knots' between the lengthened chains in order to make the classic Solomon's Knot fabric, see page 83.

## Placement of Stitches

All crochet stitches (except chains) require the hook to be inserted into existing work. It has already been shown how to work into a chain and into the top of a stitch, however stitches can also be worked into the following places.

### Working into Chain Spaces

When a stitch, group, shell, cluster or bobble etc. is positioned over a chain or chains, the hook is often inserted into the space under the chain.

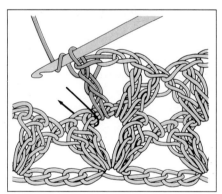

It is important to notice, however, if the pattern instructions stipulate working **into** a particular chain as this will change the appearance of the design.

If necessary information of this kind has been given as notes with the diagram.

A bobble, popcorn or cluster that is worked into a chain space is shown in the diagram spread out more than one worked **into** a stitch, therefore on the diagrams they will not be closed at the base.

**5 treble bobble into a stitch or space**

### Working Around the Stem of a Stitch

Inserting the hook round the whole stem of a stitch creates raised or relief effects.

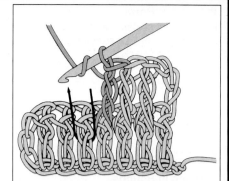

Working around the front of stem gives a stitch that lies on the front of the work.

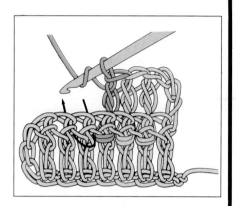

Working around the back of stem gives a stitch that lies on the back of the work.

## Working Under the Front or Back Loop Only

Inserting the hook under one loop at the top of the stitch leaves the other loop as a horizontal bar.

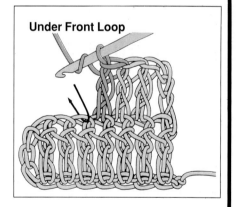

**Under Front Loop**

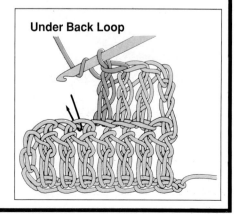

**Under Back Loop**

# Stitch Variations

### Working in Rows

If you work consistently into the front loop only you will make a series of ridges alternately on the back and front of the work. Working into the back loop only makes the ridges appear alternately on the front and back of the work.

If however you work alternately into the front loop only on one row and then the back loop only on the next row, the horizontal bars will all appear on the same side of the fabric.

### Working in Rounds

Working always into the front loop only will form a bar on the back of the work, and vice versa.

## Working Between Stitches

Inserting the hook between the stems of the stitches produces an open effect.

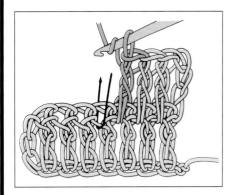

Ensure the number of stitches remains constant after each row.

## Marguerites (Stars)

A popular form of 'spiked' cluster - often called a 'Marguerite' or 'Star' - is formed by inserting the hook 3, 4, 5 or perhaps even more times, partly into the side of the previous stitch and partly into the next few stitches of the previous row.

### 4 'Spike' Marguerites
**First Marguerite**

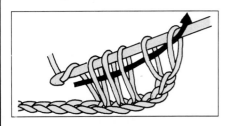

1. Insert the hook into the second chain from the hook, wrap the yarn round the hook and draw a loop through; repeat this step 3 more times into the 4th, 5th and 6th chains from the hook, (5 loops on the hook); wrap the yarn and draw through all the loops.

2. Make one chain firmly to close the Marguerite.

**2nd and subsequent Marguerites**

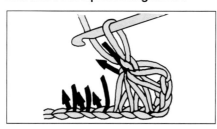

3. Insert the hook, wrap the yarn and draw through as follows: into the loop which closed the previous Marguerite; into the same place as the previous Marguerite finished; and into each of the next 2 stitches (5 loops on the hook).

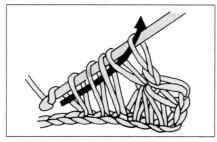

4. Wrap the yarn, draw through all the loops on the hook and make a chain firmly to close the Marguerite.

## Spikes

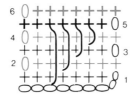

'Spikes' are made by inserting the hook further down into the fabric than usual, either below the next stitch, or to one side of it.

1. A loop is drawn through and up to the height of the current row.

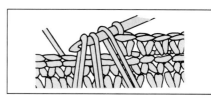

2. The stitch is then completed normally.

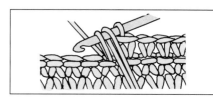

3. Spikes can be worked singly, in sequence, or in clusters by inserting the hook in different places, drawing a loop through each and finishing by drawing a loop through all the loops so collected. They add interest to fabric texture, but are most dramatic when worked in contrasting colours.

**Note:** It is important to work 'spike' loops loosely enough to avoid squashing the fabric, but with sufficient tension to maintain the stability of the fabric. When a sequence of stitches is 'spiked', it may help to work each one as a 'twin' cluster together with a stitch worked normally under the top 2 loops of the stitches as follows:

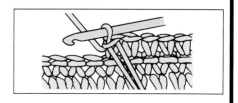

4. Insert the hook as indicated for the 'Spike' wrap the yarn around the hook and draw a loop through and up to the height of the current row; insert the hook under the top 2 loops of the next stitch, wrap the yarn and draw a loop through, (3 loops on the hook).

5. Wrap the yarn and draw through all the loops on the hook to complete.

## Corded or Reversed Double Crochet

Corded double crochet is used as a decorative texture (Corded Rib), or edging (Corded Edge). It consists of working double crochet stitches in the 'wrong' direction, ie from left to right for right-handers.

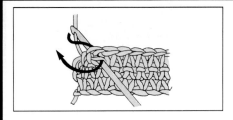

1. After a right side row do not turn. Always starting with the hook facing downwards insert the hook back into the next stitch to the right. Pull the yarn through twisting the hook to face upwards at the same time.

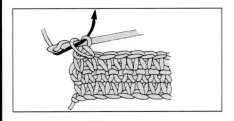

2. Wrap the yarn and draw through to finish off the double crochet as normally.

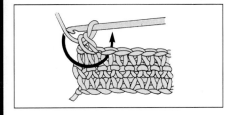

3. Insert the hook ready for the next stitch.

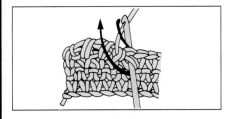

4. The direction of working causes the stitches to twist and create the decorative effect.

## Linked Stitches

The stems of all basic stitches, except double crochet, may be linked to each other in the middle. This gives the resulting fabric greater firmness and stability.

### Linked Double Treble

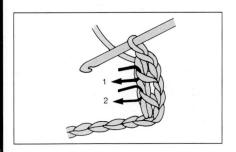

1. Insert the hook down through the upper of 2 horizontal loops round the stem of the

previous stitch, wrap the yarn over the hook and draw through; insert the hook down through the lower horizontal loop of the same stitch, wrap the yarn draw another loop through.

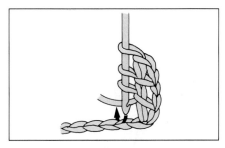

2. Treat these 2 loops as the wrappings which are required for an ordinary double treble and complete the stitch in the normal way.

To make the first linked double treble following the turning chain, insert the hook into the 2nd then 4th chains from the hook in order to pick up the 2 preliminary loops.

Trebles and longer stitches are made in the same way with the appropriate number of preliminary linked and wrapped loops.

# Pattern Instructions

In order to follow crochet instructions you should know how to make the basic stitches and to be familiar with basic fabric-making procedures.

Any unusual stitches or combinations of stitches have been given as a Special Abbreviation with the particular pattern.

Any specific techniques - for example working with padding threads - are given at the start of the relevant section, in this case Irish Style Crochet.

All the patterns in this book have been given in the form of both written instructions and diagrams, so that you can choose to follow either method.

However, if you are more used to written instructions it is still a good idea to look at the diagram to get an overall picture of how the design has been put together.

Diagram followers may find it helpful to refer to the written instructions to confirm their interpretation of the diagram.

# Working from a Diagram

Diagrams should be read exactly as the crochet is worked. For example, motifs are worked from the centre outwards and all-over patterns from the bottom to the top. Where the direction of work, within a design, is not obvious an extra line drawing or arrows are given to show where the direction changes (for example Curved Fan Stitch on page 43). Each stitch is

represented by a symbol that has been drawn to resemble its crocheted equivalent. The position of the symbol shows where the stitch should be worked.

Stitch symbols are drawn and laid out as realistically as possible but there are times when they have to be distorted for the sake of clarity. For example stitches may look extra long to show clearly where they are to be placed, but you should not try to make artificially long stitches. This distortion is particularly apparent on diagrams that represent fabrics not intended to lie flat (for example Tooth Stitch on page 45). Sometimes it has been necessary to use a coloured arrow to indicate where particular stitches should be worked. This occurs most often in the Irish Style Crochet section, because many of the designs are three-dimensional.

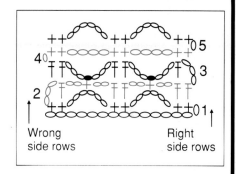

Wrong side rows     Right side rows

# Right Side and Wrong Side Rows

Where the work is turned after each row only alternate rows are worked with the right side of the work facing. These 'right side rows' are printed in black on stitch diagrams and read from right to left. Wrong side rows are printed in blue and read from left to right. Row numbers are shown at the side of the diagrams at the **beginning** of the row.

Patterns worked in rounds have the right side rows facing on every round. To make them easier to follow we have printed alternate rounds in black and blue.

# Starting Chains and Pattern Repeats

The number of starting chain required is given with each pattern. It may be given in the form of a multiple, for example:-
**Starting chain: Multiple of 7 sts + 3.** This means you can make any length of chain that is a multiple of 7 + 3, such as 14 + 3ch, 21 + 3ch, 28 + 3ch etc.

In the written instructions the stitches that should be repeated are contained within brackets [ ] or follow an asterisk *. These stitches are repeated across the row or round the required number of times. On the diagrams the stitches that have to be repeated can be easily visualised. The

# Pattern Instructions

extra stitches not included in the pattern repeat are there to balance the row or make it symmetrical and are only worked once. Obviously turning chains are only worked at the beginning of each row. Some diagrams consist of more than one pattern repeat so that you can see more clearly how the design is worked.

## Working in Colour

Capital letters A, B, C etc. are used to indicate different yarn colours in both written instructions and diagrams. They do not refer to any particular colour. See page 7 for instructions on changing colour within a pattern.

## Tension (or Gauge)

This refers to the number of stitches and rows in a given area. When following a pattern for a garment or other article the instructions will include a specified tension. If you do not produce fabric with the same number of stitches and rows as indicated, your work will not come to the measurements given.

To ensure that you achieve the correct tension work a tension sample or swatch before starting the main part of the crochet. The hook size quoted in the pattern is a suggestion only. You must use whichever hook gives you the correct tension.

If you are going to use a stitch pattern from this book to design an article of your own, it is still important to work a tension sample in order to calculate the number of stitches you will require. It is worth experimenting with different hook sizes so that you find the best tension for your chosen pattern and yarn. Some stitches look and feel better worked loosely and others need to be worked more firmly to be at their best.

## Shaping

If you are working crochet to make something which requires shaping, such as decreasing for the neckline of a garment or increasing to add width for a sleeve, you need to know something about shaping.

Increasing is generally achieved by working two or more stitches in the pattern where there would normally be one stitch. Conversely, decreasing is achieved by working two or more stitches together, or missing one or more stitches. However it can be difficult to know exactly where these adjustments are best made, and a visual guide would make the work easier!

On the diagrams below we show you some examples of shapings which cover a variety of possibilities. We recommend that you use this method yourself when planning a project. First pencil trace the diagram given with the stitch. If necessary repeat the tracing to match the repeat

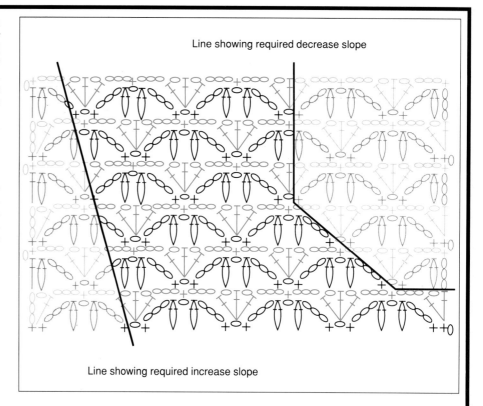

Line showing required decrease slope

Line showing required increase slope

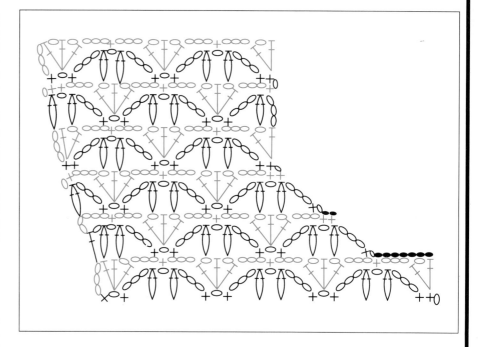

of the pattern until you have a large enough area to give you the shape you require. Once this is correct **ink it in** so that you can draw over it in pencil without destroying it. Now draw over this the shaping you require matching as near as possible the style of the particular pattern you are using.

## Joining Seams

Various methods can be used to join pieces of crochet. The use of the item will often dictate the method used, the seam could be invisible or decorative. Below are a few suggestions for joining pieces of crochet.

To join with an invisible sewn seam, place

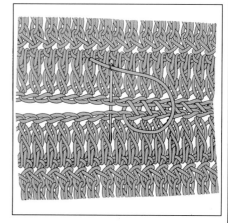

pieces edge to edge with the wrong sides uppermost and whip stitch together.

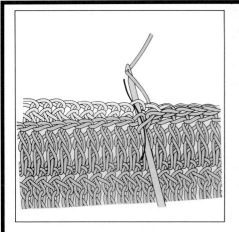

To join invisibly using a crochet hook, place right sides of pieces together and slip stitch through one loop of each piece as illustrated.

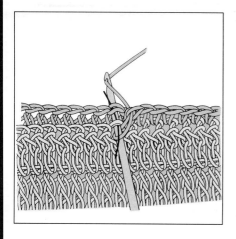

To create a decorative ridged seam on the right side of the work, place wrong sides together and join with double crochet working under two strands of each piece as illustrated.

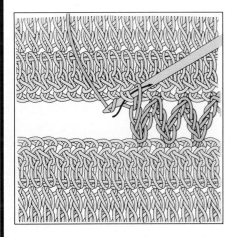

Alternatively with the right side of both pieces uppermost they can be joined with a row of fancy openwork chains.

## Pressing and Finishing

The methods you use to finish your crochet depend largely on what you are using it for and what yarn you have used.

### Cotton

Cotton yarns benefit from being wetted or thoroughly steamed. If you are using household starch (as opposed to spray starch) now is the time to apply it, either by immersing the crocheted piece or dabbing the wet starch on to the material. Pin out very near to the edge, at very close intervals, stretching or easing the material to ensure that it is even. Picots, bobbles or other intrinsic features should be carefully placed with a pin at this stage. Having satisfied yourself that the shape is correct, the work can now be pressed using a hot iron. Do not allow the full weight of the iron to rest on the work especially where interesting textures are involved. Remove the pins and if required make fine adjustments to the edges of the material to ensure that they are straight. Now leave until the work is **thoroughly** dry.

### Motifs and Irish Style Pieces

Work as given above but leave the pins in position until the work is **thoroughly** dry. Ensure that all three-dimensional features show to their best advantage.

### Other Yarns

In principal the methods given for working with cotton yarns apply, but you must read the finishing or pressing information usually included with your yarn. Not every yarn will be suitable for or require starching and some yarns cannot be pressed with a hot iron.

# Abbreviations and Symbols

Listed below are the standard abbreviations and symbols that have been used for pages 15 to 160 of this book. Refer to pages 4 to 14 for more detailed instructions of these and other stitch variations. If a pattern contains an unusual combinations of stitches these are explained in the Special Abbreviation at the beginning of that pattern.

Separate abbreviations and symbols have been used for the Tunisian stitches in this book and these have been given at the beginning of that section on pages 161 to 172.

## Abbreviations

**Alt** = alternate, **beg** = begin(ning), **ch(s)** = chain(s), **ch sp** = chain space, **cm** = centimetre(s), **dec** = decrease, **dc** = double crochet, **dtr** = double treble, **htr** = half treble, **inc** = increase, **ins** = inches, **quadtr** = quadruple treble, **quintr** = quintuple treble, **rep** = repeat, **sl st** = slip stitch, **sp(s)** = space(s), **st(s)** = stitch(es), **tog** = together, **tr** = treble, **ttr** = triple treble, **yo** = yarn over.

**dc2(3)tog**

*insert hook as indicated, yo, draw loop through* = 3(4) loops on hook.

**htr2(3/4)tog**

*yo, insert hook as indicated, yo, draw loop through* = 5(7/9) loops on hook.

**tr2(3/4/5)tog**

*yo, insert hook as indicated, yo, draw loop through, yo, draw loop through 2 loops* = 3(4/5/6) loops on hook.

**dtr2(3/4/5)tog**

*yo twice, insert hook as indicated, yo, draw loop through, (yo, draw through 2 loops) twice* = 3(4/5/6) loops on hook.

**ttr2(3/4/5/etc)tog**

*yo 3 times, insert hook as indicated, yo, draw loop through, (yo, draw through 2 loops) 3 times* = 3(4/5/6etc) loops on hook.

## Basic Symbols used in Diagrams

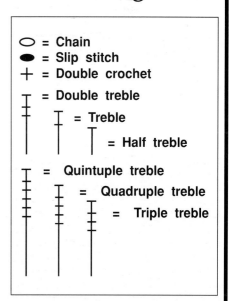

The number of strokes crossing the stems of stitches longer than a half treble represents the number of times the yarn is wrapped over the hook **before** the hook is inserted into the work.

# Basic Stitches

## Basic Double Crochet

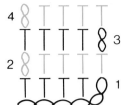

Any number of sts.
(add 1 for base chain)

**1st row:** Miss 2ch (count as 1dc), 1dc into next and each ch to end, turn.

**2nd row:** 1ch (counts as 1dc), miss 1 st, 1dc into next and each st to end working last st into tch, turn.

Rep 2nd row.

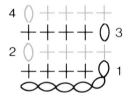

**Hint:** In some patterns the turning chain does **not** count as a stitch when working double crochet. In these cases the first dc is worked into the second ch from hook on the first row, and thereafter into the first dc of the previous row.

## Basic Half Treble

Any number of sts.
(add 1 for base chain)

**1st row:** Miss 2ch (count as 1htr), 1htr into next and each ch to end, turn.

**2nd row:** 2ch (count as 1htr), miss 1 st, 1htr into next and each st to end working last st into top of tch, turn.

Rep 2nd row.

## Basic Trebles

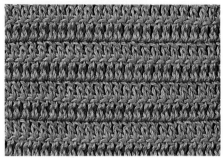

Any number of sts.
(add 2 for base chain)

**1st row:** Miss 3ch (count as 1tr), 1tr into next and each ch to end, turn.

**2nd row:** 3ch (count as 1tr), miss 1 st, 1tr into next and each st to end working last st into top of tch, turn.

Rep 2nd row.

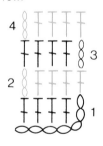

## Basic Double Trebles

Any number of sts.
(add 3 for base chain)

**1st row:** Miss 4ch (count as 1dtr), 1dtr into next and each ch to end, turn.

**2nd row:** 4ch (count as 1dtr), miss 1 st, 1dtr into next and each st to end , working last st into top of tch, turn.

Rep 2nd row.

## Back Loop Double Crochet

Worked as Basic Double Crochet except from 2nd row insert hook into back loop only of each st.

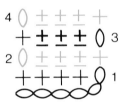

## Front Loop Double Crochet

Worked as Basic Double Crochet except from 2nd row insert hook into front loop only of each st.

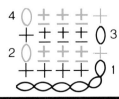

Stitch Variations, Abbreviations and Symbols on pages 7 to 15.

## Back and Front Loop Double Crochet

Multiple of 2 sts.
(add 1 for base chain)

**1st row:** Miss 2ch (count as 1dc), 1dc into next and each ch to end, turn.

**2nd row:** 1ch (counts as 1dc), miss 1 st, *1dc into back loop only of next st, 1dc into front loop only of next st; rep from * ending 1dc into top of tch, turn.

Rep 2nd row.

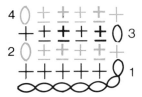

## Shallow Double Crochet

Worked as Basic Double Crochet except from 2nd row insert hook low into body of each st below 3 horizontal loops and between 2 vertical threads.

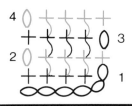

## Back Loop Half Treble

Worked as Basic Half Treble except from 2nd row insert hook into back loop only of each st.

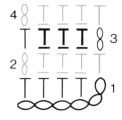

## Back and Front Loop Half Treble

Multiple of 2 sts.
(add 1 for base chain)

**1st row:** Miss 2ch (count as 1htr), 1htr into next and each ch to end, turn.

**2nd row:** 2ch (count as 1htr), miss 1 st, *1htr into back loop only of next st, 1htr into front loop only of next st; rep from * ending 1htr into top of tch, turn.

Rep 2nd row.

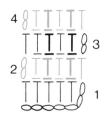

## Linked Half Trebles

Any number of sts.
(add 1 for base chain)

**Special Abbreviation**

**Lhtr (Linked Half Treble)** = insert hook into single vertical thread at left-hand side of previous st, yo, draw loop through, insert hook normally into next st, yo, draw loop through st, yo, draw through all 3 loops on hook.

**Note:** To make first Lhtr at beg of row treat 2nd ch from hook as a single vertical thread.

**1st row:** 1Lhtr into 3rd ch from hook (picking up loop through 2nd ch from hook), 1Lhtr into next and each ch to end, turn.

**2nd row:** 2ch (count as 1htr), miss 1 st, 1Lhtr into next and each st to end, working last st into top of tch, turn.

Rep 2nd row.

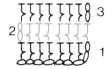

## Herringbone Half Treble

Any number of sts.
(add 1 for base chain)

**Special Abbreviation**

**HBhtr (Herringbone Half Treble)** = yo, insert hook, yo, draw through st and first loop on hook yo, draw through both loops on hook.

**1st row:** Miss 2ch (count as 1htr), 1HBhtr into next and each ch to end, turn.

**2nd row:** 2ch (count as 1htr), miss 1 st, 1HBhtr into next and each st to end working last st into top of tch, turn.

Rep 2nd row.

# Stitch Variations

## Wide Trebles

Worked as Basic Trebles but after 1st row insert hook between stems and below all horizontal threads connecting sts.

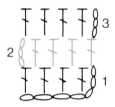

**Note:** Base chain should be worked loosely to accomodate extra width.

## Herringbone Trebles

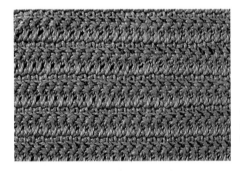

Any number of sts.
(add 2 for base chain)

### Special Abbreviation

**HBtr (Herringbone Treble)** = yo, insert hook, yo, draw through st and first loop on hook, yo, draw through 1 loop, yo, draw through both loops on hook.

**1st row:** Miss 3ch (count as 1tr), 1HBtr into next and each ch to end, turn.

**2nd row:** 3ch (count as 1tr), miss 1 st, 1HBtr into next and each st to end, working last st into top of tch, turn.

Rep 2nd row.

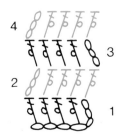

## Alternative Trebles

Any number of sts.
(add 2 for base chain)

### Special Abbreviation

**Alt tr (Alternative Treble)** = yo, insert hook, yo, draw loop through, yo, draw through 1 loop only, yo, draw through all 3 loops on hook.

**1st row:** Miss 3ch (count as 1tr), 1tr into next and each ch to end, turn.

**2nd row:** 3ch (count as 1tr), miss 1 st, work 1 Alt tr into next and each st to end, working last st into top of tch, turn.

Rep 2nd row.

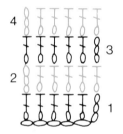

## Linked Double Trebles

Any number of sts.
(add 3 for base chain)

### Special Abbreviation

**Ldtr (Linked Double Treble)** = insert hook down through upper of 2 horizontal loops round stem of last st made, yo, draw loop through, insert hook down through lower horizontal loop of same st, yo, draw loop through, insert hook normally into next st, yo, draw loop through st, (4 loops on hook), [yo, draw through 2 loops] 3 times

**Note:** To make first Ldtr (at beg of row), treat 2nd and 4th chs from hook as upper and lower horizontal loops.

**1st row:** 1Ldtr into 5th ch from hook (picking up loops through 2nd and 4th chs from hook), 1Ldtr into next and each ch to end, turn.

**2nd row:** 4ch (count as 1dtr), miss 1 st, 1Ldtr into next and each st to end, working last st into top of tch, turn.

Rep 2nd row.

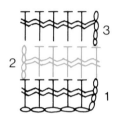

## Doubles and Trebles

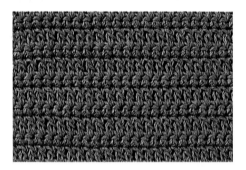

Any number of sts.
(add 1 for base chain)

**1st row** (wrong side): Miss 2ch (count as 1dc), 1dc into next and each ch to end, turn.

**2nd row:** 3ch (counts as 1tr), miss 1 st, 1tr into next and each st to end, working last st into top of tch, turn.

**3rd row:** 1ch (counts as 1dc), miss 1 st, 1dc into next and each st to end, working last st into top of tch, turn.

Rep 2nd and 3rd rows.

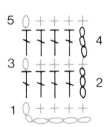

**Hint:** This is one of the simplest and most effective combination stitch patterns. It is also one of the easiest to get wrong! Concentration is required as you work the ends of the rows to avoid increasing or decreasing, or working two rows of the same stitch running by mistake.

Stitch Variations, Abbreviations and Symbols on pages 7 to 15.

## Track Stitch

Any number of sts.
(add 1 for base chain)

**1st row** (wrong side): Miss 2ch (count as 1dc), 1dc into next and each ch to end, turn.

**2nd row:** 5ch (count as 1ttr), miss 1 st, 1ttr into next and each st to end, working last st into top of tch, turn.

**3rd, 4th and 5th rows:** 1ch (counts as 1dc), miss 1 st, 1dc into next and each st to end, working last st into top of tch, turn.

Rep 2nd to 5th rows.

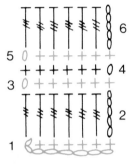

## Double Crochet Cluster Stitch I

Multiple of 2 sts + 1.
(add 1 for base chain)

**1st row** (wrong side): 1dc into 2nd ch from hook, *1ch, miss 1ch, 1dc into next ch; rep from * to end, turn.

**2nd row:** 1ch, 1dc into first st, 1ch, dc2tog inserting hook into each of next 2 ch sps, 1ch, *dc2tog inserting hook first into same ch sp as previous st, then into next ch sp, 1ch; rep from * ending 1dc into last st, miss tch, turn.

**3rd row:** 1ch, 1dc into first st, *1ch, miss 1ch, 1dc into next st; rep from * to end, miss tch, turn.

Rep 2nd and 3rd rows.

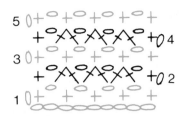

## Double Crochet Cluster Stitch II

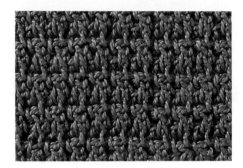

Multiple of 2 sts + 1.
(add 1 for base chain)

**1st row:** Miss 1ch, *dc2tog inserting hook into each of next 2ch, 1ch; rep from * ending 1dc into last ch, turn.

**2nd row:** 1ch, dc2tog inserting hook into first st then into next ch sp, 1ch, *dc2tog inserting hook first before and then after the vertical thread between the next 2 clusters, 1ch; rep from * ending 1dc into last dc, miss tch, turn.

Rep 2nd row.

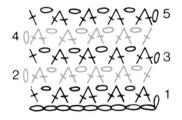

## Double Crochet Cluster Stitch III

Multiple of 2 sts.
(add 1 for base chain)

**1st row:** Miss 2ch (count as 1htr), *dc2tog inserting hook into each of next 2ch, 1ch; rep from * ending with 1htr into last ch, turn.

**2nd row:** 2ch (count as 1htr), miss 1 st, *dc2tog inserting hook into back loop only of next ch then into back loop only of next st, 1ch; rep from * ending with 1htr into top of tch, turn.

Rep 2nd row.

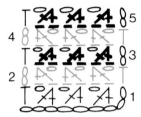

## Double Crochet Cluster Stitch IV

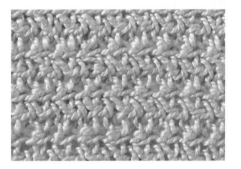

Multiple of 2 sts + 1.
(add 1 for base chain)

**Special Abbreviation**

**SC (Slip Cluster)** = insert hook into ch or st as indicated, yo, draw loop through, insert hook again as indicated, yo, draw loop through st and through next loop on hook, yo, draw through last 2 loops on hook.

**1st row:** 1SC inserting hook into 2nd and then 3rd ch from hook, 1ch; *1SC inserting hook into each of next 2ch, 1ch; rep from * ending 1dc into last ch, turn.

**2nd row:** 1ch (counts as 1dc), miss 1 st, *1SC inserting hook into front loop only of next ch then front loop only of next st, 1ch; rep from * ending 1dc into top of tch, turn.

Rep 2nd row.

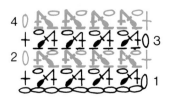

# Clusters

## Trinity Stitch I

Multiple of 2 sts + 1.
(add 1 for base chain)

**1st row:** 1dc into 2nd ch from hook, dc3tog inserting hook first into same ch as previous dc, then into each of next 2ch, *1ch, dc3tog inserting hook first into same ch as 3rd leg of previous cluster, then into each of next 2ch; rep from * to last ch, 1dc into same ch as 3rd leg of previous cluster, turn.
**2nd row:** 1ch, 1dc into first st, dc3tog inserting hook first into same place as previous dc, then into top of next cluster, then into next ch sp, *1ch, dc3tog inserting hook first into same ch sp as 3rd leg of previous cluster, then into top of next cluster, then into next ch sp; rep from * to end working 3rd leg of last cluster into last dc, 1dc into same place, miss tch, turn.
Rep 2nd row.

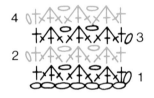

## Trinity Stitch II

Worked as Trinity Stitch I.
Work 1 row each in colours A, B and C throughout.

> **Hint:** Normally the maximum number of stitches which may be worked together into a double crochet cluster is 3. (Longer stitches may have more).
> Remember that working stitches together into clusters is often the best way to decrease.

## Half Treble Cluster Stitch I

Any number of sts.
(add 1 for base chain)

**1st row:** Miss 2ch (count as 1htr), *htr2tog all into next ch; rep from * to end, turn.
**2nd row:** 2ch (count as 1htr), miss 1 st, htr2tog all into next and each st, ending with htr2tog into top of tch, turn.
Rep 2nd row.

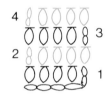

## Half Treble Cluster Stitch II

Any number of sts.
(add 2 for base chain)

**1st row:** Miss 2ch (count as 1htr), htr2tog inserting hook into each of next 2ch, *htr2tog inserting hook first into same ch as previous cluster then into next ch; rep from * until 1ch remains, 1htr into last ch, turn.
**2nd row:** 2ch (count as 1htr), htr2tog inserting hook first into first st then into next st, *htr2tog inserting hook first into same st as previous cluster then into next st; rep from * ending 1htr into top of tch, turn.
Rep 2nd row.

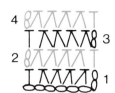

## Half Treble Cluster Stitch III

Multiple of 2 sts.
(add 1 for base chain)

**1st row:** Miss 2ch (count as 1htr), *htr2tog inserting hook into each of next 2ch, 1ch; rep from * ending 1htr into last ch, turn.
**2nd row:** 2ch (count as 1htr), miss 1 st, *htr2tog inserting hook into next ch sp then into next st, 1ch; rep from * ending 1htr into top of tch, turn.
Rep 2nd row.

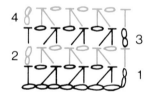

## Forked Cluster Stitch

Any number of sts.
(add 2 for base chain)

Stitch Variations, Abbreviations and Symbols on pages 7 to 15.

## Special Abbreviation

⅄ **FC (Forked Cluster)** = [yo, insert hook into ch or st as indicated, yo, draw loop through] twice (5 loops on hook), [yo, draw through 3 loops] twice.

**1st row:** Miss 2ch (count as 1tr), work 1FC inserting hook into each of next 2ch, *work 1FC inserting hook into same ch as previous FC then into next ch; rep from * until 1ch remains, 1tr into last ch, turn.

**2nd row:** 3ch (count as 1tr), 1FC inserting hook into each of first 2 sts, *1FC inserting hook into same st as previous FC then into next st; rep from * ending 1tr into top of tch, turn.

Rep 2nd row.

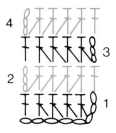

## Odd Forked Cluster Stitch

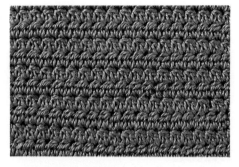

Any number of sts.
(add 2 for base chain)

## Special Abbreviation

⅄ **OFC (Odd Forked Cluster)** = yo, insert hook into ch or st as indicated, yo, draw loop through, yo, draw through 2 loops, insert hook into next ch or st, yo, draw loop through, yo, draw through all 3 loops on hook.

**1st row:** Miss 2ch (count as 1htr), 1OFC inserting hook first into 3rd then 4th ch from hook, *1OFC inserting hook first into same ch as previous OFC then into next ch; rep from * until 1ch remains, 1htr into last ch, turn.

**2nd row:** 2ch (count as 1htr), 1OFC inserting hook into first st then into next st, *1OFC inserting hook into same st as previous OFC then into next st; rep from * ending 1htr into top of tch, turn.

Rep 2nd row.

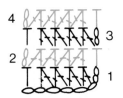

# Mixed Cluster Stitch

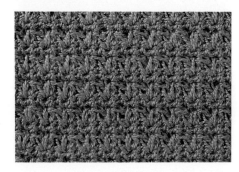

Multiple of 2 sts + 1.
(add 1 for base chain)

## Special Abbreviation

⅄ **MC (Mixed Cluster)** = yo, insert hook into first st as indicated, yo, draw loop through, yo, draw through 2 loops, miss 1 st, [yo, insert hook into next st, yo, draw loop through] twice all into same st, (6 loops on hook), yo, draw through all loops on hook.

**1st row** (wrong side): Miss 2cn (count as 1dc), 1dc into next and each ch to end, turn.

**2nd row:** 2ch (count as 1htr), 1MC inserting hook into first then 3rd st, *1ch, 1MC inserting hook first into same st as previous MC; rep from * ending last rep in top of tch, 1htr into same place, turn.

**3rd row:** 1ch (counts as 1dc), miss 1 st, 1dc into next and each st to end, working last st into top of tch, turn.

Rep 2nd and 3rd rows.

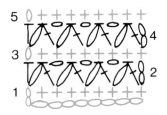

# Treble Cluster Stitch I

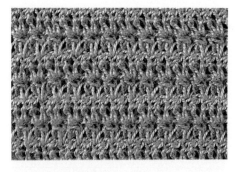

Multiple of 2 sts.
(add 2 for base chain)

## Special Abbreviation

**TrC (Treble Cluster)** = *yo, insert hook into ch or st as indicated, yo, draw loop through, yo, draw through 2 loops*, miss 1 ch or st, rep from * to * into next st, yo, draw

through all 3 loops on hook.

**1st row:** Miss 2ch (count as 1tr), work 1TrC inserting hook first into 3rd ch, 1ch, *work 1TrC inserting hook first into same ch as previous TrC, 1ch; rep from * ending 1tr into last ch, turn.

**2nd row:** 3ch (counts as 1tr), 1TrC inserting hook first into first st, 1ch, *1TrC inserting hook first into same st as previous TrC, 1ch; rep from * ending 1tr into top of tch, turn.

Rep 2nd row.

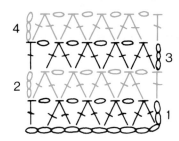

# Treble Cluster Stitch II

Multiple of 2 sts.
(add 2 for base chain)

## Special Abbreviation

**TrC (Treble Cluster)** worked as under Treble Cluster Stitch I.

**1st row** (right side): Miss 2ch (count as 1tr), work 1TrC inserting hook into 3rd ch then 5th ch, 1ch, *work 1TrC inserting hook first into same ch as previous TrC, 1ch; rep from * ending 1tr into last ch, turn.

**2nd row:** 1ch (counts as 1dc), miss 1 st, *1dc into next ch sp, 1ch, miss 1 st; rep from * ending 1dc into top of tch, turn.

**3rd row:** 3ch (count as 1tr), 1TrC inserting hook first into first st, 1ch, *1TrC inserting hook first into same st as previous TrC, 1ch; rep from * ending 1tr into top of tch, turn.

Rep 2nd and 3rd rows.

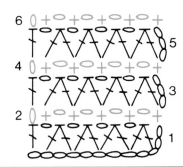

# Patterns for Texture and Colour

## Treble Cluster Stitch III

Any number of sts.
(add 2 for base chain)

**1st row:** Miss 3ch (count as 1tr), work tr2tog into next and each ch until 1ch remains, 1tr into last ch, turn.

**2nd row:** 3ch (count as 1tr), tr2tog between first tr and next cluster, *tr2tog between next 2 clusters; rep from * ending 1tr into top of tch, turn.

Rep 2nd row.

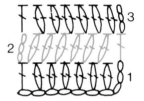

## Crunch Stitch

Multiple of 2 sts.
(add 1 for base chain)

**1st row:** Miss 2ch (count as 1htr), *sl st into next ch, 1htr into next ch; rep from * ending sl st into last ch, turn.

**2nd row:** 2ch (count as 1htr), miss 1 st, *sl st into next htr, 1htr into next sl st; rep from * ending sl st into top of tch, turn.

Rep 2nd row.

## Floret Stitch I

Multiple of 2 sts + 1.
(add 2 for base chain)

**1st row** (right side): Miss 3ch (count as 1tr), 1tr into next and each ch to end, turn.

**2nd row:** 1ch, miss 1 st, *1tr into next st, sl st into next st; rep from * ending last rep into top of tch, turn.

**3rd row:** 3ch (count as 1tr), miss 1 st, *1tr into next tr, 1tr into next sl st; rep from * ending last rep into tch, turn.

Rep 2nd and 3rd rows.

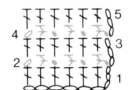

## Floret Stitch II

Worked as Floret Stitch I.
Work 1 row each in colours A and B alternately throughout.

## Floret Stitch III

Worked as Floret Stitch I.
Work 1 row each in colours A, B and C throughout.

## Griddle Stitch

Multiple of 2 sts.
(add 2 for base chain)

**1st row:** Miss 3ch (count as 1tr), *1dc into next ch, 1tr into next ch; rep from * ending 1dc into last ch, turn.

**2nd row:** 3ch (count as 1tr), miss 1 st, *1dc into next tr, 1tr into next dc; rep from * ending 1dc into top of tch, turn.

Rep 2nd row.

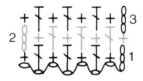

## Crumpled Griddle Stitch

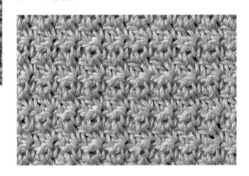

Multiple of 2 sts + 1.
(add 2 for base chain)

**1st row:** Miss 3ch (count as 1tr), *1dc into next ch, 1tr into next ch; rep from * to end, turn.

**2nd row:** 3ch (count as 1tr), miss 1 st, *1dc into next dc, 1tr into next tr; rep from * ending last rep into top of tch, turn.

Rep 2nd row.

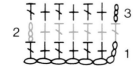

Stitch Variations, Abbreviations and Symbols on pages 7 to 15.

# Patterns for Texture and Colour

## Solid Shell Stitch

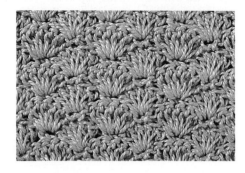

Multiple of 6 sts + 1.
(add 1 for base chain)

**1st row:** 1dc into 2nd ch from hook, *miss 2ch, 5tr into next ch, miss 2ch, 1dc into next ch; rep from * to end, turn.

**2nd row:** 3ch (count as 1tr), 2tr into first st, *miss 2tr, 1dc into next tr, miss 2tr, 5tr into next dc; rep from * ending last rep with 3tr into last dc, miss tch, turn.

**3rd row:** 1ch, 1dc into first st, *miss 2tr, 5tr into next dc, miss 2tr, 1dc into next tr; rep from * ending last rep with 1dc into top of tch, turn.

Rep 2nd and 3rd rows.

1dc into each of last 4 dc, miss tch, turn.

**4th row:** 1ch, 1dc into first st, 1dc into next and each st to end, miss tch, turn.

**5th row:** 3ch (count as 1tr), 3tr into first st, *miss 3 sts, 1dc into each of next 7 sts, miss 3 sts, 7tr into next st; rep from * ending last rep with 4tr into last dc, miss tch, turn.

Rep 2nd, 3rd, 4th and 5th rows.

## Wavy Shell Stitch II

Worked as Wavy Shell Stitch I.
Work 1 row each in colours A, B and C throughout.

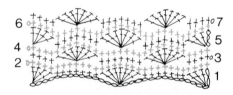

## Wavy Shell Stitch I

Multiple of 14 sts + 1.
(add 2 for base chain)
**Note:** See Wavy Shell Stitch II for stitch diagram.

**1st row** (right side): Miss 2ch (count as 1tr), 3tr into next ch, *miss 3ch, 1dc into each of next 7ch, miss 3ch, 7tr into next ch; rep from * ending last rep with 4tr into last ch, turn.

**2nd row:** 1ch, 1dc into first st, 1dc into each st to end, finishing with 1dc into top of tch, turn.

**3rd row:** 1ch, 1dc into each of first 4 sts, *miss 3 sts, 7tr into next st, miss 3 sts, 1dc into each of next 7 sts; rep from * to last 11 sts, miss 3 sts, 7tr into next st, miss 3 sts,

## Catherine Wheel I

Multiple of 10 sts + 6.
(add 1 for base chain)
**Special Abbreviation**
**CL (Cluster)** = work [yo, insert hook, yo, draw loop through, yo, draw through 2 loops] over the number of sts indicated, yo, draw through all loops on hook

**1st row** (wrong side): 1dc into 2nd ch from hook, 1dc into next ch, *miss 3ch, 7tr into next ch, miss 3ch, 1dc into each of next 3ch; rep from * to last 4 ch, miss 3 ch, 4tr into last ch, turn.

**2nd row:** 1ch, 1dc into first st, 1dc into next st, *3ch, 1CL over next 7sts, 3ch, 1dc into

each of next 3 sts; rep from * to last 4 sts, 3ch, 1CL over last 4 sts, miss tch, turn.

**3rd row:** 3ch (count as 1tr), 3tr into first st, *miss 3ch, 1dc into each of next 3dc, miss 3ch, 7tr into loop which closed next CL; rep from * to end finishing with miss 3ch, 1dc into each of last 2dc, miss tch, turn.

**4th row:** 3ch (count as 1tr) miss first st, 1CL over next 3 sts, *3ch, 1dc into each of next 3 sts, 3ch, 1CL over next 7 sts; rep from * finishing with 3ch, 1dc into next st, 1dc into top of tch, turn.

**5th row:** 1ch, 1dc into each of first 2dc, *miss 3ch, 7tr into loop which closed next CL, miss 3ch, 1dc into each of next 3dc; rep from * ending miss 3ch, 4tr into top of tch, turn.

Rep 2nd, 3rd, 4th and 5th rows.

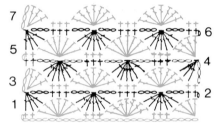

## Catherine Wheel II

Worked as Catherine Wheel I.
Make base chain and work first row in colour A. Thereafter work 2 rows each in colour B and colour A.

## Catherine Wheel III

Worked as Catherine Wheel I.
Work 1 row each in colours A, B and C throughout.

# Patterns for Texture and Colour

## Catherine Wheel IV

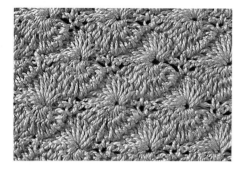

Multiple of 8 sts + 1.
(add 1 for base chain)

**Special Abbreviation**

**CL (Cluster)** worked as under Catherine Wheel I.

**1st row** (right side): 1dc into 2nd ch from hook, *miss 3ch, 9tr into next ch, miss 3ch, 1dc into next ch; rep from * to end, turn.

**2nd row:** 3ch (count as 1tr), miss first st, 1CL over next 4 sts, *3ch, 1dc into next st, 3ch, 1CL over next 9 sts; rep from * ending last rep with 1CL over last 5 sts, miss tch, turn.

**3rd row:** 3ch (count as 1tr), 4tr into first st, *miss 3ch, 1dc into next dc, miss 3ch, 9tr into loop which closed next CL; rep from * ending last rep with 5tr into top of tch, turn.

**4th row:** 1ch, 1dc into first st, *3ch, 1CL over next 9 sts, 3ch, 1dc into next st; rep from * ending last rep with 1dc into top of tch, turn.

**5th row:** 1ch, 1dc into first st, *miss 3ch, 9tr into loop which closed next CL, miss 3ch, 1dc into next dc; rep from * to end, miss tch, turn.

Rep 2nd, 3rd, 4th and 5th rows.

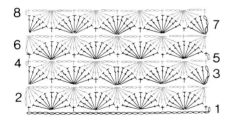

## Silt Stitch

Multiple of 3 sts + 1.
(add 2 for base chain)

**1st row** (right side): Miss 3ch (count as 1tr), 1tr into next and each ch to end, turn.

**2nd row:** 1ch (counts as 1dc), 2tr into first st, *miss 2 sts, work [1dc, 2tr] into next st; rep from * to last 3 sts, miss 2 sts, 1dc into top of tch, turn.

**3rd row:** 3ch (count as 1tr), miss 1 st, 1tr into next and each st to end, working last st into top of tch, turn.

Rep 2nd and 3rd rows.

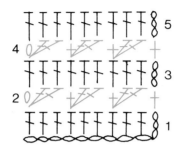

## Hexagon Stitch

Multiple of 8 sts + 4.
(add 1 for base chain)

**Special Abbreviations**

**CL (Cluster)** = work [yo, insert hook, yo, draw loop through loosely], over number and position of sts indicated, ending yo, draw through all loops, 1ch tightly to close Cluster.

**Picot** = 5ch, 1dc into 2nd ch from hook, 1dc into each of next 3ch.

**1st row** (wrong side): 1dc into 2nd ch from hook, 1dc into each of next 3ch (counts as Picot), miss 3ch, 3tr into next ch, miss 3ch, 1dc into next ch, *miss 3ch, into next ch work [3tr, 1 Picot, 3tr], miss 3ch, 1dc into next ch; rep from * to end, turn.

**2nd row:** 4ch (count as 1dtr), 1CL over each of first 8 sts, 3ch, 1dc into top of Picot, *3ch, 1CL over next 15 sts inserting hook into underside of each of 4ch of Picot, into next 3tr, 1dc, 3tr and 4dc of next Picot, then 3ch, 1dc into top of Picot; rep from * to end, turn.

**3rd row:** 1ch, 1dc into first st, *miss 3ch, into loop which closed next CL work [3tr, 1 Picot, 3tr], miss 3ch, 1dc into next dc; rep from * ending miss 3ch, 4tr into loop which closed last CL, miss tch, turn.

**4th row:** 7ch (count as 1dtr and 3ch), starting into 5th ch from hook work 1CL over next 15 sts as before, *3ch, 1dc into top of Picot, 3ch, 1CL over next 15 sts; rep from * ending last rep with 1CL over last 8 sts, miss tch, turn.

**5th row:** 8ch, 1dc into 2nd ch from hook, 1dc into each of next 3ch (counts as 1tr and 1 Picot), 3tr into first st, miss 3ch, 1dc into next dc, *miss 3ch, into loop which closed next CL work [3tr, 1 Picot, 3tr], miss 3ch, 1dc into next dc; rep from * ending last rep with 1dc into 4th ch of tch, turn.

Rep 2nd, 3rd, 4th and 5th rows.

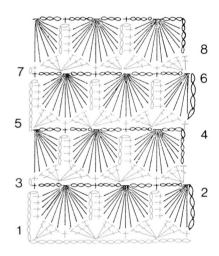

## Grit Stitch I

Multiple of 2 sts + 1.
(add 2 for base chain)

**1st row:** Miss 2ch (count as 1dc), 1dc into next ch, *miss 1ch, 2dc into next ch; rep from * to last 2ch, miss 1ch, 1dc into last ch, turn.

**2nd row:** 1ch (counts as 1dc), 1dc into first st, *miss 1dc, 2dc into next dc; rep from * to last 2 sts, miss 1dc, 1dc into top of tch, turn.

Rep 2nd row.

24

Stitch Variations, Abbreviations and Symbols on pages 7 to 15.

# Patterns for Texture and Colour

## Grit Stitch II

Multiple of 2 sts + 1.
(add 2 for base chain)

**1st row:** Miss 2ch (count as 1dc), 1tr into next ch, *miss 1ch, work [1dc and 1tr] into next ch; rep from * to last 2ch, miss 1ch, 1dc into last ch, turn.

**2nd row:** 1ch (counts as 1dc), 1tr into first st, *miss 1tr, work [1dc and 1tr] into next dc; rep from * to last 2 sts, miss 1tr, 1dc into top of tch, turn.

Rep 2nd row.

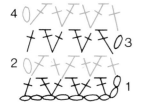

## Sedge Stitch I

Multiple of 3 sts + 1.
(add 2 for base chain)

**1st row:** Miss 2ch (count as 1dc), work [1htr, 1tr] into next ch, *miss 2ch, work [1dc, 1htr, 1tr] into next ch; rep from * to last 3ch, miss 2ch, 1dc into last ch, turn.

**2nd row:** 1ch (counts as 1dc), work [1htr, 1tr] into first st, *miss [1tr and 1htr], work [1dc, 1htr, 1tr] into next dc; rep from * to last 3 sts, miss [1tr and 1htr], 1dc into top of tch, turn.

Rep 2nd row.

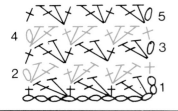

## Sedge Stitch II

Multiple of 3 sts + 1.
(add 2 for base chain)

**1st row:** Miss 2ch (count as 1dc), 2tr into next ch, *miss 2ch, [1dc, 2tr] into next ch; rep from * to last 3ch, miss 2ch, 1dc into last ch, turn.

**2nd row:** 1ch (counts as 1 dc), 2tr into first st, *miss 2tr, [1dc, 2tr] into next dc; rep from * to last 3 sts, miss 2tr, 1dc into top of tch, turn.

Rep 2nd row.

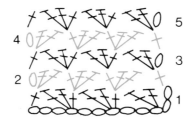

## Wattle Stitch

Multiple of 3 sts + 2.
(add 1 for base chain)

**1st row:** Miss 2ch (count as 1dc), *work [1dc, 1ch, 1tr] into next ch, miss 2ch; rep from * ending 1dc into last ch, turn.

**2nd row:** 1ch (counts as 1dc), miss first dc and next tr, *work [1dc, 1ch, 1tr] into next ch sp, miss 1dc and 1tr; rep from * ending with [1dc, 1ch, 1tr] into last ch sp, miss next dc, 1dc into top of tch, turn.

Rep 2nd row.

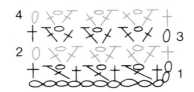

## Wedge Stitch I

Multiple of 6 sts + 1.
(add 1 for base chain)

**Special Abbreviation**

**WP (Wedge Picot)** = work 6ch, 1dc into 2nd ch from hook, 1htr into next ch, 1tr into next ch, 1dtr into next ch, 1ttr into next ch.

**1st row** (wrong side): 1dc into 2nd ch from hook, *1WP, miss 5ch, 1dc into next ch; rep from * to end, turn.

**2nd row:** 5ch (count as 1ttr), *1dc into top of WP, over next 5ch at underside of WP work 1dc into next ch, 1htr into next ch, 1tr into next ch, 1dtr into next ch, 1ttr into next ch, miss next dc; rep from * omitting 1ttr at end of last rep when 2 sts remain, **[yo] 3 times, insert hook into last ch at underside of WP, yo, draw loop through, [yo, draw through 2 loops] 3 times, rep from ** into next dc, yo, draw through all 3 loops on hook, miss tch, turn.

**3rd row:** 1ch, 1dc into first st, *1WP, miss next 5 sts, 1dc into next st; rep from * ending last rep with 1dc into top of tch, turn.

Rep 2nd and 3rd rows.

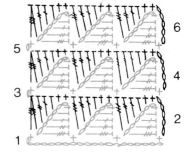

## Wedge Stitch II

Worked as Wedge Stitch I.
Make base chain and work first row in colour A. Thereafter work 2 rows each in colour B and colour A.

25

# Patterns for Texture and Colour

## Crosshatch Stitch I

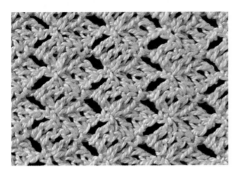

Multiple of 7 sts + 4.
(add 3 for base chain)

**1st row:** Miss 2ch (count as 1tr), 2tr into next ch, *miss 3ch, 1dc into next ch, 3ch, 1tr into each of next 3ch; rep from * to last 4ch, miss 3ch, 1dc into last ch, turn.

**2nd row:** 3ch (count as 1tr), 2tr into first dc, *miss 3trc, 1dc into first of 3ch, 3ch, 1tr into each of next 2ch, 1tr into next dc; rep from * ending miss 2tr, 1dc into top of tch, turn.
Rep 2nd row.

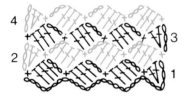

## Crosshatch Stitch II

Worked as Crosshatch Stitch I.
Work 1 row each in colours A, B and C throughout.

## Ridged Chevron Stitch

---

Multiple of 12 sts.
(add 3 for base chain)

**1st row:** Miss 3ch (count as 1tr), 1tr into next ch, *1tr into each of next 3ch, [over next 2ch work tr2tog] twice, 1tr into each of next 3ch, [2tr into next ch] twice; rep from * ending last rep with 2tr once only into last ch, turn.

**2nd row:** 3ch (count as 1tr), 1tr into first st, always inserting hook into back loop only of each st *1tr into each of next 3 sts, [over next 2 sts work tr2tog] twice, 1tr into each of next 3 sts, [2tr into next st] twice; rep from * ending last rep with 2tr once only into top of tch, turn.
Rep 2nd row.

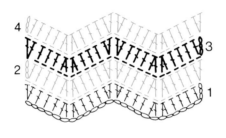

## Sharp Chevron Stitch

Multiple of 14 sts.
(add 2 for base chain)

**1st row:** Miss 2ch (count as 1tr), 2tr into next ch, *1tr into each of next 3ch, [over next 3ch work tr3tog] twice, 1tr into each of next 3ch, [3tr into next st] twice; rep from * ending last rep with 3tr once only into last ch, turn.

**2nd row:** 3ch (count as 1tr), 2tr into first st, *1tr into each of next 3 sts, [over next 3 sts work tr3tog] twice, 1tr into each of next 3 sts, [3tr into next st] twice; rep from * ending last rep with 3tr once only into top of tch, turn.
Rep 2nd row.

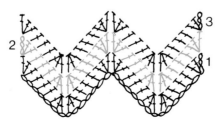

---

## Close Chevron Stitch

Multiple of 11 sts + 1.
(add 1 for base chain)
Work 4 rows each in colours A and B alternately throughout.

**1st row** (right side): 2dc into 2nd ch from hook, *1dc into each of next 4ch, miss 2ch, 1dc into each of next 4ch, 3dc into next ch; rep from * ending last rep with 2dc only into last ch, turn.

**2nd row:** 1ch, 2dc into first st, *1dc into each of next 4 sts, miss 2 sts, 1dc into each of next 4 sts, 3dc into next st; rep from * ending last rep with 2dc only into last st, miss tch, turn.
Rep 2nd row.

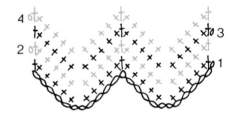

## Peephole Chevron Stitch

Multiple of 10 sts.
(add 2 for base chain)

**1st row:** Miss 2ch (count as 1tr), 1tr into each of next 4ch, *miss 2ch, 1tr into each of next 4ch, 2ch, 1tr into each of next 4ch; rep from * to last 6ch, miss 2ch, 1tr into each of next 3ch, 2tr into last ch, turn.

**2nd row:** 3ch (count as 1tr), 1tr into first st, 1tr into each of next 3 sts, *miss 2 sts, 1tr into each of next 3 sts, [1tr, 2ch, 1tr] into 2ch sp, 1tr into each of next 3 sts; rep from * to

---

Stitch Variations, Abbreviations and Symbols on pages 7 to 15.

# Patterns for Texture and Colour

last 6 sts, miss 2 sts, 1tr into each of next 3 sts, 2tr into top of tch, turn.
Rep 2nd row.

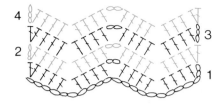

## Crunchy Chevron Stitch

Multiple of 8 sts.
(add 1 for base chain)

Work 1 row each in colours A, B, C, D and E throughout.
**1st row:** 1dc into 2nd ch from hook, 1dc into each of next 3ch, *htr2tog all into each of next 4ch, 1dc into each of next 4ch; rep from * to last 4ch, htr2tog all into each of last 4ch, turn.
**2nd row:** 1ch, then starting in first st, *1dc into each of next 4 sts, htr2tog all into each of next 4dc; rep from * to end, miss tch, turn.
Rep 2nd row.

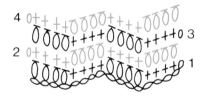

## Simple Chevron Stitch

Multiple of 10 sts + 1.
(add 2 for base chain)

**1st row:** Miss 2ch (count as 1tr), 1tr into next ch, *1tr into each of next 3ch, over next 3ch work tr3tog, 1tr into each of next 3ch, 3tr into next ch; rep from * ending last rep with 2tr into last ch, turn.
**2nd row:** 3ch (count as 1tr), 1tr into first st, *1tr into each of next 3tr, over next 3 sts work tr3tog, 1tr into each of next 3tr, 3tr into next tr; rep from * ending last rep with 2tr into top of tch, turn.
Rep 2nd row.

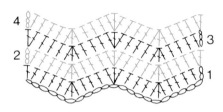

## Textured Wave Stitch

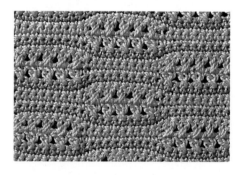

Multiple of 20 sts.
(add 1 for base chain)

**Special Abbreviation**
**2Ctr (2 crossed trebles)** = miss next st, 1tr into next st, 1tr into missed st working over previous tr.

Work 2 rows each in colours A and B alternately throughout.
**1st base row** (right side): Miss 2ch (count as 1dc), 1dc into next and each ch to end, turn.
**2nd base row:** 1ch (counts as 1dc), miss 1 st, 1dc into next and each st to end working last st into tch, turn.

**Commence Pattern**
**1st row:** 3ch (count as 1tr), miss 1 st, over next 4 sts work [2Ctr] twice, *1dc into each of next 10 sts, over next 10 sts work [2Ctr] 5 times; rep from * to last 15 sts, 1dc into each of next 10 sts, over next 4 sts work [2Ctr] twice, 1tr into tch, turn.
**2nd row:** As 1st row.
**3rd and 4th rows:** As 2nd base row.
**5th row:** 1ch (counts as 1dc), miss 1 st, 1dc into each of next 4 sts, *over next 10 sts work [2Ctr] 5 times, 1dc into each of next 10 sts; rep from * to last 15 sts, over next

10sts work [2Ctr] 5 times, 1dc into each of last 5 sts working last st into tch, turn.
**6th row:** As 5th row.
**7th and 8th rows:** As 2nd base row.
Rep these 8 rows.

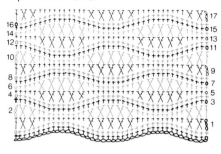

2 rows each in colours A and B

## Long Wave Stitch

Multiple of 14 sts + 1.
(add 1 for base chain)
**Special Abbreviation**
**Gr (Group)** (worked over 14 sts) = 1dc into next st, [1htr into next st] twice, [1tr into next st] twice, [1dtr into next st] 3 times, [1tr into next st] twice, [1htr into next st] twice, [1dc into next st] twice.
**Rev Gr (Reverse Group)** (worked over 14 sts) = 1dtr into next st, [1tr into next st] twice, [1htr into next st] twice, [1dc into next st] 3 times, [1htr into next st] twice, [1tr into next st] twice, [1dtr into next st] twice.

Work 2 rows each in colours A and B alternately throughout.
**1st row** (right side): Miss 2ch (count as 1dc), *1Gr over next 14ch; rep from * to end, turn.
**2nd row:** 1ch (counts as 1dc), miss first st, 1dc into next and each st to end working last st into top of tch, turn.
**3rd row:** 4ch (count as 1dtr), miss first st, *1 Rev Gr over next 14 sts; rep from * ending last rep in tch, turn.
**4th row:** As 2nd row.
**5th row:** 1ch (counts as 1dc), miss first st, *1Gr over next 14 sts; rep from * ending last rep in tch, turn.
**6th row:** As 2nd row.
Rep 3rd, 4th, 5th and 6th rows.

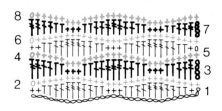

# Patterns for Texture and Colour

## Smooth Wave Stitch

Multiple of 8 sts + 4.
(add 1 for base chain)
Work 2 rows each in colours A and B alternately throughout.

**1st row** (right side): Miss 2ch (count as 1dc), 1dc into each of next 3ch, *1tr into each of next 4ch, 1dc into each of next 4ch; rep from * to end, turn.

**2nd row:** 1ch (counts as 1dc), miss first st, 1dc into each of next 3 sts, *1tr into each of next 4 sts, 1dc into each of next 4 sts; rep from * to end working last st into top of tch, turn.

**3rd row:** 3ch (count as 1tr), miss first st, 1tr into each of next 3 sts, *1dc into each of next 4 sts, 1tr into each of next 4 sts; rep from * to end working last st into top of tch, turn.

**4th row:** As 3rd row.

**5th and 6th rows:** As 2nd row.
Rep 3rd, 4th, 5th and 6th rows.

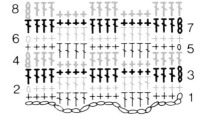

## Wave and Chevron Stitch

Multiple of 6 sts + 1.
(add 1 for base chain)

Work 2 rows each in colours A, B, C and D throughout.

**Base row:** (right side): Miss 2ch (count as 1dc), 1dc into next and each ch to end, turn.

### Commence Pattern

**1st row:** 1ch (counts as 1dc), miss 1 st, *1htr into next st, 1tr into next st, 3dtr into next st, 1tr into next st, 1htr into next st, 1dc into next st; rep from * to end, turn.

**2nd row:** 1ch, miss 1 st, 1dc into next st (counts as dc2tog), 1dc into each of next 2 sts, *3dc into next st, 1dc into each of next 2 sts, over next 3 sts work dc3tog, 1dc into each of next 2 sts; rep from * to last 5 sts, 3dc into next st, 1dc into each of next 2 sts, over last 2 sts work dc2tog, miss tch, turn.

**3rd row:** As 2nd row.

**4th row:** 4ch, miss 1 st, 1dtr into next st (counts as dtr2tog), *1tr into next st, 1htr into next st, 1dc into next st, 1htr into next st, 1tr into next st**, over next 3 sts work dtr3tog; rep from * ending last rep at **, over last 2 sts work dtr2tog, miss tch, turn.

**5th row:** 1ch (counts as 1dc), miss 1 st, 1dc into next and each st to end, turn.

**6th row:** As 5th row.
Rep these 6 rows.

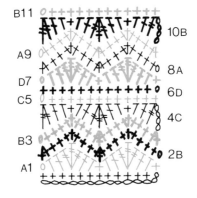

## Crossed Treble Stitch

Multiple of 2 sts.
(add 2 for base chain)

### Special Abbreviation

**2Ctr (2 crossed trebles)** worked as under Textured Wave Stitch

**1st row** (right side): Miss 3ch (count as 1tr), *2Ctr over next 2ch; rep from * ending 1tr into last ch, turn.

**2nd row:** 1ch (counts as 1dc), miss 1 st, 1dc into next and each st to end, working last st into top of tch, turn.

**3rd row:** 3ch (count as 1tr), miss 1 st, *work 2Ctr over next 2 sts; rep from * ending 1tr into tch, turn.

Rep 2nd and 3rd rows.

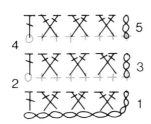

## Woven Shell Stitch

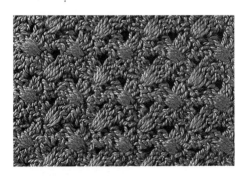

Multiple of 6 sts + 1.
(add 2 for base chain)

### Special Abbreviation

**CGr (Crossed Group)** = miss 3tr and next st, 3tr into 2nd of next 3tr, 3ch, 3tr into 2nd of 3tr just missed working back over last 3tr made.

**1st row:** Miss 3ch (count as 1tr), *miss next 3ch, 3tr into next ch, 3ch, 3tr into 2nd of 3ch just missed working back over last 3tr made, miss 1ch, 1tr into next ch; rep from * to end, turn.

**2nd row:** 3ch (count as 1tr), 3tr into first st, 1dc into next 3ch arch, *1CGr, 1dc into next 3ch arch; rep from * ending 4tr into top of tch, turn.

**3rd row:** 3ch (count as 1tr), miss 1 st, 1CGr, *1dc into next 3ch loop, 1CGr; rep from * ending 1tr into top of tch, turn.

Rep 2nd and 3rd rows.

## Crossbill Stitch

Stitch Variations, Abbreviations and Symbols on pages 7 to 15.

# Patterns for Texture and Colour

Multiple of 4 sts + 1.
(add 2 for base chain)

**Special Abbreviation**

**2Ctr (2 crossed trebles)** = miss 2sts, 1tr into next st, 1ch, 1tr into first of 2sts just missed working back over last tr made.

**1st row:** Miss 3ch (count as 1tr), *work 2Ctr over next 3ch, 1tr into next ch; rep from * to end, turn.

**2nd row:** 3ch (count as 1tr), 1tr into first st, miss 1tr, *1tr into next ch, work 2Ctr over next 3tr, rep from * ending 1tr into last ch, miss 1tr, 2tr into top of tch, turn.

**3rd row:** 3ch (count as 1tr), miss 1 st, *work 2Ctr over next 3tr, 1tr into next ch; rep from * ending last rep into top of tch, turn.

Rep 2nd and 3rd rows.

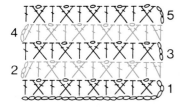

## Sidesaddle Cluster Stitch

Multiple of 5 sts + 1.
(add 1 for base chain)

**1st row:** 1dc into 2nd ch from hook, *3ch, tr4tog over next 4ch, 1ch, 1dc into next ch; rep from * to end, turn.

**2nd row:** 5ch, 1dc into next cluster, *3ch, tr4tog all into next 3ch arch, 1ch, 1dc into next cluster; rep from * ending 3ch, tr4tog all into next 3ch arch, 1tr into last dc, miss tch, turn.

**3rd row:** 1ch, miss 1 st, 1dc into next CL, *3ch, 1CL into next 3ch arch, 1ch, 1dc into next CL; rep from * ending last rep with 1dc into tch arch, turn.

Rep 2nd and 3rd rows.

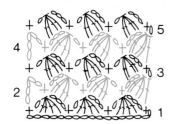

## Crossed Cluster Stitch

Multiple of 8 sts + 4.
(add 1 for base chain)

**Special Abbreviation**

**2CC (2 crossed clusters)** = miss 1 st, into next st work *[yo, insert hook, yo, draw loop through] twice, yo, draw through all 5 loops on hook; rep from * into st just missed working over previous cluster.

**1st row** (wrong side): Miss 2ch (count as 1dc), 1dc into next and each ch to end, turn.

**2nd row:** 3ch (count as 1tr), miss 1 st, *2CC over next 2 sts, 1tr into each of next 6 sts, rep from * to last 3 sts, 2CC over next 2 sts, 1tr into tch, turn.

**3rd row:** 1ch (counts as 1dc), miss 1 st, 1dc into next and each st to end, working last st into top of tch, turn.

**4th row:** 3ch (counts as 1tr), miss 1 st, 1tr into each of next 4 sts, *2CC over next 2 sts, 1tr into each of next 6 sts; rep from * to last 7 sts, 2CC over next 2 sts, 1tr into each of last 5 sts, working last st into tch, turn.

**5th row:** As 3rd row.

Rep 2nd, 3rd, 4th and 5th rows.

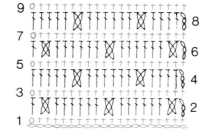

## Diagonal Shell Stitch

Multiple of 4 sts + 1.
(add 1 for base chain)

**Special Abbreviation**

**Shell** = [1dc, 3ch, 4tr] all into same st.

**1st row** (right side): Work 1 shell into 2nd ch from hook, *miss 3ch, 1 shell into next ch; rep from * to last 4ch, miss 3ch, 1dc into last ch, turn.

**2nd row:** 3ch (count as 1tr), miss 1 st, *miss 1tr, over next 2 sts work tr2tog, 3ch, miss 1tr, 1dc into top of 3ch; rep from * to end, turn.

**3rd row:** 1ch, 1 shell into first st, *miss 3ch and next st, 1 shell into next dc; rep from * ending miss 3ch and next st, 1dc into top of tch, turn.

Rep 2nd and 3rd rows.

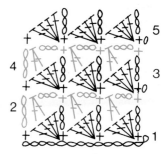

## Sidesaddle Shell Stitch

Multiple of 6 sts + 1.
(add 3 for base chain)

**Special Abbreviation**

**Shell** = 3tr, 1ch, [1dc, 1htr, 1tr] all into side of last of 3tr just made.

**1st row** (wrong side): Miss 3ch (count as 1tr), 3tr into next ch, miss 2ch, 1dc into next ch, *miss 2ch, Shell into next ch, miss 2ch, 1dc into next ch; rep from * to last 3ch, miss 2ch, 4tr into last ch, turn.

**2nd row:** 1ch (counts as 1dc), miss 1 st, *miss next 3 sts, Shell into next dc, miss 3 sts, 1dc into next ch sp; rep from * ending last rep with 1dc into top of tch, turn.

**3rd row:** 3ch (count as 1tr), 3tr into first st, miss 3 sts, 1dc into next ch sp, *miss 3 sts, Shell into next dc, miss 3 sts, 1dc into next ch sp; rep from * ending miss 3 sts, 4tr into tch, turn.

Rep 2nd and 3rd rows.

# Patterns for Texture and Colour

## Interlocking Block Stitch I

Multiple of 6 sts + 3.
(add 2 for base chain)

**Special Abbreviation**

**Str (Spike treble)** = work tr over ch sp by inserting hook into top of next row below (or base chain).

Work 1 row each in colours A, B and C throughout.

**1st row:** Miss 3ch (count as 1tr), 1tr into each of next 2ch, *3ch, miss 3ch, 1tr into each of next 3ch; rep from * to end, turn.
**2nd row:** *3ch, miss 3 sts, 1Str over each of next 3 sts; rep from * to last 3 sts, 2ch, miss 2 sts, sl st into top of tch, turn.
**3rd row:** 3ch (count as 1Str), miss 1 st, 1Str over each of next 2 sts, *3ch, miss 3 sts, 1Str over each of next 3 sts; rep from * to end, turn.
Rep 2nd and 3rd rows.

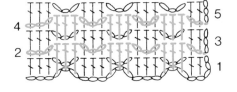

## Diagonal Spike Stitch

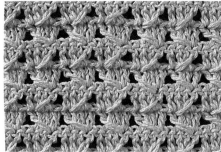

Multiple of 4 sts + 2.
(add 2 for base chain)

**Special Abbreviation**

**Str (Spike treble)** = yo, insert hook into same place that first tr of previous 3tr block was worked, yo draw loop through and up so as not to crush 3tr block, [yo, draw through 2 loops] twice.

**1st row:** Miss 3ch (count as 1tr), *1tr into each of next 3ch, miss next ch and work 1Str over it instead; rep from * ending 1tr into last ch, turn.
**2nd row:** 3ch (count as 1tr), miss 1 st, *1tr into each of next 3 sts, miss next st and work 1Str over it instead; rep from * ending 1tr into top of tch, turn.
Rep 2nd row.

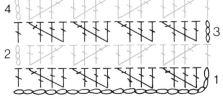

through and up to height of present row, yo, draw through both loops on hook

**1st row:** Miss 2ch (count as 1dc), 1dc into next and each ch to end, turn.
**2nd row:** 1ch (counts as 1dc), miss 1 st, *1dc into next st, 1Sdc over next st; rep from * ending 1dc into tch, turn.
Rep 2nd row.

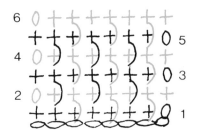

## Alternating Spike Stitch II

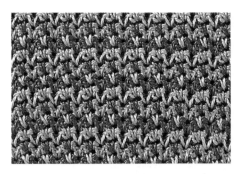

Worked as Alternating Spike Stitch I.
Work 1 row each in colours A, B and C throughout.

## Interlocking Block Stitch II

Worked as Interlocking Block Stitch I.
Work 1 row each in colours A and B alternately throughout. Do not break yarn when changing colour, but begin row at same end as colour.

## Alternating Spike Stitch I

Multiple of 2 sts.
(add 1 for base chain)

**Special Abbreviation**

**Sdc (Spike double crochet)** = insert hook below next st 1 row down (i.e. into same place as that st was worked), yo, draw loop

## Arrowhead Spike Stitch

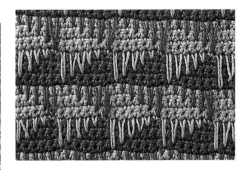

Multiple of 6 sts + 2.
(add 1 for base chain)

**Special Abbreviation**

**Sdc (Spike double crochet)** = insert hook below next st 1 or more rows down (indicated thus: Sdc1, Sdc2, Sdc3, etc), yo, draw loop through and up to height of current row,

Stitch Variations, Abbreviations and Symbols on pages 7 to 15.

# Patterns for Texture and Colour

yo, draw through both loops on hook

Work 6 rows each in colours A and B alternately throughout.

**Base row** (right side): Using A 1dc into 2nd ch from hook, 1dc into each ch to end, turn.

**Commence pattern**

**1st row:** 1ch, 1dc into first and each st to end, miss tch, turn.

Work 4 rows as 1st row.

**6th row:** Using B 1ch, 1dc into first st, *1dc into next st, 1Sdc1 over next st, 1Sdc2 over next st, 1Sdc3 over next st, 1Sdc4 over next st, 1Sdc5 over next st; rep from * ending 1dc into last st, miss tch, turn.

Work 5 rows as 1st row.

**12th row:** Using A 1ch, 1dc into first st, *1Sdc5 over next st, 1Sdc4 over next st, 1Sdc3 over next st, 1Sdc2 over next st, 1Sdc1 over next st, 1dc into next st; rep from * ending 1dc into last st, miss tch, turn.

Rep these 12 rows.

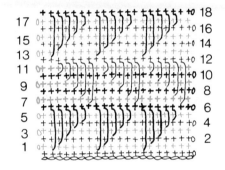

## Spiked Squares

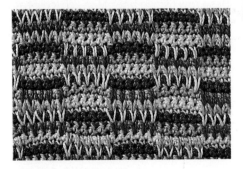

Multiple of 10 sts + 1.
(add 1 for base chain)

**Special Abbreviation**

**Sdc (Spike double crochet)** worked as under Arrowhead Spike Stitch. Note: when working Sdcs over previous Sdcs be careful to insert hook in centres of previous Sdcs.

Work 2 rows each in colours A, B and C throughout.

**Base row** (right side): 1dc into 2nd ch from hook, 1dc into next and each ch to end, turn.

**Commence Pattern**

**1st row:** 1ch, 1dc into first and each st to end, miss tch, turn.

**2nd row:** 1ch, 1dc into first st, *1Sdc2 over each of next 5 sts, 1dc into each of next 5

sts; rep from * ending 1dc into last dc, miss tch, turn.

Rep the last 2 rows 3 times more.

**9th row:** As 1st row.

**10th row:** 1ch, 1dc into first st, *1dc into each of next 5 sts, 1Sdc2 over each of next 5 sts; rep from * ending 1dc into last dc, miss tch, turn.

Rep the last 2 rows 3 times more.

Rep these 16 rows.

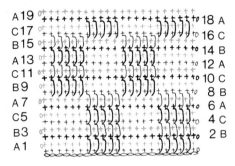

## Spike Cluster Stitch

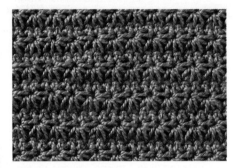

Multiple of 8 sts + 5.
(add 1 for base chain)

**Special Abbreviation**

**SPC (Spike Cluster)** = over next st pick up 5 spike loops by inserting hook as follows: 2 sts to right of next st and 1 row down; 1 st to right and 2 rows down; directly below and 3 rows down; 1 st to left and 2 rows down; 2 sts to left and 1 row down, (6 loops on hook); now insert hook into top of next st itself, yo, draw loop through, yo, draw through all 7 loops on hook

Work 4 rows each in colours A and B alternately throughout.

**Base row** (right side): 1dc into 2nd ch from hook, 1dc into each ch to end, turn.

**Commence Pattern**

**1st row:** 1ch, 1dc into first and each st to end, miss tch, turn.

**2nd and 3rd rows:** As 1st row.

**4th row:** 1ch, 1dc into each of first 4 sts, *1SPC over next st, 1dc into each of next 7 sts (Hint: be careful not to pick up any of the spikes of the previous SPC); rep from * ending 1dc into last st, miss tch, turn.

**5th, 6th and 7th rows:** As 1st row.

**8th row:** 1ch, 1dc into each of first 8 sts, *1SPC over next st, 1dc into each of next 7 sts; rep from * to last 5 sts, 1SPC over next st, 1dc into each of last 4 sts, miss tch, turn.

Rep these 8 rows.

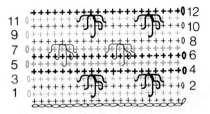

## 5-Star Marguerite Stitch

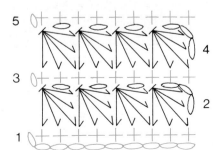

Multiple of 2 sts + 1.
(add 1 for base chain)

**Special Abbreviation**

**M5C (Marguerite Cluster with 5 spike loops)** = pick up spike loops (ie: yo and draw through) inserting hook as follows: into loop which closed previous M5C, under 2 threads of last spike loop of same M5C, into same place that last spike loop of same M5C was worked, into each of next 2 sts (6 loops on hook), yo, draw through all loops on hook

**1st row** (wrong side): 1dc into 2nd ch from hook, 1dc into next and each ch to end, turn.

**2nd row:** 3ch, 1M5C inserting hook into 2nd and 3rd chs from hook and then first 3 sts to pick up 5 spike loops, *1ch, 1M5C; rep from * to end, miss tch, turn.

**3rd row:** 1ch, 1dc into loop which closed last M5C, *1dc into next ch, 1dc into loop which closed next M5C; rep from * ending 1dc into each of next 2ch of tch, turn.

Rep 2nd and 3rd rows.

# Patterns for Texture and Colour

## Simple Marguerite Stitch

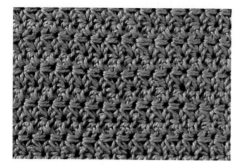

Multiple of 2 sts + 1.
(add 2 for base chain)

**Special Abbreviation**

↖ **M3C (Marguerite Cluster with 3 spike loops)**

**1st row:** Make a spike loop (i.e. yo and draw through) into 2nd, 3rd and 5th chs from hook, yo and through all 4 loops (1M3C made), *1ch, make 1M3C picking up 1 loop in ch which closed previous M3C, 2nd loop in same place as last spike of previous M3C, miss 1ch, then last loop in next ch, yo and through all 4 loops; rep from * to end, turn.

**2nd row:** 3ch, make 1M3C picking up loops in 2nd and 3rd ch from hook and in ch which closed 2nd M3C on previous row, *1ch, work 1M3C picking up first loop in ch which closed previous M3C, 2nd loop in same place as last spike of previous M3C and last loop in ch which closed next M3C on previous row; rep from * to end, picking up final loop in top of ch at beg of previous row.
Rep 2nd row.

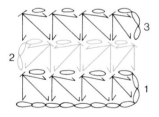

## Granule Stitch

Multiple of 4 sts + 1.
(add 1 for base chain)

**Special Abbreviation**

**Pdc (Picot double crochet)** = insert hook, yo, draw loop through, [yo, draw through 1 loop] 3 times to make 3ch, yo, draw through both loops on hook. Note: draw picot chain

loops to the back (right side) of fabric.

**1st row** (right side): 1dc into 2nd ch from hook, 1dc into each ch to end, turn.

**2nd row:** 1ch, 1dc into first st, *1Pdc into next st, 1dc into next st; rep from * to end, miss tch, turn.

**3rd row:** 1ch, 1dc into first and each st to end, miss tch, turn. Hint: Hold down the picot chains at the front and you will see the top 2 loops of the Pdc where you are to insert the hook.

**4th row:** 1ch, 1dc into each of first 2 sts, *1Pdc into next st, 1dc into next st; rep from * to last st, 1dc into last st, miss tch, turn.

**5th row:** As 3rd row.
Rep 2nd, 3rd, 4th and 5th rows.

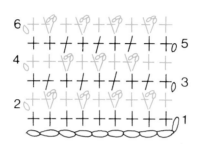

## Relief Arch Stitch

Multiple of 8 sts + 1.
(add 1 for base chain)

**1st row** (wrong side): 1dc into 2nd ch from hook, 1dc into each of next 2ch, *7ch, miss 3ch, 1dc into each of next 5ch; rep from * to last 6ch, 7ch, miss 3ch, 1dc into each of last 3ch, turn.

**2nd row:** 3ch (count as 1tr), miss 1 st, 1tr into each of next 2 sts, *going behind 7ch loop work 1dtr into each of next 3 base ch**, 1tr into each of next 5dc; rep from * ending last rep at ** when 3 sts remain, 1tr into each of last 3 sts, miss tch, turn.

**3rd row:** 1ch, 1dc into first st, *7ch, miss 3 sts, 1dc into next st at same time catching in centre of 7ch loop of last-but-one row, 7ch, miss 3 sts, 1dc into next st; rep from * to end, turn.

**4th row:** 3ch (count as 1tr), miss 1 st, *going behind 7ch loop of last row work 1dtr into each of next 3 sts of last-but-one row, 1tr into next dc; rep from * to end, miss tch, turn.

**5th row:** 1ch, 1dc into each of first 2 sts, *1dc into next st at same time catching in centre of 7ch loop of last-but-one row, 7ch, miss 3 sts, 1dc into next st at same time catching in centre of 7ch loop of last-but-one row**, 1dc into each of next 3 sts; rep from

* ending last rep at ** when 2 sts remain, 1dc into each of last 2 sts, turn.

**6th row:** As 2nd row working dtrs into last-but-one row.
Rep 3rd, 4th, 5th and 6th rows.

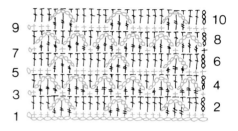

## Thistle Pattern

Multiple of 10 sts + 1.
(add 1 for base chain)

**Special Abbreviation**

**Catch Loop** = Catch 10ch loop of Thistle by inserting hook under ch at tip of loop **at the same time** as under the next st.

**Base row** (wrong side): Miss 2ch (count as 1dc), 1dc into each of next 4ch, *into next st work a Thistle of 1dc, [10ch, 1dc] 3 times**, 1dc into each of next 9ch; rep from * ending last rep at **, 1dc into each of last 5dc, turn.

**Commence Pattern**

**Note:** Hold loops of Thistle down at front of work on right side rows.

**1st row:** 1ch (count as 1dc), miss 1dc, 1dc into each of next 4dc, *miss 1dc of Thistle, work dc2tog over next 2dc, miss last dc of Thistle**, work 1dc into each of next 9 sts; rep from * ending last rep at **, 1dc into each of next 4dc, 1dc into tch, turn.

**2nd, 4th, 8th and 10th rows:** 1ch, miss 1 st, 1dc into each st to end, turn.

**3rd row:** 1ch, miss 1 st, 1dc into next dc, *catch first loop of Thistle in next dc, 1dc into each of next 5dc, miss centre loop of Thistle, catch 3rd loop in next st**, 1dc into each of next 3dc; rep from * ending last rep at **, 1dc into each of last 2 sts, turn.

**5th row:** 1ch, miss 1 st, 1dc into each of next 4dc, *work 6tr into next dc and at the same time catch centre loop**, 1dc into each of next 9dc; rep from * ending last rep at **, 1dc into each of last 5 sts, turn.

**6th row:** 1ch, miss 1 st, 1dc into each of first 4dc, *1ch, miss 6tr, 1dc into each of next 4dc**, work a Thistle into next dc, 1dc into each of next 4dc; rep from * ending last rep

Stitch Variations, Abbreviations and Symbols on pages 7 to 15.

at **, 1dc into last st, turn.

**7th row:** 1ch, miss 1 st, 1dc into each of next 9 sts, *work dc2tog over centre 2 of next 4dc, miss 1dc, 1dc into each of next 9 sts; rep from * to last st, 1dc into last st, turn.

**9th row:** 1ch, miss 1 st, 1dc into each of next 6dc, *catch first loop into next dc, 1dc into each of next 5dc, catch 3rd loop into next dc**, 1dc into each of next 3dc; rep from * ending last rep at **, 1dc into each st to end, turn.

**11th row:** 1ch, miss 1 st, 1dc into each of next 9 sts, *work 6tr into next dc and catch centre loop at the same time, 1dc into each of next 9dc; rep from * to last st, 1dc in last st, turn.

**12th row:** 1ch, miss 1 st, 1dc into each of next 4dc, *work a Thistle into next dc, 1dc into each of next 4dc**, 1ch, miss 6tr, 1dc into each of next 4dc; rep from * ending last rep at **, 1dc into last st, turn.

Rep these 12 rows.

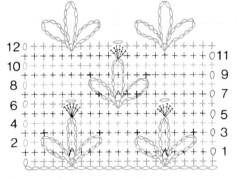

## Corded Ridge Stitch

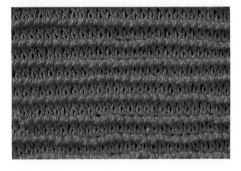

Any number of sts.
(add 2 for base chain)

**Note:** work all rows with right side facing, i.e. work even numbered rows from left to right

**1st row** (right side): Miss 3ch (count as 1tr), 1tr into next and each ch to end. Do not turn.

**2nd row:** 1ch, 1dc into front loop only of last tr made, *1dc into front loop only of next tr to right; rep from * ending sl st into top of tch at beginning of row. Do not turn.

**3rd row:** 3ch (count as 1tr), miss 1 st, 1tr into back loop only of next and each st of last-but-one row to end. Do not turn.

Rep 2nd and 3rd rows.

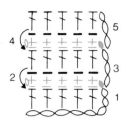

## Astrakhan Stitch

Any number of sts.
(add 2 for base chain)

**Note:** work all rows with right side facing, i.e. work even numbered rows from left to right.

**1st row** (right side): Miss 3ch (count as 1tr), 1tr into each ch to end. Do not turn.

**2nd row:** *7ch, sl st into front loop only of next tr to right; rep from * ending 7ch, sl st into top of tch at beginning of row. Do not turn.

**3rd row:** 3ch (count as 1tr), miss 1 st, 1tr into back loop only of next and each st of last-but-one row to end. Do not turn.

Rep 2nd and 3rd rows.

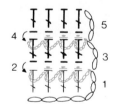

## Embossed Roundels

Multiple of 8 sts + 5.
(add 2 for base chain)

**Special Abbreviation**
**ERd (Embossed Roundel)** = work [1tr, 2ch] 9 times all into same st, remove hook from working loop, insert hook from back through top of first tr of Roundel and, keeping sts of Roundel at back of fabric, pick up working loop again and draw through to close Roundel.

**1st row** (right side): Miss 3ch (count as 1tr), 1tr into next and each ch to end, turn.

**2nd row:** 3ch (count as 1tr), miss 1 st, 1tr into each of next 3 sts, *1ERd into next st, 1tr into each of next 7 sts; rep from * ending 1tr into top of tch, turn.

**3rd row:** 3ch (count as 1tr), miss 1 st, 1tr into next and each st to end, working last st into top of tch, turn.

**4th row:** 3ch (count as 1tr), miss 1 st, *1tr into each of next 7 sts, 1ERd into next st; rep from * to last 4 sts, 1tr into each of last 4 sts, turn.

**5th row:** As 3rd row.
Rep 2nd, 3rd, 4th and 5th rows.

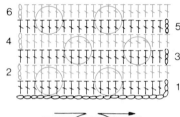

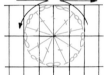

## Embossed Pockets

Multiple of 3 sts + 1.
(add 2 for base chain)

**Special Abbreviation**
**PGr (Pocket Group)** = work [1dc, 1htr, 3tr] round stem of indicated st.

**1st row:** (wrong side): Miss 3ch (count as 1tr), 1tr into each ch to end, turn.

**2nd row:** 1PGr round first st, miss 2 sts, sl st into top of next st, *1PGr round same st as sl st, miss 2 sts, sl st into top of next st; rep from * to end, turn.

**3rd row:** 3ch (count as 1tr), miss 1 st, 1tr into each st to end, turn.

Rep 2nd and 3rd rows.

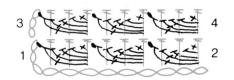

# Patterns for Texture and Colour

## Single Rib

Multiple of 2 sts.
(add 2 for base chain)

**1st row** (wrong side): Miss 3ch (count as 1tr), 1tr into next and each ch to end, turn.
**2nd row:** 2ch (count as 1tr), miss first st, *1tr/rf round next st, 1tr/rb round next st; rep from * ending 1tr into top of tch, turn.
Rep 2nd row.

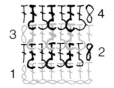

## Zig-Zag Rib

Multiple of 4 sts + 2.
(add 2 for base chain)

**Base row** (wrong side): Miss 3ch (count as 1tr), 1tr into next and each ch to end, turn.
**Commence Pattern**
**1st row:** 2ch (count as 1tr), miss first st, *1tr/rf round each of next 2 sts, 1tr/rb round each of next 2 sts; rep from * ending 1tr into top of tch, turn.
**2nd row:** 2ch (count as 1tr), miss first st, 1tr/rb round next st, *1tr/rf round each of next 2 sts**, 1tr/rb round each of next 2 sts; rep from * ending last rep at ** when 2 sts remain, 1tr/rb round next st, 1tr into top of tch, turn.
**3rd row:** 2ch (count as 1tr), miss first st, *1tr/rb round each of next 2sts, 1tr/rf round each of next 2 sts; rep from * ending 1tr into top of tch, turn.

**4th row:** 2ch (count as 1tr), miss first st, 1tr/rf round next st, *1tr/rb round each of next 2 sts**, 1tr/rf round each of next 2 sts; rep from * ending last rep at ** when 2 sts remain, 1tr/rf round next st, 1tr into top of tch, turn.
**5th row:** As 3rd row.
**6th row:** As 2nd row.
**7th row:** As 1st row.
**8th row:** As 4th row.
Rep these 8 rows.

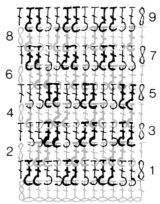

## Ripple Stitch I

Multiple of 2 sts + 1.
(add 2 for base chain)

**1st row** (right side): miss 3ch (count as 1tr), 1tr into each ch to end, turn.
**2nd row:** 1ch (counts as 1dc), miss first st, 1dc into each st to end, working last st into top of tch, turn.
**3rd row:** 3ch (count as 1tr), miss first st, *1dtr/rf round tr below next st, 1tr into next st; rep from * to end, turn.
**4th row:** As 2nd row.
**5th row:** 3ch (count as 1tr), miss first st, *1tr into next st, 1dtr/rf round tr below next st; rep from * to last 2 sts, 1tr into each of last 2 sts, turn.
Rep 2nd, 3rd, 4th and 5th rows.

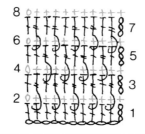

## Ripple Stitch II

Worked as Ripple Stitch I.
Work 2 rows each in colours A and B alternately throughout.

## Basketweave Stitch

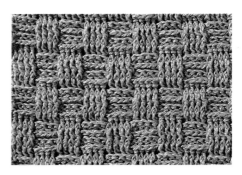

Multiple of 8 sts + 2.
(add 2 for base chain)

**Base row** (wrong side): Miss 3ch (count as 1tr), 1tr into next and each ch to end, turn.
**Commence Pattern**
**1st row:** 2ch (count as 1tr), miss first st, *1tr/rf round each of next 4 sts, 1tr/rb round each of next 4 sts; rep from * ending 1tr into top of tch, turn.
Rep the last row 3 times.
**5th row:** 2ch (count as 1tr), miss first st, *1tr/rb round each of next 4 sts, 1tr/rf round each of next 4 sts; rep from * ending 1tr into top of tch, turn.
Rep the last row 3 times.

Rep these 8 rows.

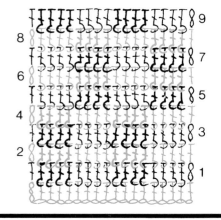

Stitch Variations, Abbreviations and Symbols on pages 7 to 15.

# Patterns for Texture and Colour

## Raised Chevron Stitch

Multiple of 16 sts + 1.
(add 2 for base chain)

**1st row** (right side): Miss 3ch, tr2tog over next 2ch (counts as tr3tog), *1tr into each of next 5ch, [2tr, 1ch, 2tr] into next ch, 1tr into each of next 5ch**, tr5tog over next 5ch; rep from * ending last rep at ** when 3ch remain, tr3tog, turn.

**2nd row:** 3ch, miss first st, tr/rb2tog over next 2 sts (all counts as tr/rb3tog), *1tr/rf round each of next 5 sts, [2tr, 1ch, 2tr] into next ch sp, 1tr/rf round each of next 5 sts**, tr/rb5tog over next 5 sts; rep from * ending last rep at ** when 3 sts remain, tr/rb3tog, turn.

**3rd row:** 3ch, miss first st, tr/rf2tog over next 2 sts (all counts as tr/rf3tog), *1tr/rb round each of next 5 sts, [2tr, 1ch, 2tr] into next ch sp, 1tr/rb round each of next 5 sts**, tr/rf5tog over next 5 sts; rep from * ending last rep at ** when 3 sts remain, tr/rf3tog, turn.

Rep 2nd and 3rd rows.

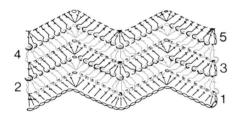

## Crinkle Stitch I

Multiple of 2 sts.
(add 1 for base chain)

**1st row** (wrong side): Miss 2ch (count as 1htr), 1htr into each ch to end, turn.
**2nd row:** 1ch, 1dc into first st, *1dc/rf round next st, 1dc/rb round next st; rep from * ending 1dc into top of tch, turn.
**3rd row:** 2ch (count as 1htr), miss first st, 1htr into next and each st to end, miss tch, turn.
**4th row:** 1ch, 1dc into first st, *1dc/rb round next st, 1dc/rf round next st; rep from * ending 1dc into top of tch, turn.
**5th row:** As 3rd row.
Rep 2nd, 3rd, 4th and 5th rows.

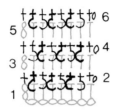

## Crinkle Stitch II

Worked as Crinkle Stitch I, but using wrong side of fabric as right side.

## Crossed Ripple Stitch

Multiple of 3 sts + 2.
(add 1 for base chain)

**1st base row** (wrong side): 1dc into 2nd ch from hook, 1dc into each ch to end, turn.
**2nd base row:** 3ch (count as 1tr), miss first st, *miss next 2 sts, 1tr into next st, 1ch, 1tr back into first of 2 sts just missed — called Crossed Pair; rep from * ending 1tr into last st, miss tch, turn.
**Commence Pattern**
**1st row:** 1 ch, 1dc into first st, 1dc into next and each st and each ch sp to end working last st into top of tch, turn.
**2nd row:** As 2nd base row, except as 2nd st of each Crossed Pair work 1tr/rf loosely round first st of corresponding Crossed Pair 2 rows below.
Rep these 2 rows.

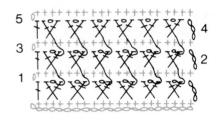

## Leafhopper Stitch

Multiple of 4 sts + 1.
(add 2 for base chain)

**Special Abbreviation**
**LCL (Leafhopper Cluster)** = *[yo, insert hook at front and from right to left behind stem of st before next st, yo, draw loop through and up to height of htr] twice, yo, draw through 4 loops**, miss next st, rep from * to ** round stem of next st, ending yo, draw through all 3 loops on hook.

**1st row** (wrong side): Miss 3ch (count as 1tr), 1tr into next and each ch to end, turn.
**2nd Row:** 3ch (count as 1tr), miss first st, 1tr into next st, *1LCL over next st, 1tr into each of next 3 sts; rep from * omitting 1tr from end of last rep, turn.
**3rd row:** 3ch (count as 1tr), miss first st, 1tr into next and each st to end, working last st into top of tch, turn.
**4th row:** 3ch (count as 1tr), miss first st, *1tr into each of next 3 sts, 1LCL over next st; rep from * ending 1tr into each of last 4 sts, working last st into top of tch, turn.
**5th row:** As 3rd row.
Rep 2nd, 3rd, 4th and 5th rows.

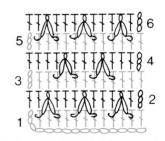

# Patterns for Texture and Colour

## Gwenyth's Cable

Worked over 19 sts on a background of basic trebles with any number of sts.

**1st row** (right side): 1dtr/rf round first st, 1tr into next st, miss next 3 sts, 1ttr into each of next 3 sts, going behind last 3ttrs work 1ttr into each of 3 sts just missed, 1tr into next st, 1dtr/rf round next st, 1tr into next st, miss next 3 sts, 1ttr into each of next 3 sts, going in front of last 3ttrs but not catching them, work 1ttr into each of 3 sts just missed, 1tr into next st, 1dtr/rf round next st.

**2nd row:** As 1st row, except work 1dtr/rb instead of rf over first, 10th and 19th sts to keep raised ridges on right side of fabric.
Rep 1st and 2nd rows.

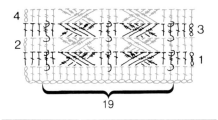

## Dots and Diamonds

Multiple of 4 sts + 3.
(add 1 for base chain)
### Special Abbreviation
**Pdc (Picot double crochet)** = insert hook, yo, draw loop through, [yo, draw through 1 loop] 3 times, yo, draw through both loops on hook. Note: draw picot ch loops to front (right side) of fabric.

**Base row** (right side): 1dc into 2nd ch from hook, 1dc into each of next 2ch, *pdc into

next ch, 1dc into each of next 3ch; rep from * to end, turn.
### Commence Pattern
**1st row:** 3ch (count as 1tr), miss first st, 1tr into each st to end, miss tch, turn.

**2nd row:** 1ch, 1dc into first st, *pdc into next st, 1dc into next st**, dtr/rf2tog over next st inserting hook round 2nd dc in last-but-one row for first leg and round following 4th dc for 2nd leg (missing 3 sts between), 1dc into next st; rep from * ending last rep at ** in top of tch, turn.

**3rd row:** As 1st row.

**4th row:** 1ch, 1dc into first st, 1dtr/rf over next st inserting hook round top of first raised cluster 2 rows below, *1dc into next st, pdc into next st, 1dc into next st**, dtr/rf2tog over next st inserting hook round same cluster as last raised st for first leg and round top of next raised cluster for 2nd leg; rep from * ending last rep at ** when 2 sts remain, 1dtr/rf over next st inserting hook round top of same cluster as last raised st, 1dc into top of tch, turn.

**5th row:** As 1st row.

**6th row:** As 2nd row, except to make new raised clusters insert hook round previous raised clusters instead of dcs.
Rep 3rd, 4th, 5th and 6th rows.

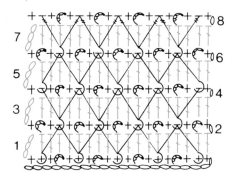

## Crossed Puff Cables

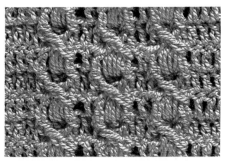

Worked over 11 sts on a background of basic trebles with any number of sts.

**1st row** (right side): 1tr into each st.

**2nd row:** *1dtr/rb round next st, work a Puff st of htr5tog all into next st, 1dtr/rb round next st**, 1tr into next st; rep from * once and from * to ** again.

**3rd row:** *Leaving last loop of each st on hook work [1tr into next st, miss Puff st, work 1dtr/rf round next st] ending yo, draw through all 3 loops on hook, 1tr into top of Puff st, leaving last loop of each st on hook work [1dtr/rf round st before same Puff st

and 1tr into top of st after Puff st], ending yo, draw through all 3 loops on hook**, 1tr into next st; rep from * once and from * to ** again.

**4th row:** As 2nd row, but make new dtr/rbs by inserting hook under raised stems only of previous sts.
Rep 3rd and 4th rows.

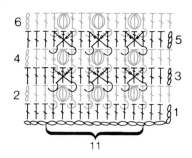

## Tulip Cable

Worked over 15 sts on a background of basic trebles with any number of sts.

### Special Abbreviations

**FCL (Forward Cluster)** = leaving last loop of each st on hook work 1tr into next st and 1dtr/rf or rb (see Note below) round next st after that, ending yo, draw through all 3 loops on hook.

**BCL (Backward Cluster)** = leaving last loop of each st on hook work 1dtr/rf or rb round st below tr just made and 1tr into next st.

**Note:** Raised legs of these clusters are to be worked at front (rf) on right side rows and at back (rb) on wrong side rows as indicated in the text thus: FCL/rf, FCL/rb, BCL/rf, BCL/rb.

**TCL (Triple Cluster)** = leaving last loop of each st on hook work 1dtr/rf round st below tr just made, 1tr/rf round next Puff st, and 1dtr/rf round next st, ending yo, draw through all 4 loops on hook.

**1st row** (right side): 1dtr/rf round next st, 1tr into next st, 1dtr/rf round next st, 1tr into each of next 2 sts, [1FCL/rf] twice, 1tr into next st, [1BCL/rf] twice, 1tr into each of next 2 sts, 1dtr/rf round next st, 1tr into next st, 1dtr/rf round next st.

**2nd row:** [1dtr/rb round next st, 1tr into next st] twice, [1FCL/rb] twice, 1tr into each of next 3 sts, [1BCL/rb] twice, [1tr into next st, 1dtr/rb round next st] twice.

**3rd row:** [1dtr/rf round next st, 1tr into next st] twice, 1dtr/rf round each of next 2 sts, 1tr into each of next 3 sts, 1dtr/rf round each

Stitch Variations, Abbreviations and Symbols on pages 7 to 15.

of next 2 sts, [1tr into next st, 1dtr/rf round next st] twice.

**4th row:** 1dtr/rb round next st, 1tr into next st, 1dtr/rb round next st, 1tr into each of next 2 sts, [1BCL/rb] twice, work a Puff st of htr5tog all into next st, [1FCL/rb] twice, 1tr into each of next 2 sts, 1dtr/rb round next st, 1tr into next st, 1dtr/rb round next st.

**5th row:** 1dtr/rf round next st, 1tr into next st, 1dtr/rf round next st, 1tr into each of next 3 sts, 1BCL/rf, 1TCL, 1FCL/rf, 1tr into each of next 3 sts, 1dtr/rf round next st, 1tr into next st, 1dtr/rf round next st.

**6th row:** *1dtr/rb round next st, 1tr into next st, 1dtr/rb round next st**, 1tr into each of next 9 sts, rep from * to **.

Rep these 6 rows.

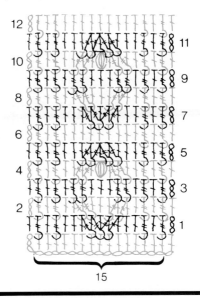

## Puff Stitch Plaits

Multiple of 8 sts + 1.
(add 1 for base chain)

**1st row** (right side): Miss 2ch (count as 1htr), 1htr into each of next 2ch, *1ch, miss 1ch, htr3tog all into next ch, 1ch, miss 1ch**, 1htr into each of next 5ch; rep from * ending last rep at ** when 3ch remain, 1htr into each of last 3ch, turn.

**2nd row:** 2ch (count as 1htr), miss first st, 1htr into each of next 2 sts, *htr3tog into next ch sp, 1ch, miss 1 st, htr3tog into next ch sp**, 1htr into each of next 5 sts; rep from * ending last rep at ** when 3 sts remain including tch, 1htr into each of last 3 sts, turn.

**3rd row:** 2ch (count as 1htr), miss first st, 1htr into each of next 2 sts, *1ch, miss 1 st, htr3tog into next ch sp, 1ch, miss 1 st**, 1htr into each of next 5 sts; rep from * ending

last rep at ** when 3 sts remain including tch, 1htr into each of last 3 sts, turn.

Rep 2nd and 3rd rows.

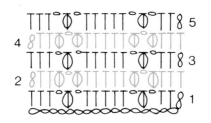

## Aligned Puff Stitch

Multiple of 2 sts + 1.
(add 1 for base chain)

**1st row** (right side): 1dc into 2nd ch from hook, *1ch, miss 1ch, 1dc into next ch; rep from * to end, turn.

**2nd row:** 2ch (count as 1htr), miss first st, *htr4tog all into next ch sp, 1ch, miss 1dc; rep from * ending htr4tog into last ch sp, 1htr into last dc, miss tch, turn.

**3rd row:** 1ch, 1dc into first st, *1ch, miss 1 st, 1dc into next ch sp; rep from * ending in top of tch, turn.

Rep 2nd and 3rd rows.

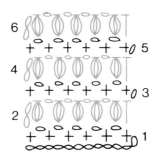

## Boxed Puff Stitch

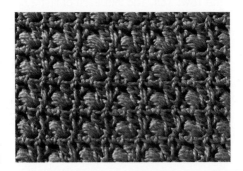

Multiple of 3 sts + 1.
(add 4 for base chain)

**Special Abbreviation**

**Puff Stitch** = htr4tog all into same st and closed with 1ch drawn tightly.

**1st row** (right side): Puff st into 5th ch from hook, *miss 2ch, [1tr, 2ch, puff st] all into next ch; rep from * ending miss 2ch, 1tr into last ch, turn.

**2nd row:** 1ch, miss first st, *work 1tr loosely over next row into first of 2 missed sts in row below, 1dc into puff st, 1dc into next 2ch sp; rep from * ending 1dc into 3rd ch of tch, turn.

**3rd row:** 5ch (count as 1tr and 2ch), puff st into first st, *miss 2dc, [1tr, 2ch, puff st] all into next tr; rep from * ending miss 2dc, 1tr into last tr, miss tch, turn.

Rep 2nd and 3rd rows.

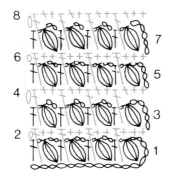

## Aligned Cobble Stitch

Multiple of 2 sts + 1.
(add 1 for base chain)

**1st row** (right side): 1dc into 2nd ch from hook, 1dc into each ch to end, turn.

**2nd row:** 1ch, 1dc into first st, *1dtr into next st, 1dc into next st; rep from * to end, miss tch, turn.

**3rd row:** 1ch, 1dc into first st, 1dc into next and each st to end, miss tch, turn.

Rep 2nd and 3rd rows.

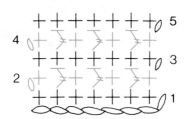

# Patterns for Texture and Colour

## Wavy Puff Stitch Sprays

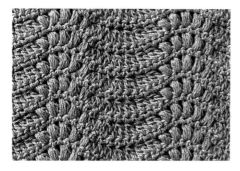

Multiple of 17 sts.
(add 2 for base chain)

**1st row** (right side): 1tr into 4th ch from hook (counts as tr2tog), [tr2tog over next 2ch] twice, *[1ch, work htr4tog into next ch] 5 times, 1ch**, [tr2tog over next 2ch] 6 times; rep from * ending last rep at ** when 6ch remain, [tr2tog over next 2ch] 3 times, turn.
**2nd row:** 1ch, 1dc into first st and then into each st and each ch sp to end excluding tch, turn.
**3rd row:** 3ch, miss first st, 1tr into next st (counts as tr2tog), [tr2tog over next 2 sts] twice, *[1ch, work htr4tog into next st] 5 times, 1ch**, [tr2tog over next 2 sts] 6 times; rep from * ending last rep at ** when 6 sts remain, [tr2tog over next 2 sts] 3 times, miss tch, turn.
Rep 2nd and 3rd rows.

## V-Twin Popcorn Stitch

Multiple of 11 sts + 3.
(add 2 for base chain)

**1st row** (right side): Miss 3ch (count as 1tr), 1tr into each of next 2ch, *2ch, miss 3ch, 5tr popcorn into next ch, 1ch, 5tr popcorn into next ch, 1ch, miss 2ch, 1tr into each of next 3ch; rep from * to end, turn.
**2nd row:** 3ch (count as 1tr), miss first st, 1dtr/rb round next st, 1tr into next st, *3ch, miss 1ch and 1 popcorn, 2dc into next ch sp, 3ch, miss 1 popcorn and 2ch, 1tr into next st, 1dtr/rb round next st, 1tr into next st; rep from * ending last rep in top of tch, turn.
**3rd row:** 3ch (count as 1tr), miss first st, 1dtr/rf round next st, 1tr into next st, *2ch, miss 3ch, 5tr popcorn into next dc, 1ch, 5tr popcorn into next dc, 1ch, miss 3ch, 1tr into next st, 1dtr/rf round next st, 1tr into next st; rep from * ending last rep in top of tch, turn.
Rep 2nd and 3rd rows.

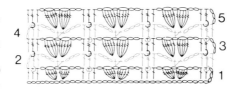

## Blackberry Salad Stitch

Multiple of 4 sts + 1.
(add 2 for base chain)

**1st row** (right side): Miss 3ch (count as 1tr), 1tr into each ch to end, turn.
**2nd row:** 1ch, 1dc into each of first 2 sts, *work tr5tog into next st, 1dc into each of next 3 sts; rep from * to last 3 sts, work tr5tog into next st, 1dc into each of last 2 sts (including top of tch), turn.
**3rd row:** 3ch (count as 1tr), miss first st, 1tr into each st to end, miss tch, turn.
**4th row:** 1ch, 1dc into each of first 4 sts, *work tr5tog into next st, 1dc into each of next 3 sts; rep from * ending 1dc into top of tch, turn.
**5th row:** As 3rd row.
Rep 2nd, 3rd, 4th and 5th rows.

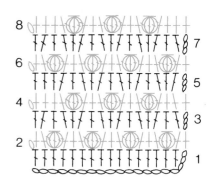

## Bullion Diagonals

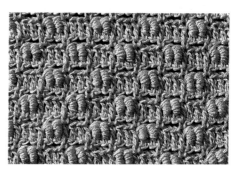

Multiple of 6 sts + 2.
(add 1 for base chain)

**1st row** (wrong side): 1dc into 2nd ch from hook, 1ch, miss 1ch, 1dc into next ch, *2ch, miss 2ch, 1dc into next ch; rep from * to last 2ch, 1ch, miss 1ch, 1dc into last ch, turn.
**2nd row:** 3ch (count as 1tr), miss first st, 1tr into next ch sp, *1tr into next dc, 1 Bullion st into each of next 2ch, 1tr into next dc**, 1tr into each of next 2ch; rep from * ending last rep at ** when 1 ch sp remains, 1tr into next ch, 1tr into last dc, miss tch, turn.
**3rd row:** 1ch, 1dc into first st, 1ch, miss 1 st, 1dc into next st, *2ch, miss 2 sts, 1dc into next st; rep from * to last 2 sts, 1ch, miss 1 st, 1dc into top of tch, turn.
**4th row:** 3ch (count as 1tr), miss first st, 1 Bullion st into next ch sp, *1tr into next dc, 1tr into each of next 2ch, 1tr into next dc**, 1 Bullion st into each of next 2ch; rep from * ending last rep at ** when 1ch sp remains, 1 Bullion st into next sp, 1tr into last dc, miss tch, turn.
**5th row:** As 3rd row.
Rep 2nd, 3rd, 4th and 5th rows.

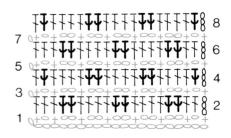

**Diagram Note**
Bullion Stitch with [yo] 7 times.

Stitch Variations, Abbreviations and Symbols on pages 7 to 15.

# Patterns for Texture and Colour

## Popcorn Waffle Stitch

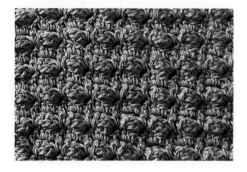

Multiple of 4 sts + 1.
(add 1 for base chain)

**1st row** (right side): 1dc into 2nd ch from hook, *3ch, 5tr popcorn into same place as previous dc, miss 3ch, 1dc into next ch; rep from * to end, turn.

**2nd row:** 3ch (count as 1tr), miss first st, *1dc into each of next 2ch, 1htr into next ch, 1tr into next dc; rep from * to end, miss tch, turn.

**3rd row:** 1ch, 1dc into first st, *3ch, 5tr popcorn into same place as previous dc, miss next 3 sts, 1dc into next tr; rep from * ending last rep in top of tch, turn.

Rep 2nd and 3rd rows.

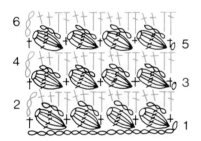

## Diagonal Trip Stitch

Multiple of 6 sts + 2.
(add 1 for base chain)

**1st row** (right side): 1dc into 2nd ch from hook, 1dc into each ch to end, turn.

**2nd row:** 1ch, 1dc into first st, *1dtr into next

st, 1dc into next st, 1dtr into next st, 1dc into each of next 3 sts; rep from * ending 1dc into last dc, miss tch, turn.

**3rd row:** 1ch, 1dc into first st, 1dc into next and each st to end, miss tch, turn.

**4th row:** 1 ch, 1dc into each of first 2 sts, *1dtr into next st, 1dc into next st, 1dtr into next st, 1dc into each of next 3 sts; rep from * to end, miss tch, turn.

**5th row:** As 3rd row.

**6th row:** 1 ch, 1dc into each of first 3 sts, *1dtr into next st, 1dc into next st, 1dtr into next st, 1dc into each of next 3 sts; rep from * to end, omitting 1dc at end of last rep, miss tch, turn.

Continue in this way, working the pairs of dtr 1 st further to the left on every wrong side row.

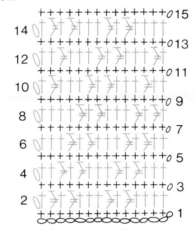

## Bobble Braid Stitch

Worked over 13 sts on a background of any number of sts worked in basic treble crochet on right side rows and double crochet on wrong side rows.

**1st row** (right side): 1tr into each of first 4 sts, [1ch, miss 1 st, 1tr into next st] 3 times, 1tr into each of last 3 sts.

**2nd row:** 1dc into each of first 4 sts, work tr5tog into next ch sp, 1dc into next tr, 1dc into next sp, 1dc into next tr, tr5tog into next sp, 1dc into each of last 4 sts.

**3rd row:** 1dtr/rf round first st 2 rows below (ie: 1st row), 1tr into next st on previous (ie: 2nd) row, 1dtr/rf round next st 2 rows below,

[1ch, miss 1 st, 1tr into next st on previous row] 3 times, 1ch, miss 1 st, 1dtr/rf round next st 2 rows below, 1tr into next st on previous row, 1dtr/rf round next st 2 rows below.

**4th row:** 1dc into each of first 6 sts, work tr5tog into next st, 1dc into each of last 6 sts.

**5th row:** [1dtr/rf round corresponding raised st 2 rows below, 1tr into next st] twice, [1ch, miss 1 st, 1tr into next st] 3 times, 1dtr/rf round corresponding raised st 2 rows below, 1tr into next st, 1dtr/rf round corresponding raised st 2 rows below.

Continue as set on 2nd, 3rd, 4th and 5th rows.

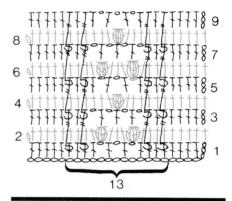

## Loop or Fur Stitch

Multiple of 8 sts.
(add 2 for base chain)

**1st row** (right side): Miss 3ch (count as 1tr), 1tr into next and each ch to end, turn.

**2nd row:** 1ch, 1dc into each of first 2 sts, *1 Loop st into each of next 4 sts**, 1dc into each of next 4 sts; rep from * ending last rep at **, 1dc into each of last 2 sts including top of tch, turn.

**3rd row:** 3ch (count as 1tr), miss 1 st, 1tr into next and each st to end, miss tch, turn.

Rep 2nd and 3rd rows.

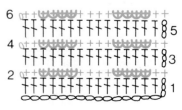

**Diagram Note**
⊎  Dc Loop Stitch

# Patterns for Texture and Colour

## Interweave Stitch

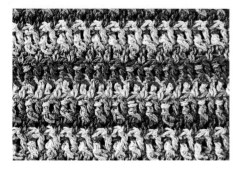

Multiple of 2 sts + 1.
(add 2 for base chain)

**1st row** (right side): Miss 3ch (count as 1tr), 1tr into next and each ch to end, turn.

**2nd row:** 3ch (count as 1tr), miss first st, *1dtr/rf round next st, 1tr into next st; rep from * ending last rep in top of tch, turn.
Rep 2nd row.

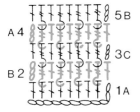

## Little Wave Stitch

Multiple of 4 sts + 1.
(add 1 for base chain)

Work 2 rows each in colours A and B alternately.

**1st row** (right side): 1dc into 2nd ch from hook, *1htr into next ch, 1tr into next ch, 1htr into next ch, 1dc into next ch; rep from * to end, turn.

**2nd row:** 1ch, 1dc into first st, *1htr into next htr, 1tr into next tr, 1htr into next htr, 1dc into next dc; rep from * to end, miss tch, turn.

**3rd row:** 3ch (count as 1tr), miss first st, *1htr into next htr, 1dc into next tr, 1htr into next htr, 1tr into next dc; rep from * to end, miss tch, turn.

**4th row:** 3ch (count as 1tr), miss first st, *1htr into next htr, 1dc into next dc, 1htr into

next htr, 1tr into next tr; rep from * ending last rep in top of tch, turn.

**5th row:** 1ch, 1dc into first st, *1htr into next htr, 1tr into next dc, 1htr into next htr, 1dc into next tr; rep from * ending last rep in top of tch, turn.

Rep 2nd, 3rd, 4th and 5th rows.

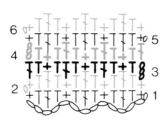

## Interlocking Diamond Stitch

Multiple of 6 sts + 1.
(add 1 for base chain)

Work 1st row in colour A, then 2 rows each in colours B and A alternately throughout.

**1st row** (wrong side): Sl st into 2nd ch from hook, *3ch, miss 2ch, 1tr into next ch, 3ch, miss 2ch, sl st into next ch; rep from * to end, turn.

**2nd row:** 4ch (count as 1tr and 1ch), 1tr into first sl st, *miss 3ch, sl st into next tr**, miss 3ch, work [1tr, 1ch, 1tr, 1ch, 1tr] into next sl st; rep from * ending last rep at ** in last tr, miss 3ch, work [1tr, 1ch, 1tr] into last sl st, turn.

**3rd row:** 6ch (count as 1tr and 3ch), miss [first st, 1ch and 1tr], *sl st into next sl st**, 3ch, miss 1tr and 1ch, 1tr into next tr, 3ch, miss 1ch and 1tr; rep from * ending last rep at ** in last sl st, 3ch, miss 1tr and 1ch, 1tr into next ch of tch, turn.

**4th row:** Sl st into first st, *miss 3ch, [1tr, 1ch, 1tr, 1ch, 1tr] all into next sl st, miss 3ch, sl st into next tr; rep from * ending in 3rd ch of tch loop, turn.

**5th row:** *3ch, miss 1tr and 1ch, 1tr into next tr, 3ch, miss 1ch and 1tr, sl st into next sl st; rep from * to end, turn.

Rep 2nd, 3rd, 4th and 5th rows.

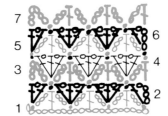

## Interlocking Shell Stitch

Multiple of 6 sts + 1.
(add 2 for base chain)

Work 1 row each in colours A and B alternately; fasten off each colour at end of each row.

**1st row** (right side): Miss 2ch (count as 1tr), 2tr into next ch, miss 2ch, 1dc into next ch, *miss 2ch, 5tr into next ch, miss 2ch, 1dc into next ch; rep from * to last 3ch, miss 2ch, 3tr into last ch, turn.

**2nd row:** 1ch, 1dc into first st, *2ch, tr5tog over next 5 sts, 2ch, 1dc into next st; rep from * ending last rep in top of tch, turn.

**3rd row:** 3ch (count as 1tr), 2tr into first st, miss 2ch, 1dc into next cluster, *miss 2ch, 5tr into next dc, miss 2ch, 1dc into next cluster; rep from * to last cluster, miss 2ch, 3tr into last dc, miss tch, turn.

Rep 2nd and 3rd rows.

## Zig-Zag Pip Stitch

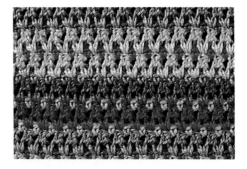

Multiple of 4 sts + 1.
(add 1 for base chain)

Work 1 row each in colours A, B, C, D and E throughout.

**1st row** (right side): 1dc into 2nd ch from hook, *1ch, miss 1ch, 1dc into next ch; rep from * to end, turn.

---

Stitch Variations, Abbreviations and Symbols on pages 7 to 15.

# Patterns for Texture and Colour

**2nd row:** 3ch, 1tr into next ch sp (counts as tr2tog), *1ch, tr2tog inserting hook into same sp as previous st for first leg and into next sp for 2nd leg; rep from * to last sp, ending 1ch, tr2tog over same sp and last dc, miss tch, turn.

**3rd row:** 1ch, 1dc into first st, *1dc into next sp, 1ch, miss next cluster; rep from * ending 1dc into last sp, 1dc into last st, miss tch, turn.

**4th row:** 3ch (count as 1tr), tr2tog inserting hook into first st for first leg and into next sp for 2nd leg, *1ch, tr2tog inserting hook into same sp as previous st for first leg and into next sp for 2nd leg; rep from * ending with 2nd leg of last cluster in last dc, 1tr into same place, miss tch, turn.

**5th row:** 1ch, 1dc into first st, *1ch, miss next cluster, 1dc into next sp; rep from * working last dc into top of tch, turn.

Rep 2nd, 3rd, 4th and 5th rows.

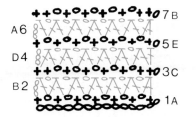

## Aligned Railing Stitch

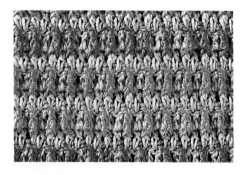

Multiple of 2 sts + 1.
(add 2 for base chain)

On a background of basic trebles in colour M work raised rows - one row each in colours A, B, and C throughout.

Work 2 rows basic trebles in M.
**Commence Pattern**
**1st row** (right side): Put working loop temporarily on a stitch holder or safety pin, draw loop of contrast colour through top of last background st completed, 1ch, work 1dtr/rf round stem of 2nd st in last-but-one row, *1ch, miss 1 st, 1dtr/rf round stem of next st in last-but-one row; rep from * ending sl st into top of tch at beg of last background row worked. Fasten off but do not turn work.

**2nd row:** Replace hook in working loop of M. 3ch, work 1tr inserting hook through top of raised st and background st at the same time, *work 1tr inserting hook under contrast colour ch and top of next st in background colour at the same time, work 1tr inserting

hook under top of next raised st and background st as before; rep from * to end. Work 1 row in basic trebles.
Rep these 3 rows.

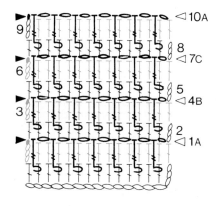

## Shadow Tracery Stitch

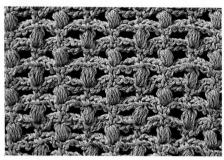

Multiple of 6 sts + 1.
(add 1 for base chain)

**Special Abbreviation**
**Puff stitch** = work htr5tog all into same place ending with 1ch drawn tightly to close.

Work 1 row each in colours A and B alternately throughout. Do not break yarn when changing colour, but fasten off temporarily and begin row at same end as new colour.
**1st row** (right side in A): 1dc into 2nd ch from hook, *3ch, miss 2ch, puff st into next ch, 3ch, miss 2ch, 1dc into next ch; rep from * to end. Do not turn.
**2nd row** (right side in B): Join yarn into first st, 1ch, 1dc into first st, *3ch, miss 3ch, 1dc into next puff st, 3ch, miss 3ch, 1dc into next dc; rep from * to end, turn.
**3rd row** (wrong side in A): 6ch (count as 1tr and 3ch), miss first st and 3ch, 1dc into next dc, *3ch, miss 3ch, puff st into next dc, 3ch, miss 3ch, 1dc into next dc; rep from * ending 3ch, miss 3ch, 1tr into last dc. Do not turn.
**4th row** (wrong side in B): Pick up yarn in 3rd ch of tch, 1ch, 1dc into same place, *3ch, miss 3ch, 1dc into next dc, 3ch, miss 3ch, 1dc into next st; rep from * to end, turn.
**5th row** (right side in A): 1ch, 1dc into first st, *3ch, miss 3ch, puff st into next dc, 3ch, miss 3ch, 1dc into next dc; rep from * to end. Do not turn.
Rep 2nd, 3rd, 4th and 5th rows.

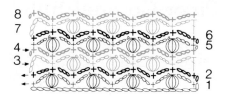

## Fleur de Lys Stitch

Multiple of 6 sts + 1.
(add 2 for base chain)
**Special Abbreviation**
**FC/rf (Fleur Cluster raised at front)** = leaving last loop of each st on hook work 1tr/rf round next tr, miss 1ch, 1tr into top of next dc, miss 1ch, 1tr/rf round next tr, (4 loops on hook), yo, draw through all loops.
**FC/rb (Fleur Cluster raised at back)** = as for FC/rf except insert hook at back for first and 3rd legs.

Work 1 row each in colours A and B alternately throughout. Do not break yarn when changing colour, but fasten off temporarily and begin row at same end as new colour.

**1st row** (right side in A): Miss 2ch (count as 1tr), 1tr into next ch, *1ch, miss 2ch, 1dc into next ch, 1ch, miss 2ch**, 3tr into next ch; rep from * ending last rep at **, 2tr into last ch. Do not turn.

**2nd row** (right side in B): Join new yarn into top of tch, 1ch, 1dc into same place, *2ch, FC/rb, 2ch, 1dc into next tr; rep from * to end, turn.

**3rd row** (wrong side in A): 3ch (count as 1tr), 1tr into first st, *1ch, miss 2ch, 1dc into next cluster, 1ch, miss 2ch**, 3tr into next dc; rep from * ending last rep at **, 2tr into last dc. Do not turn.

**4th row** (wrong side in B): Rejoin new yarn at top of 3ch, 1ch, 1dc into same place, *2ch, FC/rf, 2ch, 1dc into next tr; rep from * to end, turn.

**5th row** (right side in A): 3ch (count as 1tr), 1tr into first st, *1ch, miss 2ch, 1dc into next cluster, 1ch, miss 2ch**, 3tr into next dc; rep from * ending last rep at **, 2tr into last dc. Do not turn.

Rep 2nd, 3rd, 4th and 5th rows.

# Patterns for Texture and Colour

## Picot Coronet Stitch

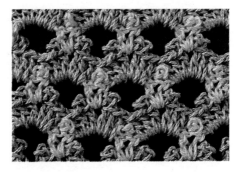

Multiple of 7 sts + 1.
(add 3 for base chain)

Work 1 row each with colours A and B alternately throughout; fasten off each colour at end of each row.

**1st row** (right side): Miss 3ch (count as 1tr), 1tr into next ch, work a picot of [3ch, insert hook down through top of tr just made and work a sl st to close], 2tr into same ch, *miss 6ch, work a Coronet of [3tr, picot, 1ch, 1tr, picot, 2tr] into next ch; rep from * to last 7ch, miss 6ch, [3tr, picot, 1tr] into last ch, turn.

**2nd row:** 3ch (count as 1tr), 1tr into first st, *3ch, work a picot V st of [1tr, picot, 1tr] into 1ch sp at centre of next Coronet; rep from * ending 3ch, 2tr into top of tch, turn.

**3rd row:** 2ch (count as 1htr), miss first 2 sts, *Coronet into next 3ch sp, miss next picot V st; rep from * ending Coronet into last sp, 1htr into top of tch, turn.

**4th row:** 4ch (count as 1tr and 1ch), *picot V st into sp at center of next Coronet, 3ch; rep from * ending picot V st into last Coronet, 1ch, 1tr into top of tch, turn.

**5th row:** 3ch (count as 1tr), miss first st, [1tr, picot, 2tr] into next ch sp, *miss next picot V st, Coronet into next sp; rep from * ending miss last picot V st, 3tr into next ch, picot, 1tr into next ch of tch, turn.

Rep 2nd, 3rd, 4th and 5th rows.

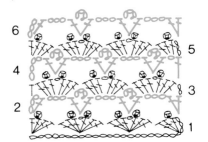

## Relief Squares

Multiple of 10 sts + 4.
(add 1 for base chain)

**1st base row** (right side): Using A, 1dc into 2nd ch from hook, 1dc into next and each ch to end, turn.

**2nd base row:** 1 ch, 1dc into first and each st to end, miss tch, turn.

**Commence Pattern**

Change to B and rep the 2nd base row twice.

Change to C and rep the 2nd base row 4 times.

**7th row:** Using B, 1 ch, 1dc into each of first 3 sts, *[1ttr/rf round st corresponding to next st 5 rows below, i.e. last row worked in B] twice, 1dc into each of next 4 sts, [1ttr/rf round st corresponding to next st 5 rows below] twice, 1dc into each of next 2 sts; rep from * ending 1dc into last st, miss tch, turn.

**8th row:** Using B rep 2nd base row.

**9th row:** Using A, 1 ch, 1dc into first st, *[1sstr/rf round st corresponding to next st 9 rows below, ie last row worked in A] twice, 1dc into each of next 8 sts; rep from * to last 3 sts, [1sstr/rf round st corresponding to next st 9 rows below] twice, 1dc into last st, miss tch, turn.

**10th row:** Using A rep 2nd base row.

Rep these 10 rows.

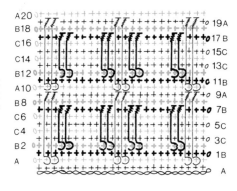

## Multi-Coloured Parquet Stitch

Multiple of 3 sts + 1.
(add 1 for base chain)

Work 1 row each in colours A, B and C alternately throughout.

**1st row** (right side): 1dc into 2nd ch from hook, *3ch, 1tr into same place as previous dc, miss 2ch, 1dc into next ch; rep from * to end, turn.

**2nd row:** 3ch (count as 1tr), 1tr into first st, 1dc into next 3ch arch, *3ch, 1tr into same 3ch arch, 1dc into next 3ch arch; rep from

* ending 2ch, 1tr into last dc, miss tch, turn.

**3rd row:** 1ch, 1dc into first st, 3ch, 1tr into next 2ch sp, *work [1dc, 3ch, 1tr] into next 3ch arch; rep from * ending 1dc into top of tch, turn.

Rep 2nd and 3rd rows.

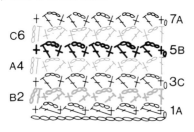

## Zig-Zag Lozenge Stitch

Multiple of 2 sts + 1.
(add 2 for base chain)

Work 1 row each in colours A, B and C alternately throughout.

**1st row** (wrong side): Miss 2ch (count as 1htr), 1htr into next ch, *miss 1ch, [1htr, 1ch, 1htr] into next ch; rep from * to last 2 ch, miss 1ch, 2htr into last ch, turn.

**2nd row:** 3ch, 1tr into first st (counts as tr2tog), *1ch, work tr3tog into next ch sp; rep from * to last sp, ending 1ch, tr2tog into top of tch, turn.

**3rd row:** 2ch (count as 1htr), miss first st, *work [1htr, 1ch, 1htr] into next ch sp; rep from * ending 1htr into top of tch, turn.

**4th row:** 3ch (count as 1tr), miss first st, *work tr3tog into next sp, 1ch; rep from * ending 1tr into top of tch, turn.

**5th row:** 2ch (count as 1htr), 1htr into first st, *work [1htr, 1ch, 1htr] into next ch sp; rep from * ending 2htr into top of tch, turn.

Rep 2nd, 3rd, 4th and 5th rows.

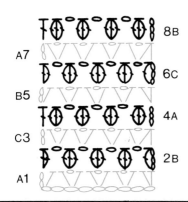

Stitch Variations, Abbreviations and Symbols on pages 7 to 15.

# Patterns for Texture and Colour

## Chevron Stitch I

Starting chain: Multiple of 16 sts + 2.

**1st row** (right side): Work 2dc into 2nd ch from hook, *1dc into each of next 7ch, miss 1ch, 1dc into each of next 7ch, 3dc into next ch; rep from * to end omitting 1dc at end of last rep, turn.

**2nd row:** 1ch, work 2dc into first dc, *1dc into each of next 7dc, miss 2dc, 1dc into each of next 7dc, 3dc into next dc; rep from * to end omitting 1dc at end of last rep, turn.

Rep 2nd row only.

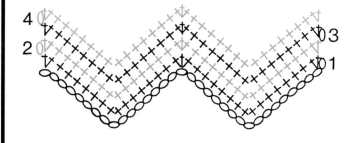

**Diagram only:** Rep 2nd and 3rd rows.

---

## Chevron Stitch II

Work as given for Chevron Stitch I, working 1 row each in A, B and C throughout.

## Curve Fan Stitch

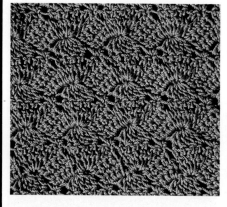

Starting chain: Multiple of 6 sts + 3.

**Special Abbreviations**

**Tr2tog** = work 1tr into each of next 2 sts until 1 loop of each remains on hook, yo and through all 3 loops on hook.

**Half Cluster** = work 1tr into each of next 3 sts until 1 loop of each remains on hook, yo and through all 4 loops on hook.

**Cluster** = work 1tr into each of next 5 sts until 1 loop of each remains on hook, yo and through all 6 loops on hook.

**1st row** (right side): Work tr2tog working into 4th and 5th ch from hook, *3ch, 1dc into next ch, turn, 1ch, 1dc into last dc worked, 3dc into last 3ch sp formed, [turn, 1ch, 1dc into each of the 4dc] 3 times, work 1 cluster over next 5ch; rep from * to end but working half cluster at end of last rep, turn.

**2nd row:** 4ch (count as 1dtr), work 2dtr into top of first half cluster, miss 3dc, 1dc into next dc, *5dtr into top of next cluster, miss 3dc, 1dc into next dc; rep from * to last tr2tog, 3dtr into top of 3ch at beg of previous row, turn.

**3rd row:** 3ch (count as 1tr), miss first dtr, work tr2tog over next 2dtr, *3ch, 1dc into next dc, turn, 1ch, 1dc into last dc worked, 3dc into last 3ch sp formed, [turn, 1ch, 1dc into each of the 4dc] 3 times, work 1 cluster over next 5dtr; rep from * to end but working half cluster at end of last rep placing last tr of half cluster into 4th of 4ch at beg of previous row, turn.

Rep 2nd and 3rd rows ending with a 2nd row.

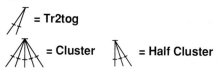

= Tr2tog

= Cluster   = Half Cluster

Line shows direction of work for first part of first row.

## Bar Stitch

Starting chain: Multiple of 3 sts + 3.

**Special Abbreviation**

**1tr/rf** = work 1tr around stem of next st 2 rows below inserting hook round stem from right to left to draw up loops.

**1st row** (right side): Work 1dc into 2nd ch from hook, 1dc into each ch to end, turn.

**2nd row:** 1ch, work 1dc into each dc to end, turn.

**3rd row:** 1ch, work 1dc into each of first 2dc, *1tr/rf round next dc 2 rows below, 1dc into each of next 2dc; rep from * to end, turn.

**4th row:** 1ch, work 1dc into each st to end, turn.

**5th row:** 1ch, work 1dc into each of first 2dc, *1tr/rf round stem of next tr/rf 2 rows below, 1dc into each of next 2dc; rep from * to end, turn.

Rep 4th and 5th rows.

= 1tr/rf

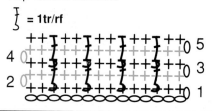

# Patterns for Texture and Colour

## Dot and Bar Stitch

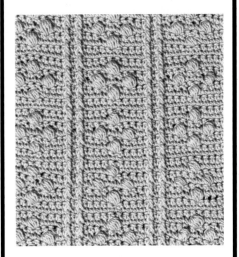

Starting chain: Multiple of 12 sts + 8.

**Special Abbreviations**

**Puff st** = *yo, insert hook into next st, yo and draw a loop through; rep from * 4 times more inserting hook into same st as before (11 loops on hook), yo and draw through 10 loops, yo and draw through 2 remaining loops.

**1tr/rf** = work 1tr around stem of next st 2 rows below inserting hook round stem from right to left to draw up loops.

**1st row** (right side): Work 1dc into 2nd ch from hook, 1dc into each ch to end, turn.

**2nd and every alt row:** 1ch, work 1dc into each st to end, turn.

**3rd row:** 1ch, work 1dc into each of first 2dc, 1tr/rf, 1dc into next dc, 1tr/rf, *1dc into each of next 4dc, 1 puff st into next dc, 1dc into each of next 4dc, 1tr/rf, 1dc into next dc, 1tr/rf; rep from * to last 2dc, 1dc into each of last 2dc, turn.

**5th row:** 1ch, work 1dc into each of first 2dc, 1tr/rf, 1dc into next dc, 1tr/rf, *1dc into each of next 2dc, 1 puff st into next dc, 1dc into each of next 3dc, 1 puff st into next dc, 1dc into each of next 2dc, 1tr/rf, 1dc into next dc, 1tr/rf; rep from * to last 2dc, 1dc into each of last 2dc, turn.

**7th row:** As 3rd row.

**9th row:** 1ch, 1dc into each of first 2dc, 1tr/rf, 1dc into next dc, 1tr/rf, *1dc into each of next 9dc, 1tr/rf, 1dc into next dc, 1tr/rf; rep from * to last 2dc, 1dc into each of last 2dc, turn.

Rep 2nd to 9th rows.

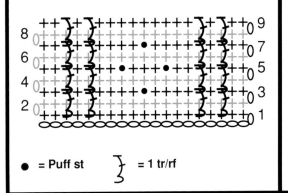

● = Puff st      ⎰⎱ = 1 tr/rf

## Lattice Stitch I

Starting chain: Multiple of 12 sts + 11.

**1st row** (right side): Using A, work 1dc into 2nd ch from hook, 1dc into each ch to end, turn.

**2nd row:** Using A, 1ch, work 1dc into each dc to end, turn.

**3rd row:** Using B, 3ch (count as 1tr), miss first dc, 1tr into next dc, 1htr into next dc, 1dc into next dc, *2ch, miss 2dc, 1dc into next dc, 1htr into next dc, 1tr into each of next 2dc, 1dtr into each of next 2dc, 1tr into each of next 2dc, 1htr into next dc, 1dc into next dc; rep from * to last 6dc, 2ch, miss 2dc, 1dc into next dc, 1htr into next dc, 1tr into each of last 2dc, turn.

**4th row:** Using B, 3ch, miss first tr, work 1tr into next tr, 1htr into next htr, 1dc into next dc, *2ch, 1dc into next dc, 1htr into next htr, 1tr into each of next 2tr, 1dtr into each of next 2dtr, 1tr into each of next 2tr, 1htr into next htr, 1dc into next dc; rep from * to last 6 sts, 2ch, 1dc into next dc, 1htr into next htr, 1tr into next tr, 1tr into 3rd of 3ch at beg of previous row, turn.

**5th row:** Using A, 1ch, work 1dc into each of first 4 sts, [inserting hook from front of work, work 1dc into each of 2 free dc in A 3 rows below], *1dc into each of next 10 sts on previous row, work 2dc 3 rows below as before; rep from * to last 4 sts, 1dc into each of next 3 sts, 1dc into 3rd of 3ch at beg of previous row, turn.

**6th row:** Using A, 1ch, work 1dc into each dc to end, turn.

**7th row:** Using B, 1ch, *work 1dc into first dc, 1htr into next dc, 1tr into each of next 2dc, 1dtr into each of next 2dc, 1tr into each of next 2dc, 1htr into next dc, 1dc into next dc, 2ch, miss 2dc; rep from * to end omitting 2ch at end of last rep, turn.

**8th row:** Using B, 1ch, *work 1dc into next dc, 1htr into next htr, 1tr into each of next 2tr, 1dtr into each of next 2dtr, 1tr into each of next 2tr, 1htr into next htr, 1dc into next dc, 2ch; rep from * to end omitting 2ch at end of last rep, turn.

**9th row:** Using A, 1ch, *1dc into each of next 10 sts, inserting hook from front of work, work 1dc into each of 2 free dc in A 3 rows below; rep from * to end omitting 2dc at end of last rep, turn.

Rep 2nd to 9th rows.

---

## Lattice Stitch II

Work as given for Lattice Stitch I **but** working 2 rows in A, 2 rows in B, 2 rows in A and 2 rows in C throughout.

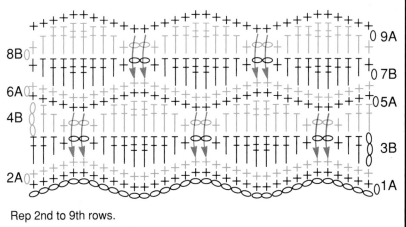

Rep 2nd to 9th rows.

Stitch Variations, Abbreviations and Symbols on pages 7 to 15

# Patterns for Texture and Colour

## Tooth Pattern

Starting chain: Multiple of 4 sts + 4.

**1st row** (right side): Using A, work 1tr into 4th ch from hook, 1tr into each ch to end, turn.

**2nd row:** Using A, 1ch, work 1dc into each tr to end working last dc into top of 3ch, turn.

**3rd row:** Using B, 3ch (count as 1tr), miss first dc, 1tr into next dc, *2ch, miss 2dc, 1tr into each of next 2dc; rep from * to end, turn.

**4th row:** Using B, 1ch, work 1dc into each of first 2tr, *2ch, 1dc into each of next 2tr; rep from * to end working last dc into 3rd of 3ch at beg of previous row, turn.

**5th row:** Using C, 1ch, 1dc into each of first 2dc, *1dtr into each of the 2 missed dc 3 rows below, 1dc into each of next 2dc; rep from * to end, turn.

**6th row:** Using C, 1ch, 1dc into each dc and each dtr to end, turn.

**7th row:** Using A, 3ch, miss first dc, 1tr into each dc to end, turn.

**8th row:** Using A, 1ch, 1dc into each tr to end working last dc into 3rd of 3ch at beg of previous row, turn.

Rep 3rd to 8th rows.

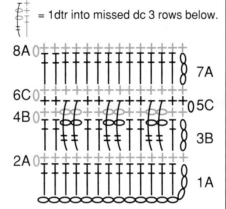

= 1dtr into missed dc 3 rows below.

## Crown Pattern

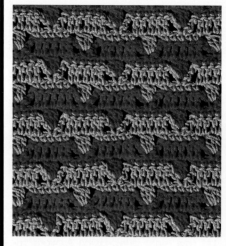

Starting chain: Multiple of 8 sts + 7.

**Special Abbreviation**

**Bobble** = work 3tr into next dc until last loop of each tr remains on hook, yo and through all 4 loops.

**Note:** Count each dc, ch sp and bobble as 1 st throughout.

**1st row** (wrong side): Using A, work 1tr into 4th ch from hook, 1tr into each of next 3ch, *3ch, miss 1ch, 1dc into next ch, 3ch, miss 1ch, 1tr into each of next 5ch; rep from * to end, turn.

**2nd row:** Using B, 1ch, work 1dc into each of first 5tr, *1ch, 1 bobble into next dc, 1ch, 1dc into each of next 5tr; rep from * to end placing last dc into top of 3ch, turn.

**3rd row:** Using B, 6ch (count as 1tr, 3ch), miss first 2dc, 1dc into next dc, 3ch, *miss 1dc, 1tr into each of next 5 sts (see note above), 3ch, miss 1dc, 1dc into next dc, 3ch; rep from * to last 2dc, miss 1dc, 1tr into last dc, turn.

**4th row:** Using A, 1ch, work 1dc into first tr, 1ch, 1 bobble into next dc, 1ch, *1dc into each of next 5tr, 1ch, 1 bobble into next dc, 1ch; rep from * to last tr, 1dc into 3rd of 6ch at beg of previous row, turn.

**5th row:** Using A, 3ch (count as 1tr), miss first dc, 1tr into each of next 4 sts, *3ch, miss 1dc, 1dc into next dc, 3ch, miss 1dc, 1tr into each of next 5 sts; rep from * to end, turn.

Rep 2nd to 5th rows.

 = **Bobble**

## Mirror Stitch

Starting chain: Multiple of 4 sts + 2.

**1st row** (right side): Using A, work 1dc into 2nd ch from hook, 1dc into next ch, *1ch, miss 1ch, 1dc into each of next 3ch; rep from * to end omitting 1dc at end of last rep, turn.

**2nd row:** Using A, 3ch (count as 1tr), miss first dc, work 1tr into next dc, *1ch, miss 1ch, 1tr into each of next 3dc; rep from * to end omitting 1tr at end of last rep, turn.

**3rd row:** Using B, 1ch, work 1dc into each of first 2tr, 1dtr into first missed starting ch, *1dc into next tr, 1ch, miss 1tr, 1dc into next tr, 1dtr into next missed starting ch; rep from * to last 2tr, 1dc into next tr, 1dc into 3rd of 3ch at beg of previous row, turn.

**4th row:** Using B, 3ch, miss first dc, work 1tr into each of next 3 sts, *1ch, miss 1ch, 1tr into each of next 3 sts; rep from * to last dc, 1tr into last dc, turn.

**5th row:** Using C, 1ch, work 1dc into each of first 2tr, *1ch, miss 1tr, 1dc into next tr, 1dtr into next missed tr 3 rows below, 1dc into next tr; rep from * to last 3tr, 1ch, miss 1tr, 1dc into next tr, 1dc into 3rd of 3ch at beg of previous row, turn.

**6th row:** Using C, 3ch, miss first dc, 1tr into next dc, *1ch, miss 1ch, 1tr into each of next 3 sts; rep from * to end omitting 1tr at end of last rep, turn.

**7th row:** Using A, 1ch, 1dc into each of first 2tr, 1dtr into next missed tr 3 rows below, *1dc into next tr, 1ch, miss 1tr, 1dc into next tr, 1dtr into next missed tr 3 rows below; rep from * to last 2tr, 1dc into each of last 2tr, turn.

**8th row:** As 4th row **but** using A instead of B.

Rep 5th to 8th rows continuing to work 2 rows each in colours B, C and A as set.

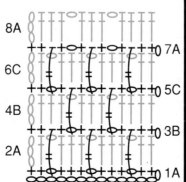

= Work dtr into missed st 3 rows below.

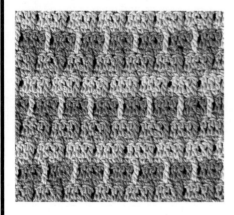

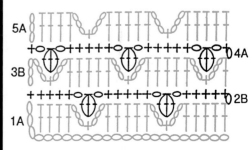

# Patterns for Texture and Colour

## Slot Stitch

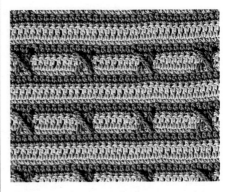

Starting chain: Multiple of 10 sts + 1.

Using A make the required number of chain.

**1st row** (right side): Using A, work 1dc into 2nd ch from hook, 1dc into each ch to end, turn.

**2nd row:** Using A, 3ch (count as 1tr), miss first dc, work 1tr into each dc to end, turn.

**3rd row:** Using B, 1ch, work 1dc into each tr to end placing last dc into 3rd of 3ch at beg of previous row, turn.

**4th row:** Using B, 1ch, work 1dc into each dc to end, turn.

**5th row:** Using A, 1ch, work 1dc into each of first 3dc, *1ch, miss 1dc, 1dc into each of next 2dc, 1ch, miss 1dc, 1dc into each of next 6dc; rep from * to end omitting 3dc at end of last rep, turn.

On 6th row work tr into ch **not** ch space. Rep 2nd to 9th rows.

 = 1ttr into missed dc 3 rows below.

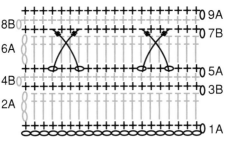

**6th row:** Using A, 3ch (count as 1tr), miss first dc, 1tr into each dc and into each ch to end, turn.

**7th row:** Using B, 1ch, 1dc into each of first 3tr, *work 1ttr into 2nd missed dc 3 rows below, miss 1tr, 1dc into each of next 2tr, 1ttr into first missed dc 3 rows below (thus crossing 2ttr), miss 1tr, 1dc into each of next 6tr; rep from * to end omitting 3dc at end of last rep and placing last dc into 3rd of 3ch at beg of previous row, turn.

**8th row:** Using B, 1ch, work 1dc into each st to end, turn.

**9th row:** Using A, 1ch, work 1dc into each dc to end, turn.

Rep 2nd to 9th rows.

## Half Moon Stitch

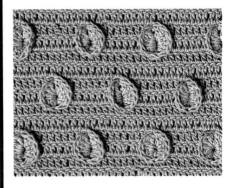

Starting chain: Multiple of 10 sts + 12.

**Special Abbreviation**

**1 Circle** = rotating work as required work 6tr **down** and around stem of next tr 1 row below, then work 6tr **up** and around stem of previous tr 1 row below.

**1st row** (right side): Work 1tr into 4th ch from hook, 1tr into each ch to end, turn.

**2nd row:** 3ch (count as 1tr), miss first tr, work 1tr into each tr to end working last tr into 3rd of 3ch at beg of previous row, turn.

**3rd row:** 3ch, miss first tr, work 1tr into each of next 4tr, *work 1 circle, working behind circle work 1tr into each of next 10tr; rep from * to end omitting 5tr at end of last rep and working last tr into 3rd of 3ch at beg of previous row, turn.

**4th, 5th and 6th rows:** 3ch, miss first tr, work 1tr into each tr to end working last tr into 3rd of 3ch at beg of previous row, turn.

**7th row:** 3ch, miss first tr, work 1tr into each of next 9tr, *work 1 circle, 1tr into each of next 10tr; rep from * to end working last tr into 3rd of 3ch, turn.

**8th and 9th rows:** 3ch, miss first tr, work 1tr into each tr to end working last tr into 3rd of 3ch, turn.

Rep 2nd to 9th rows.

 = 1 Circle

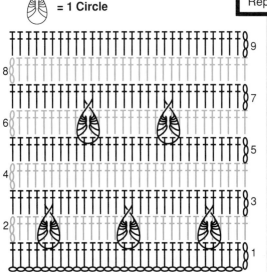

## Herringbone Box

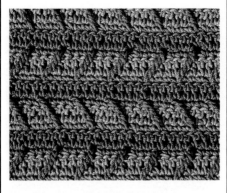

Starting chain: Multiple of 4 sts + 3.

Using A make the required number of chain.

**1st row** (right side): Using A, work 1dc into 2nd ch from hook, 1dc into each ch to end, turn.

**2nd row:** Using A, 3ch (count as 1tr), miss first dc, work 1tr into each dc to end, turn.

**3rd row:** Using B, 1ch, 1dc into each of first 4tr, 1ch, miss 1tr, *1dc into each of next 3tr, 1ch, miss 1tr; rep from * to last tr, 1dc into 3rd of 3ch at beg of previous row, turn.

**4th row:** Using B, 3ch, miss first dc, work 1tr into each ch and each dc to end, turn.

**5th row:** Using A, 1ch, 1dc into first tr, *1ttr into next missed tr 3 rows below, miss 1tr on 4th row, 1dc into each of next 3tr; rep from * to last tr, 1dc into 3rd of 3ch at beg of previous row.

**6th row:** Using A, 3ch, miss first dc, work 1tr into each dc and each ttr to end, turn.

**7th row:** Using B, 1ch, work 1dc into first tr, *1ch, miss 1tr, 1dc into each of next 3tr; rep from * to last tr, 1dc into 3rd of 3ch, turn.

**8th row:** Using B, 3ch, miss first dc, work 1tr into each dc and each ch to end, turn.

**9th row:** Using A, 1ch, 1dc into each of first 4tr, work 1ttr into first missed tr 3 rows below, miss next tr, *1dc into each of next 3tr, 1ttr into next missed tr 3 rows below, miss next tr; rep from * to last tr, 1dc into 3rd of 3ch, turn.

**10th row:** Using A, 3ch, miss first dc, work 1tr into each ttr and each dc to end, turn.

Rep 3rd to 10th rows.

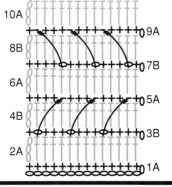

or  = 1ttr into missed tr 3 rows below.

On 4th and 8th rows work tr into ch, **not** ch space.

# Patterns for Texture and Colour

## Compass Point

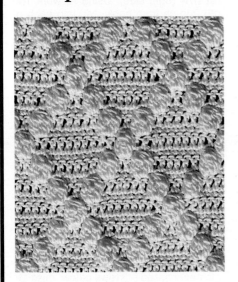

Starting chain: Multiple of 12 sts + 6.

**Special Abbreviation**

**Bobble** = working in front of work, work 5dtr into ch sp 2 rows below until 1 loop of each dtr remains on hook, yo and through all 6 loops.

**1st row** (right side): Work 1dc into 2nd ch from hook, 1dc into next ch, 1ch, miss 1ch, *1dc into each of next 11ch, 1ch, miss 1ch; rep from * to last 2ch, 1dc into each of last 2ch, turn.

**2nd row:** 3ch (count as 1tr), miss first dc, work 1tr into next dc, 1ch, miss 1ch sp, *1tr into each of next 11 sts, 1ch, miss 1ch sp; rep from * to last 2dc, 1tr into each of last 2dc, turn.

**3rd row:** 1ch, work 1dc into each of first 2tr, 1 bobble into ch sp 2 rows below, *1dc into next tr, 1ch, miss 1tr, 1dc into each of next 7tr, 1ch, miss 1tr, 1dc into next tr, 1 bobble into next ch sp 2 rows below; rep from * to last 2tr, 1dc into next tr, 1dc into 3rd of 3ch at beg of previous row, turn.

**4th row:** 3ch, miss first dc, 1tr into each of next 3 sts, *1ch, miss 1ch sp, 1tr into each of next 7 sts, 1ch, miss 1ch sp, 1tr into each of next 3 sts; rep from * to last dc, 1tr into last dc, turn.

**5th row:** 1ch, work 1dc into each of first 4tr, *1 bobble into ch sp 2 rows below, 1dc into next tr, 1ch, miss 1tr, 1dc into each of next 3tr, 1ch, miss 1tr, 1dc into next tr, 1 bobble into ch sp 2 rows below, 1dc into each of next 3tr; rep from * to last st, 1dc into 3rd of 3ch at beg of previous row, turn.

**6th row:** 3ch, miss first dc, work 1tr into each of next 5 sts, *1ch, miss 1ch sp, 1tr into each of next 3 sts, 1ch, miss 1ch sp, 1tr into each of next 7 sts; rep from * to end omitting 1tr at end of last rep, turn.

**7th row:** 1ch, work 1dc into each of first 6tr, *1 bobble into ch sp 2 rows below, 1dc into next tr, 1ch, miss 1tr, 1dc into next tr, 1 bobble into ch sp 2 rows below, 1dc into each of next 7tr; rep from * to end omitting 1dc at end of last rep, turn.

**8th row:** 3ch, miss first dc, work 1tr into each of next 7 sts, 1ch, miss 1ch sp, *1tr into each of next 11 sts, 1ch, miss 1ch sp; rep from * to last 8 sts, 1tr into each of last 8 sts, turn.

**9th row:** 1ch, work 1dc into each of first 6tr, *1ch, miss 1tr, 1dc into next tr, 1 bobble into ch sp 2 rows below, 1dc into next tr, 1ch, miss 1tr, 1dc into each of next 7tr; rep from * to end omitting 1dc at end of last rep, turn.

**10th row:** As 6th row.

**11th row:** 1ch, work 1dc into each of first 4tr, *1ch, miss 1tr, 1dc into next tr, 1 bobble into ch sp 2 rows below, 1dc into each of next 3tr, 1 bobble into ch sp 2 rows below, 1dc into next tr, 1ch, miss 1tr, 1dc into each of next 3tr; rep from * to last tr, 1dc into 3rd of 3ch, turn.

**12th row:** As 4th row.

**13th row:** 1ch, 1dc into each of first 2tr, 1ch, miss 1tr, 1dc into next tr, *1 bobble into ch sp 2 rows below, 1dc into each of next 7tr, 1 bobble into ch sp 2 rows below, 1dc into next tr, 1ch, miss 1tr, 1dc into next tr; rep from * to last tr, 1dc into 3rd of 3ch, turn.

Rep 2nd to 13th rows.

 = Bobble

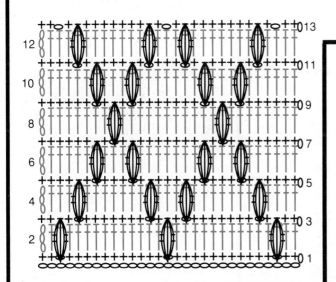

## Cross Slot Stitch

Starting chain: Multiple of 10 sts + 1.
Using A make the required number of chain.

**1st row** (wrong side): Using A, work 1dc into 2nd ch from hook, 1dc into each ch to end, turn.

**2nd row:** Using B, 1ch, work 1dc into each of first 8dc, *1ch, miss 1dc, 1dc into each of next 2dc, 1ch, miss 1dc, 1dc into each of next 6dc; rep from * to last 2dc, 1 dc into each dc to end, turn.

**3rd row:** Using B, 3ch (count as 1tr), miss first dc, work 1tr into each dc and into each ch to end, turn.

**4th row:** Using A, 1ch, work 1dc into each of first 8tr *work 1ttr into 2nd missed dc 3 rows below, miss 1tr, 1dc into each of next 2tr, 1ttr into first missed dc 3 rows below (thus crossing 2ttr), miss 1tr, 1dc into each of next 6tr; rep from * to last 2tr, 1dc into next tr, 1dc into 3rd of 3ch at beg of previous row, turn.

**5th row:** Using A, 1ch, work 1dc into each st to end, turn.

**6th row:** Using B, 1ch, work 1dc into each of first 3dc, *1ch, miss 1dc, 1dc into each of next 2dc, 1ch, miss 1dc, 1dc into each of next 6dc; rep from * to end omitting 3dc at end of last rep, turn.

**7th row:** Using B, 3ch, miss first dc, 1tr into each dc and into each ch to end, turn.

**8th row:** Using A, 1ch, 1dc into each of first 3tr, *work 1ttr into 2nd missed dc 3 rows below, miss 1tr, 1dc into each of next 2tr, 1ttr into first missed dc 3 rows below (thus crossing 2ttr), miss 1tr, 1dc into each of next 6tr; rep from * to end omitting 3dc at end of last rep and placing last dc into 3rd of 3ch at beg of previous row, turn.

**9th row:** Using A, 1ch, work 1dc into each st to end, turn.

Rep 2nd to 9th rows.

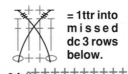 = 1ttr into missed dc 3 rows below.

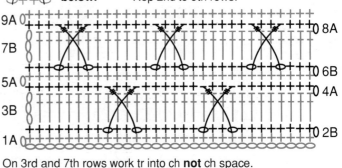

On 3rd and 7th rows work tr into ch **not** ch space.

# Patterns for Texture and Colour

## Oval Cluster Stitch

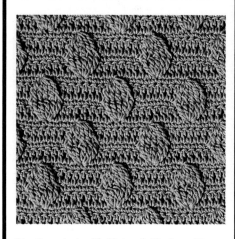

Starting chain: Multiple of 10 sts + 10.

**Special Abbreviations**

**Lower Cluster** = work 5dtr into next missed dc 2 rows below.

**Upper Cluster** = *[yo] twice then insert hook from right to left round stem of next dtr 2 rows below, work 1dtr in usual way until last loop of dtr remains on hook; rep from * 4 times more, yo and through all 6 loops.

**Note:** Count each ch sp as 1 st throughout.

**1st row** (right side): Work 1dc into 2nd ch from hook, 1dc into each ch to end, turn.

**2nd row:** 3ch (count as 1tr), miss first dc, work 1tr into each of next 3dc, *1ch, miss 1dc, 1tr into each of next 9 sts; rep from * to end omitting 5tr at end of last rep, turn.

**3rd row:** 1ch, work 1dc into each of first 2tr, *work lower cluster, **miss 5 sts of previous row,** 1dc into each of next 5tr; rep from * to end omitting 3dc at end of last rep and placing last dc into 3rd of 3ch at beg of previous row, turn.

**4th row:** 3ch, miss first dc, work 1tr into each st to end, turn.

**5th row:** 1ch, work 1dc into each of first 4tr, *work upper cluster over next 5dtr 2 rows below, miss next tr on previous row, 1dc into each of next 9tr; rep from * to end omitting 5dc at end of last rep and placing last dc into 3rd of 3ch at beg of previous row, turn.

**6th row:** 3ch, miss first dc, work 1tr into each of next 8 sts, *1ch, miss 1dc, 1tr into each of next 9 sts; rep from * to end.

## Quiver Stitch I

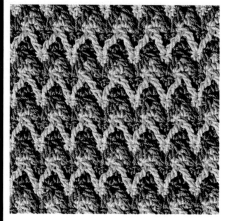

Starting chain: Multiple of 4 sts + 4.

**Special Abbreviation**

**Dtr2tog 3 rows below** = work 1dtr into same st as last dtr until last loop of dtr remains on hook, miss 3 sts, work 1dtr into next missed st 3 rows below until last loop of dtr remains on hook, yo and through all 3 loops. **Note:** Sts either side of dtr2tog must be worked behind dtr2tog.

**7th row:** 1ch, work 1dc into each of first 7tr, *work lower cluster, **miss 5 sts of previous row,** 1dc into each of next 5tr; rep from * to last 2tr, 1dc into each of last 2tr, working last dc into 3rd of 3ch at beg of previous row, turn.

**8th row:** 3ch, miss first dc, work 1tr into each st to end, turn.

**9th row:** 1ch, work 1dc into each of first 9tr, *work upper cluster over next 5dtr 2 rows below, miss next tr on previous row, 1dc into each of next 9tr; rep from * to end placing last dc into 3rd of 3ch at beg of previous row, turn.

Rep 2nd to 9th rows.

 = Lower cluster

= Upper cluster

Using A make required number of chain.

**1st row** (right side): Using A, work 1dc into 2nd ch from hook, 1dc into each of next 2ch, *1ch, miss 1ch, 1dc into each of next 3ch; rep from * to end, turn.

**2nd row:** Using A, 3ch (count as 1tr), miss first dc, work 1tr into each st to end (working into actual st of each ch, not into ch sp), turn.

**3rd row:** Using B, 1ch, 1dc into first tr, 1dtr into first missed starting ch, miss 1tr on 2nd row, 1dc into next tr, 1ch, miss 1tr, 1dc into next tr, *dtr2tog 3 rows below (into missed starting ch), miss 1tr on 2nd row, 1dc into next tr, 1ch, miss 1tr, 1dc into next tr; rep from * to last 2tr, 1dtr into same ch as 2nd leg of last dtr2tog, miss 1tr, 1dc into 3rd of 3ch at beg of previous row, turn.

**4th row:** Using B, 3ch, miss first dc, work 1tr into each st to end, turn.

**5th row:** Using A, 1ch, 1dc into first tr, 1dtr into next missed tr 3 rows below, miss 1tr on previous row, 1dc into next tr, 1ch, miss 1tr, 1dc into next tr, *dtr2tog 3 rows below, miss 1tr on previous row, 1dc into next tr, 1ch, miss 1tr, 1dc into next tr; rep from * to last 2tr, 1dtr into same tr as 2nd leg of last dtr2tog, miss 1tr, 1dc into 3rd of 3ch at beg of previous row, turn.

**6th row:** As 4th row **but** using A instead of B.

**7th row:** As 5th row **but** using B instead of A.

Rep 4th to 7th rows.

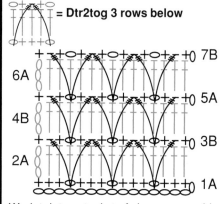

= Dtr2tog 3 rows below

Work tr into actual st of ch on wrong side rows, not into ch sp.

---

## Quiver Stitch II

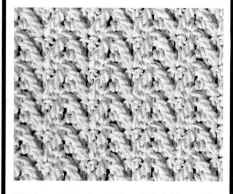

Work as given for Quiver Stitch I but using one colour throughout.

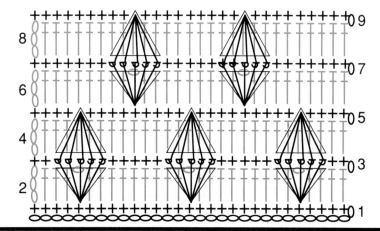

# Patterns for Texture and Colour

## Key Tab Stitch

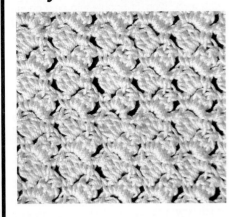

Starting chain: Multiple of 4 sts + 6.

**Special Abbreviation**
**Cluster** = work 3tr into next st until 1 loop of each remains on hook, yo and through all 4 loops on hook.

**1st row** (right side): Work 1 cluster into 5th ch from hook (1tr, 1ch formed at beg of row), 1ch, miss 2ch, 1dc into next ch, *3ch, 1 cluster into next ch, 1ch, miss 2ch, 1dc into next ch; rep from * to last 2ch, 2ch, 1tr into last ch, turn.

**2nd row:** 4ch (count as 1tr, 1ch), 1 cluster into first 2ch sp, 1ch, *1dc into next 3ch sp, 3ch, 1 cluster into same sp as last dc, 1ch; rep from * to last ch sp, 1dc into last ch sp, 2ch, 1tr into 3rd of 4ch at beg of previous row, turn.

Rep 2nd row only.

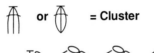

**Diagram only:** Rep 2nd and 3rd rows.

## Broadway

Starting chain: Multiple of 8 sts + 2.

**Special Abbreviations**
**Cr3R (Cross 3 Right)** = miss 2dc, work 1dtr into next dc, working behind last dtr work 1tr into each of 2 missed dc.

**Cr3L (Cross 3 Left)** = miss 1dc, work 1tr into each of next 2dc, working in front of last 2tr work 1dtr into missed dc.

**1st row** (wrong side): Work 1dc into 2nd ch from hook, 1dc into each ch to end, turn.

**2nd row:** 3ch (count as 1tr), miss first dc, *Cr3R, 1tr into next dc, Cr3L, 1tr into next dc; rep from * to end, turn.

**3rd row:** 1ch, work 1dc into each st to end placing last dc into 3rd of 3ch at beg of previous row, turn.

Rep 2nd and 3rd rows.

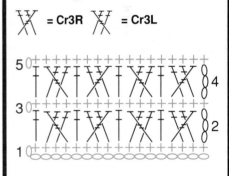

## Connected Spiral

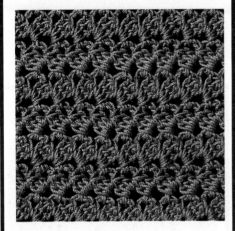

Starting chain: Multiple of 3 sts + 5.

**Special Abbreviation**
**Cluster4** = work 3tr over stem of tr just worked but leaving last loop of each tr on hook, then work 4th tr as indicated leaving last loop as before (5 loops on hook), yo and through all 5 loops.

**1st row** (right side): Work 1tr into 6th ch from hook, *3ch, miss 2ch, work cluster4 placing 4th tr into next ch; rep from * to last 2ch, 3ch, work cluster4 placing 4th tr in last ch, turn.

**2nd row:** 3ch (count as 1tr), 1tr into next 3ch sp, *3ch, work cluster4 placing 4th tr into next 3ch sp; rep from * to end placing final tr into top of ch at beg of previous row, turn.

Rep 2nd row.

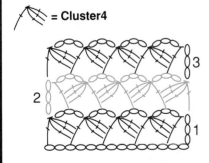 = Cluster4

**Diagram only:** Rep 2nd and 3rd rows.

## Global Connection

Starting chain: Multiple of 8 sts + 2.

**Special Abbreviation**
**Popcorn** = work 4tr into next st, drop loop from hook, insert hook from the front into top of first of these tr, pick up dropped loop and draw through tr, 1ch to secure popcorn.

**1st row** (right side): Work 1dc into 2nd ch from hook, *1ch, miss 3ch, 1tr into next ch, 1ch, into same ch as last tr work [1tr, 1ch, 1tr], 1ch, miss 3ch, 1dc into next ch; rep from * to end, turn.

**2nd row:** 6ch (count as 1tr, 3ch), miss 1tr, 1dc into next tr, *3ch, 1 popcorn into next dc, 3ch, miss 1tr, 1dc into next tr; rep from * to last dc, 3ch, 1tr into last dc, turn.

**3rd row:** 1ch, 1dc into first tr, *1ch, 1tr into next dc, 1ch, into same st as last tr work [1tr, 1ch, 1tr], 1ch, 1dc into top of next popcorn; rep from * to end, placing last dc into 3rd of 6ch at beg of previous row, turn.

Rep 2nd and 3rd rows.

 = Popcorn

# Patterns for Texture and Colour

## Triangle Stitch

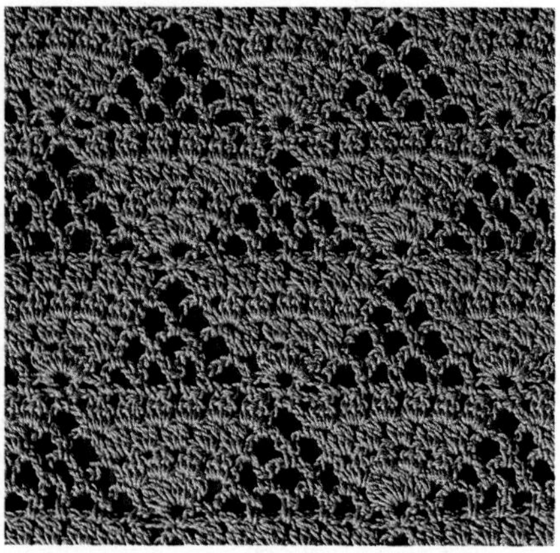

Starting chain: Multiple of 20 sts + 25.

**Special Abbreviations**

**Tr2tog** = work 2tr into next st until 1 loop of each remains on hook, yo and through all 3 loops on hook.

**Bobble** = work 3tr into next st until 1 loop of each remains on hook, yo and through all 4 loops on hook.

**1st row** (right side): Work 1dc into 7th ch from hook, 5ch, miss 3ch, 1dc into next ch, 1ch, miss 3ch, into next ch work [1 bobble, 1ch] 3 times, *miss 3ch, 1dc into next ch, [5ch, miss 3ch, 1dc into next ch] 3 times, 1ch, miss 3ch, into next ch work [1 bobble, 1ch] 3 times; rep from * to last 10ch, miss 3ch, 1dc into next ch, 5ch, miss 3ch, 1dc into next ch, 2ch, 1tr into last ch, turn.

**2nd row:** 1ch, 1dc into first tr, 5ch, 1dc into first 5ch arch, 1ch, [1 bobble into next ch sp, 1ch] 4 times, *1dc into next 5ch arch, [5ch, 1dc into next 5ch arch] twice, 1ch, [1 bobble into next ch sp, 1ch] 4 times; rep from * to last 2 arches, 1dc into next 5ch arch, 5ch, miss 2ch, 1dc into next ch, turn.

**3rd row:** 5ch (count as 1tr, 2ch), 1dc into first 5ch arch, 1ch, [1 bobble into next ch sp, 1ch] 5 times, *1dc into next 5ch arch, 5ch, 1dc into next 5ch arch, 1ch, [1 bobble into next ch sp, 1ch] 5 times; rep from * to last arch, 1dc into last arch, 2ch, 1tr into last dc, turn.

**4th row:** 1ch, 1dc into first tr, miss 2ch sp, *2ch, [1 bobble into next ch sp, 2ch] 6 times, 1dc into next 5ch arch; rep from * to end placing last dc into 3rd of 5ch at beg of previous row, turn.

**5th row:** 5ch (count as 1tr, 2ch), miss first 2ch sp, 1dc into next 2ch sp, [5ch, 1dc into next 2ch sp] 4 times, *1ch, into next dc work [1tr, 1ch] twice, miss next 2ch sp, 1dc into next 2ch sp, [5ch, 1dc into next 2ch sp] 4 times; rep from * to last 2ch sp, 2ch, 1tr into last dc, turn.

**6th row:** 3ch (count as 1tr), into first tr work [1tr, 1ch, 1 bobble], 1ch, 1dc into next 5ch arch, [5ch, 1dc into next 5ch arch] 3 times, *1ch, miss 1ch sp, into next ch sp work [1 bobble, 1ch] 3 times, 1dc into next 5ch arch, [5ch, 1dc into next 5ch arch] 3 times; rep from * to last sp, 1ch, into 3rd of 5ch at beg of previous row work [1 bobble, 1ch, tr2tog], turn.

**7th row:** 3ch (count as 1tr), [1 bobble into next ch sp, 1ch] twice, 1dc into first 5ch arch, [5ch, 1dc into next 5ch arch] twice, *1ch, [1 bobble into next ch sp, 1ch] 4 times, 1dc into next 5ch arch, [5ch, 1dc into next 5ch arch] twice; rep from * to last bobble, [1ch, 1 bobble into next ch sp] twice, 1tr into 3rd of 3ch at beg of previous row, turn.

**8th row:** 3ch, 1tr into first tr, 1ch, [1 bobble into next ch sp, 1ch] twice, 1dc into next 5ch arch, 5ch, 1dc into next 5ch arch, *1ch, [1 bobble into next ch sp, 1ch] 5 times, 1dc into next 5ch arch, 5ch, 1dc into next 5ch arch; rep from * to last 2 bobbles, 1ch, [1 bobble into next ch sp, 1ch] twice, tr2tog into 3rd of 3ch at beg of previous row, turn.

**9th row:** 4ch (count as 1tr, 1ch), [1 bobble into next ch sp, 2ch] 3 times, 1dc into next 5ch arch, *2ch, [1 bobble into next ch sp, 2ch] 6 times, 1dc into next 5ch arch; rep from * to last 2 bobbles, [2ch, 1 bobble into next ch sp] 3 times, 1ch, 1tr into 3rd of 3ch at beg of previous row, turn.

**10th row:** 1ch, 1dc into first tr, 5ch, miss first ch sp, 1dc into next 2ch sp, 5ch, 1dc into next 2ch sp, 1ch, into next dc work [1tr, 1ch] twice, *miss next 2ch sp, 1dc into next 2ch sp, [5ch, 1dc into next 2ch sp] 4 times, 1ch, into next dc work [1tr, 1ch] twice; rep from * to last 3 bobbles, miss next 2ch sp, [1dc into next 2ch sp, 5ch] twice, 1dc into 3rd of 4ch at beg of previous row, turn.

**11th row:** 5ch (count as 1tr, 2ch), 1dc into first 5ch arch, 5ch, 1dc into next 5ch arch, 1ch, miss 1ch sp, into next ch sp work [1 bobble, 1ch] 3 times, *1dc into next 5ch arch, [5ch, 1dc into next 5ch arch] 3 times, 1ch, miss 1ch sp, into next ch sp work [1 bobble, 1ch] 3 times; rep from * to last 2 arches, 1dc into next 5ch arch, 5ch, 1dc into next 5ch arch, 2ch, 1tr into last dc, turn.

Rep 2nd to 11th rows.

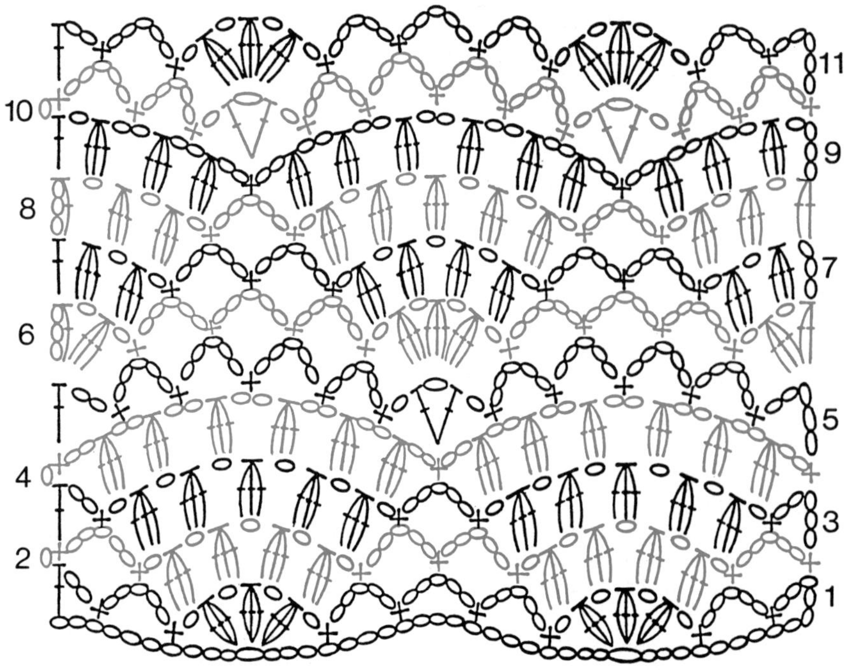


= Dc2tog    = Bobble    Rep 2nd to 11th rows.

## Spatter Pattern

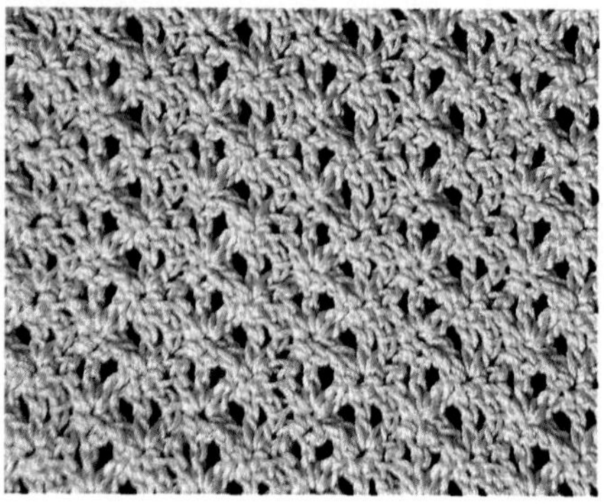

Starting chain: Multiple of 6 sts + 2.

**1st row** (right side): Work 1dc into 2nd ch from hook, *miss 2ch, 1tr into next ch, 2ch, into same ch as last tr work [1tr, 2ch, 1tr], miss 2ch, 1dc into next ch; rep from * to end, turn.

**2nd row:** 5ch (count as 1tr, 2ch), 1tr into first dc, miss 1tr, 1dc into next tr, *1tr into next dc, 2ch, into same st as last tr work [1tr, 2ch, 1tr], miss 1tr, 1dc into next tr; rep from * to last dc, into last dc work [1tr, 2ch, 1tr], turn.

**3rd row:** 1ch, 1dc into first tr, *1tr into next dc, 2ch, into same st as last tr work [1tr, 2ch, 1tr], miss 1tr, 1dc into next tr; rep from * to end placing last dc into 3rd of 5ch at beg of previous row, turn.

Rep 2nd and 3rd rows.

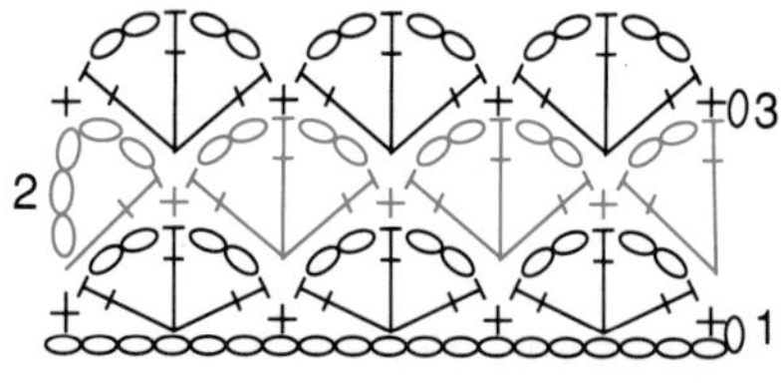




Stitch variations, Abbreviations and symbols on pages 7 to 15

# Patterns for Texture and Colour

## Wheatsheaf

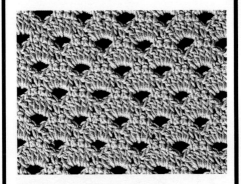

Starting chain: Multiple of 5 sts + 2.

**1st row** (wrong side): Work 1dc into 2nd ch from hook, 1dc into next ch, *3ch, miss 2ch, 1dc into each of next 3ch; rep from * to end omitting 1dc at end of last rep, turn.

**2nd row:** 1ch, 1dc into first dc, *5tr into next 3ch arch, miss 1dc, 1dc into next dc; rep from * to end, turn.

**3rd row:** 3ch (count as 1htr, 1ch), miss first 2 sts, 1dc into each of next 3tr, *3ch, miss next 3 sts, 1dc into each of next 3tr; rep from * to last 2 sts, 1ch, 1htr into last dc, turn.

**4th row:** 3ch (count as 1tr), 2tr into first ch sp, miss 1dc, 1dc into next dc, *5tr into next 3ch arch, miss 1dc, 1dc into next dc; rep from * to last sp, 2tr into last sp, 1tr into 2nd of 3ch at beg of previous row, turn.

**5th row:** 1ch, 1dc into each of first 2tr, *3ch, miss 3 sts, 1dc into each of next 3tr; rep from * to end omitting 1dc at end of last rep and placing last dc into 3rd of 3ch at beg of previous row, turn.

Rep 2nd to 5th rows.

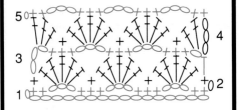

## Petal Pattern I

Starting chain: Multiple of 11 sts + 3.

**Special Abbreviation**

**Tr2tog** = Work 2tr into next st until 1 loop of each remains on hook, yo and through all 3 loops on hook.

**1st row** (right side): Work 1dc into 2nd ch from hook, 1ch, miss 1ch, 1dc into next ch, [3ch, miss 3ch, 1dc into next ch] twice, *2ch, miss 2ch, 1dc into next ch, [3ch, miss 3ch, 1dc into next ch] twice; rep from * to last 2ch, 1ch, miss 1ch, 1dc into last ch, turn.

**2nd row:** 3ch (count as 1tr), into first ch sp work [tr2tog, 2ch, tr2tog], 1ch, miss 1dc, 1dc into next dc, *1ch, miss 3ch sp, tr2tog into next 2ch sp, into same sp as last tr2tog work [2ch, tr2tog] 3 times, 1ch, miss 3ch sp, 1dc into next dc; rep from * to last 2 sps, 1ch, miss 3ch sp, into last ch sp work [tr2tog, 2ch, tr2tog], 1tr into last dc, turn.

**3rd row:** 1ch, 1dc into first tr, *3ch, work 1tr2tog into top of each of next 4tr2tog, 3ch, 1dc into next 2ch sp; rep from * to end placing last dc into 3rd of 3ch at beg of previous row, turn.

**4th row:** 1ch, 1dc into first dc, *3ch, 1dc into top of next tr2tog, 2ch, miss 2tr2tog, 1dc into top of next tr2tog, 3ch, 1dc into next dc; rep from * to end, turn.

**5th row:** 1ch, work 1dc into first dc, *1ch, miss 3ch sp, tr2tog into next 2ch sp, into same sp as last tr2tog work [2ch, tr2tog]

3 times, 1ch, miss 3ch sp, 1dc into next dc; rep from * to end, turn.

**6th row:** 3ch, work 1tr2tog into top of each of next 2tr2tog, 3ch, 1dc into next 2ch sp, 3ch, *tr2tog into top of each of next 4tr2tog, 3ch, 1dc into next 2ch sp, 3ch; rep from * to last 2tr2tog, work 1tr2tog into each of last 2tr2tog, 1tr into last dc, turn.

**7th row:** 1ch, 1dc into first tr, 1ch, miss 1tr2tog, 1dc into next tr2tog, 3ch, 1dc into next dc, 3ch, *1dc into top of next tr2tog, 2ch, miss 2tr2tog, 1dc into top of next tr2tog, 3ch, 1dc into next dc, 3ch; rep from * to last 2tr2tog, 1dc into next tr2tog, 1ch, miss 1tr2tog, 1dc into 3rd of 3ch at beg of previous row, turn.

Rep 2nd to 7th rows.

 = Tr2tog

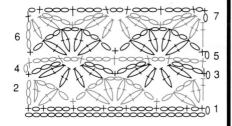

## Petal Pattern II

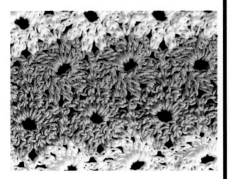

Work as Petal Pattern I **but** working 1st and 2nd rows in A, then work 3 rows each in B, C and A throughout.

## Petal Pattern III

Work as Petal Pattern I **but** working 1st and 2nd rows in A then 3 rows each in B and A throughout. **Note:** Cut yarn after each colour change.

## Cabbage Patch

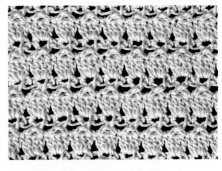

Starting chain: Multiple of 4 sts + 7.

**Special Abbreviation**

**Cross2tr** = miss 3tr, work 1tr into next tr, 2ch, working behind last tr work 1tr into the first of the missed tr.

**1st row** (right side): Work 4tr into 5th ch from hook, *miss 3ch, 4tr into next ch; rep from * to last 2ch, 1tr into last ch, turn.

**2nd row:** 3ch (count as 1tr), miss first tr, *cross2tr; rep from * to end, 1tr into top of 3ch at beg of previous row, turn.

**3rd row:** 3ch, work 4tr into each 2ch sp to end, 1tr into 3rd of 3ch at beg of previous row, turn.

Rep 2nd and 3rd rows.

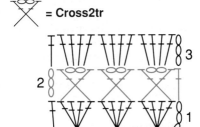 = Cross2tr

# All Over Patterns

## Triple Curve Stitch

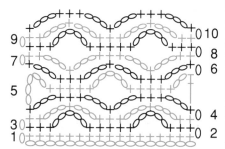

Starting chain: Multiple of 8 sts + 2.

**1st row** (wrong side): Work 1dc into 2nd ch from hook, 1dc into each ch to end, turn.

**2nd row:** 1ch, 1dc into each of first 3dc, *5ch, miss 3dc, 1dc into each of next 5dc; rep from * to end omitting 2dc at end of last rep, turn,

**3rd row:** 1ch, 1dc into each of first 2dc, *3ch, 1dc into next 5ch arch, 3ch, miss 1dc, 1dc into each of next 3dc; rep from * to end omitting 1dc at end of last rep, turn.

**4th row:** 1ch, 1dc into first dc, *3ch, 1dc into next 3ch arch, 1dc into next dc, 1dc into next 3ch arch, 3ch, miss 1dc, 1dc into next dc; rep from * to end, turn.

**5th row:** 5ch (count as 1tr, 2ch), 1dc into next 3ch arch, 1dc into each of next 3dc, 1dc into next 3ch arch, *5ch, 1dc into next 3ch arch, 1dc into each of next 3dc, 1dc into next 3ch arch; rep from * to last dc, 2ch, 1tr into last dc, turn.

**6th row:** 1ch, 1dc into first tr, 3ch, miss 1dc, 1dc into each of next 3dc, *3ch, 1dc into next 5ch arch, 3ch, miss 1dc, 1dc into each of next 3dc; rep from * to last 2ch arch, 3ch, 1dc into 3rd of 5ch at beg of previous row, turn.

**7th row:** 1ch, 1dc into first dc, 1dc into first 3ch arch, 3ch, miss 1dc, 1dc into next dc, *3ch, 1dc into next 3ch arch, 1dc into next dc, 1dc into next 3ch arch, 3ch, miss 1dc, 1dc into next dc; rep from * to last 3ch arch, 3ch, 1dc into 3ch arch, 1dc into last dc, turn.

**8th row:** 1ch, 1dc into each of first 2dc, *1dc into next 3ch arch, 5ch, 1dc into next 3ch arch, 1dc into each of next 3dc; rep from * to end omitting 1dc at end of last rep, turn.

Rep 3rd to 8th rows.

## Jigsaw Pattern

Starting chain: Multiple of 10 sts + 2.
**Special Abbreviations**

**Bobble** = Work 4tr into next st until 1 loop of each remains on hook, yo and through all 5 loops on hook.

**Tr2tog** = Work 2tr into next st until 1 loop of each remains on hook, yo and through all 3 loops on hook.

**1st row** (right side): Work 1dc into 2nd ch from hook, 1dc into each of next 2ch, *3ch, miss 2ch, 1 bobble into next ch, 3ch, miss 2ch, 1dc into each of next 5ch; rep from * to end omitting 2dc at end of last rep, turn.

**2nd row:** 1ch, 1dc into each of first 2dc, *3ch, 1dc into next 3ch sp, 1dc into top of next bobble, 1dc into next 3ch sp, 3ch, miss 1dc, 1dc into each of next 3dc; rep from * to end omitting 1dc at end of last rep, turn.

**3rd row:** 3ch (count as 1tr), 1tr into first dc (half bobble made at beg of row), *3ch, 1dc into next 3ch sp, 1dc into each of next 3dc, 1dc into next 3ch sp, 3ch, miss 1dc, 1 bobble into next dc; rep from * to end but working half bobble of tr2tog at end of last rep, turn.

**4th row:** 1ch, 1dc into top of half bobble, 1dc into first 3ch sp, 3ch, miss 1dc, 1dc into each of next 3dc, *3ch, 1dc into next 3ch sp, 1dc into top of next bobble, 1dc into next 3ch sp, 3ch, miss 1dc, 1dc into each of next 3dc; rep from * to last 3ch sp, 3ch, 1dc into last 3ch sp, 1dc into 3rd of 3ch at beg of previous row, turn.

**5th row:** 1ch, 1dc into each of first 2dc, *1dc into next 3ch sp, 3ch, miss 1dc, 1 bobble into next dc, 3ch, 1dc into next 3ch sp, 1dc into each of next 3dc; rep from * to end omitting 1dc at end of last rep, turn.

Rep 2nd to 5th rows.

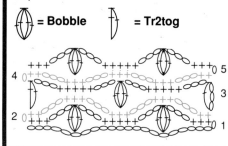

**= Bobble**      **= Tr2tog**

## Theatre Box

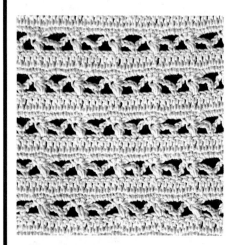

Starting chain: Multiple of 6 sts + 4.
**Special Abbreviation**

**Puff st** = [yo, insert hook into next st, yo and draw a loop through] 3 times into same st, yo and draw through 7 loops on hook, work 1 firm ch to close puff st.

**1st row** (right side): Work 1dc into 2nd ch from hook, 1dc into each ch to end, turn.

**2nd row:** 3ch (count as 1tr), miss first dc, 1tr into each dc to end, turn.

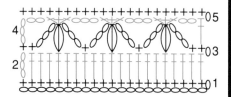

 = Puff st

**3rd row:** 1ch, 1dc into each of first 2tr, *3ch, miss 2tr, 1 puff st into next tr, 3ch, miss 2tr, 1dc into next tr; rep from * to last tr, 1dc into 3rd of 3ch at beg of previous row, turn.

**4th row:** 5ch (count as 1tr, 2ch), work 3dc into closing ch of next puff st, *3ch, 3dc into closing ch of next puff st; rep from * to last 2dc, 2ch, 1tr into last dc, turn.

**5th row:** 1ch, 1dc into first tr, 2dc into first 2ch sp, *1dc into each of next 3dc, 3dc into next 3ch sp; rep from * to end working last dc into 3rd of 5ch at beg of previous row, turn.

Rep 2nd to 5th rows.

Stitch Variations, Abbreviations and Symbols on pages 7 to 15

## Angel Stitch

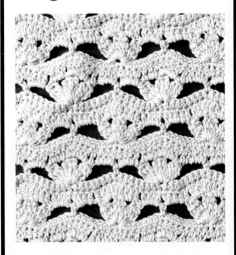

Starting chain: Multiple of 16 sts + 3.

**Special Abbreviations**

**Cluster** = work 1tr into same arch as last 3tr until 2 loops remain on hook, miss 1dc, work 1tr into next arch until 3 loops remain on hook, yo and through all 3 loops on hook.

**Bobble** = work 3dtr into next dc until 1 loop of each remains on hook, yo and through all 4 loops on hook.

**1st row** (right side): Work 1tr into 4th ch from hook, 1tr into each of 6ch, work 3tr into next ch, 1tr into each of next 6ch, *work 1tr into next ch until 2 loops remain on hook, miss 1ch, 1tr into next ch until 3 loops remain on hook, yo and through all 3 loops on hook, work 1tr into each of next 6ch, 3tr into next ch, 1tr into each of next 6ch; rep from * to last 2 ch, work 1tr into next ch until 2 loops remain on hook, 1tr into last ch until 3 loops remain on hook, yo and through all 3 loops (cluster made at end of row), turn.

**2nd row:** 1ch, work 1dc into each st to last tr, miss last tr, 1dc into top of 3ch, turn.

**3rd row:** 4ch, work 1dtr into first dc (half bobble made at beg of row), 2ch, 1 bobble into same dc as half bobble, 4ch, miss 7dc, 1dc into next dc, *4ch, miss 7dc, work 1 bobble into next dc, into same dc as last bobble work [2ch, 1 bobble] twice, 4ch, miss 7dc, 1dc into next dc; rep from * to last 8dc, 4ch, work 1 bobble into last dc, 2ch, work 2dtr into same dc as last bobble until 1 loop of each remains on hook, yo and through all 3 loops on hook (half bobble made at end of row), turn.

## Mosaic

**4th row:** 3ch (count as 1tr), 1tr into top of first half bobble, work 2tr into 2ch sp, 1tr into next bobble, 3tr into next 4ch arch, 1 cluster, 3tr into same arch as 2nd leg of last cluster, *1tr into top of next bobble, 2tr into 2ch sp, 3tr into top of next bobble, 2tr into next 2ch sp, 1tr into top of next bobble, 3tr into next 4ch arch, 1 cluster, 3tr into same arch as 2nd leg of last cluster; rep from * to last bobble, 1tr into last bobble, 2tr into next 2ch sp, 2tr into top of half bobble, turn.

**5th row:** 1ch, 1dc into each st to end, placing last dc into 3rd of 3ch at beg of previous row, turn.

**6th row:** 1ch, 1dc into first dc, *4ch, miss 7dc, 1 bobble into next dc, into same dc as last bobble work [2ch, 1 bobble] twice, 4ch, miss 7 dc, 1dc into next dc; rep from * to end, turn.

**7th row:** 3ch, 4tr into first 4ch arch, 1tr into next bobble, 2tr into next 2ch sp, 3tr into next bobble, 2tr into next 2ch sp, 1tr into next bobble, *3tr into next 4ch arch, 1 cluster, 3tr into same arch as 2nd leg of last cluster, 1tr into next bobble, 2tr into next 2ch sp, 3tr into next bobble, 2tr into next 2ch sp, 1tr into next bobble; rep from * to last 4ch arch, 3tr into last arch, 1 cluster working into last arch and last dc, turn.

Rep 2nd to 7th rows.

Starting chain: Multiple of 8 sts + 2.

**Special Abbreviation**

**Bobble** = work 4tr into next st until 1 loop of each remains on hook, yo and through all 5 loops on hook.

**1st row** (wrong side): Work 1dc into 2nd ch from hook, 1dc into each ch to end, turn.

**2nd row:** 4ch (count as 1tr, 1ch), miss first 2dc, 1 bobble into next dc, 1ch, miss 1dc, 1tr into next dc, *1ch, miss 1dc, 1 bobble into next dc, 1ch, miss 1dc, 1tr into next dc; rep from * to end, turn.

**3rd row:** 1ch, work 1dc into each tr, ch sp and bobble to end, working last 2dc into 4th and 3rd of 4ch at beg of previous row, turn.

**4th row:** 1ch, 1dc into each of first 3dc, *5ch, miss 3dc, 1dc into each of next 5dc; rep from * to end omitting 2dc at end of last rep, turn.

**5th row:** 1ch, 1dc into each of first 2dc, *3ch, 1dc into 5ch arch, 3ch, miss 1dc, 1dc into each of next 3dc; rep from * to end omitting 1dc at end of last rep, turn.

**6th row:** 1ch, 1dc into first dc, *3ch, 1dc into next 3ch arch, 1dc into next dc, 1dc into next 3ch arch, 3ch, miss 1dc, 1dc into next dc; rep from * to end, turn.

**7th row:** 5ch (count as 1tr, 2ch), 1dc into next 3ch arch, 1dc into each of next 3dc, 1dc into next 3ch arch, *5ch, 1dc into next 3ch arch, 1dc into each of next 3dc, 1dc into next 3ch arch; rep from * to last dc, 2ch, 1tr into last dc, turn.

**8th row:** 1ch, 1dc into first tr, *3ch, miss 1dc, 1dc into each of next 3dc, 3ch, 1dc into next 5ch arch; rep from * to end placing last dc into 3rd of 5ch at beg of previous row, turn.

**9th row:** 1ch, 1dc into first dc, *1dc into next 3ch arch, 3ch, miss 1dc, 1dc into next dc, 3ch, 1dc into next 3ch arch, 1dc into next dc; rep from * to end, turn.

**10th row:** 1ch, 1dc into each of first 2dc, *1dc into next 3ch arch, 3ch, 1dc into next 3ch arch, 1dc into each of next 3dc; rep from * to end omitting 1dc at end of last rep, turn.

**11th row:** 1ch, 1dc into each of first 3dc, *3ch, 3dc into next 3ch arch, 1dc into each of next 5dc; rep from * to end omitting 2dc at end of last rep, turn.

Rep 2nd to 11th rows.

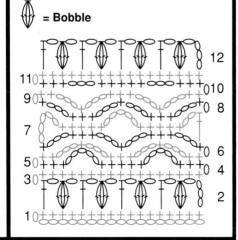

= **Bobble**

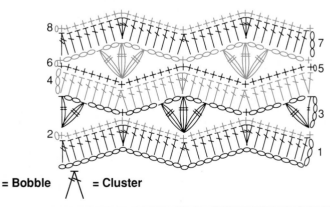

= **Bobble**      = **Cluster**

# All Over Patterns

## Roller Coaster

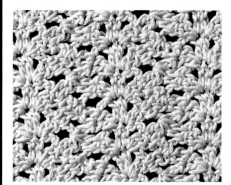

Diagram only: Rep 2nd and 3rd row.

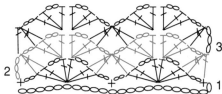

- = 2tr Cluster
- = 4tr Cluster

Starting chain: Multiple of 10 sts + 2.

### Special Abbreviations

**2tr Cluster** = work 1tr into each of next 2tr until 1 loop of each remains on hook, yo and through all 3 loops on hook.

**4tr Cluster** = work 1tr into each of next 4tr until 1 loop of each remains on hook, yo and through all 5 loops on hook.

**1st row** (right side): Work 1dc into 2nd ch from hook, *2ch, miss 4ch, 2tr into next ch, into same ch as last 2tr work [2ch, 2tr] twice, 2ch, miss 4ch, 1dc into next ch; rep from * to end, turn.

**2nd row:** 3ch (count as 1tr), work a 2tr cluster over next 2tr, 2ch, into next tr work [2tr, 2ch, 1tr], into next tr work [1tr, 2ch, 2tr], 2ch, *work a 4tr cluster over next 4tr, 2ch, into next tr work [2tr, 2ch, 1tr], into next tr work [1tr, 2ch, 2tr], 2ch; rep from * to last 2tr, work a 2tr cluster over last 2tr, 1tr into last dc, turn.

**3rd row:** 3ch (count as 1tr), miss first tr and cluster, work a 2tr cluster over next 2tr, 2ch, into next tr work [2tr, 2ch, 1tr], into next tr work [1tr, 2ch, 2tr], 2ch, *work a 4tr cluster over next 4tr (excluding 4tr cluster of previous row), 2ch, into next tr work [2tr, 2ch, 1tr], into next tr work [1tr, 2ch, 2tr], 2ch; rep from * to last 4 sts (excluding 2ch sp), work a 2tr cluster over next 2tr, 1tr into 3rd of 3ch at beg of previous row, turn.

Rep 3rd row only.

## Flame Stitch

Starting chain: Multiple of 10 sts + 2.

### Special Abbreviation

**Tr2tog** = work 2tr into next 3ch arch until 1 loop of each remains on hook, yo and through all 3 loops on hook.

**1st row** (wrong side): Work 1dc into 2nd ch from hook, *3ch, miss 3ch, 1dc into next ch, 3ch, miss 1ch, 1dc into next ch, 3ch, miss 3ch, 1dc into next ch; rep from * to end, turn.

**2nd row:** 1ch, 1dc into first dc, *1ch, miss next 3ch sp, tr2tog into next 3ch arch, into same arch as last tr2tog work [3ch, tr2tog] 4 times, 1ch, miss next 3ch sp, 1dc into next dc; rep from * to end, turn.

**3rd row:** 7ch (count as 1dtr, 3ch), miss next 3ch arch, 1dc into next 3ch arch, 3ch, 1dc into next 3ch arch, 3ch, 1dtr into next dc, *3ch, miss next 3ch arch, 1dc into next 3ch arch, 3ch, 1dc into next 3ch arch, 3ch, 1dtr into next dc; rep from * to end, turn.

**4th row:** 1ch, 1dc into first dtr, *1ch, miss next 3ch sp, tr2tog into next 3ch arch, into same arch as last tr2tog work [3ch, tr2tog] 4 times, 1ch, 1dc into next dtr; rep from * to end, working last dc into 4th of 7ch at beg of previous row, turn.

Rep 3rd and 4th rows.

- = Tr2tog

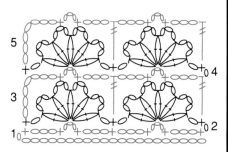

## Country Style

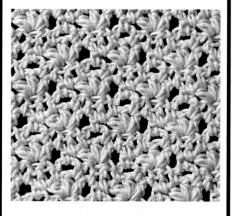

Starting chain: Multiple of 6 sts + 2.

### Special Abbreviations

**Htr2tog** = *Yo, insert hook into st, yo and draw a loop through (3 loops on hook); rep from * once more into same st, yo and through all 5 loops on hook.

**Tr2tog** = work 1tr into next ch sp until 2 loops remain on hook, work a 2nd tr into next ch sp until 3 loops remain on hook, yo and through all 3 loops on hook.

**1st row** (right side): Work 1dc into 2nd ch from hook, *1ch, miss 2ch, into next ch work [htr2tog, 1ch] 3 times, miss 2ch, 1dc into next ch; rep from * to end, turn.

**2nd row:** 4ch (count as 1tr, 1ch), miss first ch sp, 1dc into next ch sp, 3ch, 1dc into next ch sp, *1ch, tr2tog over next 2 ch sps, 1ch, 1dc into next ch sp, 3ch, 1dc into next ch sp; rep from * to last dc, 1ch, 1tr into last dc, turn.

**3rd row:** 3ch (count as 1htr, 1ch), htr2tog into first tr, 1ch, 1dc into next 3ch sp, 1ch, *into top of next tr2tog work [htr2tog, 1ch] 3 times, 1dc into next 3ch sp, 1ch; rep from * to last ch sp, into 3rd of 4ch at beg of previous row work [htr2tog, 1ch, 1htr], turn.

**4th row:** 1ch, 1dc into first htr, 1dc into first ch sp, 1ch, tr2tog over next 2 ch sps, 1ch, *1dc into next ch sp, 3ch, 1dc into next ch sp, 1ch, tr2tog over next 2 ch sps, 1ch; rep from * to last ch sp, 1dc into last ch sp, 1dc into 2nd of 3ch at beg of previous row, turn.

**5th row:** 1ch, 1dc into first dc, *1ch, into top of next tr2tog work [htr2tog, 1ch] 3 times, 1dc into next 3ch sp; rep from * to end placing last dc into last dc, turn.

Rep 2nd to 5th rows.

- = Htr2tog
- = Tr2tog

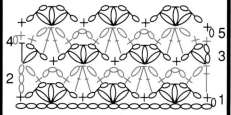

Stitch Variations, Abbreviations and Symbols on pages 7 to 15

## Shallow Curve

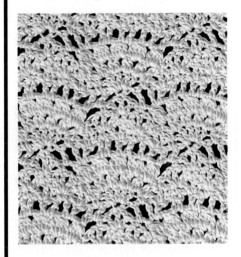

Starting chain: Multiple of 24 sts + 5.

**Special Abbreviations**

**Tr2tog** = work 2tr into next st until 1 loop of each remains on hook, yo and through all 3 loops on hook.

**Bobble** = work 4tr into next st until 1 loop of each remains on hook, yo and through all 5 loops on hook.

**Group** = work 1tr into next st, into same st as last tr work [1ch, 1tr] twice.

**1st row** (right side): Work 1tr into 5th ch from hook, miss 2ch, 1dc into next ch, miss 2ch, 1 group into next ch, miss 2ch, 1dc into next ch, miss 2ch, 5tr into next ch, *miss 2ch, 1dc into next ch, [miss 2ch, 1 group into next ch, miss 2ch, 1dc into next ch] 3 times, miss 2ch, 5tr into next ch; rep from * to last 12ch, miss 2ch, 1dc into next ch, miss 2ch, 1 group into next ch, miss 2ch, 1dc into next ch, miss 2ch, into last ch work [1tr, 1ch, 1tr], turn.

**2nd row:** 1ch, 1dc into first tr, 1 group into next dc, 1dc into centre tr of next group, miss 1tr, 2tr into each of next 5tr, *1dc into centre tr of next group, [1 group into next dc, 1dc into centre tr of next group] twice, miss 1tr, 2tr into each of next 5tr; rep from * to last group, 1dc into centre tr of next group, 1 group into next dc, miss [1tr, 1ch], 1 dc into next ch, turn.

**3rd row:** 4ch (count as 1tr, 1ch), 1tr into first dc, 1dc into centre tr of first group, 2ch, [1 bobble between next pair of tr, 2ch] 5 times, *1dc into centre tr of next group, 1 group into next dc, 1dc into centre tr of next group, 2ch, [1 bobble between next pair of tr, 2ch] 5 times; rep from * to last group, 1dc into centre tr of last group, into last dc work [1tr, 1ch, 1tr], turn.

**4th row:** 1ch, 1dc into first tr, *1ch, 1tr into next 2ch sp, [1ch, 1tr into top of next bobble, 1ch, 1tr into next 2ch sp] 5 times, 1ch, 1dc into centre tr of next group; rep from * to end placing last dc into 3rd of 4ch at beg of previous row, turn.

**5th row:** 3ch (count as 1tr), 2tr into first dc, *miss 1ch sp, 1dc into next ch sp, [miss 1ch sp, 1 group into next tr, miss 1ch sp, 1dc into next ch sp] 3 times, 5tr into next dc; rep from * to end omitting 2tr at end of last rep, turn.

**6th row:** 3ch (count as 1tr), 1tr into first tr, 2tr into each of next 2tr, 1dc into centre tr of next group, [1 group into next dc, 1dc into centre tr of next group] twice, *miss 1tr, 2tr into each of next 5tr, 1dc into centre tr of next group, [1 group into next dc, 1dc into centre tr of next group] twice; rep from * to last 5 sts, miss next tr and dc, 2tr into each of next 2tr, 2tr into 3rd of 3ch at beg of previous row, turn.

**7th row:** 3ch (count as 1tr), tr2tog between first pair of tr, 2ch, [1 bobble between next pair of tr, 2ch] twice, 1dc into centre tr of next group, 1 group into next dc, 1dc into centre tr of next group, *2ch, miss [1tr, 1dc], [1 bobble between next pair of tr, 2ch] 5 times, 1dc into centre tr of next group, 1 group into next dc, 1dc into centre tr of next group; rep from * to last 3 pairs of tr, [2ch, 1 bobble between next pair of tr] twice, 2ch, tr2tog between last pair of tr, 1tr into 3rd of 3ch at beg of previous row, turn.

**8th row:** 4ch (count as 1tr, 1ch), 1tr into first 2ch sp, 1ch, [1tr into top of next bobble, 1ch, 1tr into next 2ch sp, 1ch] twice, 1dc into centre tr of next group, *1ch, 1tr into next 2ch sp, 1ch, [1tr into top of next bobble, 1ch, 1tr into next 2ch sp, 1ch] 5 times, 1dc into centre tr of next group; rep from * to last 3 2ch sps, 1ch, 1tr into next 2ch sp, [1ch, 1tr into top of next bobble, 1ch, 1tr into next 2ch sp] twice, 1ch, 1tr into 3rd of 3ch at beg of previous row, turn.

**9th row:** 4ch (count as 1tr, 1ch), 1tr into first tr, miss 1ch sp, 1dc into next ch sp, miss 1ch sp, 1 group into next tr, miss 1ch sp, 1dc into next ch sp, 5tr into next dc, *miss 1ch sp, 1dc into next ch sp, [miss 1ch sp, 1 group into next tr, miss 1ch sp, 1dc into next ch sp] 3 times, 5tr into next dc; rep from * to last 6 ch sps, miss 1ch sp, 1dc into next ch sp, miss 1ch sp, 1 group into next tr, miss 1ch sp, 1dc into next ch sp, into 3rd of 4ch at beg of previous row work [1tr, 1ch, 1tr], turn.

Rep 2nd to 9th rows.

## Mat Stitch

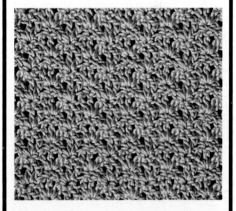

Starting chain: Multiple of 6 sts + 2.

**1st row** (right side): Work 1dc into 2nd ch from hook, *miss 2ch, 1tr into next ch, 1ch, into same ch as last tr work [1tr, 1ch, 1tr], miss 2ch, 1dc into next ch; rep from * to end, turn.

**2nd row:** 4ch (count as 1tr, 1ch), 1tr into first dc, miss 1tr, 1dc into next tr, *1tr into next dc, 1ch, into same st as last tr work [1tr, 1ch, 1tr], miss 1tr, 1dc into next tr; rep from * to last dc, into last dc work [1tr, 1ch, 1tr], turn.

**3rd row:** 1ch, 1dc into first tr, *1tr into next dc, 1ch, into same st as last tr work [1tr, 1ch, 1tr], miss 1tr, 1dc into next tr; rep from * to end placing last dc into 3rd of 4ch at beg of previous row, turn.

Rep 2nd and 3rd rows.

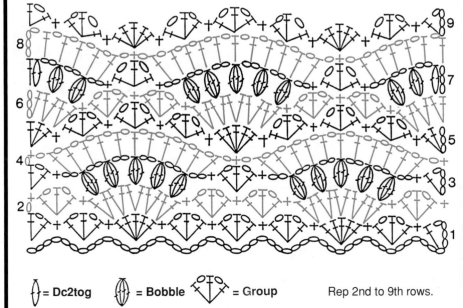

〉〈 = Dc2tog    〈〉 = Bobble    = Group    Rep 2nd to 9th rows.

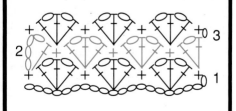

# All-over Patterns

## Rack Stitch

**Diagram only:** Rep 2nd to 7th rows.

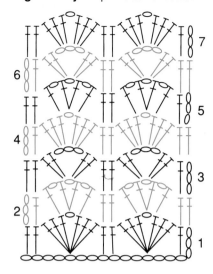

Starting chain: Multiple of 7 sts + 4.

**1st row** (right side): Work 1tr into 4th ch from hook, *miss 2ch, into next ch work [3tr, 1ch, 3tr], miss 2ch, 1tr into each of next 2ch; rep from * to end, turn.

**2nd row:** 3ch (count as 1tr), miss first tr, 1tr into next tr, *miss 2tr, 1tr into next tr, 1ch, into next ch sp work [1tr, 1ch, 1tr], 1ch, 1tr into next tr, miss 2tr, 1tr into each of next 2tr; rep from * to end placing last tr into 3rd of 3ch at beg of previous row, turn.

**3rd row:** 3ch, miss first tr, 1tr into next tr, *miss next ch sp, into next ch sp work [2tr, 3ch, 2tr], miss 2tr, 1tr into each of next 2tr; rep from * to end placing last tr into 3rd of 3ch at beg of previous row, turn.

**4th row:** 3ch, miss first tr, 1tr into next tr, *into next 3ch sp work [3tr, 1ch, 3tr], miss 2tr, 1tr into each of next 2tr; rep from * to end placing last tr into 3rd of 3ch at beg of previous row, turn.

Rep 2nd to 4th rows.

## Arch Gallery

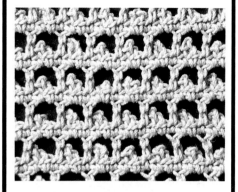

Starting chain: Multiple of 3 sts + 2.

**1st row** (right side): Work 1dc into 2nd ch from hook, 1dc into next ch, *4ch, sl st into 4th ch from hook (1 picot made), 1dc into each of next 3dc; rep from * to end omitting 1dc at end of last rep, turn.

**2nd row:** 5ch (count as 1tr, 2ch), miss 2dc, 1tr into next dc, *2ch, miss 2dc, 1tr into next dc; rep from * to end, turn.

**3rd row:** 1ch, 1dc into first tr, *into next 2ch sp work [1dc, 1 picot, 1dc], 1dc into next tr; rep from * to end placing last dc into 3rd of 5ch at beg of previous row, turn.

Rep 2nd and 3rd rows.

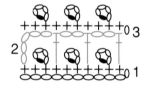

## Cool Design

**5th row:** 1ch, 1dc into first dc, *7tr into next dc, 1dc into next dc; rep from * to end, turn.

**6th row:** 6ch, miss 3tr, 1tr into next tr, 3ch, 1tr into next dc, *3ch, miss 3tr, 1tr into next tr, 3ch, 1tr into next dc; rep from * to end, turn.

**7th and 8th rows:** As 3rd and 4th rows.

**9th row:** 3ch (count as 1tr), 3tr into first dc, 1dc into next dc, *7tr into next dc, 1dc into next dc; rep from * to last dc, 4tr into last dc, turn.

Rep 2nd to 9th rows.

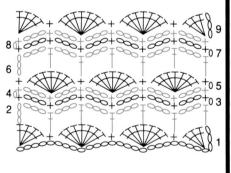

Starting chain: Multiple of 8 sts + 4.

**1st row** (right side): Work 3tr into 4th ch from hook, miss 3ch, 1dc into next ch, *miss 3ch, 7tr into next ch, miss 3ch, 1dc into next ch; rep from * to last 4ch, miss 3ch, 4tr into last ch, turn.

**2nd row:** 6ch (count as 1tr, 3ch), 1tr into next dc, *3ch, miss 3tr, 1tr into next tr, 3ch, 1tr into next dc; rep from * to last 4 sts, 3ch, 1tr into top of 3ch at beg of previous row, turn.

**3rd row:** 1ch, *1dc into next tr, 3ch; rep from * to last st, 1dc into 3rd of 6ch at beg of previous row, turn.

**4th row:** 1ch, 1dc into first dc, *3ch, 1dc into next dc; rep from * to end, turn.

## Tortoise Shell

Starting chain: Multiple of 5 sts + 2.

**1st row** (wrong side): Work 1dc into 2nd ch from hook, *5ch, miss 4ch, 1dc into next ch; rep from * to end, turn.

**2nd row:** 5ch (count as 1dtr, 1ch), *into next 5ch arch work [1dtr, 1tr, 4ch, sl st into 4th ch from hook, 1tr, 1dtr], 2ch; rep from * to end omitting 1ch at end of last rep, 1dtr into last dc, turn.

**3rd row:** 1ch, 1dc into first dtr, *5ch, 1dc into next 2ch sp; rep from * to end placing last dc into 4th of 5ch at beg of previous row, turn.

Rep 2nd and 3rd rows.

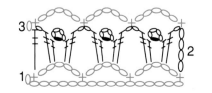

Stitch Variations, Abbreviations and Symbols on pages 7 to 15

## Fossil Stitch

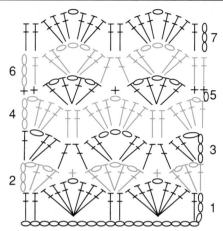

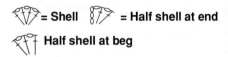

Starting chain: Multiple of 9 sts + 4.

**Special Abbreviations**

**Shell** = work 1tr into next tr, 1ch, between last tr and next tr work [1tr, 1ch, 1tr], 1ch, 1tr into next tr.

**Half shell at beg of row** = 4ch (count as 1tr, 1ch), 1tr between first 2tr, 1ch, 1tr into next tr.

**Half shell at end of row** = 1tr into next tr, 1ch, 1tr between last tr worked into and last tr (the 3ch at beg of previous row), 1ch, 1tr into 3rd of 3ch at beg of previous row.

**1st row** (right side): Work 1tr into 4th ch from hook, *miss 3ch, into next ch work [3tr, 1ch, 3tr], miss 3ch, 1tr into each of next 2ch; rep from * to end, turn.

**2nd row:** Work half shell over first 2tr, 1dc into next ch sp, *miss 3tr, 1 shell over next 2tr, 1dc into next ch sp; rep from * to last 5 sts, miss 3tr, half shell over last 2tr, turn.

**3rd row:** 4ch (count as 1tr, 1ch), 2tr into first ch sp, miss 1tr, 1tr into each of next 2tr, *miss 1ch sp, into next ch sp work [2tr, 3ch, 2tr], miss 1tr, 1tr into each of next 2tr; rep from * to last 2tr, 2tr into last ch sp, 1ch, 1tr into 3rd of 4ch at beg of previous row, turn.

$\lessdot$ = Shell   $\lessgtr$ = Half shell at end

$\lessdot$ Half shell at beg

**4th row:** 4ch (count as 1tr, 1ch), 3tr into first ch sp, miss 2tr, 1tr into each of next 2tr, *into next 3ch sp work [3tr, 1ch, 3tr], miss 2tr, 1tr into each of next 2tr; rep from * to last 3tr, work 3tr into last ch sp, 1ch, 1tr into 3rd of 4ch at beg of previous row, turn.

**5th row:** 1ch, 1dc into first tr, 1dc into first ch sp, *miss 3tr, 1 shell over next 2tr, 1dc into next ch sp; rep from * to end, 1dc into 3rd of 4ch at beg of previous row, turn.

**6th row:** 3ch (count as 1tr), miss first dc, 1tr into next dc, miss 1ch sp, into next ch sp work [2tr, 3ch, 2tr], *miss 1tr, work 1tr into each of next 2tr, miss 1ch sp, into next ch sp work [2tr, 3ch, 2tr]; rep from * to last 2tr, 1tr into each of last 2dc, turn.

**7th row:** 3ch (count as 1tr), miss first tr, 1tr into next tr, *into next 3ch sp work [3tr, 1ch, 3tr], miss 2tr, 1tr into each of next 2tr; rep from * to end placing last tr into 3rd of 3ch at beg of previous row, turn.

Rep 2nd to 7th rows.

## Rose Buds

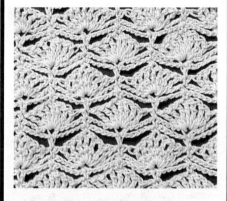

Starting chain: Multiple of 12 sts + 6.

**1st row** (right side): Work [1dtr, 1ch] 3 times into 6th ch from hook, miss 5ch, 1dc into next ch, *1ch, miss 5ch, into next ch work [1dtr, 1ch] 7 times, miss 5ch, 1dc into next ch; rep from * to last 6ch, 1ch, into last ch work [1dtr, 1ch] 3 times, 1dtr into same ch as last 3dtr, turn.

**2nd row:** 1ch, 1dc into first dtr, *6ch, 1dc into next dc, 6ch, miss 3dtr, 1dc into next dtr; rep from * to end placing last dtr into 4th of 5ch at beg of previous row, turn.

**3rd row:** 1ch, 1dc into first dc, *6ch, 1dc into next dc; rep from * to end, turn.

**4th row:** 1ch, 1dc into first dc, *1ch, into next dc work [1dtr, 1ch] 7 times, 1dc into next dc; rep from * to end, turn.

**5th row:** 1ch, 1dc into first dc, *6ch, miss 3dtr, 1dc into next dtr, 6ch, 1dc into next dc; rep from * to end, turn.

**6th row:** 1ch, 1dc into first dc, *6ch, 1dc into next dc; rep from * to end, turn.

**7th row:** 5ch (count as 1dtr, 1ch), into first dc work [1dtr, 1ch] 3 times, 1dc into next dc, *1ch, into next dc work [1dtr, 1ch] 7 times, 1dc into next dc; rep from * to last dc, into last dc work [1ch, 1dtr] 4 times, turn.

Rep 2nd to 7th rows.

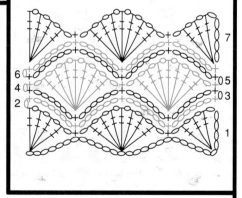

## Garland Pattern

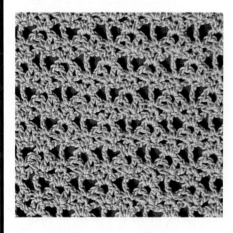

Starting chain: Multiple of 8 sts + 2.

**1st row** (right side): Work 1dc into 2nd ch from hook, *miss 3ch, into next ch work [1tr, 1ch, 1tr, 3ch, 1tr, 1ch, 1tr], miss 3ch, 1dc into next ch; rep from * to end, turn.

**2nd row:** 7ch (count as 1dtr, 3ch), *miss 1ch sp, into next 3ch sp work [1dc, 3ch, 1dc], 3ch, 1dtr into next dc, 3ch; rep from * to end omitting 3ch at end of last rep, turn.

**3rd row:** 4ch (count as 1tr, 1ch), into first dtr work [1tr, 1ch, 1tr], miss 3ch sp, 1dc into next 3ch sp, *into next dtr work [1tr, 1ch, 1tr, 3ch, 1tr, 1ch, 1tr], miss 3ch sp, 1dc into next 3ch sp; rep from * to last sp, miss 3ch, 1tr into next ch, work [1ch, 1tr] twice into same ch as last tr, turn.

**4th row:** 1ch, 1dc into first tr, 1dc into first ch sp, 3ch, 1dtr into next dc, *3ch, miss 1ch sp, into next 3ch sp work [1dc, 3ch, 1dc], 3ch, 1dtr into next dc; rep from * to last 3tr, 3ch, miss 1ch sp, 1dc into each of next 2ch, turn.

**5th row:** 1ch, 1dc into first dc, *into next dtr work [1tr, 1ch, 1tr, 3ch, 1tr, 1ch, 1tr], miss 3ch sp, 1dc into next 3ch sp; rep from * to end placing last dc into last dc, turn.

Rep 2nd to 5th rows.

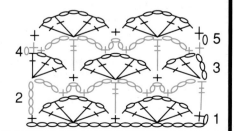

# All-over Patterns

## Flying Stitch

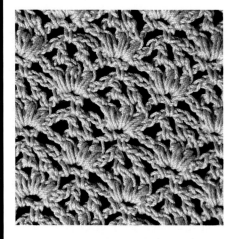

 = Puff st

Starting chain: Multiple of 10 sts + 14.

**Special Abbreviation**

**Puff st** = [yo, insert hook into sp, yo and draw a loop through] 3 times into same space, yo and through all 7 loops on hook, work 1 firm ch to close puff st.

**1st row** (wrong side): Work 1dc into 9th ch from hook, (first 3ch sp made), 1ch, miss 1ch, 1dc into next ch, *3ch, miss 2ch, 1tr into next ch, 1ch, miss 1ch, 1tr into next ch, 3ch, miss 2ch, 1dc into next ch, 1ch, miss 1ch, 1dc into next ch; rep from * to last 3ch, 3ch, miss 2ch, 1tr into last ch, turn.

**2nd row:** 1ch, 1dc into first tr, *3ch, miss 3ch sp, 1 puff st into next ch sp, 2ch, into same ch sp as last puff st work [1 puff st, 2ch, 1 puff st], 3ch, miss 3ch sp, 1dc into next ch sp; rep from * to end working last dc into 4th ch, turn.

**3rd row:** 1ch, 1dc into first dc, 3ch, miss first 3ch arch, 1tr into next 2ch arch, 1ch, 1tr into next 2ch arch, 3ch, 1dc into next 3ch arch, *1ch, 1dc into next 3ch arch, 3ch, 1tr into next 2ch arch, 1ch, 1tr into next 2ch arch, 3ch, 1dc into next 3ch arch; rep from * to end placing last dc into last dc, turn.

**4th row:** 6ch (count as 1tr, 3ch), miss 3ch arch, 1dc into next ch sp, *3ch, miss 3ch arch, 1 puff st into next ch sp, 2ch, into same ch sp as last puff st work [1 puff st, 2ch, 1 puff st], 3ch, miss 3ch arch, 1dc into next ch sp; rep from * to last 3ch arch, 3ch, 1tr into last dc, turn.

**5th row:** 6ch (count as 1tr, 3ch), 1dc into first 3ch arch, 1ch, 1dc into next 3ch arch, *3ch, 1tr into next 2ch arch, 1ch, 1tr into next 2ch arch, 3ch, 1dc into next 3ch arch, 1ch, 1dc into next 3ch arch; rep from * to end, 3ch, 1tr into 3rd of 6ch at beg of previous row, turn.

Rep 2nd to 5th rows.

## Crown Stitch

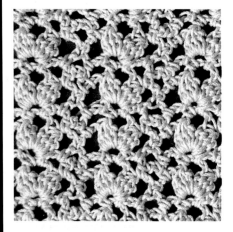

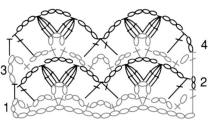

= Cluster    Tr2tog over next 3 3ch arches

Starting chain: Multiple of 9 sts + 14.

**Special Abbreviations**

**Cluster** = work 4tr into next 3ch arch until 1 loop of each remains on hook, yo and through all 5 loops on hook.

**Tr2tog over next 3 3ch arches** = work 1tr into next 3ch arch until 2 loops remain on hook, miss next 3ch arch, 1tr into next 3ch arch until 3 loops remain on hook, yo and through all 3 loops on hook.

**1st row** (wrong side): Work 1dc into 6th ch from hook, 3ch, miss 2ch, into next ch work [1dc, 3ch, 1dc], *[3ch, miss 2ch, 1dc into next ch] twice, 3ch, miss 2ch, into next ch work [1dc, 3ch, 1dc]; rep from * to last 5ch, 3ch, miss 2ch, 1dc into next dc, 1ch, miss 1ch, 1tr into last ch, turn.

**2nd row:** 2ch (count as 1htr), 1tr into first 3ch arch, 3ch, into next 3ch arch work [1 cluster, 4ch, 1 cluster], 3ch, *tr2tog over next 3 3ch arches, 3ch, into next 3ch arch work [1 cluster, 4ch, 1 cluster], 3ch; rep from * to last 2 arches, work 1tr into next 3ch arch, miss 1ch, 1htr into next ch, turn.

**3rd row:** 4ch (count as 1tr, 1ch), 1dc into next 3ch arch, 3ch, into next 4ch arch work [1dc, 3ch, 1dc], *3ch, [1dc into next 3ch arch, 3ch] twice, into next 4ch arch work [1dc, 3ch, 1dc]; rep from * to last 3ch arch, 3ch, 1dc into last 3ch arch, 1ch, 1tr into 2nd of 2ch at beg of previous row, turn.

Rep 2nd and 3rd rows.

## Sprig Pattern

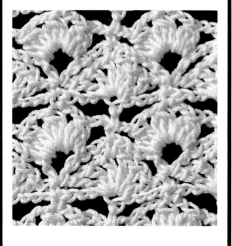

Starting chain: Multiple of 10 sts + 5.

**Special Abbreviation**

**Cluster** = work 3tr into next space until 1 loop of each remains on hook, yo and through all 4 loops on hook.

**1st row** (right side): Work [1tr, 1ch, 1tr] into 5th ch from hook (1tr and 1ch sp formed at beg of row), 1ch, miss 4ch, 1dc into next ch, *1ch, miss 4ch, into next ch work [1tr, 1ch] 6 times, miss 4ch, 1dc into next ch; rep from * to last 5ch, 1ch, 1tr into last ch, [1ch, 1tr] twice into same ch as last tr, turn.

**2nd row:** 1ch, 1dc into first tr, 3ch, into next dc work [1tr, 3ch, 1tr], *3ch, miss 3tr, 1dc into next ch sp, 3ch, into next dc work [1tr, 3ch, 1tr]; rep from * to last 3tr, 3ch, 1dc into 3rd of 4ch at beg of previous row, turn.

**3rd row:** 1ch, 1dc into first dc, *2ch, miss 3ch sp, 1 cluster into next 3ch sp, 2ch, into same sp as last cluster work [1 cluster, 2ch] twice, 1dc into next dc; rep from * to end, turn.

**4th row:** 7ch (count as 1tr, 4ch), *miss 1 cluster, 1dc into next cluster, 4ch, 1tr into next dc, 4ch; rep from * to end omitting 4ch at end of last rep, turn.

**5th row:** 4ch (count as 1tr, 1ch), into first tr work [1tr, 1ch] twice, 1dc into next dc, *1ch, into next tr work [1tr, 1ch] 6 times, 1dc into next dc; rep from * to last tr, 1ch, work 1tr into 3rd of 7ch at beg of previous row, [1ch, 1tr] twice into same ch as last tr, turn.

Rep 2nd to 5th rows.

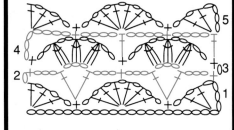 = Cluster

Stitch Variations, Abbreviations and Symbols on pages 7 to 15

## Open Fan

**Starting chain:** Multiple of 30 sts + 32.

**1st row** (right side): Work 1dc into 2nd ch from hook, [miss 2ch, 5tr into next ch, miss 2ch, 1dc into next ch] twice, miss 2ch, 1tr into next ch, 1ch, into same ch as last tr work [1tr, 1ch, 1tr], *miss 2ch, 1dc into next ch, [miss 2ch, 5tr into next ch, miss 2ch, 1dc into next ch] 4 times, miss 2ch, 1tr into next ch, 1ch, into same ch as last tr work [1tr, 1ch, 1tr]; rep from * to last 15ch, miss 2ch, 1dc into next ch, [miss 2ch, 5tr into next ch, miss 2ch, 1dc into next ch] twice, turn.

**2nd row:** 3ch (count as 1tr), 2tr into first dc, miss 2tr, 1dc into next tr, 5tr into next dc, miss 2tr, 1dc into next tr, 1ch, miss 2tr, 1tr into next tr, 1ch, [1tr into next ch sp, 1ch, 1tr into next tr, 1ch] twice, *miss 2tr, 1dc into next tr, [5tr into next dc, miss 2tr, 1dc into next tr] 3 times, 1ch, miss 2tr, 1tr into next tr, 1ch, [1tr into next ch sp, 1ch, 1tr into next tr, 1ch] twice; rep from * to last 2 groups of 5tr, miss 2tr, 1dc into next tr, 5tr into next dc, miss 2tr, 1dc into next tr, 3tr into last dc, turn.

**3rd row:** 1ch, 1dc into first tr, 5tr into first dc, miss 2tr, 1dc into next tr, 2ch, miss 2tr, [1tr into next tr, 2ch] 5 times, *miss 2tr, 1dc into next tr, [5tr into next dc, miss 2tr, 1dc into next tr] twice, 2ch, miss 2tr, [1tr into next tr, 2ch] 5 times; rep from * to last group of 5tr, miss 2tr, 1dc into next tr, 5tr into next dc, 1dc into 3rd of 3ch at beg of previous row, turn.

**4th row:** 3ch (count as 1tr), 2tr into first dc, miss 2tr, 1dc into next tr, 1ch, 1tr into next 2ch sp, [1ch, 1tr into next tr, 1ch, 1tr into next 2ch sp] 5 times, *1ch, miss 2tr, 1dc into next tr, 5tr into next dc, miss 2tr, 1dc into next tr, 1ch, 1tr into next 2ch sp, [1ch, 1tr into next tr, 1ch, 1tr into next 2ch sp] 5 times; rep from * to last group of 5tr, 1ch, miss 2tr, 1dc into next tr, 3tr into last dc, turn.

**5th row:** 1ch, 1dc into first tr, *5tr into next dc, miss 1ch sp, 1dc into next ch sp, [miss 1ch sp, 5tr into next tr, miss 1ch sp, 1dc into next ch sp] 3 times, 5tr into next dc, 1dc into centre tr of next group of 5; rep from * to end placing last dc into 3rd of 3ch at beg of previous row, turn.

**6th row:** 4ch (count as 1tr, 1ch), 1tr into first dc, 1dc into centre tr of first group of 5, [5tr into next dc, 1dc into centre tr of next group of 5] 4 times, *1tr into next dc, 1ch, into same st as last tr work [1tr, 1ch, 1tr], 1dc into centre tr of next group of 5, [5tr into next dc, 1dc into centre tr of next group of 5] 4 times; rep from * to last dc, into last dc work [1tr, 1ch, 1tr], turn.

**7th row:** 4ch (count as 1tr, 1ch), 1tr into first ch sp, 1ch, 1tr into next tr, 1ch, 1dc into centre tr of first group of 5, [5tr into next dc, 1dc into centre tr of next group of 5] 3 times, *1ch, miss 2tr, 1tr into next tr, 1ch, [1tr into next ch sp, 1ch, 1tr into next tr, 1ch] twice, 1dc into centre tr of next group of 5, [5tr into next dc, 1dc into centre tr of next group of 5] 3 times; rep from * to last 4tr, 1ch, miss 2tr, 1tr into next tr, 1ch, 1tr into last ch sp, 1ch, 1tr into 3rd of 4ch at beg of previous row, turn.

**8th row:** 5ch (count as 1tr, 2ch), miss first tr, [1tr into next tr, 2ch] twice, 1dc into centre tr of group of 5, [5tr into next dc, 1dc into centre tr of next group of 5] twice, *2ch, miss 2tr, [1tr into next tr, 2ch] 5 times, 1dc into centre tr of next group of 5, [5tr into next dc, 1dc into centre tr of next group of 5] twice; rep from * to last 5tr, 2ch, miss 2tr, [1tr into next tr, 2ch] twice, 1tr into 3rd of 4ch at beg of previous row, turn.

**9th row:** 4ch (count as 1tr, 1ch), 1tr into first 2ch sp, 1ch, [1tr into next tr, 1ch, 1tr into next 2ch sp, 1ch] twice, 1dc into centre tr of first group of 5, 5tr into next dc, 1dc into centre tr of next group of 5, *1ch, 1tr into next 2ch sp, 1ch, [1tr into next tr, 1ch, 1tr into next 2ch sp, 1ch] 5 times, 1dc into centre tr of next group of 5, 5tr into next dc, 1dc into centre tr of next group of 5; rep from * to last 5tr, 1ch, 1tr into next 2ch sp, 1ch, [1tr into next tr, 1ch, 1tr into next 2ch sp, 1ch] twice, 1tr into 3rd of 5ch at beg of previous row, turn.

**10th row:** 3ch (count as 1tr), 2tr into first tr, miss 1ch sp, 1dc into next ch sp, miss 1ch sp, 5tr into next tr, miss 1ch sp, 1dc into next ch sp, 5tr into next dc, 1dc into centre tr of next group of 5, *miss 1ch sp, 1dc into next ch sp, [miss 1ch sp, 5tr into next tr, miss 1ch sp, 1dc into next ch sp] 3 times, 5tr into next dc, 1dc into centre tr of next group of 5, 5tr into next dc; rep from * to last 6tr, miss 1ch sp, 1dc into next ch sp, miss 1ch sp, 5tr into next tr, miss 1ch sp, 1dc into next ch sp, 3tr into 3rd of 4ch at beg of previous row, turn.

**11th row:** 1ch, 1dc into first tr, [5tr into next dc, 1dc into centre tr of next group of 5] twice, 1tr into next dc, 1ch, into same st as last tr work [1tr, 1ch, 1tr], *1dc into centre tr of next group of 5, [5tr into next dc, 1dc into centre tr of next group of 5] 4 times, 1tr into next dc, 1ch, into same st as last tr work [1tr, 1ch, 1tr]; rep from * to last 2 groups of 5tr, [1dc into centre tr of next group of 5, 5tr into next dc] twice, 1dc into 3rd of 3ch at beg of previous row, turn.
Rep 2nd to 11th rows.

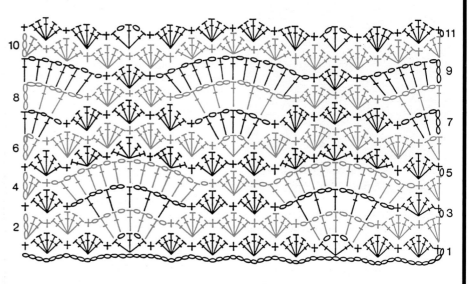

# All-over Patterns

## Column and Bowl

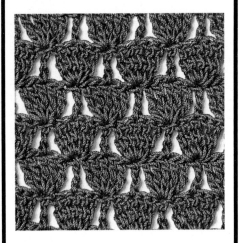

Starting chain: Multiple of 8 sts + 12.

**1st row** (right side): Work 5dtr into 8th ch from hook, miss 3ch, 1dtr into next ch, *miss 3ch, 5dtr into next ch, miss 3ch, 1dtr into next ch; rep from * to end, turn.

**2nd row:** 4ch (count as 1dtr), 2dtr into first dtr, miss 2dtr, 1dtr into next dtr, *miss 2dtr, 5dtr into next dtr, miss 2dtr, 1dtr into next dtr; rep from * to last 3 sts, miss 2dtr, 3dtr into next ch, turn.

**3rd row:** 4ch, *miss 2dtr, 5dtr into next dtr, miss 2dtr, 1dtr into next dtr; rep from * to end placing last dtr into 4th of 4ch at beg of previous row, turn.

Rep 2nd and 3rd rows.

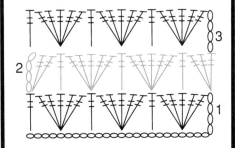

## Column Stitch

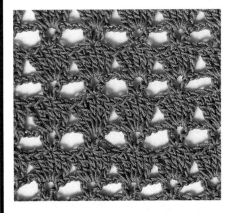

Starting chain: Multiple of 5 sts + 6.

**1st row** (wrong side): Work [1tr, 2ch, 1tr] into 8th ch from hook, *3ch, miss 4ch, work [1tr, 2ch, 1tr] into next ch; rep from * to last 3ch, 2ch, 1tr into last ch, turn.

## Cone Stitch

Starting chain: Multiple of 8 sts + 3.

**1st row** (wrong side): Work 1tr into 4th ch from hook, *1ch, miss 2ch, into next ch work [1tr, 3ch, 1tr], 1ch, miss 2ch, 1tr into each of next 3ch; rep from * to end omitting 1tr at end of last rep, turn.

**2nd row:** 4ch (count as 1tr, 1ch), work 7tr into next 3ch arch, *1ch, miss 2tr, 1tr into next tr, 1ch, 7tr into next 3ch arch; rep from * to last 3tr, 1ch, miss 2tr, 1tr into top of 3ch, turn.

**3rd row:** 4ch, 1tr into first tr, 1ch, miss 2tr, 1tr into each of next 3tr, *1ch, miss 2tr, into next tr work [1tr, 3ch, 1tr], 1ch, miss 2tr, 1tr into each of next 3tr; rep from * to last 3tr, miss 2tr, into 3rd of 4ch at beg of previous row work [1tr, 1ch, 1tr], turn.

**4th row:** 3ch (count as 1tr), 3tr into first ch sp, 1ch, miss 2tr, 1tr into next tr, *1ch, 7tr into next 3ch arch, 1ch, miss 2tr, 1tr into next tr; rep from * to last 3tr, 1ch, miss 2tr, 3tr into last ch sp, 1tr into 3rd of 4ch at beg of previous row, turn.

**5th row:** 3ch, miss first tr, 1tr into next tr, *1ch, miss 2tr, into next tr work [1tr, 3ch, 1tr], 1ch, miss 2tr, 1tr into each of next 3tr; rep from * to end omitting 1tr at end of last rep and placing last tr into 3rd of 3ch at beg of previous row, turn.

Rep 2nd to 5th rows.

**2nd row:** 4ch (count as 1dtr), miss first 2ch sp, work 5dtr into next 2ch sp, *miss 3ch sp, work 5dtr into next 2ch sp; rep from * to last sp, miss 2ch, 1dtr into next ch, turn.

**3rd row:** 5ch (count as 1tr, 2ch), miss first 3dtr, into next dtr work [1tr, 2ch, 1tr], *3ch, miss 4dtr, into next dtr work [1tr, 2ch, 1tr]; rep from * to last 3dtr, 2ch, 1tr into 4th of 4ch at beg of previous row, turn.

Rep 2nd and 3rd rows.

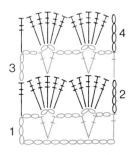

## Umbrella Stitch

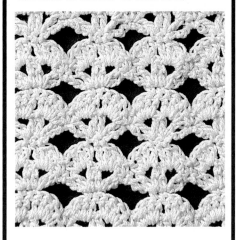

Rep 2nd to 5th rows.

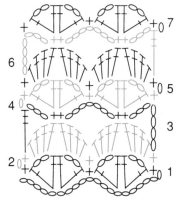

Starting chain: Multiple of 9 sts + 2.

**1st row** (right side): Work 1dc into 2nd ch from hook, *miss 3ch, into each of next 2ch work [1tr, 2ch, 1tr], miss 3ch, 1dc into next ch; rep from * to end, turn.

**2nd row:** 1ch, 1dc into first dc, *into next 2ch sp work [1htr, 3tr], into next 2ch sp work [3tr, 1htr], 1dc into next dc; rep from * to end, turn.

**3rd row:** 7ch (count as 1dtr, 3ch), miss first 4 sts, 1dc into each of next 2tr, *7ch, miss 7 sts, 1dc into each of next 2tr; rep from * to last 4 sts, 3ch, 1dtr into last dc, turn.

**4th row:** 1ch, 1dc into first dtr, *into each of next 2dc work [1tr, 2ch, 1tr], 1dc into 7ch arch; rep from * to end placing last dc into 4th of 7ch at beg of previous row, turn.

Rep 2nd to 4th rows.

**Diagram only:** Rep 2nd to 7th rows.

Stitch Variations, Abbreviations and Symbols on pages 7 to 15

## Medallion Pattern

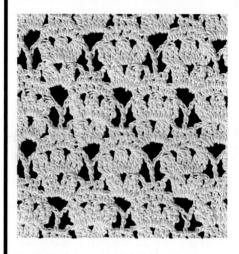

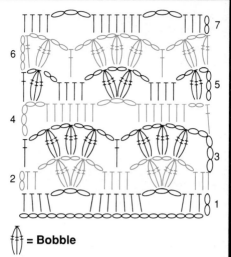

Starting chain: Multiple of 10 sts + 2.

**Special Abbreviation**

**Bobble** = work 3dtr into next st until 1 loop of each remains on hook, yo and through all 4 loops on hook.

**1st row** (right side): Work 1htr into 3rd ch from hook, 1htr into each of next 2ch, *3ch, miss 3ch, 1htr into each of next 7ch; rep from * to end omitting 3htr at end of last rep, turn.

**2nd row:** 2ch (count as 1htr), working between sts work 1htr between first and 2nd htr then between 2nd and 3rd htr, 2ch, into next 3ch sp work [1 bobble, 2ch] twice, *miss 1htr, [1htr between next 2htr] 4 times, 2ch, into next 3ch sp work [1 bobble, 2ch] twice; rep from * to last 4 sts, miss 1htr, 1htr between next 2htr, 1htr between last htr and 2ch, 1htr into top of 2ch, turn.

**3rd row:** 5ch (count as 1tr, 2ch), *1 bobble into next bobble, 2ch, 1 bobble into next 2ch sp, 2ch, 1 bobble into next bobble, 2ch, 1tr between 2nd and 3rd htr, 2ch; rep from * to end omitting 2ch at end of last rep and placing last tr into 2nd of 2ch at beg of previous row, turn.

**4th row:** 5ch, *1htr into next bobble, [2htr into next 2ch sp, 1htr into next bobble] twice, 3ch; rep from * to end omitting 1ch at end of last rep, work 1tr into 3rd of 5ch at beg of previous row, turn.

**5th row:** 4ch (count as 1tr, 1ch), 1 bobble into first 2ch sp, 2ch, miss 1htr, [1htr between next 2htr] 4 times, *2ch, into next 3ch sp work [1 bobble, 2ch] twice, miss 1htr, [1htr between next 2htr] 4 times; rep from * to last 2ch sp, 2ch, work 1 bobble into last 2ch sp, 1ch, 1tr into 3rd of 5ch at beg of previous row, turn.

**6th row:** 4ch (count as 1dtr), 1dtr into first ch sp, 2ch, 1 bobble into next bobble, 2ch, miss 1htr, 1tr between next 2htr, 2ch, *1 bobble into next bobble, 2ch, 1 bobble into next 2ch sp, 2ch, 1 bobble into next bobble, 2ch, miss 1htr, 1tr between next 2htr; rep from * to last bobble, 2ch, 1 bobble into next bobble, 2ch, work 1dtr into last ch sp until last loop of dtr remains on hook, 1dtr into 3rd of 4ch until 3 loops remain on hook, yo and through all 3 loops on hook, turn.

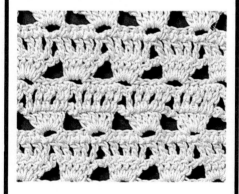

= Bobble

**7th row:** 2ch, 2htr into first 2ch sp, 1htr into next bobble, 3ch, *1htr into next bobble, [2htr into next 2ch sp, 1htr into next bobble] twice, 3ch; rep from * to last bobble, 1htr into last bobble, 2htr into next 2ch sp, 1htr into 4th of 4ch at beg of previous row, turn.

Rep 2nd to 7th rows.

## Candelabra

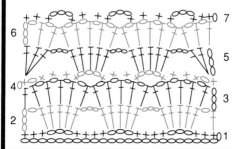

Starting chain: Multiple of 7 sts + 3.

**1st row** (right side): Work 1dc into 2nd ch from hook, 1dc into each of next 2ch, *3ch, miss 3ch, 1dc into each of next 4ch; rep from * to end omitting 1dc at end of last rep, turn.

**2nd row:** 4ch (count as 1tr, 1ch), work 5tr into first 3ch sp, *3ch, 5tr into next 3ch sp; rep from * to last 3dc, 1ch, 1tr into last dc, turn.

**3rd row:** 3ch (count as 1tr), miss first tr, *1tr into next tr, [1ch, 1tr into next tr] 4 times; rep from * to last tr, 1tr into 3rd of 4ch at beg of previous row, turn.

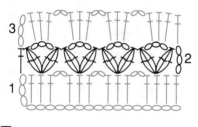

## Paradise Stitch

Starting chain: Multiple of 4 sts + 3.

**Special Abbreviation**

**Bobble** = work 3tr into next st until 1 loop of each remains on hook, yo and through all 4 loops on hook.

**1st row** (wrong side): Work 1tr into 4th ch from hook, 1tr into each of next 2ch, *2ch, miss 1ch, 1tr into each of next 3ch; rep from * to last ch, 1tr into last ch, turn.

**2nd row:** 3ch (count as 1tr), miss first 2tr, into next tr work [1 bobble, 3ch, 1 bobble], *miss 2tr, into next tr work [1 bobble, 3ch, 1 bobble]; rep from * to last 2tr, 1tr into 3rd of 3ch at beg of previous row, turn.

**3rd row:** 3ch, work 3tr into first 3ch arch, *2ch, 3tr into next 3ch arch; rep from * to last 2 sts, 1tr into 3rd of 3ch at beg of previous row, turn.

Rep 2nd and 3rd rows.

= Bobble

**4th row:** 1ch, 1dc into first tr, 1ch, [1dc into next ch sp, miss 1tr] 4 times, *3ch, [1dc into next ch sp, miss 1tr] 4 times; rep from * to last 2tr, 1ch, 1dc into 3rd of 3ch at beg of previous row, turn.

**5th row:** 3ch, 2tr into first dc, 3ch, *5tr into next 3ch sp, 3ch; rep from * to last dc, 3tr into last dc, turn.

**6th row:** 4ch, miss first tr, 1tr into next tr, 1ch, 1tr into next tr, *1tr into next tr, [1ch, 1tr into next tr] 4 times; rep from * to last 3tr, [1tr into next tr, 1ch] twice, 1tr into 3rd of 3ch at beg of previous row, turn.

**7th row:** 1ch, 1dc into first tr, [1dc into next ch sp, miss 1tr] twice, 3ch, *[1dc into next ch sp, miss 1tr] 4 times, 3ch; rep from * to last 3tr, 1dc into next ch sp, miss 1tr, 1dc into next ch sp, 1dc into 3rd of 4ch at beg of previous row, turn.

Rep 2nd to 7th rows.

# All-over Patterns

## Acorn Stitch

## Carpet Bag Stitch

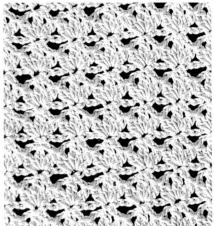

Starting chain: Multiple 5 sts + 6.

**Special Abbreviation**

**Tr2tog** = work 2tr into next st until 1 loop of each remains on hook, yo and through all 3 loops on hook.

**1st row** (right side): Work tr2tog into 6th ch from hook, (1tr and 2ch sp at beg of row), *miss 4ch, tr2tog into next ch, 2ch, into same ch as last tr2tog work [tr2tog, 2ch, tr2tog]; rep from * to last 5ch, miss 4ch, into last ch work [tr2tog, 2ch, 1tr], turn.

**2nd row:** 1ch, 1dc into first tr, *4ch, miss 2 tr2tog, 1dc into top of next tr2tog; rep from * to end placing last dc into 3rd ch, turn.

**3rd row:** 5ch (count as 1tr, 2ch), work tr2tog into first dc, *work tr2tog into next dc, 2ch, into same st as last tr2tog work [tr2tog, 2ch, tr2tog]; rep from * to last dc, into last dc work [tr2tog, 2ch, 1tr], turn.

Rep 2nd and 3rd rows.

 = Tr2tog

Starting chain: Multiple of 6 sts + 5.

**Special Abbreviations**

**Tr2tog** = work 2tr into next st until 1 loop of each remains on hook, yo and through all 3 loops on hook.

**Shell** = work [tr2tog, 1tr, tr2tog] all into next st.

**Group** = into first tr2tog of shell work 2tr until 1 loop of each remains on hook, 1tr into tr of same shell until 4 loops remain on hook, into 2nd tr2tog of shell work 2tr until 1 loop of each remains on hook, yo and through all 6 loops.

**1st row** (right side): Work 1tr into 8th ch from hook (1tr and 2ch sp at beg of row), *1ch, miss 2ch, work 1 shell into next ch, 1ch, miss 2ch, 1tr into next ch; rep from * to last 3ch, 2ch, miss 2ch, 1tr into last ch, turn.

**2nd row:** 5ch (count as 1tr, 2ch), miss first tr, 1tr into next tr, 2ch, *work 1 group over next shell, 2ch, 1tr into next tr, 2ch; rep from * to last tr, miss 2ch, 1tr into next ch, turn.

**3rd row:** 4ch (count as 1tr, 1ch), miss first tr, *work 1 shell into next tr, 1ch, 1tr into top of next group, 1ch; rep from * to end omitting 1ch at end of last rep and placing last tr into 3rd of 5ch at beg of previous row, turn.

**4th row:** 5ch, *work 1 group over next shell, 2ch, 1tr into next tr, 2ch; rep from * to end omitting 2ch at end of last rep and placing last tr into 3rd of 4ch at beg of previous row, turn.

**5th row:** 5ch, 1tr into top of next group, *1ch, work 1 shell into next tr, 1ch, 1tr into top of next group; rep from * to last tr, 2ch, 1tr into 3rd of 5ch at beg of previous row, turn.

Rep 2nd to 5th rows.

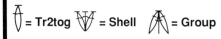 = Tr2tog   = Shell   = Group

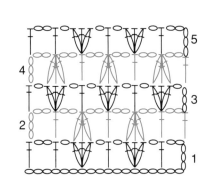

## Metric Stitch

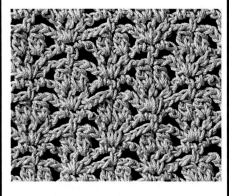

Starting chain: Multiple of 10 sts + 2.

**Special Abbreviation**

**Tr2tog** = work 2tr into next st until 1 loop of each remains on hook, yo and through all 3 loops on hook.

**1st row** (right side): Work 1dc into 2nd ch from hook, 1dc into next ch, 3ch, miss 2ch, tr2tog into next ch, 1ch, miss 1ch, tr2tog into next ch, *3ch, miss 2ch, 1dc into next ch, 1ch, miss 1ch, 1dc into next ch, 3ch, miss 2ch, tr2tog into next ch, 1ch, miss 1ch, tr2tog into next ch; rep from * to last 4ch, 3ch, miss 2ch, 1dc into each of last 2ch, turn.

**2nd row:** 4ch (count as 1tr, 1ch), 1tr into first dc, 3ch, miss next 3ch sp, 1dc into next ch sp, *3ch, miss next 3ch sp, 1tr into next ch sp, 1ch, into same ch sp as last tr work [1tr, 1ch, 1tr], 3ch, miss next 3ch sp, 1dc into next ch sp; rep from * to last 3ch sp, 3ch, into last dc work [1tr, 1ch, 1tr], turn.

**3rd row:** 3ch (count as 1tr), tr2tog into first ch sp, 3ch, 1dc into next 3ch sp, 1ch, 1dc into next 3ch sp, *3ch, tr2tog into next ch sp, 1ch, tr2tog into next ch sp, 3ch, 1dc into next 3ch sp, 1ch, 1dc into next 3ch sp; rep from * to last ch sp, 3ch, tr2tog into last ch sp, 1tr into 3rd of 4ch at beg of previous row, turn.

**4th row:** 1ch, 1dc into first tr, *miss next 3ch sp, 3ch, 1tr into next ch sp, 1ch, into same ch sp as last tr work [1tr, 1ch, 1tr], 3ch, miss next 3ch sp, 1dc into next ch sp; rep from * to end placing last dc into 3rd of 3ch at beg of previous row, turn.

**5th row:** 1ch, 1dc into first dc, 1dc into first 3ch sp, 3ch, tr2tog into next ch sp, 1ch, tr2tog into next ch sp, *3ch, 1dc into next 3ch sp, 1ch, 1dc into next 3ch sp, 3ch, tr2tog into next ch sp, 1ch, tr2tog into next ch sp; rep from * to last 3ch sp, 3ch, 1dc into last 3ch sp, 1dc into last dc, turn.

Rep 2nd to 5th rows.

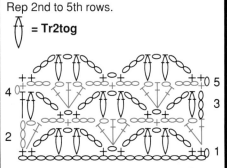 = Tr2tog

Stitch Variations, Abbreviations and Symbols on pages 7 to 15

## Rover Stitch

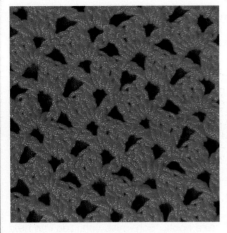

Starting chain: Multiple of 6 sts + 5.

**1st row** (right side): Work 1tr into 6th ch from hook, 1tr into each of next 2ch, 3ch, 1tr into next ch, *miss 2ch, 1tr into each of next 3ch, 3ch, 1tr into next ch; rep from * to last 2ch, miss 1ch, 1tr into last ch, turn.

## Candy Cover

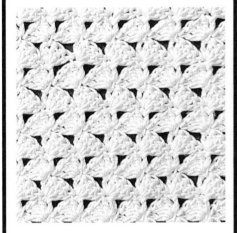

Starting chain: Multiple of 4 sts + 4.

**1st row** (right side): Work 4tr into 4th ch from hook, miss 3ch, 1dc into next ch, *2ch, 4tr into same ch as last dc, miss 3ch, 1dc into next ch; rep from * to end, turn.

**2nd row:** 5ch, work 4tr into 4th ch from hook, *miss 4tr, 1dc between last tr missed and next 2ch, 2ch, 4tr to side of last dc worked; rep from * to last 4tr, miss 4tr, 1dc into next ch, turn.

Rep 2nd row.

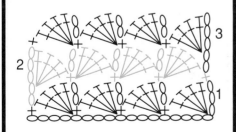

**Diagram only:** Rep 2nd and 3rd rows.

**Diagram only:** Rep 2nd and 3rd rows.

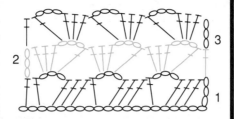

**2nd row:** 3ch (count as 1tr), *into next 3ch arch work [3tr, 3ch, 1tr]; rep from * to last 3tr, miss 3tr, 1tr into next ch, turn.

**3rd row:** 3ch, *into next 3ch arch work [3tr, 3ch, 1tr]; rep from * to last 4tr, miss 3tr, 1tr into 3rd of 3ch at beg of previous row, turn.

Rep 3rd row only.

## Warm Glow

Starting chain: Multiple of 13 sts + 9.

**1st row** (right side): Work 3tr into 4th ch from hook, miss 4ch, 4tr into next ch, *3ch, miss 3ch, 1dc into next ch, 3ch, miss 3ch, 4tr into next ch, miss 4ch, 4tr into next ch; rep from * to end, turn.

**2nd row:** 3ch (count as 1tr), 3tr into first tr, miss 6tr, work 4tr into next tr, *3ch, 1dc into next dc, 3ch, 4tr into next tr, miss 6tr, 4tr into next tr; rep from * to end placing last group of 4tr into top of 3ch, turn.

**3rd row:** 6ch (count as 1tr, 3ch), work 1dc between next 2 groups of 4tr, *3ch, miss 3tr, 4tr into each of next 2tr, 3ch, 1dc between next 2 groups of 4tr; rep from * to last group, 3ch, 1tr into 3rd of 3ch at beg of previous row, turn.

**4th row:** 6ch, work 1dc into first dc, 3ch, *4tr into next tr, miss 6tr, 4tr into next tr, 3ch, 1dc into next dc, 3ch; rep from * to last arch, 1tr into 3rd of 6ch at beg of previous row, turn.

**5th row:** 3ch, 3tr into first tr, work 4tr into next tr, *3ch, 1dc between next 2 groups of 4tr, 3ch, miss 3tr, 4tr into each of next 2tr; rep from * to end placing last group of 4tr into 3rd of 6ch at beg of previous row, turn.

Rep 2nd to 5th rows.

## Vine Leaf

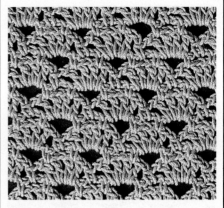

Starting chain: Multiple of 7 sts + 4.

**1st row** (wrong side): Work 1dc into 5th ch from hook, 3ch, miss 3ch, 1dc into next ch, *3ch, miss 2ch, 1dc into next ch, 3ch, miss 3ch, 1dc into next ch; rep from * to last 2ch, 1ch, 1htr into last ch, turn.

**2nd row:** 1ch, 1dc into first htr, *1ch, into next 3ch arch work [1tr, 1ch] 4 times, 1dc into next 3ch arch; rep from * to end placing last dc into 2nd ch, turn.

**3rd row:** 4ch (count as 1tr, 1ch), miss first ch sp, 1dc into next ch sp, 3ch, miss 1ch sp, 1dc into next ch sp, *3ch, miss 2ch sps, 1dc into next ch sp, 3ch, miss 1ch sp, 1dc into next ch sp; rep from * to last ch sp, 1ch, 1tr into last dc, turn.

**4th row:** 3ch (count as 1tr), work [1tr, 1ch] twice into first ch sp, 1dc into next 3ch arch, *1ch, work [1tr, 1ch] 4 times into next 3ch arch, 1dc into next 3ch arch; rep from * to last sp, 1ch, work [1tr, 1ch, 1tr] into last ch sp, 1tr into 3rd of 4ch at beg of previous row, turn.

**5th row:** 3ch (count as 1htr, 1ch), 1dc into first ch sp, 3ch, miss 2ch sps, 1dc into next ch sp, *3ch, miss 1ch sp, 1dc into next ch sp, 3ch, miss 2ch sps, 1dc into next ch sp; rep from * to last 2tr, 1ch, 1htr into 3rd of 3ch at beg of previous row, turn.

Rep 2nd to 5th rows.

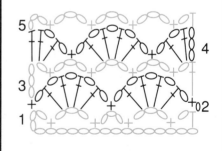

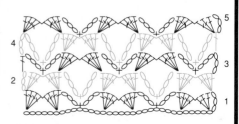

# Openwork and Lace Patterns

## Starburst

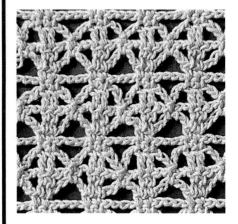

Starting chain: Multiple of 6 sts + 3.

**1st row** (right side): Work 1dc into 2nd ch from hook, 1dc into next ch, *6ch, miss 4ch, 1dc into each of next 2ch; rep from * to end, turn.

**2nd row:** 3ch (count as 1tr), miss first dc, 1tr into next dc, *2ch, 1dc into 6ch arch, 2ch, 1tr into each of next 2dc; rep from * to end, turn.

**3rd row:** 3ch, miss first tr, 1tr into next tr, *3ch, 1 sl st into next dc, 3ch, 1tr into each of next 2 tr; rep from * to end placing last tr into 3rd of 3ch at beg of previous row, turn.

**4th row:** 1ch, 1dc into each of first 2tr, *4ch, 1dc into each of next 2 tr; rep from * to end placing last dc into 3rd of 3ch at beg of previous row, turn.

**5th row:** 1ch, 1dc into each of first 2dc, *6ch, 1dc into each of next 2dc; rep from * to end, turn.

Rep 2nd to 5th rows.

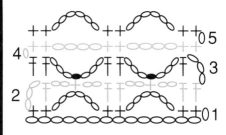

## Inverted Triangle

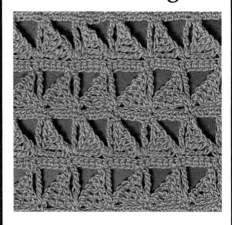

Starting chain: Multiple of 6 sts + 2.

**1st row** (right side): Work 1dc into 2nd ch from hook, 1dc into each ch to end, turn.

**2nd row:** 1ch, 1dc into first dc, *6ch, work 1dc into 2nd ch from hook, then working 1 st into each of next 4ch work 1htr, 1tr, 1dtr and 1ttr, miss 5dc on previous row, 1dc into next dc; rep from * to end, turn.

**3rd row:** 5ch (count as 1ttr), *1dc into ch at top of next triangle, 4ch, 1ttr into next dc; rep from * to end, turn.

**4th row:** 1ch, work 1dc into each [ttr, ch and dc] to end, placing last dc into top of 5ch at beg of previous row, turn.

Rep 2nd to 4th rows.

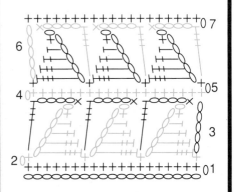

**Diagram only:** Rep 2nd to 7th rows.

## Square Coin

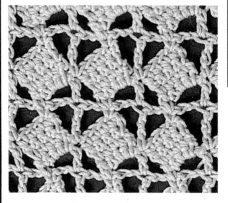

Starting chain: Multiple of 6 sts + 6.

**1st row** (right side): Work 1dc into 9th ch from hook (1tr and 3ch sp formed at beg of row), turn, 1ch, 1dc into dc, 3dc into 3ch sp, [turn, 1ch, 1dc into each of the 4dc] 3 times, miss next 2ch on starting chain, 1tr into next ch, *3ch, miss next 2ch on starting ch, 1dc into next ch, turn, 1ch, 1dc into dc, 3dc into 3ch sp, [turn, 1ch, 1dc into each of the 4dc] 3 times, miss next 2ch on starting ch, 1tr into next ch; rep from * to end, turn.

**2nd row:** 6ch (count as 1dtr, 2ch), miss 1tr and 3dc, 1dc into next dc, 2ch, 1dtr into next tr, *2ch, miss 3dc, 1dc into next dc, 2ch, 1dtr into next tr; rep from * to end placing last dtr into top of ch at beg of previous row, turn.

## Bridge Stitch

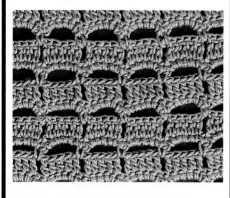

Starting chain: Multiple of 5 sts + 2.

**1st row** (right side): Work 1dc into 2nd ch from hook, *5ch, miss 4ch, 1dc into next ch; rep from * to end, turn.

**2nd row:** 1ch, work 1dc into first dc, *5dc into 5ch sp, 1dc into next dc; rep from * to end, turn.

**3rd row:** 3ch (count as 1tr), miss first dc, work 1tr into each of next 5dc, *1ch, miss 1dc, 1tr into each of next 5dc; rep from * to last dc, 1tr into last dc, turn.

**4th row:** 1ch, 1dc into first tr, *5ch, 1dc into next ch sp; rep from * to end placing last dc into 3rd of 3ch at beg of previous row, turn.

Rep 2nd to 4th rows.

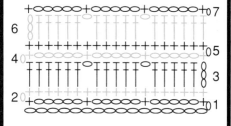

**Diagram only:** Rep 2nd to 7th rows.

**3rd row:** 6ch (count as 1tr, 3ch), 1dc into first dc, turn, 1ch, 1dc into dc, 3dc into 3ch sp, [turn, 1ch, 1dc into each of the 4dc] 3 times, 1tr into next dtr, *3ch, 1dc into next dc, turn, 1ch, 1dc into dc, 3dc into 3ch sp, [turn, 1ch, 1dc into each of the 4dc] 3 times, 1tr into next dtr; rep from * to end placing last tr into 4th of 6ch at beg of previous row, turn.

Rep 2nd and 3rd rows ending with a 2nd row.

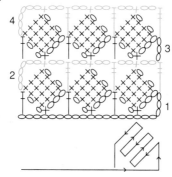

Line shows direction of work for first part of first row.

Stitch Variations, Abreviations and Symbols on pages 7 to 15

# Openwork and Lace Patterns

## Two Leaf Bar

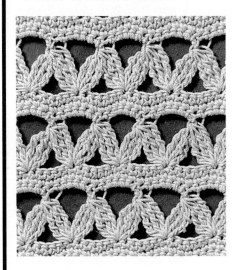

Starting chain: Multiple of 6 sts + 2.

**Special Abbreviations**

**Ttr group** = work 3ttr into next dc until 1 loop of each remains on hook, yo and through all 4 loops on hook.

**Double ttr group** = work 3ttr into same dc as last group until 1 loop of each remains on hook (4 loops on hook), miss 5 dc, into next dc work 3ttr until 1 loop of each remains on hook, yo and through all 7 loops on hook.

**1st row** (right side): Work 1dc into 2nd ch from hook, 1dc into each ch to end, turn.

**2nd row:** 1ch, work 1dc into each dc to end, turn.

**3rd row:** 5ch (count as 1ttr), miss first 3dc, work 1ttr group into next dc, 5ch, *1 double ttr group, 5ch; rep from * to last 3dc, into same dc as last group work 3ttr until 1 loop of each remains on hook (4 loops on hook), 1ttr into last dc until 5 loops remain on hook, yo and through all 5 loops, turn.

**4th row:** 1ch, 1dc into top of first group, 5dc into 5ch arch, *1dc into top of next group, 5dc into next 5ch arch; rep from * to last group, 1dc into 5th of 5ch at beg of previous row, turn.

**5th row:** 1ch, work 1dc into each dc to end, turn.

Rep 2nd to 5th rows.

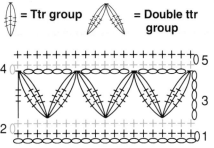

= Ttr group    = Double ttr group

## Braided Pattern

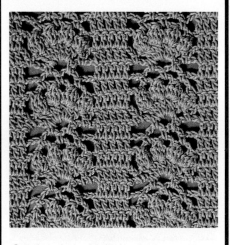

Starting chain: Multiple of 16 sts + 7.

**Special Abbreviation**

**Bobble** = work 4tr into next st until 1 loop of each remains on hook, yo and through all 5 loops on hook.

**1st row** (right side): Work 1tr into 4th ch from hook, 1tr into each of next 3ch, *4ch, miss 4ch, 1dc into next ch, 3ch, miss 1ch, 1dc into next ch, 4ch, miss 4ch, 1tr into each of next 5ch; rep from * to end, turn.

**2nd row:** 3ch (count as 1tr), miss first tr, 1tr into each of next 4tr, *2ch, 1dc into next 4ch arch, 1ch, work 7tr into next 3ch arch, 1ch, 1dc into next 4ch arch, 2ch, 1tr into each of next 5tr; rep from * to end placing last tr into top of 3ch at beg of previous row, turn.

**3rd row:** 3ch, miss first tr, 1tr into each of next 4tr, *1ch, 1 bobble into next tr, [3ch, miss 1tr, 1 bobble into next tr] 3 times, 1ch, 1tr into each of next 5tr; rep from * to end placing last tr into 3rd of 3ch at beg of previous row, turn.

**4th row:** 3ch, miss first tr, 1tr into each of next 4tr, *2ch, 1dc into next 3ch arch, [3ch, 1dc into next 3ch arch] twice, 2ch, 1tr into each of next 5tr; rep from * to end placing last tr into 3rd of 3ch at beg of previous row, turn.

**5th row:** 3ch, miss first tr, 1tr into each of next 4tr, *4ch, miss 2ch sp, 1dc into next 3ch arch, 3ch, 1dc into next 3ch arch, 4ch, 1tr into each of next 5tr; rep from * to end placing last tr into 3rd of 3ch at beg of previous row.

Rep 2nd to 5th rows.

## Clover Leaf

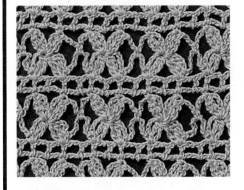

Starting chain: Multiple of 12 sts + 11.

**Special Abbreviation**

**Dtr2tog** = work 2dtr into next st until 1 loop of each remains on hook, yo and through all 3 loops on hook.

**1st row** (right side): Work 1tr into 8th ch from hook, *2ch, miss 2ch, 1tr into next ch; rep from * to end, turn.

**2nd row:** 1ch, 1dc into first tr, *9ch, miss 1tr, into next tr work [1dc, 4ch, dtr2tog], miss 1tr, into next tr work [dtr2tog, 4ch, 1dc]; rep from * to last 2 sps, 9ch, miss 1tr, 1dc into 3rd ch, turn.

**3rd row:** 10ch (count as quadtr, 4ch), 1dc into first 9ch arch, *4ch, into top of next dtr2tog work [dtr2tog, 4ch, 1 sl st, 4ch, dtr2tog], 4ch, 1dc into next 9ch arch; rep from * to end, 4ch, 1quadtr into last dc, turn.

**4th row:** 1ch, 1dc into first quadtr, *5ch, 1dc into top of next dtr2tog; rep from * to end placing last dc into 6th of 10ch at beg of previous row, turn.

**5th row:** 5ch (count as 1tr, 2ch), 1tr into next 5ch arch, 2ch, 1tr into next dc, *2ch, 1tr into next 5ch arch, 2ch, 1tr into next dc; rep from * to end, turn.

Rep 2nd to 5th rows.

= Dtr2tog

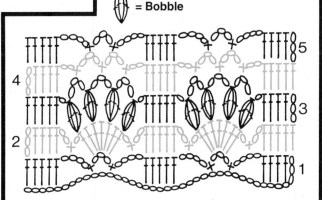

= Bobble

# Openwork and Lace Patterns

## Plaid Diagonal

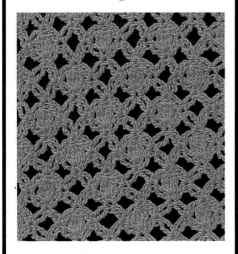

Starting chain: Multiple of 12 sts + 8.

**Special Abbreviations**

**Cluster** = 3ch, 1dtr worked until 2 loops remain on hook (first leg), 1dtr worked until 3 loops remain, yo and through all 3 loops, 3ch, 1dc into same st as last dtr (2nd leg).

**Bobble on cluster** = work first leg of cluster then work 4dtr into next dc until 1 loop of each remains on hook (6 loops on hook), work 2nd leg of cluster but bringing yarn through all 7 loops on hook to finish dtr, complete 2nd leg as for cluster.

**1st row** (right side): Work 1dc into 2nd ch from hook, *work first leg of cluster into same ch as last dc, miss 5ch, work 2nd leg of cluster into next ch; rep from * to end, turn.

**2nd row:** 4ch (count as 1dtr), into top of first cluster work [1dtr, 3ch, 1dc], *work next cluster placing 2nd leg into top of next cluster; rep from * finishing with 2nd leg worked into top of last cluster, work first leg of cluster, 1dtr into last dc until 3 loops remain, yo and through all 3 loops, turn.

**3rd row:** 1ch, 1dc into first st, *work cluster placing 2nd leg into top of next cluster; rep from * to end **but** working bobble on next and every alt cluster, turn.

**4th row:** As 2nd row.

**5th row:** As 3rd row **but** working bobble on first then every alt cluster, turn.

Rep 2nd to 5th rows.

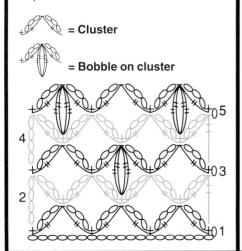

## Wider View

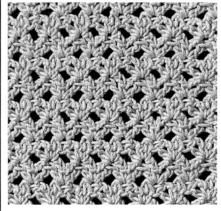

Starting chain: Multiple of 4 sts + 2.

**1st row** (right side): Work 1dc into 2nd ch from hook, *2ch, into same ch as last dc work 1tr until 2 loops remain on hook, miss 3ch, work 1tr into next ch until 3 loops remain on hook, yo and through all 3 loops, 2ch, 1dc into same ch as last tr, (1 cluster made); rep from * to end, turn.

**2nd row:** 3ch (count as 1tr), work 1tr into top of first cluster, *2ch, into same cluster as last tr work [1dc, 2ch, 1tr until 2 loops remain on hook], 1tr into top of next cluster until 3 loops remain on hook, yo and through all 3 loops; rep from * to end placing last tr into last dc, turn.

**3rd row:** 1ch, into first cluster work [1dc, 2ch, 1tr until 2 loops remain on hook], 1tr into top of next cluster until 3 loops remain on hook, yo and through all 3 loops, *2ch, into same cluster as last tr work [1dc, 2ch, 1tr until 2 loops remain on hook], 1tr into next cluster until 3 loops remain on hook, yo and through all 3 loops; rep from * to end, 2ch, 1dc into 3rd of 3ch at beg of previous row, turn.

Rep 2nd and 3rd rows.

## Crossbar Diamond

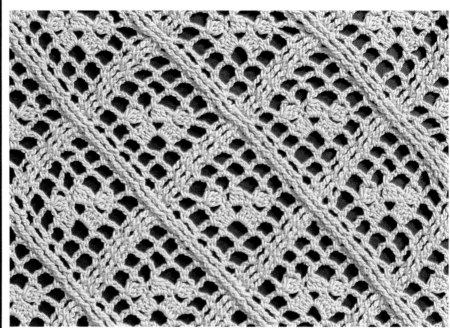

Starting chain: Multiple of 24 sts + 6.

**Special Abbreviations**

**Bobble** = work 3tr into next st until 1 loop of each tr remains on hook, yo and through all 4 loops on hook.

**Dtr/rf (Double treble round front)** = on a right side row: **working from front of work**, work 1dtr inserting hook from right to left under stem of next tr or dtr in previous row.

**Dtr/rb (Double treble round back)** = on a wrong side row: **working at back** (right side of work), work 1dtr inserting hook from right to left under stem of next tr or dtr in previous row. (See page 10).

**Cross 4dtr/rf (Cross 4 double treble round front)** = miss next 2dtr, work 1dtr/rf round each of next 2dtr, 1ch, work 1dtr/rf around each of the 2 missed dtr.

**1st row** (right side): Work 1dc into 2nd ch from hook, 3ch, miss 1ch, 2tr into next ch, miss 1ch, 1dc into next ch, 5ch, miss 3ch, 1dc into next ch, 4ch, 1 bobble into side of last dc worked, miss 3ch, 1dc into next ch, 2ch, miss 1ch, 1 bobble into next ch, 2ch, miss 1ch, 1dc into next ch, 4ch, 1 bobble into side of last dc worked, miss 3ch, 1dc into next ch, 5ch, miss 3ch, 1dc into next ch, miss 1ch, *into next ch work [2tr, 1ch, 2tr], miss 1ch, 1dc into next ch, 5ch, miss 3ch, 1dc into next ch, 4ch, 1 bobble into side of last dc worked, miss

Stitch Variations, Abreviations and Symbols on pages 7 to 15

# Openwork and Lace Patterns

3ch, 1dc into next ch, 2ch, miss 1ch, 1 bobble into next ch, 2ch, miss 1ch, 1dc into next ch, 4ch, 1 bobble into side of last dc worked, miss 3ch, 1dc into next ch, 5ch, miss 3ch, 1dc into next ch, miss 1ch; rep from * to last 3ch, 2tr into next ch, 3ch, miss 1ch, 1dc into last ch, turn.

**2nd row:** 6ch (count as 1dtr, 2ch), 1dc into next 3ch arch, *3ch, 1dtr/rb around each of next 2tr, 1dc into next 5ch arch, 5ch, 1dc into next 4ch arch, 5ch, 1dc into top of next bobble, 5ch, 1dc into next 4ch arch, 5ch, 1dc into next 5ch arch, 1dtr/rb around each of next 2tr, 3ch, 1dc into next ch sp; rep from * to last dc placing last dc into last 3ch arch, 2ch, 1dtr into last dc, turn.

**3rd row:** 1ch, 1dc into first dtr, 5ch, miss 2ch arch, *1dc into next 3ch arch, 3ch, 1dtr/rf around each of next 2dtr, 1dc into next 5ch arch, [5ch, 1dc into next 5ch arch] 3 times, 1dtr/rf around each of next 2dtr, 3ch, 1dc into next 3ch arch, 5ch; rep from * to last 2ch sp, 1dc into 4th of 6ch at beg of previous row, turn.

**4th row:** 6ch, 1dc into next 5ch arch, *5ch, 1dc into next 3ch arch, 3ch, 1dtr/rb around each of next 2dtr, 1dc into next 5ch arch, [5ch, 1dc into next 5ch arch] twice, 1dtr/rb around each of next 2dtr, 3ch, 1dc into next 3ch arch, 5ch, 1dc into next 5ch arch; rep from * to last dc, 2ch, 1dtr into last dc, turn.

**5th row:** 1ch, 1dc into first dtr, 5ch, 1dc into next 5ch arch, 5ch, 1dc into next 3ch arch, 3ch, 1dtr/rf around each of next 2dtr, 1dc into next 5ch arch, 5ch, 1dc into next 5ch arch, 1dtr/rf around each of next 2dtr, *3ch, 1dc into next 3ch arch, 5ch, [1dc into next 5ch arch, 5ch] twice, 1dc into next 3ch arch, 3ch, 1dtr/rf around each of next 2dtr, 1dc into next 5ch arch, 5ch, 1dc into next 5ch arch, 1dtr/rf around each of next 2dtr; rep from * to last 3 arches, 3ch, 1dc into next 3ch arch, 5ch, 1dc into next 5ch arch, 5ch, 1dc into 4th of 6ch at beg of previous row, turn.

**6th row:** 4ch (count as 1dtr), work [1tr, 2ch, 3tr] into first 5ch arch, 1dc into next 5ch arch, 5ch, 1dc into next 3ch arch, 3ch, 1dtr/rb around each of next 2dtr, 1dc into next 5ch arch, 1dtr/rb around each of next 2dtr, *3ch, 1dc into next 3ch arch, 5ch, 1dc into next 5ch arch, into next 5ch arch work [3tr, 3ch, 3tr], 1dc into next 5ch arch, 5ch, 1dc into next 3ch arch, 3ch, 1dtr/rb around each of next 2dtr, 1dc into next 5ch arch, 1dtr/rb around each of next 2dtr; rep from * to last 3 arches, 3ch, 1dc into next 3ch arch, 5ch, 1dc into next 5ch arch, work [3tr, 2ch, 1tr] into last 5ch arch, 1dtr into last dc, turn.

**7th row:** 1ch, 1dc into first dtr, 2ch, 1 bobble into first 2ch sp, 2ch, 1dc into next tr, *4ch, 1 bobble into side of last dc worked, 1dc into next 5ch arch, 5ch, 1dc into next 3ch arch, cross 4dtr/rf, 1dc into next 3ch arch, 5ch, 1dc into next 5ch arch, 4ch, 1 bobble into side of last dc worked, miss 2tr, 1dc into next tr, 2ch, 1 bobble into next 3ch arch, 2ch, 1dc into next tr; rep from * to end placing last bobble into last 2ch sp and last dc into 4th of 4ch at beg of previous row, turn.

**8th row:** 6ch, work 1dc into top of first bobble, *5ch, 1dc into next 4ch arch, 5ch, 1dc into next 5ch arch, 1dtr/rb around each of next 2dtr, 3ch, 1dc into ch sp, 3ch, 1dtr/rb around each of next 2dtr, 1dc into next 5ch arch, 5ch, 1dc into next 4ch arch, 5ch, 1dc into top of next bobble; rep from * to last dc, 2ch, 1dtr into last dc, turn.

**9th row:** 1ch, 1dc into first dtr, [5ch, 1dc into next 5ch arch] twice, 1dtr/rf around each of next 2dtr, 3ch, 1dc into next 3ch arch, 5ch, 1dc into next 3ch arch, 3ch, 1dtr/rf around each of next 2dtr, *1dc into next 5ch arch, [5ch, 1dc into next 5ch arch] 3 times, 1dtr/rf around each of next 2dtr, 3ch, 1dc into next 3ch arch, 5ch, 1dc into next 3ch arch, 3ch, 1dtr/rf around each of next 2dtr; rep from * to last 3 arches, [1dc into next 5ch arch, 5ch] twice, 1dc into 4th of 6ch, turn.

**10th row:** 6ch, 1dc into first 5ch arch, 5ch, 1dc into next 5ch arch, 1dtr/rb around each of next 2dtr, 3ch, 1dc into next 3ch arch, 5ch, 1dc into next 5ch arch, 3ch, 1dtr/rb around each of next 2dtr, *1dc into next 5ch arch, [5ch, 1dc into next 5ch arch] twice, 1dtr/rb around each of next 2dtr, 3ch, 1dc into next 3ch arch, 5ch, 1dc into next 5ch arch, 3ch, 1dtr/rb around each of next 2dtr; rep from * to last 2 arches, 1dc into next 5ch arch, 5ch, 1dc into last 5ch arch, 2ch, 1dtr into last dc, turn.

**11th row:** 1ch, 1dc into first dtr, 5ch, 1dc into next 5ch arch, *1dtr/rf around each of next 2dtr, 3ch, 1dc into next 3ch arch, 5ch, [1dc into next 5ch arch, 5ch] twice, 1dc into next 3ch arch, 3ch, 1dtr/rf around each of next 2dtr, 1dc into next 5ch arch, 5ch, 1dc into next 5ch arch; rep from * to end placing last dc into 4th of 6ch, turn.

**12th row:** 6ch, 1dc into first 5ch arch, *1dtr/rb around each of next 2dtr, 3ch, 1dc into next 3ch arch, 5ch, 1dc into next 5ch arch, into next 5ch arch work [3tr, 3ch, 3tr], 1dc into next 5ch arch, 5ch, 1dc into next 3ch arch, 3ch, 1dtr/rb around each of next 2dtr, 1dc into next 5ch arch; rep from * to last dc, 2ch, 1dtr into last dc, turn.

**13th row:** 1ch, 1dc into first dtr, 1dtr/rf around each of next 2dtr, 3ch, 1dc into next 3ch arch, 5ch, 1dc into next 5ch arch, 4ch, 1 bobble into side of last dc worked, miss 2tr, 1dc into next tr, 2ch, 1 bobble into next 3ch arch, 2ch, 1dc into next tr, 4ch, 1 bobble into side of last dc worked, 1dc into next 5ch arch, 5ch, 1dc into next 3ch arch, *cross 4dtr/rf, 1dc into next 3ch arch, 5ch, 1dc into next 5ch arch, 4ch, 1 bobble into side of last dc worked, miss 2tr, 1dc into next tr, 2ch, 1 bobble into next 3ch arch, 2ch, 1dc into next tr, 4ch, 1 bobble into side of last dc worked, 1dc into next 5ch arch, 5ch, 1dc into next 3ch arch; rep from * to last 2dtr, 3ch, 1dtr/rf around each of next 2dtr, 1dc into 4th of 6ch, turn.

**14th row:** 6ch, 1dc into first 3ch arch, 3ch, 2dtr into same 3ch arch as last dc, 1dc into next 5ch arch, 5ch, 1dc into next 4ch arch, 5ch, 1dc into top of next bobble, 5ch, 1dc into next 4ch arch, 5ch, 1dc into next 5ch arch, *1dtr/rb around each of next 2dtr, 3ch, 1dc into next ch sp, 3ch, 1dtr/rb around each of next 2dtr, 1dc into next 5ch arch, 5ch, 1dc into next 4ch arch, 5ch, 1dc into top of next bobble, 5ch, 1dc into next 4ch arch, 5ch, 1dc into next 5ch arch; rep from * to last 3ch arch, into last 3ch arch work [2dtr, 3ch, 1dc], 2ch, 1dtr into last dc, turn.

Rep 3rd to 14th rows.

= Dtr/rf   = Dtr/rb   = Bobble   = Cross 4 dtr/rf

= 1dc, 4ch, work 1 bobble into side of dc just worked

# Openwork and Lace Patterns

## Eight Bar Stitch

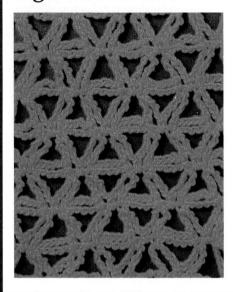

Starting chain: Multiple of 8 sts + 4.

**1st row** (right side): Work 1dc into 2nd ch from hook, 1dc into next ch, 9ch, 1dc into next ch, 5ch, miss 5ch, 1dc into next ch, *[9ch, 1dc into next ch] twice, 5ch, miss 5ch, 1dc into next ch; rep from * to last 2ch, 9ch, 1dc into each of last 2ch, turn.

**2nd row:** 7ch (count as 1dtr, 3ch), *1dc into next 9ch loop, 1ch, 1dc into next 9ch loop, 5ch; rep from * to end omitting 2ch at end of last rep, 1dtr into last dc, turn.

**3rd row:** 1ch, 1dc into first dtr, 3ch, *1dc into next dc, 9ch, 1dc into next ch sp, 9ch, 1dc into next dc, 5ch; rep from * to end omitting 2ch at end of last rep, 1dc into 4th of 7ch at beg of previous row, turn.

**4th row:** 5ch (count as 1dtr, 1ch), *1dc into next 9ch loop, 5ch, 1dc into next 9ch loop, 1ch; rep from * to end, 1dtr into last dc, turn.

**5th row:** 1ch, 1dc into first dtr, 1dc into next ch sp, 9ch, 1dc into next dc, 5ch, *1dc into next dc, 9ch, 1dc into next ch sp, 9ch, 1dc into next dc, 5ch; rep from * to last dc, 1dc into last dc, 9ch, 1dc into ch sp, 1dc into 4th of 5ch at beg of previous row, turn.

Rep 2nd to 5th rows ending with a 2nd or 4th row.

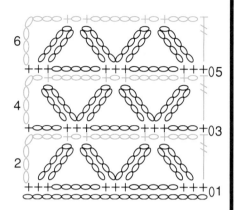

## Open Link

Starting chain: Multiple of 18 sts + 8.

**1st row** (right side): Work 1tr into 8th ch from hook, *2ch, miss 2ch, 1tr into next ch; rep from * to end, turn.

**2nd row:** 5ch (count as 1tr, 2ch), miss first tr, 1tr into next tr, *4ch, 1dtr into each of next 4tr, 4ch, 1tr into next tr, 2ch, 1tr into next tr; rep from * to end placing last tr into 3rd turning ch at beg of previous row, turn.

**3rd row:** 5ch, miss first tr, 1tr into next tr, *4ch, 1dc into each of next 4dtr, 4ch, 1tr into next tr, 2ch, 1tr into next tr; rep from * to end placing last tr into 3rd of 5ch at beg of previous row, turn.

**4th row:** 5ch, miss first tr, 1tr into next tr, *4ch, 1dc into each of next 4dc, 4ch, 1tr into next tr, 2ch, 1tr into next tr; rep from * to end placing last tr into 3rd of 5ch at beg of previous row, turn.

**5th row:** As 4th row.

**6th row:** 5ch, miss first tr, 1tr into next tr, *2ch, [1dtr into next dc, 2ch] 4 times, 1tr into next tr, 2ch, 1tr into next tr; rep from * to end placing last tr into 3rd of 5ch at beg of previous row, turn.

**7th row:** 5ch, miss first tr, 1tr into next tr, *2ch, [1tr into next dtr, 2ch] 4 times, 1tr into next tr, 2ch, 1tr into next tr; rep from * to end placing last tr into 3rd of 5ch at beg of previous row, turn.

Rep 2nd to 7th rows.

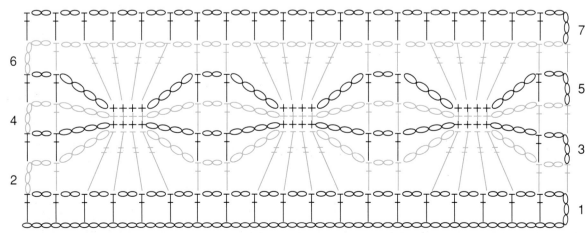

Stitch Variations, Abbreviations and Symbols on pages 7 to 15

# Openwork and Lace Patterns

## Block Trellis Stitch

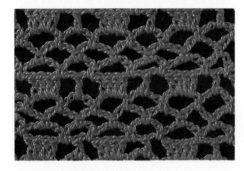

Multiple of 8 sts + 5.
(add 1 for base chain)

**1st row** (right side): 1dc into 2nd ch from hook, *5ch, miss 3ch, 1dc into next ch; rep from * to end, turn.

**2nd row:** *5ch, 1dc into next 5ch arch; rep from * ending 2ch, 1tr into last dc, miss tch, turn.

**3rd row:** 3ch (count as 1tr), 1tr into first st, 2ch, 1tr into next 5ch arch, *2ch, 4tr into next arch, 2ch, 1tr into next arch; rep from * to end, turn.

**4th row:** *5ch, 1dc into next 2ch sp; rep from * ending 2ch, 1tr into top of tch, turn.

**5th row:** 1ch, 1dc into first st, *5ch, 1dc into next 5ch arch; rep from * to end, turn.

Rep 2nd, 3rd, 4th and 5th rows.

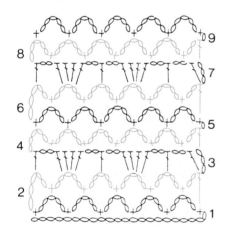

## Bullion Trellis Stitch

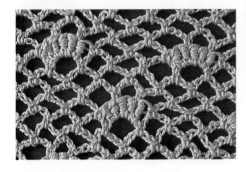

Multiple of 16 sts + 5.
(add 1 for base chain)

**Base row** (right side): 1dc into 2nd ch from hook, *[5ch, miss 3ch, 1dc into next ch] twice, miss 3ch, work 5 Bullion sts into next ch, miss 3ch, 1dc into next ch; rep from * to last 4ch, 5ch, miss 3ch, 1dc into last ch, turn.

**Commence Pattern**

**1st row:** 5ch, 1dc into next 5ch arch, *5ch, 1dc into 2nd of next 5 Bullion sts, 5ch, 1dc into 4th Bullion st of same group, [5ch, 1dc into next arch] twice; rep from * ending 2ch, 1tr into last dc, miss tch, turn.

**2nd row:** 1ch, 1dc into first st, *5ch, 1dc into next arch; rep from * to end, turn.

**3rd row:** *5ch, 1dc into next arch; rep from * ending 2ch, 1tr into last dc, miss tch, turn.

**4th row:** 1ch, 1dc into first st, miss 2ch sp, *5 Bullion sts into next 5ch arch, 1dc into next arch, [5ch, 1dc into next arch] twice; rep from * ending 5ch, 1dc into tch arch, turn.

**5th row:** 5ch, 1dc into next 5ch arch, *[5ch, 1dc into next arch] twice, 5ch, 1dc into 2nd of next 5 Bullion sts, 5ch, 1dc into 4th Bullion st of same group; rep from * ending 2ch, 1tr into last dc, miss tch, turn.

**6th row:** As 2nd row.

**7th row:** As 3rd row.

**8th row:** 1ch, 1dc into first st, *[5ch, 1dc into next 5ch arch] twice, 5 Bullion sts into next arch, 1dc into next arch; rep from * ending 5ch, 1dc into tch arch, turn.

Rep these 8 rows.

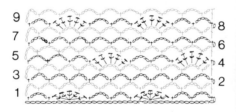

Bullion st with [yo] 7 times.

## Shell Trellis Stitch

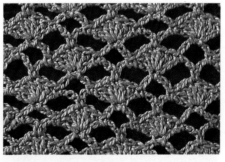

Multiple of 12 sts + 1.
(add 2 for base chain)

**1st row** (right side): 2tr into 3rd ch from hook, *miss 2ch, 1dc into next ch, 5ch, miss 5ch, 1dc into next ch, miss 2ch, 5tr into next ch; rep from * ending last rep with only 3tr into last ch, turn.

**2nd row:** 1ch, 1dc into first st, *5ch, 1dc into next 5ch arch, 5ch, 1dc into 3rd tr of next 5tr; rep from * ending last rep with 1dc into top of tch, turn.

**3rd row:** *5ch, 1dc into next 5ch arch, 5tr into next dc, 1dc into next arch; rep from * ending 2ch, 1tr into last dc, miss tch, turn.

**4th row:** 1ch, 1dc into first st, *5ch, 1dc into 3rd tr of next 5tr, 5ch, 1dc into next 5ch arch; rep from * to end, turn.

**5th row:** 3ch (count as 1tr), 2tr into first st, *1dc into next arch, 5ch, 1dc into next arch, 5tr into next dc; rep from * ending last rep with only 3tr into last dc, miss tch, turn.

Rep 2nd, 3rd, 4th and 5th rows.

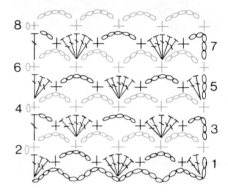

## Puff Cluster Trellis Stitch

Multiple of 6 sts + 2.
(add 3 for base chain)

**1st row** (right side): 1dc into 5th ch from hook, *3ch, miss 2ch, 1dc into next ch; rep from * to end, turn.

**2nd row:** 3ch, 1dc into next 3ch arch, *3ch, htr3tog into next arch, 3ch, 1dc into next arch; rep from * to end, turn.

**3rd row:** *3ch, 1dc into next 3ch arch; rep from * to end, turn.

**4th row:** *3ch, htr3tog into next 3ch arch, 3ch, 1dc into next arch; rep from * ending 3ch, htr3tog into tch arch, turn.

**5th row:** As 3rd row.

Rep 2nd, 3rd, 4th and 5th rows.

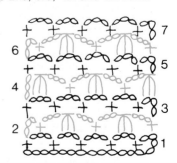

# Openwork and Lace Patterns

## Fan Trellis Stitch

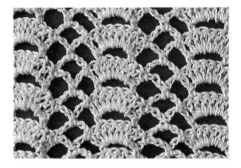

Multiple of 12 sts + 11.
(add 1 for base chain)

**1st row** (wrong side): 1dc into 2nd ch from hook, *5ch, miss 3ch, 1dc into next ch; rep from * to last 2ch, 2ch, miss 1ch, 1tr into last ch, turn.

**2nd row:** 1ch, 1dc into first st, miss 2ch sp, *7tr into next 5ch arch, 1dc into next arch**, 5ch, 1dc into next arch; rep from * ending last rep at **, 2ch, 1dtr into last dc, miss tch, turn.

**3rd row:** 1ch, 1dc into first st, *5ch, 1dc into 2nd of next 7tr, 5ch, 1dc into 6th tr of same group**, 5ch, 1dc into next 5ch arch; rep from * ending last rep at **, 2ch, 1dtr into last dc, miss tch, turn.

Rep 2nd and 3rd rows.

## Floral Trellis Stitch

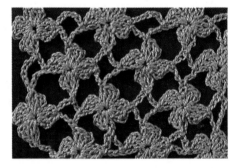

Any number of Flower Units.

**1st row** (right side): 7ch, *sl st into 4th ch from hook, 3ch, into ring just formed work a Base Flower Unit of [2tr, 3ch, sl st, 3ch, 2tr]**, 10ch; rep from * ending last rep at ** when fabric is required width, then keep same side facing and turn so as to be able to work along underside of Base Flower Units.

**2nd row** (right side): *3ch, sl st into ch ring at centre of Flower, 3ch, [2tr, 3ch, sl st — centre Petal completed, 3ch, 2tr] all into same ring, miss 2ch of base chain which connects Units, sl st into next ch, 7ch, miss

2ch, sl st into next ch; rep from * into next and each Base Flower Unit to end, turn.
**Note:** Check that each Base Flower Unit is not twisted before you work into it.

**3rd row:** 11ch, sl st into 4th ch from hook, 3ch, 2tr into ring just formed, 3ch, sl st into top of 3ch of centre Petal of last Flower made in previous row (see diagram), *10ch, sl st into 4th ch from hook, 3ch, 2tr into ring just formed, sl st into 4th of next 7ch arch of previous row, 3ch, [sl st, 3ch, 2tr] into same ch ring as last 2tr, 3ch, sl st into top of 3ch of centre Petal of next Flower in previous row; rep from * to end, turn.

**4th row:** 9ch, miss 2ch, sl st into next ch, *3ch, sl st into ch ring at centre of Flower, 3ch, work [2tr, 3ch, sl st, 3ch, 2tr] into same ring, miss 2ch, sl st into next ch, 7ch, miss [3ch, sl st and next 2ch], sl st into next ch; rep from * ending 3ch, sl st into ch ring at centre of last Flower, 3ch, 2tr into same ring, turn.

**5th row:** *10ch, sl st into 4th ch from hook, 3ch, 2tr into ring just formed, sl st into 4th ch of next arch of previous row, 3ch, [sl st, 3ch, 2tr] into same ch ring as last 2tr**, 3ch, sl st into top of 3ch of centre Petal of next Flower in previous row; rep from * ending last rep at **, turn.

Rep 2nd, 3rd, 4th and 5th rows.

When fabric is required length, finishing after a 4th (right side) row (see asterisk on diagram), continue down left side to complete edge Flowers as follows: *3ch, [sl st, 3ch, 2tr, 3ch, sl st, 3ch, 2tr] all into ch ring at centre of edge Flower, miss 3ch, sl st into next ch**, 6ch, sl st into last ch before centre Petal of next edge Flower (see diagram); rep from * ending last rep at ** after last edge Flower.

Fasten off.

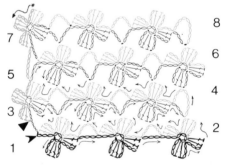

## Double Trellis Stitch

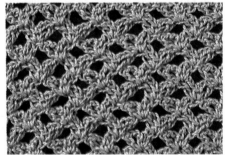

Multiple of 4 sts + 1.
(add 1 for base chain)

**1st row** (right side): 1dc into 2nd ch from hook, *3ch, tr2tog inserting hook into same place as dc just made for first leg and then into following 4th ch for 2nd leg (missing 3ch between), 3ch, 1dc into same place as 2nd leg of cluster just made; rep from * to end, turn.

**2nd row:** 4ch, 1tr into top of next cluster (counts as edge cluster), 3ch, 1dc into same place as tr just made, *3ch, tr2tog inserting hook into same place as dc just made for first leg and then into next cluster for 2nd leg, 3ch, 1dc into same place as 2nd leg of cluster just made; rep from * ending 3ch, yo, insert hook into same place as dc just made, yo, draw loop through, yo, draw through 2 loops, [yo] twice, insert hook into last dc, yo, draw loop through, [yo, draw through 2 loops] twice, yo, draw through all 3 loops on hook, miss tch, turn.

**3rd row:** 1ch, 1dc into first st, *3ch, tr2tog inserting hook into same place as dc just made for first leg and then into next cluster for 2nd leg, 3ch, 1dc into same place as 2nd leg of cluster just made; rep from * to end, turn.

Rep 2nd and 3rd rows.

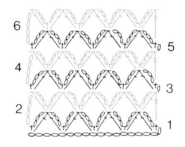

## Diamond Shell Trellis Stitch

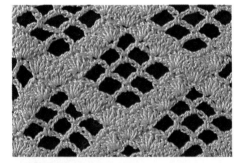

Multiple of 16 sts + 5.
(add 1 for base chain)

**Base row** (right side): 1dc into 2nd ch from hook, [5ch, miss 3ch, 1dc into next ch] twice, *miss 1ch, 5tr into next ch, miss 1ch, 1dc into next ch**, [5ch, miss 3ch, 1dc into next ch] 3 times; rep from * ending last rep at ** when 8ch remain, [5ch, miss 3ch, 1dc into next ch] twice, turn.

**Commence Pattern**

**1st row:** *[5ch, 1dc into next 5ch arch] twice, 5tr into next dc, 1dc into 3rd of next 5tr, 5tr into next dc, 1dc into next arch; rep from * ending, 5ch, 1dc into next arch, 2ch, 1tr into last dc, miss tch, turn.

Stitch Variations, Abbreviations and Symbols on pages 7 to 15.

**2nd row:** 1ch, 1dc into first st, miss 2ch, *5ch, 1dc into next 5ch arch, 5tr into next dc, 1dc into 3rd of next 5tr, 5ch, 1dc into 3rd of next 5tr, 5tr into next dc, 1dc into next arch; rep from * ending 5ch, 1dc into tch arch, turn.

**3rd row:** 3ch (count as 1tr), 2tr into first st, *1dc into next 5ch arch, 5tr into next dc, 1dc into 3rd of next 5tr, 1dc into next arch, 5ch, 1dc into 3rd of next 5tr, 5tr into next dc; rep from * ending 1dc into next arch, 3tr into last dc, miss tch, turn.

**4th row:** 1ch, 1dc into first st, *5tr into next dc, 1dc into 3rd of next 5tr, [5ch, 1dc into next arch] twice, 5ch, 1dc into 3rd of next 5tr; rep from * ending 5tr into next dc, 1dc into top of tch, turn.

**5th row:** 3ch (count as 1tr), 2tr into first st, *1dc into 3rd of next 5tr, 5tr into next dc, 1dc into next arch, [5ch, 1dc into next arch] twice, 5tr into next dc; rep from * ending 1dc into 3rd of next 5tr, 3tr into last dc, miss tch, turn.

**6th row:** 1ch, 1dc into first st, *5ch, 1dc into 3rd of next 5tr, 5tr into next dc, 1dc into next arch, 5ch, 1dc into next arch, 5tr into next dc, 1dc into 3rd of next 5tr; rep from * ending 5ch, 1dc into top of tch, turn.

**7th row:** *5ch, 1dc into next 5ch arch, 5ch, 1dc into 3rd of next 5tr, 5tr into next dc, 1dc into next arch, 5tr into next dc, 1dc into 3rd of next 5tr; rep from * ending 5ch, 1dc into next arch, 2ch, 1tr into last dc, miss tch, turn.

**8th row:** 1ch, 1dc into first st, miss 2ch, 5ch, 1dc into next 5ch arch, 5ch, 1dc into 3rd of next 5tr, *5tr into next dc, 1dc into 3rd of next 5tr, [5ch, 1dc into next arch] twice**, 5ch, 1dc into 3rd of next 5tr; rep from * ending last rep at ** in tch arch, turn.

Rep these 8 rows.

## Ruled Lattice

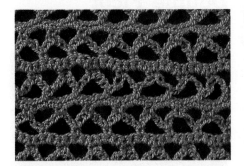

Multiple of 4 sts + 1.
(add 1 for base chain)

**1st row** (right side): 1dc into 2nd ch from hook, 1dc into each ch to end, turn.

**2nd row:** 7ch, miss first 2 sts, 1dc into next st, *7ch, miss 3 sts, 1dc into next st; rep from * to last 2 sts, 3ch, miss 1 st, 1tr into last st, miss tch, turn.

**3rd row:** 1ch, 1dc into first st, *3ch, 1dc into next 7ch arch; rep from * to end, turn.

**4th row:** 1ch, 1dc into first st, *3dc into next 3ch arch, 1dc into next dc; rep from * to end, miss tch, turn.

Rep 2nd, 3rd and 4th rows.

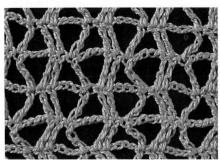

## Doubled Lattice Stitch

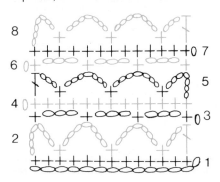

Multiple of 6 sts + 2.
(add 3 for base chain)

**1st row** (right side): Miss 6ch, 1dtr into next ch (counts as edge cluster), 4ch, 1dtr into same ch as dtr just made, *dtr2tog inserting hook into next ch for first leg and then into following 5th ch for 2nd leg (missing 4ch between), 4ch, 1dtr into same ch as 2nd leg of cluster just made; rep from * to last 4ch, dtr2tog inserting hook into next ch for first leg and into last ch for 2nd leg, (missing 2ch between), turn.

**2nd row:** 6ch (count as 1dtr and 2ch), 1dtr into first st, *dtr2tog inserting hook into next dtr for first leg and then into next cluster for 2nd leg**, 4ch, 1dtr into same place as 2nd leg of cluster just made; rep from * ending last rep at ** when 2nd leg is in edge cluster, 2ch, 1dtr into same place, turn.

**3rd row:** 4ch, miss 2ch, 1dtr into next cluster (counts as edge cluster), *4ch, 1dtr into same place as dtr just made**, dtr2tog inserting hook into next dtr for first leg and then into next cluster for 2nd leg; rep from * ending last rep at **, dtr2tog inserting hook into next dtr for first leg and then into following 3rd ch for 2nd leg, turn.

Rep 2nd and 3rd rows.

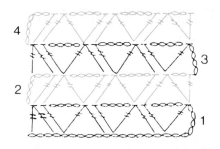

## Crown Puff Lattice

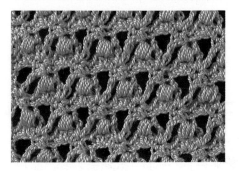

Multiple of 6 sts + 1.
(add 2 for base chain)

**1st row** (right side): 1htr into 3rd ch from hook, *1dc into next ch, dc3tog over next 3ch, 1dc into next ch, [1htr, 1tr, 1htr] into next ch; rep from * omitting 1htr at end of last rep, turn.

**2nd row:** 3ch (count as 1tr), miss first 3 sts, *[1dtr, 3ch, 1dtr] into next dc cluster, miss 2 sts**, work htr5tog into next tr; rep from * ending last rep at **, 1tr into top of tch, turn.

**3rd row:** 1ch, miss 1 st, 1dc into next dtr (all counts as dc cluster), *[1dc, 1htr, 1tr, 1htr, 1dc] into next 3ch arch**, dc3tog over next 3 sts; rep from * ending last rep at **, dc2tog over last st and top of tch, turn.

**4th row:** 5ch (count as 1dtr and 1ch), 1dtr into first st, *miss 2 sts, htr5tog into next tr, miss 2 sts**, [1dtr, 3ch, 1dtr] into next dc cluster; rep from * ending last rep at **, [1dtr, 1ch, 1dtr] into top of tch, turn.

**5th row:** 3ch (count as 1tr), 1htr into first st, 1dc into next ch sp, *dc3tog over next 3 sts**, [1dc, 1htr, 1tr, 1htr, 1dc] into next 3ch arch; rep from * ending last rep at **, 1dc into next ch of tch, [1htr, 1tr] into next ch, turn.

Rep 2nd, 3rd, 4th and 5th rows.

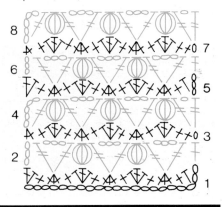

# Openwork and Lace Patterns

## Crow's Foot Lattice

Multiple of 6 sts + 1.
(add 4 for base chain)

**1st row** (wrong side): Miss 4ch (count as 1dtr and 1ch), 1tr into next ch, 1ch, miss 2ch, 1dc into next ch, *1ch, miss 2ch, work [1tr, 1ch, 1dtr, 1ch, 1tr] into next ch, 1ch, miss 2ch, 1dc into next ch; rep from * to last 3ch, 1ch, miss 2ch, [1tr, 1ch, 1dtr] into last ch, turn.

**2nd row:** 1ch, 1dc into first st, *1ch, miss 2 sps, 1dtr into next dc, 1ch, 1tr into base of dtr just made, 1ch, miss 2 sps, 1dc into next dtr; rep from * ending last rep in tch, turn.

**3rd row:** 1ch, 1dc into first st, *1ch, miss sp, work [1tr, 1ch, 1dtr, 1ch, 1tr] into next sp, 1ch, miss sp, 1dc into next dc; rep from * to end, turn.

**4th row:** 4ch (count as 1dtr), 1tr into 4th ch from hook, *1ch, miss 2 sps, 1dc into next dtr, 1ch, 1dtr into next dc**, 1ch, 1tr into base of dtr just made; rep from * ending last rep at **, 1tr into base of dtr just made, turn.

**5th row:** 5ch (count as 1dtr and 1ch), 1tr into first st, 1ch, miss sp, 1dc into next dc; *1ch, miss sp, work [1tr, 1ch, 1dtr 1ch, 1tr] into next sp, 1ch, miss sp, 1dc into next dc; rep from * ending 1ch, miss sp, [1tr, 1ch, 1dtr] into top of tch, turn.
Rep 2nd, 3rd, 4th and 5th rows.

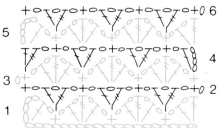

## Open Fan Stitch

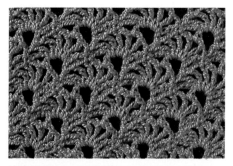

Multiple of 10 sts + 6.
(add 1 for base chain)

**1st row** (right side): 1dc into 2nd ch from hook, *1ch, miss 4ch, into next ch work a Fan of 1dtr, [2ch, 1dtr] 4 times, then 1ch, miss 4ch, 1dc into next ch; rep from * to last 5ch, 1ch, miss 4ch, into last ch work [1dtr, 2ch] twice and 1dtr, turn.

**2nd row:** 1ch, 1dc into first st, *3ch, miss next 2ch sp, 1tr into next sp**, 2ch, miss next dtr, dc and dtr and work 1tr into first 2ch sp of next Fan, 3ch, work 1dc into centre dtr of Fan; rep from * ending last rep at **, 1ch, 1dtr into last dc, miss tch, turn.

**3rd row:** 7ch (count as 1dtr and 2ch), miss first dtr, work [1dtr, 2ch, 1dtr] into next 1ch sp, 1ch, miss 3ch sp, 1dc into next dc, *1ch, miss next 3ch sp, work a Fan into next 2ch sp, 1ch, miss next 3ch sp, 1dc into next dc; rep from * to end, miss tch, turn.

**4th row:** 6ch (count as 1dtr and 1ch), miss first dtr, work 1tr into next 2ch sp, 3ch, 1dc into centre dtr of Fan, *3ch, miss next 2ch sp, 1tr into next 2ch sp, 2ch, miss next dtr, dc and dtr, work 1tr into next 2ch sp, 3ch, 1dc into centre dtr of Fan; rep from * ending last rep in 3rd ch of tch, turn.

**5th row:** 1ch, *1dc into dc, 1ch, miss next 3ch sp, Fan into next 2ch sp, 1ch, miss next 3ch sp; rep from * to last dc, 1dc into dc, 1ch, miss next 3ch sp, work [1dtr, 2ch] twice and 1dtr all into top of tch, turn.
Rep 2nd, 3rd, 4th and 5th rows.

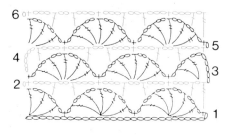

## Open Shell and Picot Stitch

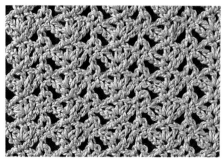

Multiple of 7 sts.
(add 1 for base chain)

**1st row** (right side): 1dc into 2nd ch from hook, *miss 2ch, work a Shell of [1tr, 1ch, 1tr, 1ch, 1tr] into next ch, miss 2ch, 1dc into next ch**, 3ch, 1dc into next ch; rep from * ending last rep at ** in last ch, turn.

**2nd row:** 7ch (count as 1dtr and 3ch), *work a Picot of [1dc, 3ch, 1dc] into centre tr of next Shell, 3ch**, 1tr into next 3ch arch; rep from * ending last rep at **, 1dtr into

last dc, miss tch, turn.

**3rd row:** 1ch, 1dc into first st, *miss next 3ch sp, Shell into centre of next Picot, miss next 3ch sp**, Picot into next tr; rep from * ending last rep at **, 1dc into next ch of tch, turn.
Rep 2nd and 3rd rows.

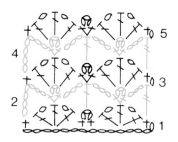

## Ridged String Network

Multiple of 4 sts + 1.
(add 1 for base chain)

**1st row** (right side): 1dc into 2nd ch from hook, *3ch, miss 3ch, 1dc into next ch; rep from * to end, turn.

**2nd row:** 1ch, working into back loop only of each st work 1dc into first st, *3ch, miss 3ch, 1dc into next dc; rep from * to end, miss tch, turn.
Rep 2nd row.

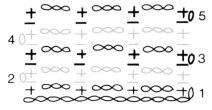

## Double Picot String Network

Stitch Variations, Abbreviations and Symbols on pages 7 to 15.

# Openwork and Lace Patterns

Multiple of 6 sts + 5.
(add 1 for base chain)

**1st row** (wrong side): 1dc into 2nd ch from hook, *3ch, miss 4ch, work a picot of [1dc, 3ch, 1dc] into next ch; rep from * to last 5ch, 3ch, miss 4ch, 1dc into last ch, turn.

**2nd row:** 1ch, 1dc into first st, *3ch, miss 3ch, 2 picots into next 3ch arch; rep from * ending 3ch, miss 3ch, 1dc into last dc, turn.

**3rd row:** 6ch (count as 1tr and 3ch), miss 3ch, *1dc into next picot arch, 3ch, 1dc into next picot arch, 3ch, miss 3ch; rep from * ending 1tr into last dc, miss tch, turn.

Rep 2nd and 3rd rows.

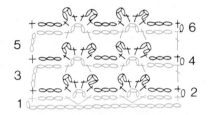

## Zig-Zag Double String Network

Multiple of 6 sts + 1.
(add 1 for base chain)

**Base row** (right side): 1dc into 2nd ch from hook, *5ch, miss 5ch, 1dc into next ch; rep from * to end, turn.

### Commence Pattern

**1st row:** 1ch, 1dc into first st, *5ch, miss 5ch, 1dc into next dc; rep from * to end, miss tch, turn.

**2nd row:** 1ch, 1dc into first st, *7ch, miss 5ch, 1dc into next dc; rep from * to end, miss tch, turn.

**3rd row:** 1ch, 1dc into first st, *7ch, miss 7ch, 1dc into next dc; rep from * to end, miss tch, turn.

**4th row:** 5ch (count as 1tr and 2ch), inserting hook under the 7ch arch made in the 2nd row, work 1dc thus binding the arches of the 2nd and 3rd rows together, *5ch, 1dc under next pair of arches as before; rep from * ending 2ch, 1tr into last dc, miss tch, turn.

**5th row:** 1ch, 1dc into first st, 2ch, miss 2ch, 1dc into next dc, *5ch, miss 5ch, 1dc into next dc; rep from * ending 2ch, miss next 2ch of tch, 1dc into next ch, turn.

**6th row:** 6ch (count as 1tr and 3ch), miss 2ch, 1dc into next dc, *7ch, miss 5ch, 1dc into next dc; rep from * ending 3ch, miss 2ch, 1tr into last dc, miss tch, turn.

**7th row:** 1ch, 1dc into first st, 3ch, miss 3ch,

1dc into next dc, *7ch, miss 7ch, 1dc into next dc; rep from * ending 3ch, miss next 3ch of tch, 1dc into next ch, turn.

**8th row:** 1ch, 1dc into first st, *5ch, 1dc under next pair of arches together; rep from * ending last rep with 1dc into last dc, miss tch, turn.

Rep these 8 rows.

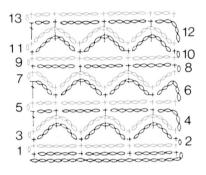

## Zig-Zag Popcorn Network

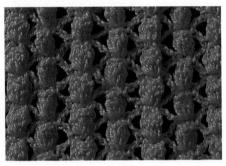

Multiple of 10 sts + 1.
(add 5 for base chain)

**1st row** (right side): 1dc into 9th ch from hook, 1dc into each of next 2ch, *3ch, miss 3ch, 5tr popcorn into next ch, 3ch, miss 3ch, 1dc into each of next 3ch; rep from * to last 4ch, 3ch, miss 3ch, 1tr into last ch, turn.

**2nd row:** 1ch, 1dc into first st, *1dc into next arch, 3ch, 5tr popcorn into 2nd of next 3dc, 3ch**, 1dc into next arch, 1dc into next Popcorn; rep from * ending last rep at **, miss 2ch of tch arch, 1dc into each of next 2ch, turn.

**3rd row:** 6ch (count as 1tr and 3ch), *1dc into next arch, 1dc into next Popcorn, 1dc into next arch, 3ch**, 5tr Popcorn into 2nd of next 3dc, 3ch; rep from * ending last rep at **, 1tr into last dc, miss tch, turn.

Rep 2nd and 3rd rows.

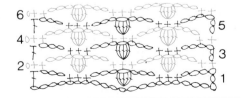

## Boxed Shell Stitch

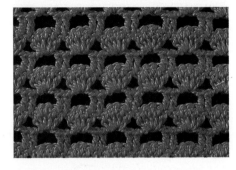

Multiple of 5 sts + 2.
(add 2 for base chain)

**1st row** (right side): Miss 3ch (count as 1tr), 1tr into next ch, *3ch, miss 3ch, 1tr into each of next 2ch; rep from * to end, turn.

**2nd row:** 3ch (count as 1tr), miss first st, *5tr into 2nd ch of next 3ch arch; rep from * ending 1tr into top of tch, turn.

**3rd row:** 3ch (count as 1tr), miss first st, 1tr into next tr, *3ch, miss 3tr, 1tr into each of next 2tr; rep from * to end, turn.

Rep 2nd and 3rd rows.

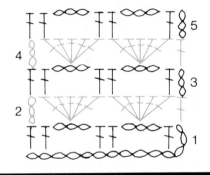

## Boxed Block Stitch

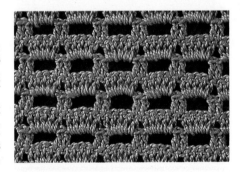

Worked as Boxed Shell Stitch, except that on 2nd and every alternate row 5tr are worked under 3ch arch instead of into actual st, thus making a block rather than a shell.

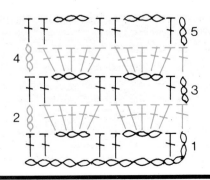

# Openwork and Lace Patterns

## Norman Arch Stitch

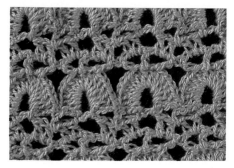

Multiple of 9 sts + 1.
(add 1 for base chain)

**1st row** (wrong side): 1dc into 2nd ch from hook, *3ch, miss 3ch, 1dc into next ch, 7ch, 1dc into next ch, 3ch, miss 3ch, 1dc into next ch; rep from * to end, turn.

**2nd row:** 1ch, 1dc into first dc, *miss 3ch, work 13tr into next 7ch arch, miss 3ch, 1dc into next dc; rep from * to end, miss tch, turn.

**3rd row:** 5ch (count as 1tr), miss first dc and next 5tr, *[1tr into next tr, 3ch] twice, 1tr into next tr**, miss [next 5tr, 1dc and 5tr]; rep from * ending last rep at **, miss next 5tr, 1ttr into last dc, miss tch, turn.

**4th row:** 3ch (count as 1tr), miss first st and next tr, *1tr into next ch, 1ch, miss 1ch, 1tr into next ch, 3ch, miss 1tr, 1tr into next ch, 1ch, miss 1ch, 1tr into next ch**, miss next 2tr; rep from * ending last rep at **, miss next tr, 1tr into top of tch, turn.

**5th row:** 6ch (count as 1tr and 3ch, *miss next 1ch sp, work [1dc, 7ch, 1dc] into next 3ch sp, 3ch, miss next 1ch sp**, 1tr between next 2tr; rep from * ending last rep at **, 1tr into top of tch, turn.

Rep 2nd, 3rd, 4th and 5th rows.

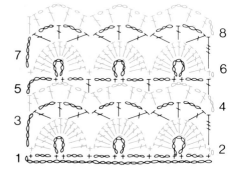

## Double Arch Ground

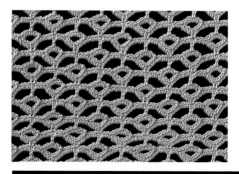

Multiple of 10 sts + 1.
(add 8 for base chain)

**1st row** (wrong side): 1dc into 14th ch from hook, *5ch, miss 4ch, 1tr into next ch**, 5ch, miss 4ch, 1dc into next ch; rep from * ending last rep at **, turn.

**2nd row:** 1ch, 1dc into first tr, *6dc into next 5ch arch, 1dc into next dc, 3dc into beginning of next 5ch arch, work a 'back double' of [4ch, then without turning work, miss 6 previous dc and work a sl st back into previous dc, now work 5dc in the normal direction into 4ch arch just worked], 3dc into remaining part of 5ch arch**, 1dc into next tr; rep from * ending last rep at **, 1dc into next ch, turn.

**3rd row:** 1ch, 1dc into first st, *5ch, 1tr into 3rd of 5dc of next 'back double', 5ch, 1dc into dc over tr of previous row; rep from * ending last rep in last dc, turn.

**4th row:** 1ch, 1dc into first st, 3dc into beginning of next 5ch arch, turn, 2ch, miss 3 previous dc, work 1tr into first dc, 1ch, turn, 1dc into tr, 2dc into 2ch arch, 3dc into remaining part of 5ch arch, *1dc into next tr, 6dc into next 5ch arch, 1dc into next dc**, 3dc into beginning of 5ch arch, 1 'back double' as before, 3dc into remaining part of 5ch arch; rep from * ending last rep at ** in last dc, 5ch, miss 3 previous dc, sl st back into next dc, 3dc in normal direction into beginning of 5ch arch, turn.

**5th row:** 8ch, *1dc into dc over tr of previous row, 5ch**, 1tr into 3rd of 5dc of next 'back double', 5ch; rep from * ending last rep at ** 1tr into last dc, miss tch, turn.

Rep 2nd, 3rd, 4th and 5th rows.

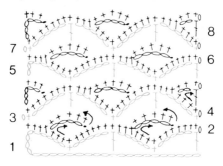

## Coronet Ground

Multiple of 8 sts.
(add 1 for base chain)

**1st row** (right side): Miss 1ch, *1dc into each of next 4ch, work a picot of [3ch, insert hook down through top of last dc made and work sl st to close], 1dc into each of next 4ch, work 9ch then without turning miss 7 previous dc, work a sl st back into previous dc, then working in the normal direction work 7dc into 9ch arch, work a Coronet of [5ch, sl st into 5th ch from hook, 7ch, sl st into 7th ch from hook, 5ch, sl st into 5th ch from hook], work 7dc into arch; rep from * ending sl st into last dc, turn.

**2nd row:** 11ch (count as 1quad tr and 4ch), *1dc into 7ch arch at centre of next Coronet, 7ch; rep from * ending 1dc into 7ch arch at centre of last Coronet, 2ch, 1quad tr into last dc, miss tch, turn.

**3rd row:** 1ch, 1dc into first st, 1dc into each of next 2ch and next dc, turn, 4ch, miss 3dc, 1dtr into last dc, turn, 8ch, sl st into 7th ch from hook, 5ch, sl st into 5th ch from hook (½ Coronet worked), 7dc into next 4ch arch, *1dc into each of next 4ch, 3ch Picot, 1dc into each of next 3ch, 1dc into next dc, work 9ch, miss 7 previous dc, sl st back into previous dc, work 7dc into 9ch arch, work a Coronet as before, then 7dc into 9ch loop; rep from * ending 1dc into each of next 4ch of tch arch, 9ch, miss previous 3dc, sl st into previous dc, work 7dc into 9ch arch, work a ½ Coronet of [5ch, sl st into 5th ch from hook], 1dc into 9ch arch, 3ch, 1dtr into last dc, turn.

**4th row:** 1ch, 1dc into top of 3ch, *7ch, 1dc into 7ch arch at centre of next Coronet; rep from * ending last rep in 8ch arch of ½ Coronet, turn.

**5th row:** 1ch, 1dc into first st, 1dc into each of next 3ch, *3ch Picot, 1dc into each of next 3ch, 1dc into next dc, 9ch, miss 7 previous dc, sl st back into previous dc, work 7dc, Coronet and 7dc into arch**, 1dc into each of next 4ch; rep from * ending last rep at **, sl st into last dc, turn.

Rep 2nd, 3rd, 4th and 5th rows.

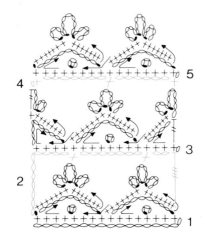

## Shell and V Stitch

Multiple of 8 sts + 1.
(add 2 for base chain)

**1st row** (right side): Miss 2ch (count as 1tr), 2tr into next ch, *miss 3ch, work a V st of

Stitch Variations, Abbreviations and Symbols on pages 7 to 15.

# Openwork and Lace Patterns

[1tr, 1ch, 1tr] into next ch, miss 3ch**, 5tr into next ch; rep from * ending last rep at **, 3tr into last ch, turn.

**2nd row:** 3ch (count as 1tr), 1tr into first st, *5tr into sp at centre of next V st**, V st into 3rd of next 5tr; rep from * ending last rep at **, 2tr into top of tch, turn.

Rep 2nd row.

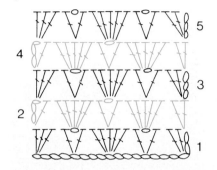

## Fan and V Stitch

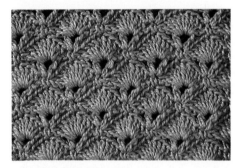

Multiple of 8 sts + 1.
(add 1 for base chain)

**1st row** (right side): 1dc into 2nd ch from hook, *miss 3ch, 9tr into next ch, miss 3ch, 1dc into next ch; rep from * to end, turn.

**2nd row:** 3ch (count as 1tr), 1tr into first st, *5ch, miss 9tr group, work a V st of [1tr, 1ch, 1tr] into next dc; rep from * ending 5ch, miss last 9tr group, 2tr into last dc, miss tch, turn.

**3rd row:** 3ch (count as 1tr), 4tr into first st, *working over next 5ch so as to enclose it, work 1dc into 5th tr of group in row below**, 9tr into sp at centre of next V st; rep from * ending last rep at ** 5tr into top of tch, turn.

**4th row:** 3ch, miss 5tr, V st into next dc, *5ch, miss 9tr group, V st into next dc; rep from * ending 2ch, sl st to top of tch, turn.

**5th row:** 1ch, 1dc over sl st into first st of row below, *9tr into sp at centre of next V st, working over next 5ch so as to enclose it work 1dc into 5th tr of group in row below; rep from * to end, turn.

Rep 2nd, 3rd, 4th and 5th rows.
End with a wrong side row working [2ch, sl st to 5th tr of group, 2ch] in place of 5ch between the V sts.

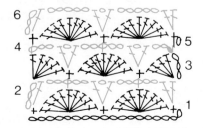

## Peacock Fan Stitch

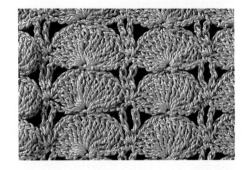

Multiple of 12 sts + 1.
(add 1 for base chain)

**1st row** (right side): 1dc into 2nd ch from hook, *miss 5ch, 13ttr into next ch, miss 5ch, 1dc into next ch; rep from * to end, turn.

**2nd row:** 5ch (count as 1ttr), 1ttr into first st, *4ch, miss 6ttr, 1dc into next ttr, 4ch, miss 6ttr**, work [1ttr, 1ch, 1ttr] into next dc; rep from * ending last rep at **, 2ttr into last dc, miss tch, turn.

**3rd row:** 1ch, 1dc into first st, *miss [1ttr and 4ch], 13ttr into next dc, miss [4ch and 1ttr], 1dc into next ch; rep from * to end, turn.

Rep 2nd and 3rd rows.

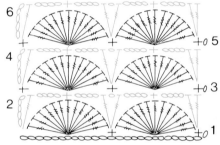

## Block and Offset Shell Stitch

Multiple of 11 sts + 4.
(add 2 for base chain)

**1st row** (right side): Miss 3ch (count as 1tr), 1tr into each of next 4ch, *miss 2ch, 5tr into next ch, 2ch, miss 3ch, 1tr into each of next 5ch; rep from * to end, turn.

**2nd row:** 3ch (count as 1tr), miss first st, 1tr into each of next 4 sts, *miss 2ch, 5tr into next tr, 2ch, miss 4tr, 1tr into each of next 5 sts; rep from * to end, turn.

Rep 2nd row.

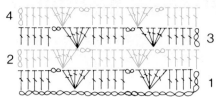

## Soft Fan Stitch

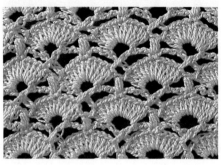

Multiple of 10 sts + 1.
(add 1 for base chain)

**1st row** (wrong side): 1dc into 2nd ch from hook, *3ch, work 2 crossed trs as follows: miss 5ch, 1tr into next ch, 5ch, inserting hook behind tr just made work 1tr into 4th of 5ch just missed, then 3ch, miss 3ch, 1dc into next ch; rep from * to end, turn.

**2nd row:** 3ch (count as 1tr), miss first st, *miss next 3ch sp, work a group of 11tr into next 5ch arch, miss next 3ch sp, work htr3tog into next dc, 1ch; rep from * omitting htr3tog and 1ch at end of last rep and working 1tr into last dc, miss tch, turn.

**3rd row:** 2ch, miss first 2 tr, 1htr into next tr, 4ch, 1htr into top of htr just made, *3ch, miss 3tr, 1dc into next tr, 3ch**, work 2 crossed trs as follows: 1tr into 2nd tr of next 11tr group, 5ch, going behind tr just made work 1tr into 10th tr of previous 11tr group; rep from * ending last rep at **, 1tr into top of tch, 2ch, going behind tr just made work 1tr into 10th tr of previous 11tr group, turn.

**4th row:** 3ch (count as 1tr), miss first st, 5tr into next 2ch sp, *miss next 3ch sp, work htr3tog into next dc, 1ch, miss next 3ch sp**, 11tr into next 5ch arch; rep from * ending last rep at **, 6tr into top of tch, turn.

**5th row:** 1ch, 1dc into first st, 3ch, 1tr into 2nd tr of next 11tr group, 5ch, going behind tr just made work 1tr into 5th tr of previous 6tr group, *3ch, miss 3tr, 1dc into next tr**, 3ch, 1tr into 2nd tr of next tr group, 5ch, going behind tr just made work 1tr into 10th tr of previous tr group; rep from * ending last rep at ** in top of tch, turn.

Rep 2nd, 3rd, 4th and 5th rows.

# Openwork and Lace Patterns

## Hotcross Bun Stitch

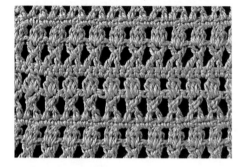

Multiple of 3 sts + 2.
(add 1 for base chain)

**Special Abbreviation**

**DtrX (double treble 'X' shape - worked over 3 sts)** = [yo] twice, insert hook into next st, yo, draw loop through, yo, draw through 2 loops; miss next st, yo, insert hook into next st, yo, draw loop through, [yo, draw through 2 loops] 4 times, 1ch, yo, insert hook half way down st just made where lower 'legs' join, yo, draw loop through, [yo, draw through 2 loops] twice

**1st row** (wrong side): 1dc into 2nd ch from hook, 1dc into next and each ch to end, turn.

**2nd row:** 4ch (count as 1dtr), miss first st, *DtrX over next 3 sts; rep from * ending 1dtr into last st, miss tch, turn.

**3rd row:** 4ch (count as 1tr and 1ch), *work tr3tog into next 1ch sp**, 2ch; rep from * ending last rep at **, 1ch, 1tr into top of tch, turn.

**4th row:** 1ch, 1dc into first st, 1dc into next ch, *1dc into next cluster, 1dc into each of next 2ch; rep from * to end, turn.

Rep 2nd, 3rd and 4th rows.

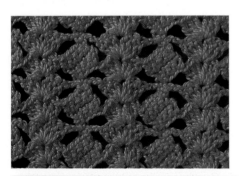

## Hearts and Diamonds Stitch

Multiple of 10 sts + 7.
(add 5 for base chain)

**Special Abbreviation**

**Diamond** = 4 rows inside a main row worked as follows: Turn, **1st row:** 1ch, 1dc into first dc, 1dc into each of next 3ch. **Next row:** 1ch, 1dc into each of next 4 dc, miss tch, turn. Rep the last row twice more.

**1st row** (wrong side): 1dc into 9th ch from hook, *2ch, miss 4ch, work a Heart of [3tr, 1ch, 3tr] into next ch, 2ch, miss 4ch, 1dc into next ch; rep from * to last 3ch, 2ch, miss 2ch, 1tr into last ch, turn.

**2nd row:** 6ch, miss first st and next 2ch, 1dc into next dc, work a Diamond, *miss 2ch, 1 Heart into ch sp at centre of next Heart, 3ch, miss 2ch, 1dc into next dc, work Diamond; rep from * ending miss 2ch, 1tr into next ch of tch, turn.

**3rd row:** 5ch (count as 1tr and 2ch), *1dc into top corner of next Diamond, 2ch**, 1 Heart into sp at centre of next Heart, 2ch; rep from * ending last rep at **, 1tr into 3rd ch of tch, turn.

Rep 2nd and 3rd rows.

## Tread Pattern Stitch

Multiple of 8 sts + 3.
(add 2 for base chain)

**1st row** (right side): Miss 3ch (count as 1tr), 1tr into each of next 2ch, *miss 2ch, 1tr into next ch, 3ch, work a block of 3tr evenly spaced into side of tr just made, miss 2ch, 1tr into each of next 3ch; rep from * to end, turn.

**2nd row:** 3ch (count as 1tr), miss first st, 1tr into each of next 2tr, *2ch, 1dc into top of 3ch at corner of next block, 2ch, miss tr which forms base of same block, 1tr into each of next 3tr; rep from * ending last rep in top of tch, turn.

**3rd row:** 3ch (count as 1tr), miss first st, 1tr into each of next 2tr, *miss 2ch, 1tr into next dc, 3ch, 3tr evenly spaced into side of tr just made, miss 2ch, 1tr into each of next 3tr; rep from * ending last rep in top of tch, turn.

Rep 2nd and 3rd rows.

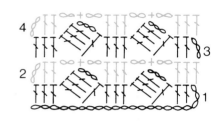

## Butterfly Lace

Multiple of 12 sts + 3.
(add 1 for base chain)

**1st row** (right side): 1dc into 2nd ch from hook, 2ch, miss 1ch, 1dc into next ch, *miss 3ch, work [3dtr, 4ch, 1dc] into next ch, 2ch, miss 1ch, work [1dc, 4ch, 3dtr] into next ch, miss 3ch, 1dc into next ch, 2ch, miss 1ch, 1dc into next ch; rep from * to end, turn.

**2nd row:** 4ch (count as 1tr and 1ch), miss first dc, 1tr into next 2ch sp, *1ch, miss 3dtr, 1dc into top of 4ch, 2ch, work tr2tog into next 2ch sp, 2ch, miss 3ch, 1dc into next ch, 1ch**, work [1tr, 1ch, 1tr] into next sp; rep from * ending last rep at **, 1tr into last sp, 1ch, 1tr into last dc, miss tch, turn.

**3rd row:** 1ch, 1dc into first st, 2ch, miss [1ch and 1tr], 1dc into next ch, *work [3dtr, 4ch, 1dc] into next 2ch sp, 2ch, miss next cluster, work [1dc, 4ch, 3dtr] into next 2ch sp, 1dc into next 1ch sp, 2ch, miss 1ch, 1dc into next 1ch sp; rep from * ending last rep in 3rd ch of tch, turn.

Rep 2nd and 3rd rows.

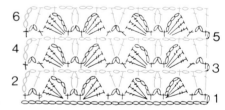

## Cluster Lace Stitch

Stitch Variations, Abbreviations and Symbols on pages 7 to 15.

# Openwork and Lace Patterns

Multiple of 8 sts + 1.
(add 1 for base chain)

**1st row** (right side): 1dc into 2nd ch from hook, 1dc into next ch, *4ch, work tr4tog over next 5ch as follows: leaving last loop of each st on hook work 1tr into each of next 2ch, miss 1ch, 1tr into each of next 2ch, yo and draw through all 5 loops on hook; 4ch, 1dc into next ch**, 1ch, miss 1ch, 1dc into next ch; rep from * ending last rep at **, 1dc into last ch, turn.

**2nd row:** 3ch (count as 1tr), 1tr into first st, *3ch, 1dc into top of next 4ch, 1ch, miss cluster, 1dc into top of next 4ch, 3ch, miss 1dc**, tr3tog into next 1ch sp; rep from * ending last rep at **, tr2tog into last dc, miss tch, turn.

**3rd row:** 1ch, 1dc into first st, *1dc into next ch, 4ch, tr4tog as follows: leaving last loop of each st on hook work 1tr into each of next 2ch, miss [1dc, 1ch and 1dc], 1tr into each of next 2ch, yo and draw through all 5 loops on hook; 4ch, 1dc into next ch**, 1ch, miss cluster, rep from * ending last rep at **, 1dc into top of tch, turn.

Rep 2nd and 3rd rows.

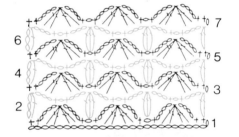

## Triple Picot V Stitch

Multiple of 11 sts + 7.
(add 3 for base chain)

**1st row** (right side): 1tr into 4th ch from hook, *3ch, miss 3ch, 1dc into next ch**, work a picot of [3ch, 1dc into next ch] 3 times, 3ch, miss 3ch, [1tr, 2ch, 1tr] into next ch; rep from * ending last rep at ** when 2ch remain, 3ch, 1dc into next ch, 1ch, 1htr into last ch, turn.

**2nd row:** 4ch (count as 1tr and 1ch), 1tr into first st, *3ch, miss 1 Picot and 3ch**, into next 2ch sp work 1dc, [3ch, 1dc] 3 times, then 3ch, miss 3ch and 1 Picot, [1tr, 2ch, 1tr] into next Picot; rep from * ending last rep at **, work [1dc, 3ch, 1dc] into top of tch, 1ch, 1htr into next ch, turn.

Rep 2nd row.

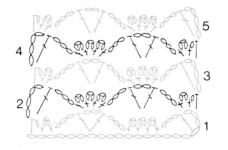

## Lacy Wave Stitch

Multiple of 11 sts + 1.
(add 1 for base chain)

**1st row** (right side): 1dc into 2nd ch from hook, *2ch, miss 2ch, 1tr into each of next 2ch, 2ch, miss 2ch, 1dc into each of next 5ch; rep from * to end, turn.

**2nd row:** 5ch (count as 1tr and 2ch), 1tr into first st, *[1ch, miss 1 st, 1tr into next st] twice, 1ch, 1tr into next 2ch sp, miss 2tr**, 5tr into next 2ch sp, 2ch, 1tr into next st; rep from * ending last rep at **, 4tr into last 2ch sp, 1tr into last dc, miss tch, turn.

**3rd row:** 5ch (count as 1tr and 2ch), 1tr into first st, *[1ch, miss 1 st, 1tr into next st] twice, 1ch, miss 1 st, 1tr into next ch, miss [1tr, 1ch, 1tr, 1ch and 1tr], 5tr into next 2ch sp**, 2ch, 1tr into next st; rep from * ending last rep at ** in tch, turn.

Rep 3rd row.

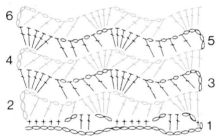

## Alternative V Stitch

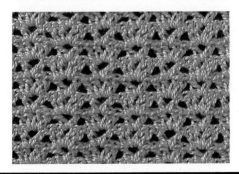

Multiple of 9 sts + 1.
(add 2 for base chain)

**1st row:** 2tr into 5th ch from hook, *1ch, 2tr into next ch, miss 3ch, work [1tr, 2ch, 1tr] into next ch**, miss 3ch, 2tr into next ch; rep from * ending last rep at ** when 2ch remain, miss 1ch, 1tr into last ch, turn.

**2nd row:** 3ch (count as 1tr), miss first st, *work [2tr, 1ch, 2tr] into next 2ch sp, work [1tr, 2ch, 1tr] into next 1ch sp; rep from * ending 1tr into top of tch, turn.

Rep 2nd row.

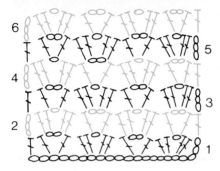

## Shell Filigree Stitch

Multiple of 5 sts + 1.
(add 2 for base chain)

**1st row** (wrong side): 2tr into 3rd ch from hook, *1ch, miss 4ch, 5tr into next ch; rep from * working only 3tr at end of last rep, turn.

**2nd row:** 1ch, 1dc into first st, *2ch, miss 2tr, work a picot V st of [1tr, 3ch, insert hook down through top of tr just made and work a sl st to close, 1tr] into next 1ch sp, 2ch, miss 2tr, 1dc into next tr; rep from * ending last rep in top of tch, turn.

**3rd row:** 3ch (count as 1tr), 2tr into first dc, *1ch, miss 2ch, Picot V st and 2ch, work 5tr into next dc; rep from * finishing with only 3tr at end of last rep, miss tch, turn.

Rep 2nd and 3rd rows.

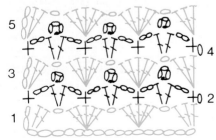

# Openwork and Lace Patterns

## Arched Lace Stitch

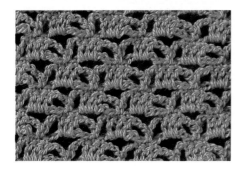

Multiple of 8 sts + 1.
(add 1 for base chain)

**1st row** (right side): 1dc into 2nd ch from hook, 1dc into next ch, *5ch, miss 5ch, 1dc into each of next 3ch; rep from * omitting 1dc at end of last rep, turn.

**2nd row:** 1ch, 1dc into first st, *3ch, miss next dc, 3tr into next 5ch arch, 3ch, miss 1dc, 1dc into next dc; rep from * to end, miss tch, turn.

**3rd row:** 6ch (count as 1dtr and 2ch), miss 3ch, *1dc into each of next 3tr**, 5ch, miss [3ch, 1dc and 3ch]; rep from * ending last rep at **, 2ch, miss 3ch, 1dtr into last dc, miss tch, turn.

**4th row:** 3ch (count as 1tr), miss first st, 1tr into 2ch sp, *3ch, miss next dc, 1dc into next dc, 3ch, miss 1dc**, 3tr into next 5ch arch; rep from * ending last rep at **, miss 1ch, 1tr into each of next 2ch of tch, turn.

**5th row:** 1ch, 1dc into first st, 1dc into next st, *5ch, miss [3ch, 1dc and 3ch], 1dc into each of next 3tr; rep from * to end, omitting 1dc at end of last rep, turn.
Rep 2nd, 3rd, 4th and 5th rows.

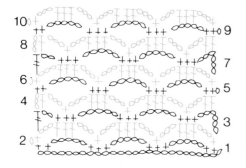

## Chain Lace Stitch

Multiple of 10 sts + 1.
(add 7 for base chain)

### Special Abbreviation

**TP (Triple Picot)** = work 1dc, [7ch, 1dc] 3 times all into same place.

**1st row** (right side): TP into 12th ch from hook, *4ch, miss 4ch, 1tr into next ch**, 4ch, miss 4ch, TP into next ch; rep from * ending last rep at ** in last ch, turn.

**2nd row:** 1ch, 1dc into first st, *1ch, 1dc into first arch of next TP, [3ch, 1dc into next arch of same TP] twice, 1ch, miss 4ch, 1dc into next tr; rep from * to end placing last dc into arch of tch, turn.

**3rd row:** 8ch, work [1dc, 7ch, 1dc] into first dc, *4ch, miss [1ch, 1dc and 3ch], 1tr into next dc, 4ch, miss [3ch, 1dc and 1ch]**, TP into next dc; rep from * ending last rep at **, work [1dc, 7ch, 1dc, 3ch and 1dtr] into last dc, miss tch, turn.

**4th row:** 1ch, 1dc into first st, 3ch, 1dc into next 7ch arch, *1ch, miss 4ch, 1dc into next tr, 1ch, 1dc into first arch of next TP**, [3ch, 1dc into next arch of same TP] twice; rep from * ending last rep at **, 3ch, 1dc into tch arch, turn.

**5th row:** 7ch, miss [3ch, 1dc and 1ch], *TP into next dc, 4ch, miss [1ch, 1dc and 3ch], 1tr into next dc**, 4ch, miss [3ch, 1dc and 1ch]; rep from * ending last rep at **, turn.
Rep 2nd, 3rd, 4th and 5th rows.

## Wavy Lace Stitch

Multiple of 12 sts + 1.
(add 4 for base chain)

**Base row** (right side): 1dc into 7th ch from hook, *3ch, miss 3ch, 1tr into next ch**, [3ch, miss 3ch, 1dc into next ch] twice; rep from * ending last rep at **, 3ch, miss 3ch, 1dc into next ch, 1ch, miss 1ch, 1tr into last ch, turn.

### Commence Pattern

**1st row:** 4ch (count as 1dtr), [1dtr, 1ch, 1dtr] all into next 1ch sp, *3ch, miss 3ch, 1dc into next tr, 3ch, miss 3ch**, work 1dtr, [1ch, 1dtr] 3 times all into next 3ch arch, rep from * ending last rep at **, 1dtr into next ch, 1ch, 2dtr into next ch of tch, turn.

**2nd row:** 4ch (count as 1tr and 1ch), miss first 2 dtr, 1dc into 1ch sp, *3ch, miss [1dtr and 3ch], 1dc into next dc, 3ch, miss [3ch and 1dtr], 1dc into next ch sp**, 4ch, miss next sp, 1dc into next sp; rep from * ending last rep at **, 1ch, miss 1dtr, 1tr into top of tch, turn.

**3rd row:** 1ch, 1dc into first st, miss 1ch, *[3ch, 1dc into next 3ch arch] twice, 3ch, 1dc into next 4ch arch; rep from * to end, turn.

**4th row:** 1ch, 1dc into first st, *3ch, miss 3ch, work 1dtr, [1ch, 1dtr] 3 times into next 3ch arch, 3ch, miss 3ch, 1dc into next dc; rep from * to end, miss tch, turn.

**5th row:** 1ch, 1dc into first st, *3ch, miss [3ch and 1dtr], 1dc into next ch sp, 4ch, miss next sp, 1dc into next sp, 3ch, miss [1dtr and 3ch], 1dc into next dc; rep from * to end, miss tch, turn.

**6th row:** 5ch (count as 1dtr and 1ch), *1dc into next 3ch arch, 3ch, 1dc into next 4ch arch, 3ch, 1dc into next arch**, 3ch; rep from * ending last rep at **, 1ch, 1dtr into last dc, miss tch, turn.
Rep these 6 rows.

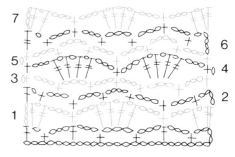

## Petal Stitch

Multiple of 8 sts + 1.
(add 1 for base chain)

**1st row** (wrong side): 1dc into 2nd ch from hook, *2ch, miss 3ch, 4dtr into next ch, 2ch, miss 3ch, 1dc into next ch; rep from * to end, turn.

**2nd row:** 1ch, 1dc into first st, *3ch, miss 2ch and 1dtr, 1dc into next dtr, 3ch, miss 2dtr and 2ch, 1dc into next dc; rep from * to end, miss tch, turn.

**3rd row:** 4ch (count as 1dtr), 1dtr into first st, *2ch, miss 3ch, 1dc into next dc, 2ch, miss 3ch, 4dtr into next dc; rep from * to end omitting 1dtr at end of last rep, miss tch, turn.

**4th row:** 1ch, 1dc into first st, *3ch, miss 2dtr and 2ch, 1dc into next dc, 3ch, miss 2ch and 1dtr, 1dc into next dtr; rep from * ending last rep in top of tch, turn.

**5th row:** 1ch, 1dc into first st, *2ch, miss 3ch, 4dtr into next dc, 2ch, miss 3ch, 1dc into next dc; rep from * to end, miss tch, turn.
Rep 2nd, 3rd, 4th and 5th rows.

Stitch Variations, Abbreviations and Symbols on pages 7 to 15.

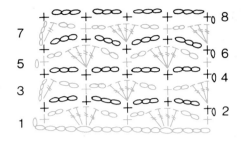

hook, *4ch, miss 5ch, 5tr into next ch; rep from * working only 3tr at end of last rep, turn.

**2nd row:** 2ch (count as 1tr), miss first 3 sts, *work [3tr, 3ch, 3tr] into next 4ch arch**, miss next 5tr; rep from * ending last rep at **, miss 2tr, 1tr into top of tch, turn.

**3rd row:** 6ch (count as 1ttr and 1ch), *5tr into next 3ch arch**, 4ch; rep from * ending last rep at **, 1ch, 1ttr into top of tch, turn.

**4th row:** 5ch (count as 1dtr and 1ch), 3tr into next 1ch sp, *miss 5tr, work [3tr, 3ch, 3tr] into next 4ch arch; rep from * ending miss 5tr, work [3tr, 1ch, 1dtr] into tch, turn.

**5th row:** 3ch (count as 1tr), 2tr into next 1ch sp, *4ch, 5tr into next 3ch arch; rep from * ending 4ch, 3tr into tch, turn.

Rep 2nd, 3rd, 4th and 5th rows.

2ch and 1dc, 1dc into each of next 3dc, 3ch, miss 1dc, 1dc into next 5ch arch; rep from * ending last rep in tch, turn.

**5th row:** 1ch, 1dc into first st, *1dc into next 3ch sp, 3ch, miss 1dc, 1dc into next dc, 3ch, miss 1dc, 1dc into next 3ch sp, 1dc into next dc; rep from * to end, miss tch, turn.

**6th row:** 1ch, 1dc into each of first 2 sts, *1dc into next 3ch sp, 5ch, 1dc into next 3ch sp**, 1dc into each of next 3dc; rep from * ending last rep at **, 1dc into each of last 2dc, miss tch, turn.

Rep these 6 rows.

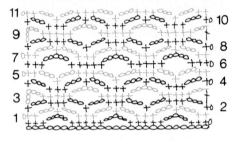

## Webbed Lace Stitch

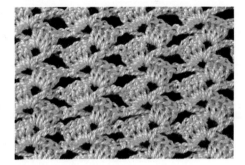

Multiple of 7 sts.
(add 4 for base chain)

**1st row:** 1tr into 5th ch from hook, *2ch, miss 5ch, 4tr into next ch**, 2ch, 1tr into next ch; rep from * ending last rep at ** in last ch, turn.

**2nd row:** 4ch, 1tr into first st, *2ch, miss [3tr, 2ch and 1tr]**, work [4tr, 2ch, 1tr] into next 2ch sp; rep from * ending last rep at **, 4tr into tch, turn.

Rep 2nd row.

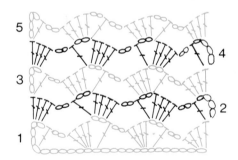

## Acrobatic Stitch

Multiple of 6 sts + 1.
(add 2 for base chain)
**1st row** (right side): 2tr into 3rd ch from

## Diamond Lace Stitch

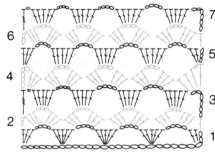

Multiple of 8 sts + 1.
(add 1 for base chain)
**Base row** (right side): 1dc into 2nd ch from hook, 1dc into each of next 2ch, *5ch, miss 3ch**, 1dc into each of next 5ch; rep from * ending last rep at **, 1dc into each of last 3ch, turn.

**Commence Pattern**

**1st row:** 1ch, 1dc into each of first 2 sts, *3ch, miss 1dc, 1dc into next 5ch arch, 3ch, miss 1dc**, 1dc into each of next 3dc; rep from * ending last rep at **, 1dc into each of last 2dc, miss tch, turn.

**2nd row:** 1ch, 1dc into first st, *3ch, miss 1dc, 1dc into next 3ch sp, 1dc into next dc, 1dc into next 3ch sp, 3ch, miss 1dc, 1dc into next dc; rep from * to end, miss tch, turn.

**3rd row:** 5ch (count as 1tr and 2ch), *1dc into next 3ch sp, 1dc into each of next 3dc, 1dc into next 3ch sp**, 5ch; rep from * ending last rep at **, 2ch, 1tr into last dc, miss tch, turn.

**4th row:** 1ch, 1dc into first st, *3ch, miss

## Picot Fan Stitch

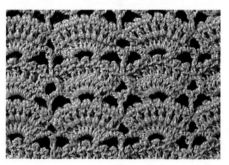

Multiple of 12 sts + 1.
(add 1 for base chain)

**1st row** (right side): 1dc into 2nd ch from hook, *5ch, miss 3ch, 1dc into next ch; rep from * to end, turn.

**2nd row:** 5ch (count as 1tr and 2ch), *1dc into next 5ch arch, 8tr into next arch, 1dc into next arch**, 5ch; rep from * ending last rep at ** in last arch, 2ch, 1tr into last dc, miss tch, turn.

**3rd row:** 1ch, 1dc into first st, miss 2ch and 1dc, *work a picot of [1tr into next tr, 3ch, insert hook down through top of tr just made and sl st to close] 7 times, 1tr into next tr, 1dc into next arch; rep from * to end, turn.

**4th row:** 8ch, miss 2 picots, *1dc into next picot, 5ch, miss 1 picot, 1dc into next picot, 5ch, miss 2 picots, 1tr into next dc**, 5ch, miss 2 picots; rep from * ending last rep at **, miss tch, turn.

Rep 2nd, 3rd and 4th rows.

# Openwork and Lace Patterns

## Crazy Diamond Stitch

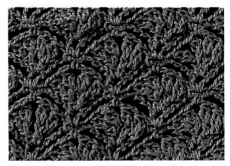

Multiple of 12 sts + 1.
(add 1 for base chain)

**Special Abbreviation**

**CRC (Crazy Cluster)** = [yo] 3 times, insert hook as indicated, yo, draw loop through, [yo, draw through 2 loops] 3 times, (2 loops on hook); yo, insert hook into centre left side of ttr in progress, yo, draw loop through, yo, draw through 2 loops, (3 loops on hook), yo, draw through all loops on hook; 1ch; [yo] twice, insert hook into lower left side of original ttr, yo, draw loop through, [yo, draw through 2 loops] twice, (2 loops on hook); yo, insert hook into centre left side of dtr in progress, yo, draw loop through, yo, draw through 2 loops, (3 loops on hook), yo, draw through all loops on hook.

**1st row** (right side): 1dc into 2nd ch from hook, *1dc into next ch, 1ch, miss 4ch, work [1CRC, 2ch, 1CRC] into next ch, 1ch, miss 4ch, 1dc into next ch**, 1ch, miss 1ch; rep from * ending last rep at **, 1dc into last ch, turn.

**2nd row:** 3ch (count as 1tr), 1tr into first st, *4ch, 1dc into 2ch sp between next 2CRCs, 4ch**, work a V st of [1tr, 1ch, 1tr] into ch sp between next 2dc; rep from * ending last rep at **, 2tr into last dc, miss tch, turn.

**3rd row:** 6ch (count as 1 quad tr), 1CRC into first st, *1ch, 1dc into next 4ch sp, 1ch, 1dc into next 4ch sp, 1ch**, work [1CRC, 2ch, 1CRC] into sp at centre of next V st; rep from * ending last rep at **, work [1CRC, 1 quad tr] into top of tch, turn.

**4th row:** 1ch, 1dc into first st, *4ch, V st into sp between next 2dc, 4ch, 1dc into 2ch sp between next 2CRCs; rep from * ending last rep in top of tch, turn.

**5th row:** 1ch, 1dc into first st, *1dc into next 4ch sp, 1ch, work [1CRC, 2ch, 1CRC] into sp at centre of next V st, 1ch, 1dc into next 4ch sp**, 1ch; rep from * ending last rep at **, 1dc into last dc, miss tch, turn.

Rep 2nd, 3rd, 4th and 5th rows.

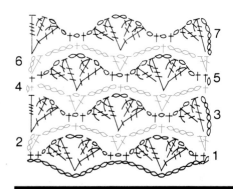

## Christmas Tree and Bauble Stitch

Multiple of 10 sts + 6.
(add 2 for base chain)

**Special Abbreviation**

**Tree** = work 1 quad tr as indicated, 1ch, 1ttr into base of stem of previous quad tr, 1ch, 1dtr into base of stem of previous ttr, 1ch, 1tr into base of stem of previous dtr, 2ch, 1htr into stem of previous tr, 1ch, 1tr into stem of previous dtr in same place as previous tr, 1ch, 1dtr into stem of previous ttr in same place as previous dtr, 1ch, 1ttr into stem of previous quad tr in same place as previous ttr.

**Base row** (right side): Miss 2ch (count as 1tr), 3tr into next ch, *miss 4ch, 1dc into next ch**, miss 4ch, 7tr into next ch; rep from * ending last rep at ** in last ch, turn.

**Commence Pattern**

**1st row:** 8ch, 1htr into 3rd ch from hook, 1ch, miss 1ch, 1tr into next ch, 1ch, 1dtr into next ch, 1ch, 1ttr into next ch, 1ch, miss 1tr, 1dc and 3tr, 1dc into next st, *1ch, miss 3tr, work 1 Tree into next dc, 1ch, miss 3tr, 1dc into next st; rep from * to end, turn.

**2nd row:** 4ch (count as 1dtr), miss first st, dtr4tog/rb round stems of next 4 branches of Tree, *4ch, 1dc into next 2ch sp**, 4ch, dtr8tog/rb round stems of 4 remaining branches of same Tree and first 4 branches of next Tree; rep from * ending last rep at ** in tch, turn.

**3rd row:** 1ch, 1dc into first st, *miss 4ch, 7tr into loop which closed next cluster, miss 4ch, 1dc into next dc; rep from * ending miss 4ch, 4tr into loop which closed half cluster at edge, turn.

**4th row:** 1ch, 1dc into first st, *1ch, miss 3tr**, Tree into next dc, 1ch, miss 3tr, 1dc into next st; rep from * ending last rep at **, work first half of Tree into last dc, omitting 2ch at top centre and ending 1ch, 1htr into stem of previous tr, turn.

**5th row:** 1ch, 1dc into first st, *4ch, dtr8tog/rf round stems of 4 branches of first Half Tree and first 4 branches of next Tree, 4ch, 1dc into next 2ch sp; rep from * ending 4ch, dtr5tog/rf round stems of 4 remaining branches of last Tree and last dc, miss tch, turn.

**6th row:** 3ch (count as 1tr), 3tr into first st, *miss 4ch, 1dc into next dc**, miss 4ch, 7tr into loop which closed next cluster; rep from * ending last rep at ** in last dc, miss tch, turn.

Rep these 6 rows.

## Clover Fan Stitch

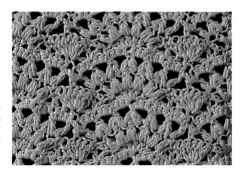

Multiple of 18 sts + 1.
(add 1 for base chain)

**Special Abbreviation**

**CVC (Clover Cluster)** = [yo, insert hook, yo, draw loop through loosely] twice as indicated for first leg, (5 loops on hook), and twice more as indicated for 2nd leg, (9 loops on hook), *yo, draw through all except last loop, yo, draw through remaining 2 loops.

**Note:** For CVC with 1 leg only, omit 2nd leg and complete as given from * to end.

**1st row** (wrong side): 1dc into 2nd ch from hook, *miss 2ch, 5tr into next ch, miss 2ch, 1dc into next ch; rep from * to end, turn.

**2nd row:** 3ch (count as 1tr), 2tr into first st, *miss 2tr, 1dc into next tr, 1ch, miss 2tr and 1dc, work CVC with 1 leg only into next tr, [2ch, 1CVC inserting hook into same place as previous CVC for first leg and into next tr for 2nd leg] 4 times, 2ch, work CVC with 1 leg only into same place as 2nd leg of previous CVC, 1ch, miss 1dc and 2tr, 1dc into next tr, miss 2tr, 5tr into next dc; rep from * ending last rep with only 3tr into last dc, miss tch, turn.

**3rd row:** 1ch, 1dc into first st, *miss 2tr, 1dc and 1ch, work CVC with 1 leg only into next CVC, [2ch, 1CVC inserting hook into same place as previous CVC for first leg and into next CVC for 2nd leg, missing 2ch between] 5 times, 2ch, work CVC with 1 leg only into same place as 2nd leg of previous CVC, miss 1ch, 1dc and 2tr, 1dc into next st; rep from * to end, turn.

**4th row:** 1ch, 1dc into first st, 1dc into each st and each ch to end, miss tch, turn.

**5th row:** 1ch, 1dc into first st, *miss 3dc, 5tr into next dc, [miss 2dc, 1dc into next dc, miss 2dc, 5tr into next dc] twice, miss 3dc, 1dc into next dc; rep from * to end, miss tch, turn.

Stitch Variations, Abbreviations and Symbols on pages 7 to 15.

# Openwork and Lace Patterns

Rep 2nd, 3rd, 4th and 5th rows.

## Open Pineapple Stitch

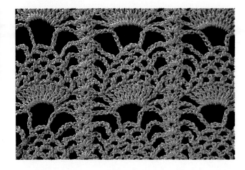

Multiple of 15 sts + 1.
(add 2 for base chain)

**Special Abbreviation**

**DV st** = Double V Stitch.

**Base row** (right side): Miss 2ch (count as 1tr), 2tr into next ch, *7ch, miss 5ch, 1dc into next ch, 3ch, miss 2ch, 1dc into next ch, 7ch, miss 5ch**, work a DV st of [2tr, 1ch, 2tr] into next ch; rep from * ending last rep at **, 3tr into last ch, turn.

**Commence Pattern**

**1st row:** 3ch (count as 1tr), 2tr into first st, *3ch, 1dc into 7ch arch, 5ch, miss 3ch, 1dc into next 7ch arch, 3ch**, DV st into sp at centre of DV st; rep from * ending last rep at **, 3tr into top of tch, turn.

**2nd row:** 3ch (count as 1tr), 2tr into first st, *miss 3ch, 11dtr into next 5ch arch, miss 3ch**, DV st into next sp; rep from * ending last rep at **, 3tr into top of tch, turn.

**3rd row:** 3ch (count as 1tr), 2tr into first st, *2ch, miss 2tr, 1dc into next dtr, [3ch, miss 1dtr, 1dc into next dtr] 5 times, 2ch, miss 2tr**, DV st into next sp; rep from * ending last rep at **, 3tr into top of tch, turn.

**4th row:** 3ch (count as 1tr), 2tr into first st, *3ch, miss 2ch, 1dc into next 3ch arch, [3ch, 1dc into next 3ch arch] 4 times, 3ch, miss 2ch**, DV st into next sp; rep from * ending last rep at **, 3tr into top of tch, turn.

**5th row:** 3ch (count as 1tr), 2tr into first st, *4ch, miss 3ch, 1dc into next 3ch arch, [3ch, 1dc into next 3ch arch] 3 times, 4ch, miss 3ch**, DV st into next sp; rep from * ending last rep at **, 3tr into top of tch, turn.

**6th row:** 3ch (count as 1tr), 2tr into first st, *5ch, miss 4ch, 1dc into next 3ch arch, [3ch,

1dc into next 3ch arch] twice, 5ch, miss 4ch**, DV st into next sp; rep from * ending last rep at **, 3tr into top of tch, turn.

**7th row:** 3ch (count as 1tr), 2tr into first st, *7ch, miss 5ch, 1dc into next 3ch arch, 3ch, 1dc into next 3ch arch, 7ch, miss 5ch**, DV st into next sp; rep from * ending last rep at **, 3tr into top of tch, turn.

Rep these 7 rows.

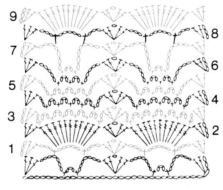

## Strawberry Lace Stitch

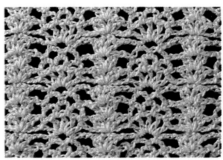

Multiple of 12 sts + 7.
(add 1 for base chain)

**1st row** (right side): 1dc into 2nd ch from hook, *3ch, miss 5ch, into next ch work a 5 group of 1tr, [1ch, 1tr] 4 times, 3ch, miss 5ch, 1dc into next ch; rep from * ending 3ch, miss 5ch, into last ch work 1tr, [1ch, 1tr] twice, turn.

**2nd row:** [3ch, 1dc into next ch sp] twice, *1ch, miss 3ch, work a DV st of [2tr, 1ch, 2tr] into next dc, 1ch, miss 3ch, 1dc into next ch sp, [3ch, 1dc into next ch sp] 3 times; rep from * ending 1ch, miss 3ch, 3tr into last dc, miss tch, turn.

**3rd row:** 3ch (count as 1tr), 2tr into first st, *2ch, miss 1ch, 1dc into next 3ch arch**, [3ch, 1dc into next 3ch arch] twice, 2ch, miss 1ch, DV st into next ch sp; rep from * ending last rep at **, 3ch, 1dc into tch, turn.

**4th row:** 4ch, 1dc into next 3ch arch, *3ch, miss 2ch, DV st into next ch sp, 3ch, miss 2ch, 1dc into next 3ch arch, 3ch, 1dc into next 3ch arch; rep from * ending 3ch, miss 2ch, 3tr into top of tch, turn.

**5th row:** 1ch, 1dc into first st, *3ch, miss 3ch, 5 group into next 3ch arch, 3ch, miss 3ch, 1dc into next ch sp; rep from * ending 3ch, miss 3ch, into tch work 1tr, [1ch, 1tr] twice, turn.

Rep 2nd, 3rd, 4th and 5th rows.

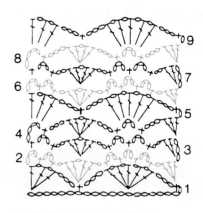

## Open Crescent

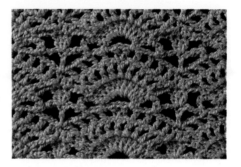

Multiple of 18 sts + 1.
(add 1 for base chain)

**1st row** (wrong side): 1dc into 2nd ch from hook, *3ch, miss 2ch, 1dc into next ch, [5ch, miss 3ch, 1dc into next ch] 3 times, 3ch, miss 2ch, 1dc into next ch; rep from * to end, turn.

**2nd row:** 3ch (count as 1tr), 1tr into first st, *3ch, miss 3ch, 1dc into next arch, 9tr into next arch, 1dc into next arch, 3ch, miss 3ch, 3tr into next dc; rep from * working only 2tr at end of last rep, miss tch, turn.

**3rd row:** 1ch, 1dc into each of first 2 sts, *1ch, miss 3ch and 1dc, 1tr into next tr, [1ch, 1tr into next tr] 8 times, 1ch, miss 1dc and 3ch, 1dc into each of next 3 sts; rep from * omitting 1dc at end of last rep, turn.

**4th row:** 1ch, 1dc into first st, *miss 1dc and 1ch, 1tr into next tr, [1ch, miss 1ch, 1tr into next tr] 3 times, 1ch, miss 1ch, work [1tr, 1ch, 1tr] into next tr, [1ch, miss 1ch, 1tr into next tr] 4 times (Crescent completed), miss 1ch and 1dc, 1dc into next dc; rep from * to end, miss tch, turn.

**5th row:** 6ch (count as 1tr and 3ch), *1dc into 3rd tr of next Crescent, 5ch, miss 1ch and 1tr, 1dc into next ch, 5ch, miss 1tr, 1ch and 1tr, 1dc into next ch, 5ch, miss 1tr and 1ch, 1dc into next tr, 3ch, miss remaining sts of same Crescent, 1tr into next dc, 3ch; rep from * omitting 3ch at end of last rep, miss tch, turn.

Rep 2nd, 3rd, 4th and 5th rows.

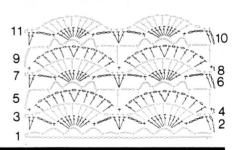

# Openwork and Lace Patterns

## Broomstick Lace

Multiple of 4 sts.
(add 1 for base chain)

**1st row** (right side): 1dc into 2nd ch from hook, 1dc into next and each ch to end, turn.

**2nd row:** 1ch, 1dc into first st, 1dc into next and each st to end, miss tch, turn.

**3rd row:** *1ch, draw loop on hook up to approx height of ttr, keeping loop on hook and not allowing it to change size through yarn slippage, insert hook into next st, yo, draw loop through; rep from * to end keeping all lace loops on hook. (Hint: slip some sts off handle end of hook if they become too numerous.) At end remove all except last lace loop from hook, yo, draw loop through, insert hook under back thread and work 1dc as for Solomon's Knot (see page 11), to lock last lace loop, turn.

**4th row:** *Always inserting hook through next 4 lace loops together work 4dc; rep from * to end, turn.

Rep 2nd, 3rd and 4th rows.

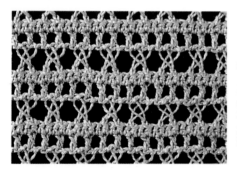

## Crossed Lace Loop Stitch

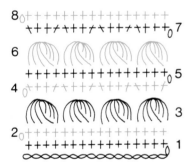

Multiple of 2 sts + 1.
(add 3 for base chain)

**1st row** (right side): 1tr into 6th ch from hook, *1ch, miss 1ch, 1tr into next ch; rep from * to end, turn.

**2nd row:** 1ch, 1dc into first st, *1dc into next ch, 1dc into next tr; rep from * ending 1dc into each of next 2ch of tch, turn.

**3rd row:** *1ch, draw loop on hook up to approx height of dtr, keeping loop on hook and not allowing it to change size through yarn slippage, insert hook into next st, yo, draw loop through, sl st into next st; rep from * to end keeping all lace loops on hook. (Hint: slip some off handle end of hook, if they become too numerous.) At end remove all except last lace loop from hook, yo, draw loop through, insert hook under back thread as though for Solomon's Knot (see page 11), but make sl st to lock last lace loop, turn.

**4th row:** *1ch, miss 1 lace loop, sl st into top of next loop, 1ch, bring forward loop just missed and sl st into top of it; rep from * ending sl st into top of last loop, turn.

**5th row:** 4ch (count as 1tr and 1ch), miss 1ch, 1tr into next sl st, *1ch, miss 1ch, 1tr into next sl st; rep from * to end, turn.

Rep 2nd, 3rd, 4th and 5th rows.

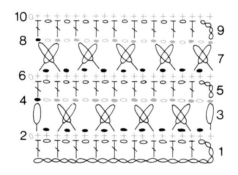

## Little Pyramid Stitch

Multiple of 4 sts + 1.
(add 1 for base chain)

**1st row** (right side): 1dc into 2nd ch from hook, *work a Pyramid of [6ch, 1dc into 3rd ch from hook, 1tr into each of next 3ch], miss 3ch, 1dc into next ch; rep from * to end, turn.

**2nd row:** 6ch (count as 1ttr and 1ch), *1dc into ch at tip of next Pyramid, 3ch; rep from * ending 1dc into ch at tip of last Pyramid, 1ch, 1ttr into last dc, miss tch, turn.

**3rd row:** 10ch, miss 1ch, 1dc into next dc, *work Pyramid, miss 3ch, 1dc into next dc; rep from * ending 5ch, miss 1ch, 1ttr into

next ch of tch, turn.

**4th row:** 1ch, 1dc into first st, *3ch, 1dc into ch at tip of next Pyramid; rep from * ending last rep in centre of 10tch, turn.

**5th row:** 1ch, 1dc into first st, *work Pyramid, miss 3ch, 1dc into next dc; rep from * to end, miss tch, turn.

Rep 2nd, 3rd, 4th and 5th rows.

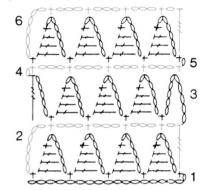

## Chevron Lattice

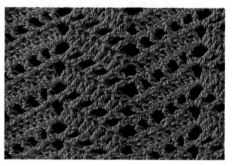

Multiple of 20 sts + 11.
(add 3 for base chain)

**Special Abbreviation**

**Tr cluster:** leaving last loop of each tr on hook work 1tr into next ch, miss 3ch, and work 1tr into next ch, then yo and draw through all 3 loops on hook.

**1st row** (wrong side): 1tr into 6th ch from hook, *[1ch, miss 1ch, 1tr into next ch] 3 times, 1ch, miss 1ch**, work [1tr, 3ch, 1tr] into next ch, [1ch, miss 1ch, 1tr into next ch] 3 times, 1ch, miss 1ch, work a tr cluster over next 1tr, 3ch and 1tr; rep from * ending last rep at **, work [1tr, 1ch, 1tr] into last ch, turn.

**2nd row:** 3ch (count as 1tr), 2tr into first st, *1tr into next ch sp, [1tr into next tr, 1tr into next ch sp] 3 times**, leaving last loop of each tr on hook work 1tr into next tr, miss tr cluster, work 1tr into next tr and complete as tr cluster, [1tr into next ch sp, 1tr into next tr] 3 times, 1tr into next ch, work [1tr, 3ch, 1tr] into next ch; rep from * ending last rep at **, work tr cluster over next 2 trs, miss tch, turn.

**3rd row:** 3ch, miss first 2 sts, 1tr into next st, *[1ch, miss 1tr, 1tr into next tr] 3 times**, 1ch, miss 1ch, work [1tr, 3ch, 1tr] into next ch, 1ch, miss 1ch, [1tr into next tr, 1ch, miss 1tr] 3 times, leaving last loop of each tr on hook work 1tr into next tr, miss 1tr, tr cluster and 1tr, work 1tr into next tr and complete as tr cluster; rep from * ending last rep at **, 1ch, miss 1tr, work [1tr, 1ch, 1tr] into top of tch, turn.

Rep 2nd and 3rd rows.

 Stitch Variations, Abbreviations and Symbols on pages 7 to 15.

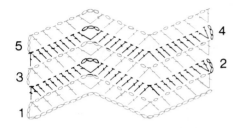

## Solomon's Knot

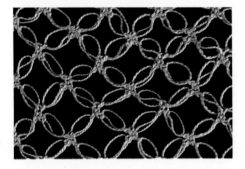

Multiple of 2 Solomon's Knots + 1.
(add 2 Solomon's Knots for base 'chain')

**Special Abbreviations**

**ESK (Edge Solomon's Knot):** these form the base 'chain' and edges of the fabric and are only two-thirds the length of MSK's.

**MSK (Main Solomon's Knot):** These form the main fabric and are half as long again as ESK's.

**Base 'chain':** 2ch, 1dc into 2nd ch from hook, now make a multiple of 2ESK's (say, 2cm), ending with 1MSK (say, 3cm).

**1st row:** 1dc into dc between 3rd and 4th loops from hook, *2MSK, miss 2 loops, 1dc into next dc; rep from * to end, turn.

**2nd row:** 2ESK and 1MSK, 1dc into dc between 4th and 5th loops from hook, *2MSK, miss 2 loops, 1dc into next dc; rep from * ending in top of ESK, turn.

Rep 2nd row.

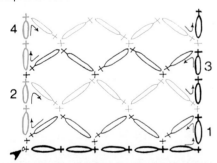

## Lacewing Network

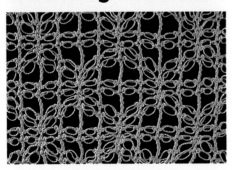

Multiple of 16 sts + 1.
(add 1 for base chain)

**Special Abbreviation**

**SK (Solomon's Knot):** loop approx 1.5cm.

**Note:** You may need to experiment with the number of ch in the base chain and length of loop, or even make the base 'chain' itself out of Knots.

**Base row** (right side): 1dc into 2nd ch from hook, *1SK, miss 3ch, 1dtr into next ch, 1SK, miss 3ch, 1 quad tr into next ch, 1SK, miss 3ch, 1dtr into next ch, 1SK, miss 3ch, 1dc into next ch; rep from * to end, turn.

**Commence Pattern**

**1st row:** 3ch, 1dc into 2nd ch from hook, *1SK, miss SK, 1tr into next st; rep from * to end, turn.

**2nd row:** 6ch, 1dc into 2nd ch from hook, *1SK, miss SK, 1dtr into next st, 1SK, miss SK, 1dc into next st, 1SK, miss SK, 1dtr into next st, 1SK, miss SK, 1 quad tr into next st; rep from * to end, turn.

Rep the last 2 rows once then work 1st row again.

**6th row:** 1ch, 1dc into first st, *1SK, miss SK, 1dtr into next st, 1SK, miss SK, 1 quad tr into next st, 1SK miss SK, 1dtr into next st, 1SK, miss SK, 1dc into next st; rep from * to end, turn.

**7th row:** As 1st row.

**8th row:** As 6th row.

Rep these 8 rows.

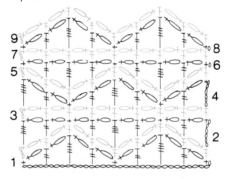

## Embossed Flower Network

Multiple of 24 sts + 4.
(add 4 for base chain)

**Note:** When working Embossed Flower always treat the various stitches and threads which form the four sides of the space as if they were the base ring of a Motif, i.e. always insert hook through centre of this 'ring' to make stitches.

**Base row** (right side): 1tr into 8th ch from hook, *2ch, miss 2ch, 1tr into each of next 4ch, [2ch, miss 2ch, 1tr into next ch] 3 times, 1tr into each of next 3ch, [2ch, miss 2ch, 1tr into next ch] twice; rep from * to end, turn.

**Commence Pattern**

**1st row:** 5ch (count as 1tr and 2ch), miss 2ch, 1tr into next st, *2tr into next 2ch sp, 1tr into next st, [2ch, miss 2 sts, 1tr into next st] twice, 2tr into next sp, 1tr into next st, [2ch, miss 2 sts, 1tr into next st] twice, 2tr into next sp, 1tr into next st, 2ch, miss 2ch, 1tr into next st; rep from * to end, turn.

**2nd row:** 3ch (count as 1tr), miss first st, 2tr into next 2ch sp, 1tr into next st, *[2ch, miss 2 sts, 1tr into next st] twice, 2tr into next sp, 1tr into next st, 2ch, miss 2tr, 1tr into next st. Now work Embossed Flower round space just completed, (see note above); with right side facing and working around anticlockwise, work 1dc into corner (top left), down left side work **3ch, 3tr, 3ch, 1dc into next corner** (bottom left), rep from ** to ** 3 more times, omitting dc at end of last rep and ending sl st to first dc, sl st to last tr made of main fabric. Continue working main fabric as follows: 2tr into next 2ch sp, 1tr into next st, [2ch, miss 2 sts, 1tr into next st] twice, 2tr into next 2ch sp, 1tr into next st; rep from * ending last rep in 3rd ch of tch, turn.

**3rd row:** As 1st row.

**4th row:** 5ch (count as 1tr and 2ch), miss 2ch, 1tr into next st, *2ch, miss 2 sts, 1tr into next st, 2tr into next 2ch sp, 1tr into next st, [2ch, miss 2 sts, 1tr into next st] 3 times, 2tr into next sp, 1tr into next st, [2ch, miss 2 sts, 1tr into next st] twice; rep from * ending last rep in 3rd ch of tch, turn.

**5th row:** 3ch (count as 1tr), miss first st, 2tr into next 2ch sp, 1tr into next st, *[2ch, miss 2 sts, 1tr into next st] twice, [2tr into next sp, 1tr into next st, 2ch, miss 2 sts, 1tr into next st] twice, 2tr into next sp, 1tr into next st, 2ch, miss 2ch, 1tr into next st, 2tr into next sp, 1tr into next st; rep from * ending last rep in 3rd ch of tch, turn.

**6th row:** 5ch (count as 1tr and 2ch), miss first 3 sts, 1tr into next st. Now work Embossed Flower round space just completed as in 3rd row. Continue working main fabric as follows: *2tr into next 2ch sp, 1tr into next st, [2ch, miss 2 sts, 1tr into next st] twice, 2tr into next sp, 1tr into next st, [2ch, miss 2 sts, 1tr into next st] twice, 2tr into next sp, 1tr into next st, 2ch, miss 2 sts, 1tr into next st. Now work Embossed Flower round space just completed as before; rep from * ending last rep of main fabric in top of tch, turn.

**7th row:** As 5th row.
**8th row:** As 4th row.
Rep these 8 rows.

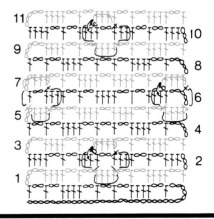

# Openwork and Lace Patterns

## Offset Filet Network

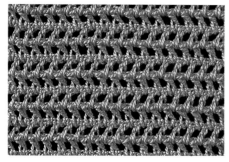

Multiple of 2 sts.
(add 3 for base chain)

**1st row** (right side): 1tr into 6th ch from hook, *1ch, miss 1ch, 1tr into next ch; rep from * ending 1tr into last ch, turn.

**2nd row:** 4ch (count as 1tr and 1ch), miss first 2 sts, 1tr into next ch sp, *1ch, miss 1tr, 1tr into next sp; rep from * to tch, 1tr into next ch, turn.

Rep 2nd row.

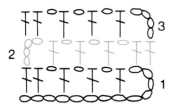

## String Network

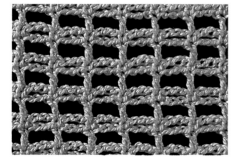

Multiple of 4 sts + 1.
(add 5 for base chain)

**1st row** (right side): 1tr into 10th ch from hook, *3ch, miss 3ch, 1tr into next ch; rep from * to end, turn.

**2nd row:** 1ch, 1dc into first st, *3ch, miss 3ch, 1dc into next tr; rep from * ending 3ch, 1dc into 4th ch of tch, turn.

**3rd row:** 6ch (count as 1tr and 3ch), miss first st and 3ch, 1tr into next dc, *3ch, miss 3ch, 1tr into next dc; rep from * to end, turn.

Rep 2nd and 3rd rows.

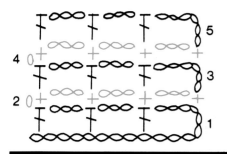

## Popcorn and Treble Squares

Multiple of 8 sts + 3.
(add 2 for base chain)

**Note**
Popcorns occur on both right and wrong side rows. Be sure to push them all out on the right side of the fabric as you complete them.

**1st row** (right side): 5tr Popcorn into 4th ch from hook, *1tr into each of next 7ch, 5tr Popcorn into next ch; rep from * ending 1tr into last ch, turn.

**2nd row:** 4ch (count as 1tr and 1ch), miss first st and next Popcorn, 1tr into next st, *2ch, miss 2 sts, 5tr Popcorn into next st, 2ch, miss 2 sts, 1tr into next st, 1ch, miss next Popcorn, 1tr into next st; rep from * ending last rep in tch, turn.

**3rd row:** 4ch (count as 1tr and 1ch), miss first st and next ch, 1tr into next st, *1ch, miss 1ch, 5tr Popcorn into next ch, 1ch, miss Popcorn, 5tr Popcorn into next ch, [1ch, miss next ch, 1tr into next st] twice; rep from * ending last rep in tch, turn.

**4th row:** 4ch (count as 1tr and 1ch), miss first st and next ch, 1tr into next st, *2ch, 5tr Popcorn into ch sp between next 2 Popcorns, 2ch, 1tr into next tr, 1ch, miss 1ch, 1tr into next st; rep from * ending last rep in tch, turn.

**5th row:** 3ch (count as 1tr), miss first st, 5tr Popcorn into next ch, *1tr into next tr, 1tr into each of next 2ch, 1tr into next Popcorn, 1tr into each of next 2ch, 1tr into next tr, 5tr Popcorn into next ch; rep from * ending 1tr into next ch of tch, turn.

Rep 2nd, 3rd, 4th and 5th rows.

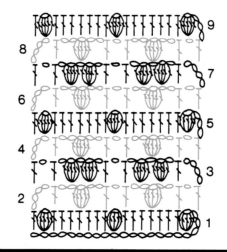

## Picot Ridge Stitch

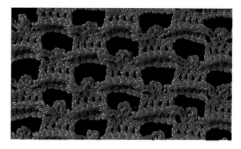

Multiple of 10 sts + 7.
(add 2 for base chain)

**1st row** (right side): Miss 3ch (count as 1tr), *1tr into each of next 5ch, 3ch, miss 2ch, [1dc, 4ch, 1dc] into next ch, 3ch, miss 2ch; rep from * ending 1tr into last ch, turn.

**2nd row:** 8ch (count as 1tr and 5ch), miss first st and next 3ch arch, *1tr/rf round each of next 5 sts, 5ch, miss next 3 arches; rep from * ending 1tr/rf round each of last 5trs, 1tr into top of tch, turn.

**3rd row:** 6ch, miss first 3 sts, *[1dc, 4ch, 1dc] into next st, 3ch, miss 2 sts, 1tr into each of next 5ch**, 3ch, miss 2 sts; rep from * ending last rep at **, 1tr into next ch of tch, turn.

**4th row:** 3ch (count as 1tr), miss first st, *1tr/rf round each of next 5 sts, 5ch**, miss next 3 arches; rep from * ending last rep at **, miss next 2 arches, 1tr into tch arch, turn.

**5th row:** 3ch (count as 1tr), miss first st, *1tr into each of next 5ch, 3ch, [1dc, 4ch, 1dc] into next st, 3ch, miss 2 sts; rep from * ending 1tr into top of tch, turn.

Rep 2nd, 3rd, 4th and 5th rows.

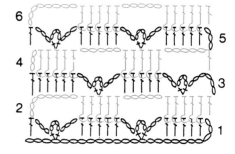

## Fancy Picot Stitch

Multiple of 10 sts + 1.
(add 2 for base chain)

**1st row** (right side): Miss 3ch (count as 1tr), *1tr into each of next 2ch, work a picot of [3ch, insert hook down through top of last st made and sl st to close], [1ch, miss 1ch,

Stitch Variations, Abbreviations and Symbols on pages 7 to 15.

# Openwork and Lace Patterns

1tr into next ch, picot] twice, 1ch, miss 1ch, 1tr into each of next 2ch**, 1ch, miss 1ch; rep from * ending last rep at **, 1tr into last ch, turn.

**2nd row:** 3ch (count as 1tr), miss first st, *1tr into each of next 2 sts, [picot, 1ch, miss next ch and picot, 1tr into next tr] 3 times, 1tr into next tr**, 1ch, miss 1ch; rep from * ending last rep at **, 1tr into top of tch, turn.

Rep 2nd row.

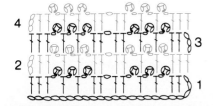

## Squares and Ladders

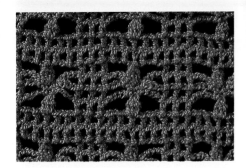

Multiple of 16 sts + 5.
(add 3 for base chain)

**Base row** (right side): 1tr into 6th ch from hook, *1ch, miss 1ch, 1tr into next ch; rep from * to end, turn.

**Commence Pattern**

**1st row:** 4ch (count as 1tr and 1ch), miss first st and next ch, 1tr into next tr, 1ch, miss 1ch, 1tr into next tr, *5ch, miss 5 sts, tr3tog into next tr, 5ch, miss 5 sts, 1tr into next tr, [1ch, miss 1ch, 1tr into next st] twice; rep from * ending last rep in tch, turn.

**2nd row:** 4ch (count as 1tr and 1ch), miss first st and next ch, 1tr into next tr, 1ch, miss 1ch, 1tr into next tr, *4ch, 1dc into 5ch arch, miss cluster, 1dc into next 5ch arch, 4ch, 1tr into next tr, [1ch, miss 1ch, 1tr into next st] twice; rep from * ending last rep in tch, turn.

**3rd row:** 4ch (count as 1tr and 1ch), miss first st and next ch, 1tr into next tr, 1ch, miss 1ch, 1tr into next tr, *4ch, 1dc into 4ch arch, 1dc between 2dc, 1dc into next 4ch arch, 4ch, 1tr into next tr, [1ch, miss 1ch, 1tr into next st] twice; rep from * ending last rep in tch, turn.

**4th row:** 4ch (counts as 1tr and 1ch), miss first st and next ch, 1tr into next tr, 1ch, miss 1ch, 1tr into next tr, *5ch, tr3tog into 2nd of 3dc, 5ch, 1tr into next tr, [1ch, miss 1ch, 1tr into next st] twice; rep from * ending last rep in tch, turn.

**5th row:** 4ch (count as 1tr and 1ch), miss first st and next ch, 1tr into next tr, *1ch, miss 1ch, 1tr into next st; rep from * ending last rep in tch, turn.

**6th row:** As 5th row.

Rep these 6 rows.

Rep these 6 rows.

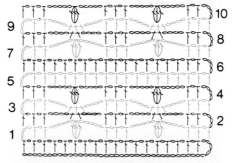

## Shell Network

Multiple of 8 sts + 3.
(add 3 for base chain)

**1st row** (right side): 1tr into 6th ch from hook, *miss 2ch, 5tr into next ch, miss 2ch, 1tr into next ch, 1ch, miss 1ch, 1tr into next ch; rep from * to end, turn.

**2nd row:** 4ch (count as 1tr and 1ch), miss first st and next ch, 1tr into next tr, *miss 2tr, 5tr into next tr, miss 2tr, 1tr into next tr, 1ch, miss 1ch, 1tr into next tr; rep from * ending last rep in 2nd ch of tch, turn.

Rep 2nd row.

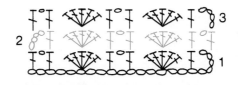

## Sieve Stitch

Multiple of 2 sts + 1.
(add 1 for base chain)

**Base row** (wrong side): 1dc into 2nd ch from hook, *1ch, miss 1ch, 1dc into next ch; rep from * to end, turn.

**Commence Pattern**

**1st row:** 1ch, miss 1 st, *2dc into next ch sp, miss next dc; rep from * until 1 ch sp remains, 1dc into last ch sp, 1dc into next dc, miss tch, turn.

**2nd row:** 1ch, miss 1 st, 1dc into next st, *1ch, miss 1 st, 1dc into next dc; rep from * until only tch remains, 1dc into tch, turn.

**3rd row:** 1ch, miss first 2 sts, *2dc into next ch sp, miss next dc; rep from * until only tch remains, 2dc into tch, turn.

**4th row:** As 2nd row.

**5th row:** 1ch, 1dc into first st, *miss next dc, 2dc into next ch sp; rep from * ending last rep in tch, turn.

**6th row:** 1ch, miss 1 st, *1dc into next dc, 1ch, miss 1dc; rep from * ending 1dc into tch, turn.

**7th row:** 1ch, miss 1 st, 1dc into next ch sp, *miss 1dc, 2dc into next sp; rep from * ending miss last dc, 1dc into tch, turn.

**8th row:** 1ch, 1dc into first st, *1ch, miss 1dc, 1dc into next st; rep from * to end working last st into top of tch, turn.

Rep these 8 rows.

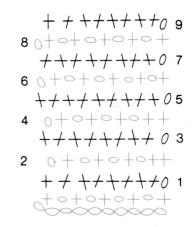

## Winkle Picot Stitch

Multiple of 3 sts + 2.
(add 4 for base chain)

**1st row** (right side): 1dc into 6th ch from hook, *miss 1ch, 1dc into next ch, 3ch, 1dc into next ch; rep from * until 3ch remain, miss 1ch, 1dc into next ch, 2ch, 1htr into last ch, turn.

**2nd row:** 4ch, 1dc into next 2ch sp, *[1dc, 3ch, 1dc] into next 3ch arch; rep from * ending [1dc, 2ch, 1htr] into last ch arch, turn.

Rep 2nd row.

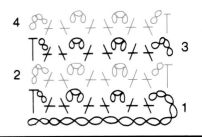

# Openwork and Lace Patterns

## Half Treble V Stitch

Multiple of 2 sts.
(add 2 for base chain)

**1st row** (right side): [1htr, 1ch, 1htr] into 4th ch from hook, *miss 1ch, [1htr, 1ch, 1htr] into next ch; rep from * until 2ch remain, miss 1ch, 1htr into last ch, turn.

**2nd row:** 2ch, *miss 2 sts, [1htr, 1ch, 1htr] into next ch sp; rep from * to last ch sp, miss 1 st, 1htr into tch, turn.

Rep 2nd row.

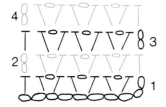

## Treble V Stitch

Multiple of 2 sts.
(add 2 for base chain)

**1st row** (right side): 2tr into 4th ch from hook, *miss 1ch, 2tr into next ch; rep from * to last 2ch, miss 1ch, 1tr into last ch, turn.

**2nd row:** 3ch, *miss 2 sts, 2tr between 2nd missed st and next st; rep from * to last 2 sts, miss 1 st, 1tr into top of tch, turn.

Rep 2nd row.

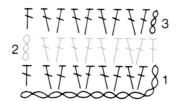

## Offset V Stitch

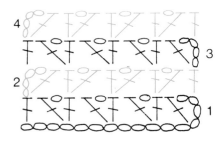

Multiple of 3 sts + 1.
(add 3 for base chain)

**1st row** (right side): 1tr into 4th ch from hook, *miss 2ch, work a V st of [1tr, 1ch, 1tr] into next ch; rep from * to last 3ch, miss 2ch, 1tr into last ch, turn.

**2nd row:** 4ch, 1tr into first st, *V st into 2nd tr of next V st; rep from * until 1tr and tch remain, miss 1tr and 1ch, 1tr into next ch, turn.

Rep 2nd row.

## Twin V Stitch

Multiple of 4 sts + 2.
(add 2 for base chain)

**1st row** (right side): 2tr into 5th ch from hook, 2tr into next ch, *miss 2ch, 2tr into each of next 2ch; rep from * to last 2ch, miss 1ch, 1tr into last ch, turn.

**2nd row:** 3ch, *miss 2 sts, 2tr into each of next 2 sts; rep from * to last 2 sts, miss 1 st, 1tr into tch, turn.

Rep 2nd row.

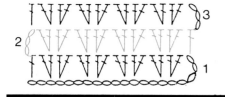

## Three-and-Two Stitch

Multiple of 6 sts + 2.
(add 2 for base chain)

**1st row** (right side): Work a V st of [1tr, 1ch, 1tr] into 5th ch from hook, *miss 2ch, 3tr into next ch, miss 2ch, work a V st into next ch; rep from * to last 5ch, miss 2ch, 3tr into next ch, miss 1ch, 1tr into last ch, turn.

**2nd row:** 3ch, *miss 2 sts, work 3tr into centre tr of next 3tr, work a V st into ch sp at centre of next V st; rep from * ending 1tr into top of tch, turn.

**3rd row:** 3ch, *V st into sp of next V st, 3tr into centre tr of next 3tr; rep from * ending 1tr into top of tch, turn.

Rep 2nd and 3rd rows.

## Basket Stitch

Multiple of 3 sts + 2.
(add 2 for base chain)

**1st row** (wrong side): Work a V st of [1tr, 1ch, 1tr] into 5th ch from hook, *miss 2ch, work V st into next ch; rep from * to last 2ch,

Stitch Variations, Abbreviations and Symbols on pages 7 to 15.

miss 1ch, 1tr into last ch, turn.

**2nd row:** 3ch, miss 2 sts, work a double V st of [2tr, 1ch, 2tr] into ch sp at centre of V st, *1ch, miss next V st, work a Double V st into sp at centre of next V st; rep from * leaving last loop of last tr of last Double V st on hook and working it together with 1tr into top of tch, turn.

**3rd row:** 3ch, work a V st into each sp to end finishing with 1tr into top of tch, turn.

**4th row:** 3ch, 1tr into first st, *1ch, miss next V st, work a Double V st into sp at centre of next V st; rep from * until 1 V st remains, 1ch, miss V st, 2tr into top of tch, turn.

**5th row:** As 3rd row.

Rep 2nd, 3rd, 4th and 5th rows.

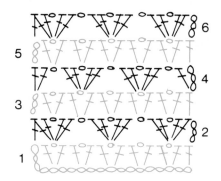

## Empress Stitch

Multiple of 18 sts + 1.
(add 3 for base chain)

**Note**

Popcorns occur on both right and wrong side rows alternately. Be sure to push them all out on the right side of the fabric as you complete them.

**1st row** (wrong side): 1tr into 4th ch from hook, *miss 2ch, work a V st of [1tr, 1ch, 1tr] into next ch; rep from * to last 3ch, miss 2ch, 2tr into last ch, turn.

**2nd row:** 3ch, 1tr into first st, V st into sp at centre of next V st, *5ch, miss next V st, 1dc into sp at centre of next V st, 5ch, miss next V st**, [V st into sp at centre of next V st] 3 times; rep from * ending last rep at **, V st into sp at centre of last V st, 2tr into top of tch, turn.

**3rd row:** 3ch, 1tr into first st, V st into sp at centre of next V st, *[3ch, 1dc into next 5ch arch] twice, 3ch**, [V st into sp at centre of next V st] 3 times; rep from * ending last rep at **, V st into sp of last V st, 2tr into top of tch, turn.

**4th row:** 3ch, 1tr into first st, V st into sp at centre of next V st, *miss next 3ch arch, [5tr Popcorn, 2ch, 5tr Popcorn, 2ch, 5tr Popcorn] into next 3ch arch, miss next 3ch arch**, [V st into sp at centre of next V st] 3 times; rep from * ending last rep at **, V st into sp at centre of last V st, 2tr into top of tch, turn.

**5th row:** 3ch, 1tr into first st, V st into sp at centre of next V st, *[3ch, 1dc into next 2ch sp] twice, 3ch**, [V st into sp at centre of next V st] 3 times; rep from * ending last rep at **, V st into sp at centre of last V st, 2tr into top of tch, turn.

**6th row:** 3ch, 1tr into first st, V st into sp at centre of next V st, *[V st into 2nd ch of next 3ch arch] 3 times**, [V st into sp at centre of next V st] 3 times; rep from * ending last rep at **, V st into sp at centre of last V st, 2tr into top of tch, turn.

Rep 2nd, 3rd, 4th, 5th and 6th rows.

## Noughts and Crosses Stitch

Multiple of 2 sts + 1.
(add 3 for base chain)

**1st row** (right side): 1tr into 6th ch from hook, *1ch, miss 1ch, 1tr into next ch; rep from * to end, turn.

**2nd row:** 3ch, miss next ch sp, work 2 crossed stitches as follows: 1tr forward into next ch sp, 1tr back into ch sp just missed going behind forward tr so as not to catch it, *1tr forward into next unoccupied ch sp, 1tr back into previous ch sp going behind forward tr as before; rep from * to end when last forward tr occupies tch, 1tr into next ch, turn.

**3rd row:** 1ch (counts as 1dc), 1dc into first st, 1dc into next and each st to end working last st into top of tch, turn.

**4th row:** 4ch (counts as 1tr and 1ch), miss 2 sts, 1tr into next st, *1ch, miss 1 st, 1tr into next st; rep from * ending last rep in tch, turn.

Rep 2nd, 3rd and 4th rows.

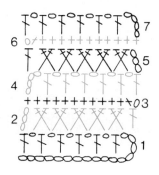

## Fantail Stitch

Multiple of 10 sts + 1.
(add 1 for base chain)

**1st row** (right side): 1dc into 2nd ch from hook, 1dc into next ch, *miss 3ch, work a Fan of [3tr, 1ch, 3tr] into next ch, miss 3ch, 1dc into next ch**, 1ch, miss 1ch, 1dc into next ch; rep from * ending last rep at **, 1dc into last ch, turn.

**2nd row:** 2ch (count as 1htr), 1htr into first st, *3ch, 1dc into ch sp at centre of next Fan, 3ch**, work a V st of [1htr, 1ch, 1htr] into next sp; rep from * ending last rep at **, 2htr into last dc, miss tch, turn.

**3rd row:** 3ch, 3tr into first st, *1dc into next 3ch arch, 1ch, 1dc into next arch**, work a Fan into sp at centre of next V st; rep from * ending last rep at **, 4tr into top of tch, turn.

**4th row:** 1ch, 1dc into first st, *3ch, V st into next sp, 3ch, 1dc into sp at centre of next Fan; rep from * ending last rep into top of tch, turn.

**5th row:** 1ch, 1dc into first st, *1dc into next arch, Fan into sp at centre of next V st, 1dc into next arch**, 1ch; rep from * ending last rep at **, 1dc into last dc, miss tch, turn.

Rep 2nd, 3rd, 4th and 5th rows.

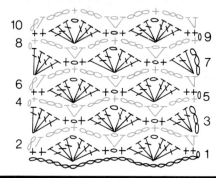

# Openwork and Lace Patterns

## Flying Shell Stitch

Multiple of 4 sts + 1.
(add 1 for base chain)

**1st row** (right side): Work a Flying Shell (called FS) of [1dc, 3ch, 3tr] into 2nd ch from hook, *miss 3ch, 1FS into next ch; rep from * to last 4ch, miss 3ch, 1dc into last ch, turn.

**2nd row:** 3ch, 1tr into first st, *miss 3 sts, 1dc into top of 3ch**, work a V st of [1tr, 1ch, 1tr] into next dc; rep from * ending last rep at **, 2tr into last dc, miss tch, turn.

**3rd row:** 3ch, 3tr into first st, miss next st, *1FS into next dc, miss next V st; rep from * ending 1dc into last dc, 3ch, tr2tog over last tr and top of tch, turn.

**4th row:** 1ch (counts as 1dc), *V st into next dc, miss 3 sts, 1dc into top of 3ch; rep from * to end, turn.

**5th row:** 1ch, FS into first st, *miss next V st, FS into next dc; rep from * ending miss last V st, 1dc into tch, turn.

Rep 2nd, 3rd, 4th and 5th rows.

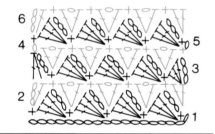

## Picot V Stitch

Multiple of 3 sts + 1.
(add 2 for base chain)

**1st row** (right side): Miss 3ch (count as 1tr), 1tr into next ch, miss 1ch, 1tr into next ch, work a picot of [3ch, insert hook down through top of tr just made and work a sl st], 1tr into same ch as last tr, *miss 2ch, [1tr, picot, 1tr] into next ch; rep from * to last 3ch, miss 2ch, 1tr into last ch, turn.

**2nd row:** 3ch (count as 1tr), 1tr into first st, *miss 1tr and Picot, [1tr, picot, 1tr] into next tr; rep from * to last 2 sts, miss next tr, 1tr into top of tch, turn.

Rep 2nd row.

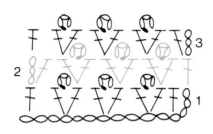

## Pebble Lace Stitch

Multiple of 4 sts + 3.
(add 1 for base chain)

**Notes**

Close dtr7tog clusters with 1ch drawn tightly, (this does not count as part of following ch loop).

Clusters always occur on wrong side rows. Be sure to push them all out to the back (right side) of the fabric as you complete them.

**1st row** (wrong side): 1dc into 2nd ch from hook, *2ch, miss 1ch, work dtr7tog into next ch, 2ch, miss 1ch, 1dc into next ch; rep from * to last 2ch, 2ch, miss 1ch, 1htr into last ch, turn.

**2nd row:** 1ch, 1dc into first st, *3ch, 1dc into next cluster; rep from * ending 1ch, 1htr into last dc, miss tch, turn.

**3rd row:** 4ch, miss first htr and ch, 1dc into next dc, *2ch, dtr7tog into 2nd of next 3ch, 2ch, 1dc into next dc; rep from * to end, miss tch, turn.

**4th row:** 3ch, miss first st and 2ch, 1dc into next cluster, *3ch, 1dc into next cluster; rep from * ending 3ch, 1dc into last 4ch arch, turn.

**5th row:** 1ch, 1dc into first st, *2ch, dtr7tog into 2nd of next 3ch, 2ch, 1dc into next dc; rep from * ending 2ch, miss 1ch, 1htr into next ch of tch, turn.

Rep 2nd, 3rd, 4th and 5th rows.

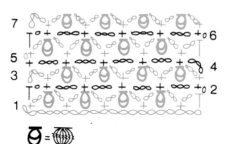

## Plain Trellis Stitch

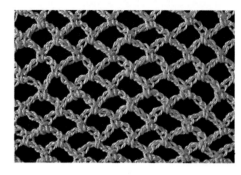

Multiple of 4 sts + 3.
(add 3 for base chain)

**1st row:** 1dc into 6th ch from hook, *5ch, miss 3ch, 1dc into next ch; rep from * to end, turn.

**2nd row:** *5ch, 1dc into next 5ch arch; rep from * to end, turn.

Rep 2nd row.

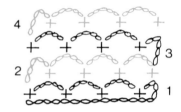

## Picot Trellis Stitch

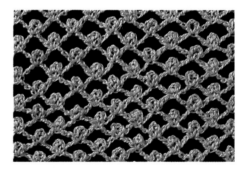

Multiple of 5 sts + 1.
(add 1 for base chain)

**1st row:** 1dc into 2nd ch from hook, *5ch, miss 4ch, 1dc into next ch; rep from * to end, turn.

**2nd row:** *5ch, work a picot of [1dc, 3ch, 1dc] into 3rd ch of next 5ch arch; rep from * ending 2ch, 1tr into last dc, miss tch, turn.

**3rd row:** 1ch, 1dc into first st, *5ch, miss picot, picot into 3rd ch of next 5ch arch; rep from * ending 5ch, miss picot, 1dc into tch arch, turn.

Rep 2nd and 3rd rows.

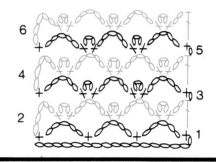

Stitch Variations, Abbreviations and Symbols on pages 7 to 15.

# Filet Charts

Filet crochet is based on a simple network or 'ground' made of treble and chain stitches. Patterns are therefore usually presented in the form of squared charts. Designs of all kinds - flowers, geometric patterns, lettering and even whole scenes - can be created by 'filling in' some of the squares or spaces with trebles instead of chains.

Like stitch diagrams, charts are read from the bottom to the top, right side rows from right to left and wrong side rows from left to right. Each open square represents an open space whilst a filled-in square represents a 'block' of stitches. Every row starts with three chain (count as one treble), bringing you to the correct height and balancing the pattern.

The basis of filet crochet is rectangular. Ideally each space or block should be square, but this is hard to achieve because of variations in tension. Small variations to the ratio between height and width can be made by changing the way you hold the yarn or hook. To test your tension first work a swatch based on sample 'b' below. This is worked so that each open square on the chart represents a space formed by two chain and a treble. The other edge of the space is formed by the last stitch of the preceeding space or block or by the three chain at the beginning of the row. When a square is filled the two chain space is replaced by two trebles making a single block of three trebles. Each additional block therefore adds three trebles, so two blocks together (with a space either side), appear as seven trebles, and three blocks, as ten trebles.

If you cannot adjust the ratio between height and width sufficiently by changing the way you hold the work it may be necessary to change the size of the blocks and spaces. A space could be reduced to a single chain and a treble with a two treble block (sample 'a'), or enlarged to a three chain and one treble space with a four treble block (sample 'c'). The photographs of the samples show the differences between the three variations.

The worked samples in this section have been made following the style of sample

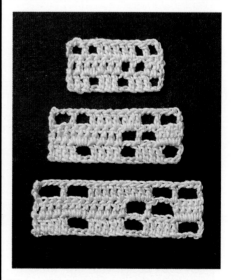

'b', but whatever your tension look at the other methods as there may be times you would wish to use these purely for their decorative effect.

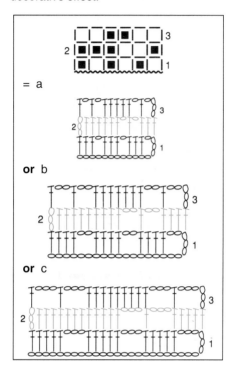

= a

or b

or c

# Starting Chain

When working as sample 'b', the number of chain required to start filet crochet is calculated by multiplying the number of squares required by three. Add five chain if the first square to be worked is a space or three chain if the first square to be worked is a block (see diagram 'b above').

To work samples 'a' or 'c', multiply the number of squares by two or four, adding four or six chain for a space and three chain for a block (see diagrams 'a' and 'c').

# Lacets and Bars

Variations on blocks and spaces include 'V' shapes known as lacets, and longer chains known as bars.

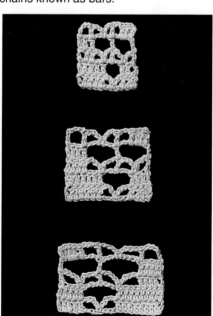

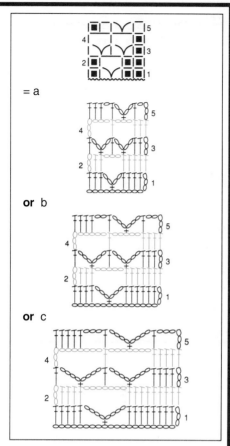

= a

or b

or c

The diagrams above show the stitches and their positioning for each variation.

# Increasing and Decreasing

In filet crochet increases are usually made in whole squares rather than stitches. If increases are made at the beginning of rows and decreases at the ends of rows no special techniques are required as the following stitch diagram shows.

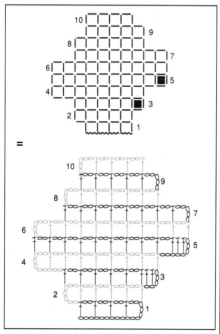

=

When increases are needed at the end of a row or decreases at the beginning of a row, the following techniques should be used.

# Filet Crochet

## To increase a space at the end of a row

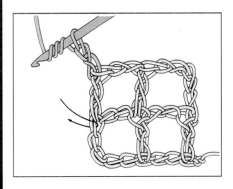

1. Work two chain, then work a triple treble into same place as previous treble.

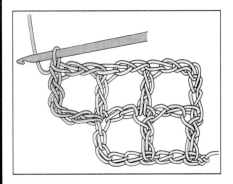

2. The triple treble makes the outer edges of the increased space.

## To increase a block at the end of a row

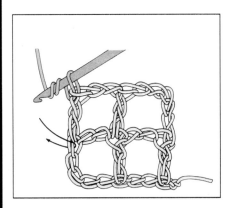

1. Work a double treble into same place as previous treble.

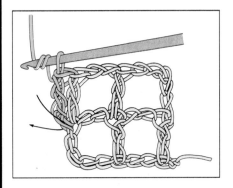

2. Then work [a double treble into bottom segment of previous double treble] twice.

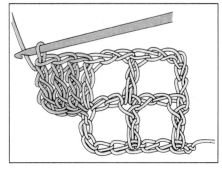

3. Thus making an increased block.

## To decrease at the beginning of a row

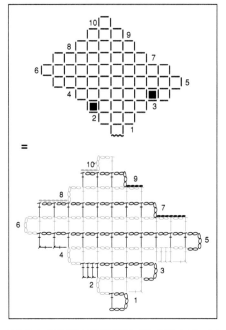

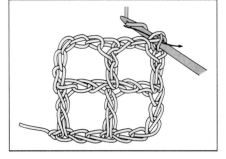

1. Turn work. Slip stitch into top of last treble worked, then into each of next two chain (or top of trebles if last square in previous row is a block) and into top of next treble.

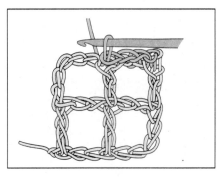

2. Hook is in position to commence row.

## Using Filet Patterns

The patterns in this book can be used exactly as they are to produce fabrics with all-over patterns, borders, insertions and motifs. Different effects can be achieved by working the charts downwards or sideways or by repeating or combining designs. Graph paper should be used to plot out any changes.

## Key

☐| = Block

|■| = Space

|☐| = Bar

|Y| = Lacet

## Pressing and Finishing Filet

The feature of Filet which distinguishes it from other styles of crochet is its rectangular appearance. For information on how to press and finish your filet crochet see the general instructions on page 12 but remember, at every stage, to check that all the vertical and horizontal lines of the work are laying at right-angles. After removing the pins and while the work is still quite damp, use your fingertips to gently ease the edges into perfectly straight lines.

Filet crochet is often used for borders, edgings and insertions on items like tablecloths and tray mats. The crochet piece is sewn on to a piece of fabric. Firstly turn under the raw edges to form a hem, and slip-stitch in place. Then whip stitch the crochet piece to the outer fold of the fabric, (see Picture Frame on page 97).

# Filet Crochet

## Mitre Block

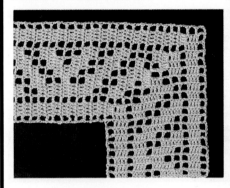

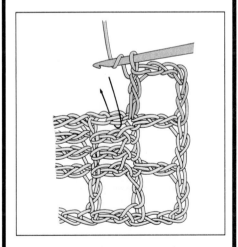

Rep these 18 rows to adjust length.

Direction of first row.

Start and finish here.

### Turning corners

Following chart work short rows to corner, then turn piece and work into the side of completed stitches.

It is important to remember when working a mitred corner that the final row, before changing direction, should be worked towards the the inner edge so that the yarn is in the correct position to turn and work at right angles to the edge.

Join the start and finish together with a neat seam.

## Space Race

Rep these 2 squares
Rep these 2 rows.

## Cross Over

Rep these 4 squares
Rep these 2 rows.

## Gull Wings

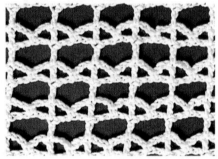

Rep these 2 squares
Rep these 2 rows.

## Chequers

Rep these 4 squares
Rep these 4 rows.

## Square Cross

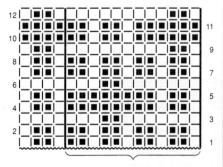

Rep these 12 squares
Rep these 12 rows.

## Penta Point

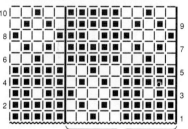

Rep these 10 squares
Rep these 10 rows.

# Filet Crochet

## Swept Back

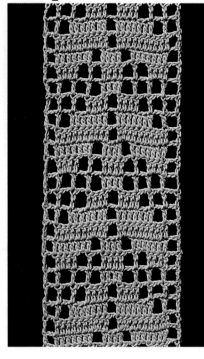

## Extra Line

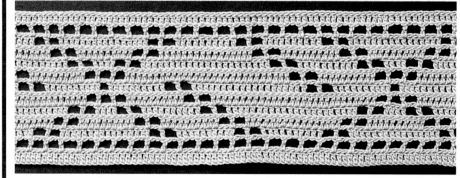

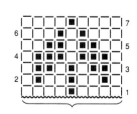

9 squares

Rep 2nd to 7th rows.

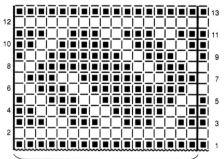

Rep these 17 squares

## Sunburst

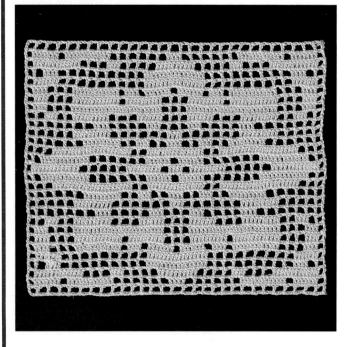

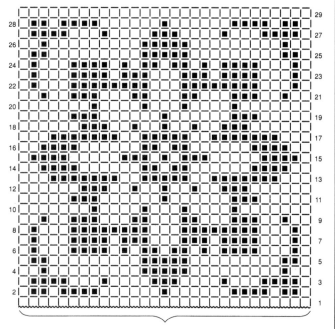

29 squares

## Double Hook

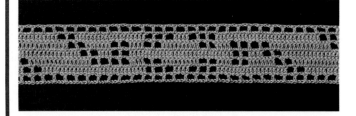

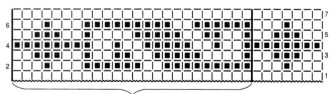

Rep these 24 squares

For more information and key to Filet Symbols see pages 89-90.

# Filet Crochet

## Icicle

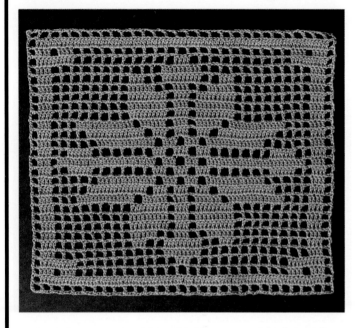

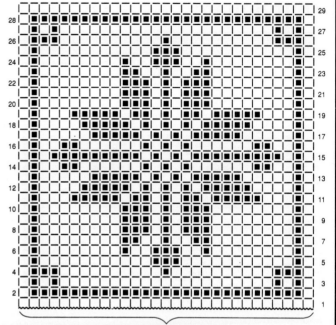

29 squares

## Board Games

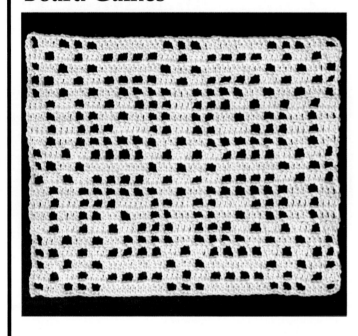

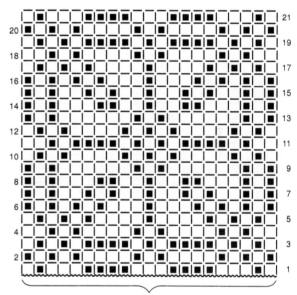

21 squares

## Love Birds

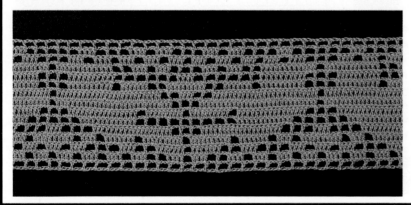

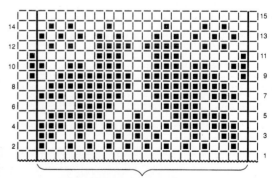

Rep these 22 squares

# Filet Crochet

## Four Square

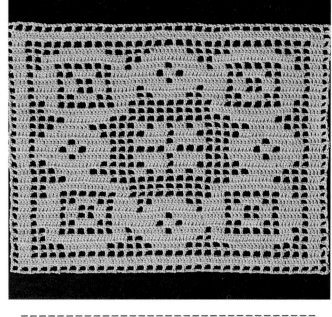

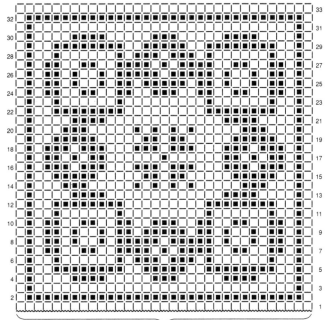

33 squares

## Falling Leaves

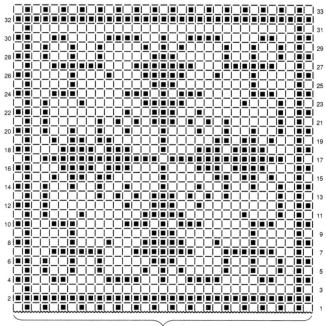

33 squares

## Bookmark

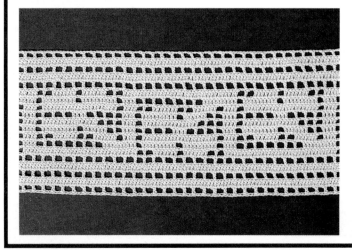

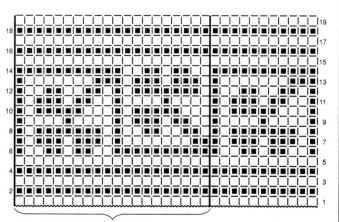

Rep these 20 squares

For more information and key to Filet symbols see pages 89-90.

## Floral Accent

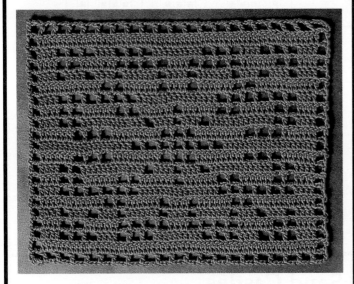

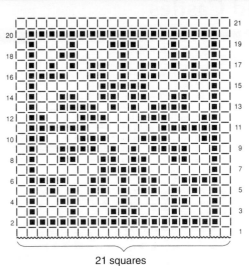

21 squares

## Hollow Shape

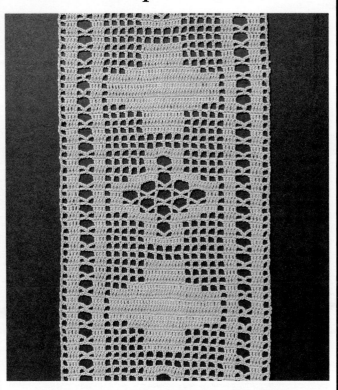

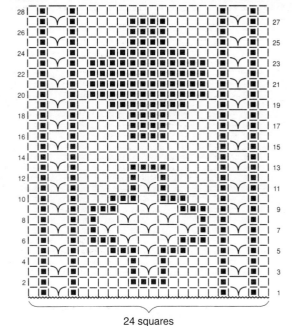

24 squares

Rep these 28 rows.

## Even Border

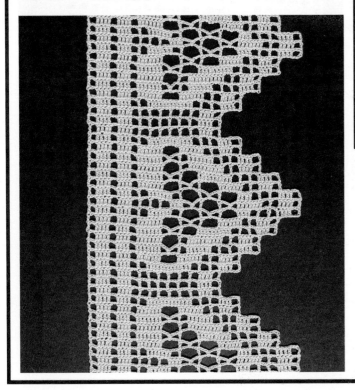

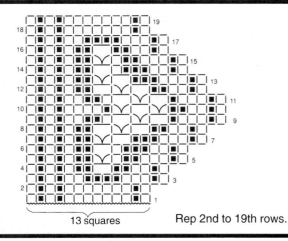

13 squares

Rep 2nd to 19th rows.

# Filet Crochet

## Union Flag

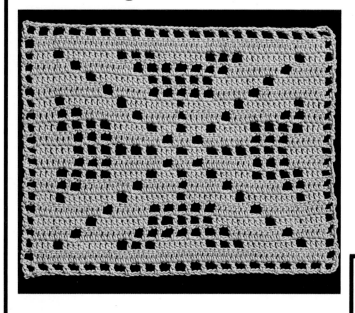

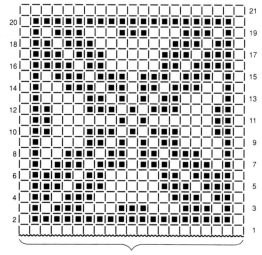

21 squares

## Poppy Seed

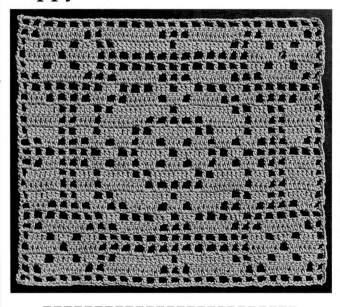

## Sand Castles

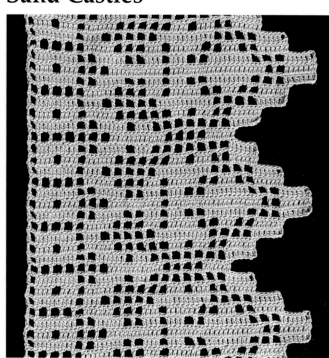

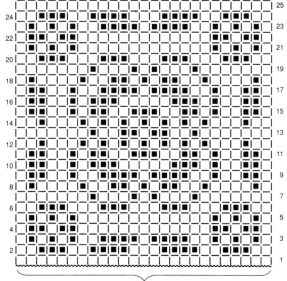

25 squares

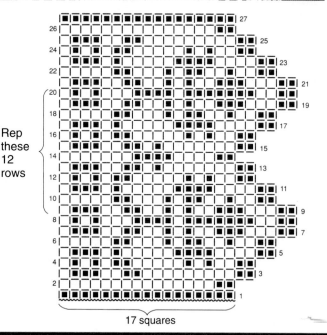

Rep these 12 rows

17 squares

For more information and key to Filet symbols see pages 89–90.

# Filet Crochet

## Pennants I

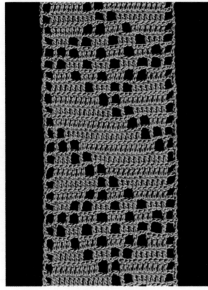

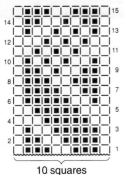

10 squares

Rep 2nd to 15th rows.

## Pennants II

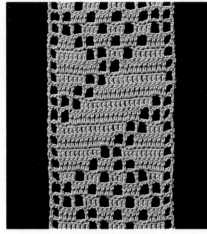

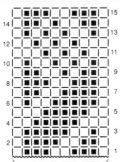

10 squares

Rep 2nd to 15th rows.

## Picture Frame

Work first 10 rows of whole diagram, then work the 10 squares of right hand side of 11th row. Continue on right hand side only, finishing with a row as 35th row. Do not turn but make a chain for base of centre top (a multiple of 14 + 11 squares). Break yarn, rejoin at X and work left side to match right but finishing on a row as 36th row. Do not turn but continue in pattern across chain already made (taking care that the chain is not twisted), then work 36th row across right side to end. Complete remaining 9 rows.

If preferred, edging may be worked starting and ending at line A with 10 squares, working first row in direction of arrow and making mitred corner at line B (see page 91).

See page 90 for attaching to fabric.

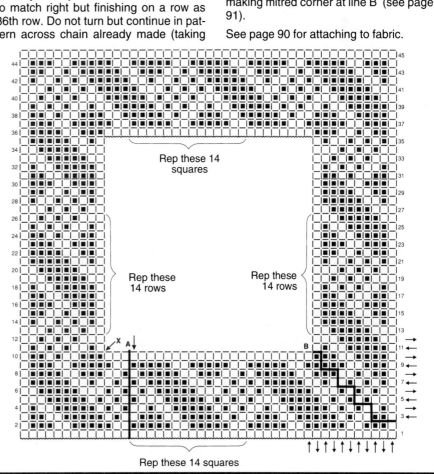

Rep these 14 squares

Rep these 14 rows

Rep these 14 rows

Rep these 14 squares

# Filet Crochet

## Filet Crochet Lace

☐ = space (2ch)
⌐ = bar
⋃ = lacet
⊡ = block

## Greek Key Frieze

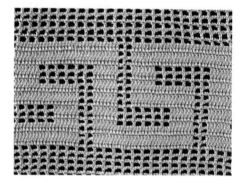

**Base Row**
Multiple of 3 sts per square + 1
Pattern Repeat = 12 squares

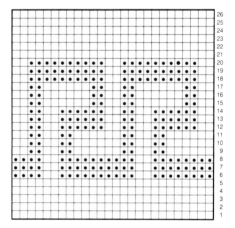

## Alternating Tiles

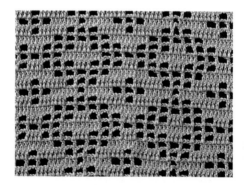

**Base Row**
Multiple of 3 sts per square + 1
Pattern Repeat = 8 squares

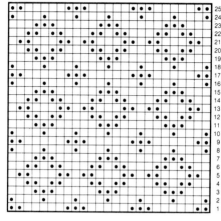

## Southern Cross

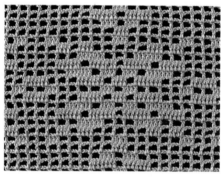

**Base Row**
Multiple of 3 sts per square + 1
Pattern Repeat = 15 squares

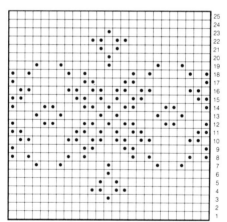

## Orchid Blooms

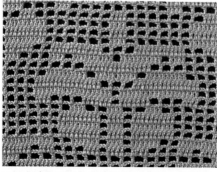

**Base Row**
Multiple of 3 sts per square + 1
Pattern Repeat = 22 squares

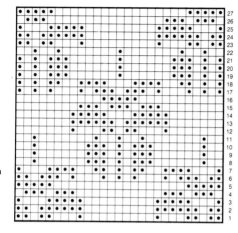

## Blocks and Lacets

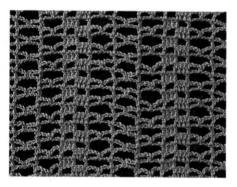

**Base Row**
Multiple of 3 sts per square + 1
Pattern Repeat = 8 squares wide by 2 squares deep

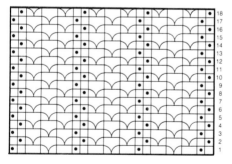

**Hint:** Larger items, such as curtains and bedspreads, can easily be made in Filet. Work a small piece of alternate blocks and spaces to ascertain the number of blocks and rows to the inch. From that you can calculate the number of squares you will need in Filet to cover the area you require and this can then be drawn onto graph paper. Any of the designs suggested here can then be added, either singly or in repeats, or you can design your own exclusive pattern!

For more information and key to Filet Symbols see pages 89 and 90.

# Filet Crochet

## Flowerpots

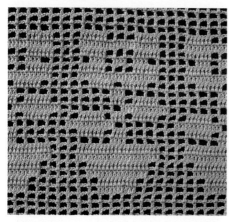

**Base Row**
Multiple of 3 sts per square + 1
Pattern Repeat = 10 squares

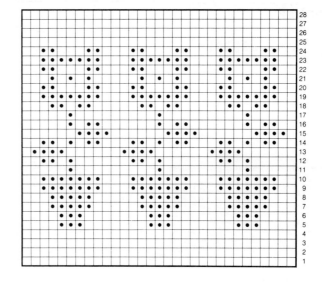

## Butterfly

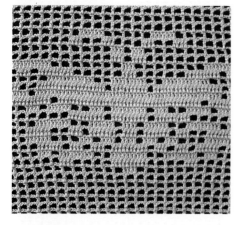

**Base Row**
Multiple of 3 sts per square + 1
Pattern Repeat = 31 squares

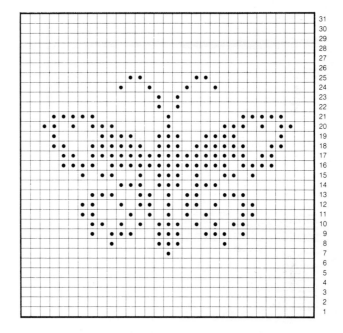

## Peace Rose

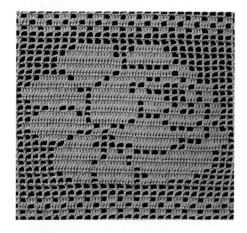

**Base Row**
Multiple of 3 sts per square + 1
Pattern Repeat = 30 squares

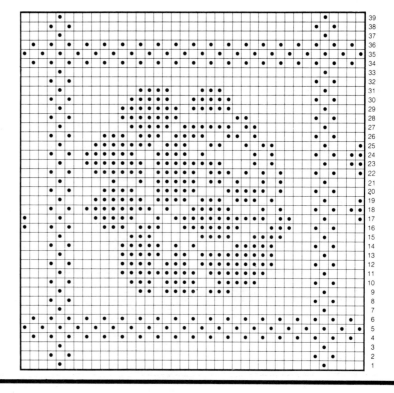

# Filet Crochet

## Pokerwork

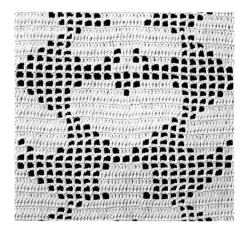

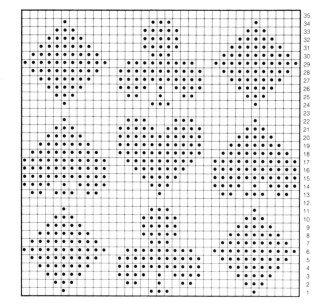

**Base Row**
Multiple of 3 sts per square + 1

Pattern Repeat = 24 squares wide by 23 squares deep

## Letterform

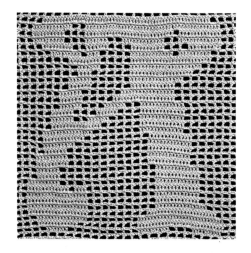

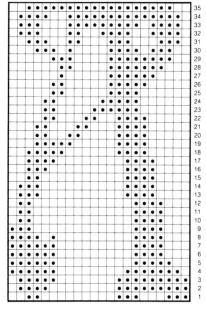

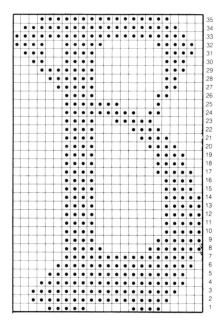

**Base Row**
Multiple of 3 sts per square + 1

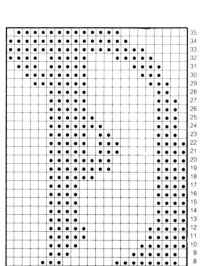

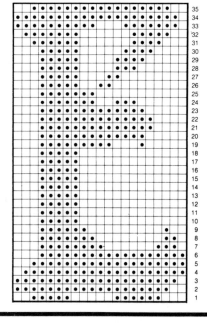

For more information and key to Filet Symbols see pages 89 and 90.

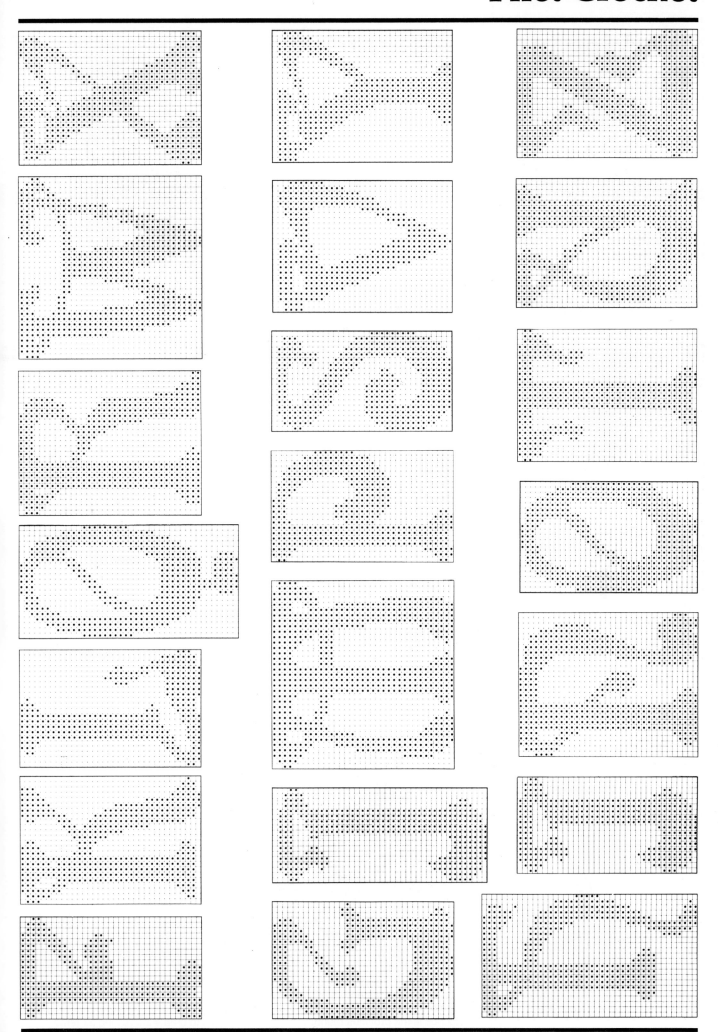

# Motifs

## Working in Rounds

Most motifs are not worked in rows but are worked from the centre outwards in rounds. Unless otherwise indicated do not turn the work between rounds but continue with the same side facing and treat this as the right side of the fabric. The centre ring is usually formed by a number of chains joined together with a slip stitch.

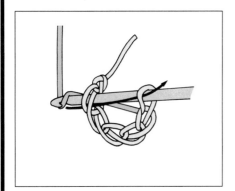

1. Insert the hook back into the first chain made.

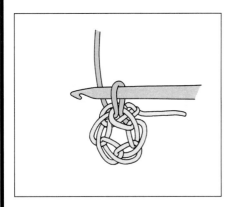

2. Make a slip stitch to join into a ring.

At the beginning of each round one or more chain can be worked to match the height of the following stitches. (This is equivalent to a turning chain).

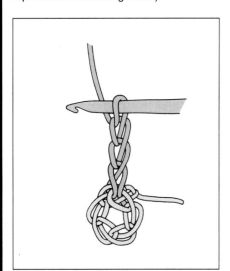

3. When working trebles three starting chain are required.

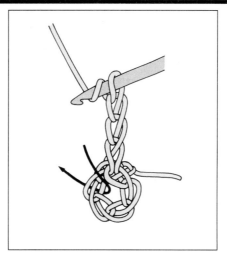

4. The stitches of the first round are worked by inserting the hook into the space at the centre of the chain ring. Occasionally the first round is worked into the first chain (Crystal Web on page 124).

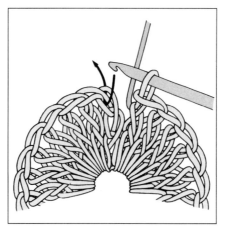

5. When each round is complete insert the hook into the top of the chain or stitch at the beginning of the round and slip stitch together.

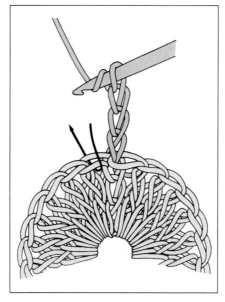

6. When working second and subsequent rounds, unless otherwise stated, insert the hook under the two top loops of the stitches in the previous round.

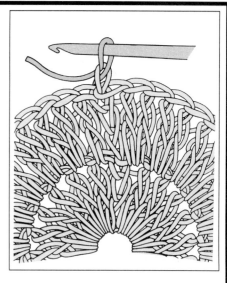

7. After joining final round with a slip stitch, fasten off by making a chain, then cutting the yarn and drawing the end through.

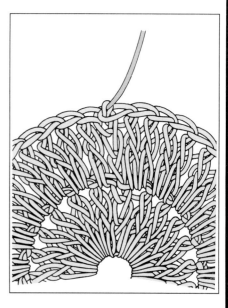

8. Tighten gently to form a knot.

## Joining Motifs

### Motif Layout

Some motifs such as triangles, squares and hexagons fit together exactly while others leave interesting spaces when joined. These spaces can themselves be a decorative part of an openwork fabric or can be filled in a variety of ways. Smaller spaces can be filled with suitable combinations of chains and stitches and larger ones with small motifs. Most motifs can be joined in more than one way so that any individual motif can form the basis of several different fabric designs. If motifs are worked in different colours they can be laid out to produce patchwork effects. Solid motifs are particularly suitable for working coloured patchwork.

Opposite are just a few examples of how motifs of various shapes can be positioned to create interesting patterns.

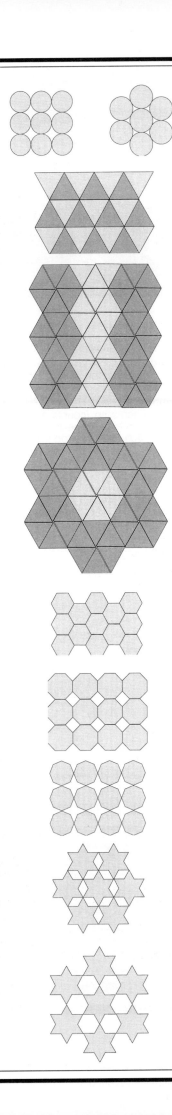

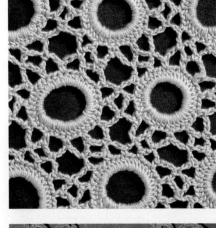

## Methods of Joining

Layouts that involve motifs fitting together along straight edges can be joined with a flat seam or by working a row of slip stitch or double crochet through both edges (see page 15). The crochet joins should be done with the right sides of the motifs together so they will be invisible on the right side of the fabric. Alternatively a crochet join can be used as a decorative feature when worked on the right side.

Some designs, particularly those with chain arches or picots round their edges, can be joined to previous motifs during the course of their final rounds. This is done by interrupting the picots or arches at half

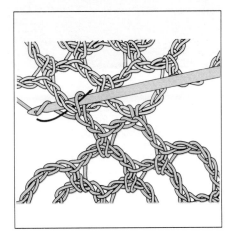

way and slip stitching to the corresponding places on the adjacent motifs.

Spaces between motifs are sometimes filled with small motifs, made and joined in at the same time as they are worked.

## Joined Motifs

We show here a few motifs joined in various ways. The possibilities are infinite and only depend on the shape of the motifs and your ingenuity.

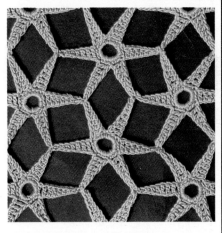

# Motifs

## Traditional Square I

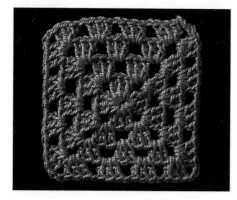

Base ring: 4ch, join with sl st.

**1st round:** 5ch (count as 1tr and 2ch), [3tr into ring, 2ch] 3 times, 2tr into ring, sl st to 3rd of 5ch.

**2nd round:** Sl st into next ch, 5ch (count as 1tr and 2ch), 3tr into same sp, *1ch, miss 3tr, [3tr, 2ch, 3tr] into next sp; rep from * twice, 1ch, miss 3 sts, 2tr into same sp as 5ch at beg of round, sl st to 3rd of 5ch.

**3rd round:** Sl st into next ch, 5ch (count as 1tr and 2ch), 3tr into same sp, *1ch, miss 3tr, 3tr into next sp, 1ch, miss 3tr**, [3tr, 2ch, 3tr] into next sp; rep from * twice and from * to ** again, 2tr into same sp as 5ch, sl st to 3rd of 5ch.

**4th round:** Sl st into next ch, 5ch (count as 1tr and 2ch), 3tr into same sp, *[1ch, miss 3tr, 3tr into next sp] twice, 1ch, miss 3tr**, [3tr, 2ch, 3tr] into next sp; rep from * twice and from * to ** again, 2tr into same sp as 5ch, sl st to 3rd of 5ch.

Fasten off.

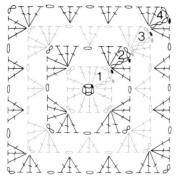

## Traditional Square II

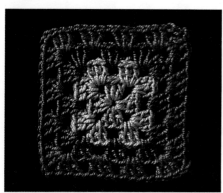

---

Worked as Traditional Square I.
Work 1 round each in colours A, B, C and D.

## Treble Square I

Base ring: 4ch, join with sl st.

**1st round:** 5ch (count as 1tr and 2ch), [3tr into ring, 2ch] 3 times, 2tr into ring, sl st to 3rd of 5ch. (4 groups of 3tr).

**2nd round:** Sl st into next ch, 7ch (count as 1tr and 4ch), *2tr into same arch, 1tr into each tr across side of square**, 2tr into next arch, 4ch; rep from * twice and from * to ** again, 1tr into same arch as 7ch, sl st to 3rd of 7ch (4 groups of 7tr).

**3rd round:** As 2nd round. (4 groups of 11tr).

**4th round:** As 2nd round. (4 groups of 15tr).

Fasten off.

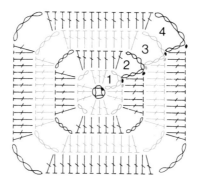

## Treble Square II

Worked as Treble Square I.
Work 1 round each in colours A, B, C and D.

---

## French Square

Base ring: 6ch, join with sl st.

**1st round:** 4ch (count as 1tr and 1ch), [1tr into ring, 1ch] 11 times, sl st to 3rd of 4ch. (12 spaces).

**2nd round:** Sl st into next ch, 3ch, work htr3tog into same sp (counts as htr4tog), *2ch, work htr4tog into next sp, 3ch, 1dtr into next tr, 3ch, work htr4tog into next sp, 2ch**, htr4tog into next sp; rep from * twice more and from * to ** again, sl st to top of first cluster.

**3rd round:** 1ch, 1dc into same place, *2ch, miss next 2ch sp, 4tr into next 3ch sp, 2ch, 1dtr into next dtr, 3ch, insert hook down through top of last dtr and work sl st, 2ch, 4tr into next 3ch sp, 2ch, miss next 2ch sp, 1dc into next cluster; rep from * 3 more times, omitting dc at end, sl st to first dc.

Fasten off.

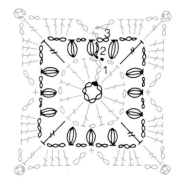

## Italian Square

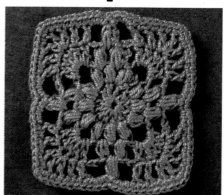

---

Stitch Variations, Abbreviations and Symbols on pages 7 to 15.

Base ring: 4ch, join with sl st.

**1st round:** 3ch (count as 1tr), 11tr into ring, sl st to top of 3ch. (12 sts).

**2nd round:** 3ch, work htr3tog into same place as 3ch (counts as htr4tog), *[1ch, work htr4tog into next st] twice, 5ch**, htr4tog into next st; rep from * twice more and from * to ** again, sl st to top of first cluster.

**3rd round:** Sl st into next sp, 3ch, work htr3tog into same sp (counts as htr4tog), *1ch, htr4tog into next sp, 2ch, 5tr into next 5ch arch, 2ch**, htr4tog into next sp; rep from * twice more and from * to ** again, sl st to top of first cluster.

**4th round:** Sl st into next sp, 3ch, work htr3tog into same sp (counts as htr4tog), *3ch, miss 2ch, [1tr into next tr, 1ch] twice, work [1tr, 1ch, 1tr, 1ch, 1tr] into next tr, [1ch, 1tr into next tr] twice, 3ch, miss 2ch**, work htr4tog into next sp; rep from * twice more and again from * to **, sl st to top of first cluster.

**5th round:** 1ch, 1dc into each ch and each st all round, but working 3dc into 3rd of 5 tr at each corner, ending sl st to first dc.
Fasten off.

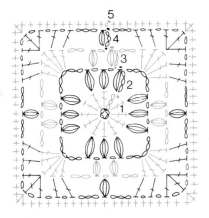

## Christmas Rose Square

Base ring: Using A, 6ch, join with sl st.

**1st round:** 5ch (count as 1tr and 2ch), [1tr into ring, 2ch] 7 times, sl st to 3rd of 5ch. (8 spaces).

**2nd round:** 3ch, work tr3tog into next sp (counts as tr4tog), [5ch, work tr4tog into next sp] 7 times, 5ch, sl st to top of first cluster. Fasten off.

**3rd round:** Using B join into same place, 1ch, 1dc into same place, *2ch, working over the 5ch arch so as to enclose it work 1tr into next tr of 1st round, 2ch, 1dc into top of next cluster; rep from * all round omitting dc at end, sl st to first dc.

**4th round:** Sl st into next ch, 1ch, 1dc into same place, *3ch, 1dc into next sp; rep from * all round omitting dc at end, sl st to first dc.

**5th round:** Sl st into next ch, 3ch (count as 1tr), [1tr, 2ch, 2tr] into same arch, *2ch, 1dc into next arch, [3ch, 1dc into next arch] twice, 2ch**, [2tr, 2ch, 2tr] into next arch; rep from * twice more and from * to ** again, sl st to top of 3ch.
Fasten off.

## Baltic Square

Base ring: 8ch, join with sl st.

**1st round:** 3ch, 4tr Popcorn into ring (counts as 5tr Popcorn), [5ch, 5tr Popcorn into ring] 3 times, 5ch, sl st to top of first Popcorn.

**2nd round:** 3ch (count as 1tr), *work [2tr, 2ch, 5tr Popcorn, 2ch, 2tr] into next 5ch arch**, 1tr into next Popcorn; rep from * twice more and from * to ** again, sl st to top of 3ch.

**3rd round:** 3ch (count as 1tr), 1tr into each of next 2 sts, *2tr into next sp, 2ch, 5tr Popcorn into next Popcorn, 2ch, 2tr into next sp**, 1tr into each of next 5tr; rep from * twice more and from * to ** again, 1tr into each of last 2tr, sl st to top of 3ch.

**4th round:** 3ch (count as 1tr), 1tr into each of next 4tr, *2tr into next sp, 2ch, 5tr Popcorn into next Popcorn, 2ch, 2tr into next sp**, 1tr into each of next 9tr; rep from * twice more and from * to ** again, 1tr into each of last 4tr, sl st to top of 3ch.
Fasten off.

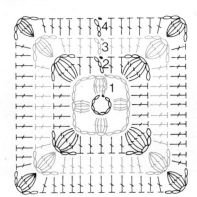

## Cranesbill Lace Square

Base ring: 6ch, join with sl st.

**1st round:** 3ch, tr2tog into ring (counts as tr3tog), [3ch, tr3tog into ring] 7 times, 3ch, sl st to top of first cluster.

**2nd round:** Sl st to centre of next 3ch arch, 1ch, 1dc into same place, [5ch, 1dc into next arch] 7 times, 2ch, 1tr into first dc.

**3rd round:** *5ch, [tr3tog, 3ch, tr3tog] into next arch**, 5ch, 1dc into next arch; rep from * twice and from * to ** again, 2ch, 1tr into tr which closed 2nd round.

**4th round:** *5ch, 1dc into next arch, 5ch, [1dc, 5ch, 1dc] into corner 3ch arch, 5ch, 1dc into next 5ch arch; rep from * 3 times, ending last rep into tr which closed 3rd round, sl st to first ch.
Fasten off.

# Motifs

## Rose Square

Base ring: Using A, 12ch, join with sl st.

**1st round:** 1ch, 18dc into ring, sl st to first dc. (18 sts).

**2nd round:** 1ch, beginning into same st as 1ch [1dc, 3ch, miss 2 sts] 6 times, sl st to first dc.

**3rd round:** 1ch, work a petal of [1dc, 3ch, 5tr, 3ch, 1dc] into each of next 6 3ch arches, sl st to first dc.

**4th round:** 1ch, [1dc between 2dc, 5ch behind petal of 3rd round] 6 times, sl st to first dc.

**5th round:** 1ch, work a petal of [1dc, 3ch, 7tr, 3ch, 1dc] into each of next 6 5ch arches, sl st to first dc. Fasten off.

**6th round:** Using B join between 2dc, 1ch, [1dc between 2dc, 6ch behind Petal of 5th round] 6 times, sl st to first dc.

**7th round:** Sl st into next ch, 3ch (count as 1tr), *[4tr, 2ch, 1tr] all into same arch, 6tr into next arch, [2tr, 2ch, 4tr] all into next arch**, 1tr into next arch; rep from * to **, sl st to top of 3ch.

**8th round:** 3ch (count as 1tr), 1tr into each tr all round with [3tr, 2ch, 3tr] into each 2ch corner sp, ending sl st to top of 3ch. Fasten off.

**9th round:** Using C join into same place, 1ch, 1dc into same st as 1ch, *1dc into next st, work a 3ch picot of [3ch, sl st down through top of last dc made] twice, 1dc into each of next 3 sts, work [3ch picot, 1dc into next st] twice, [1dc, 7ch, 1dc] into corner 2ch sp, [1dc into next st, 3ch picot] twice, 1dc into each of next 3 sts, [3ch Picot, 1dc into next st] twice, 1dc into next st; rep from * 3 times omitting dc at end of last rep, sl st to first dc.

**10th round:** Sl st across to top of next 3ch picot, 1ch, 1dc into same picot, *5ch, miss next picot, 1dc into next picot, 5ch, [1dc, 7ch, 1dc] into corner 7ch arch, [5ch, miss next picot, 1dc into next picot] twice, 5ch, 1dc into next picot; rep from * 3 times omitting dc at end of last rep, sl st to first dc. Fasten off.

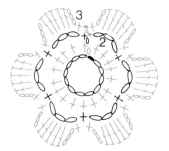

## Popcorn Wheel Square

Base ring: 6ch, join with sl st.

**1st round:** 3ch (count as 1tr), 4tr into ring and complete as for 5tr Popcorn, [3ch, 5tr Popcorn into ring] 7 times, 3ch, sl st to first Popcorn.

**2nd round:** 3ch (count as 1tr), 1tr into next 3ch arch, [9tr into next arch, 2tr into next arch] 3 times, 9tr into last arch, sl st to top of 3ch.

**3rd round:** 1ch, 1dc into same place as 1ch, 1dc into next st, *into next 9tr group work 1dc into each of first 3tr, miss 1tr, [1htr, 4tr, 1htr] into next tr, miss 1tr, 1dc into each of last 3tr**, 1dc into each of next 2 sts; rep from * twice and from * to ** again, sl st to first dc.

Fasten off.

⬡ = 5tr Popcorn

## Floribunda

Stitch Variations, Abbreviations and Symbols on pages 7 to 15.

Base ring: Using A, 6ch, join with sl st.

**1st round:** 1ch, 16dc into ring, sl st to first dc. (16 sts).

**2nd round:** 6ch (count as 1tr and 3ch arch), miss 2 sts, [1tr into next st, 3ch, miss 1 st] 7 times, sl st to 3rd of 6ch.

**3rd round:** 1ch, work a petal of [1dc, 1htr, 5tr, 1htr, 1dc] into each of next 8 3ch arches, sl st to first dc. Fasten off.

**4th round:** Using B join between 2dc, 1ch, [1dc between 2dc, 6ch behind petal of 3rd round] 8 times, sl st to first dc.

**5th round:** 1ch, work a petal of [1dc, 1htr, 6tr, 1htr, 1dc] into each of next 8 arches, sl st to first dc. Fasten off.

**6th round:** Using C join into 2nd tr of petal of 5th round, 1ch, 1dc into same place as 1ch, 6ch, miss 2tr, 1dc into next tr, [6ch, 1dc into 2nd tr of next petal, 6ch, miss 2tr, 1dc into next tr] 7 times, 3ch, 1tr into first dc.

**7th round:** 3ch (count as 1tr), 3tr into arch formed by tr which closed 6th round, *4ch, 1dc into next arch, [6ch, 1dc into next arch] twice, 4ch**, [4tr, 4ch, 4tr] into next arch; rep from * twice and from * to ** again, ending [4tr, 4ch] into last ch arch, sl st to top of 3ch.

Fasten off.

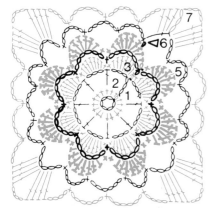

1, 2, 3 — A    4, 5 — B    6, 7 — C

## Daisy Cluster Square

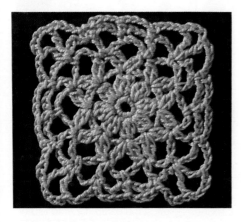

Base ring: Wrap yarn round finger.

**1st round:** 1ch, 8dc into ring, sl st to first dc. (8 sts).

**2nd round:** 3ch, tr2tog into first st (counts as tr3tog), [3ch, tr3tog into next st] 7 times, 3ch, sl st to top of first cluster.

**3rd round:** 3ch, 1tr into first st (counts as tr2tog), *miss 3ch, [tr2tog, 5ch, tr2tog] all into next cluster; rep from * 6 times, tr2tog into next cluster, 5ch, sl st to top of 3ch.

**4th round:** Sl st into next cluster, 7ch (counts as 1tr and 4ch), [1dc into next 5ch arch, 4ch, miss 1 cluster, 1tr into next cluster, 4ch] 7 times, 1dc into next arch, 4ch, sl st to 3rd of 7ch.

**5th round:** 1ch, 1dc into same place as 1ch, *4ch, miss 4ch, [1dtr, 4ch, 1dtr] into next dc, 4ch, miss 4ch, 1dc into next tr, 4ch, miss 4ch, 1htr into next dc, 4ch, miss 4ch, 1dc into next tr; rep from * 3 times, omitting dc at end of last rep, sl st to first dc.

Fasten off.

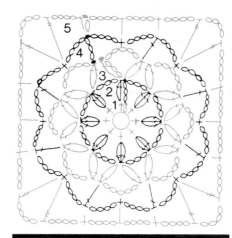

## Sow Thistle Square

Base ring: Using A, 4ch, join with sl st.

**1st round:** 4ch (count as 1tr and 1ch), [1tr, 1ch] 11 times into ring, sl st to 3rd of 4ch. Fasten off. (12 spaces).

**2nd round:** Using B join into sp, 3ch, tr2tog into same sp (counts as tr3tog), [3ch, tr3tog into next sp] 11 times, 3ch, sl st to top of first cluster. Fasten off.

**3rd round:** Using A join into 3ch arch, 1ch, 1dc into same arch, [5ch, 1dc into next arch] 11 times, 2ch, 1tr into first dc. Fasten off.

**4th round:** Using B join into same place, 1ch, 1dc into same place, *5ch, 1dc into next arch, 1ch, [5tr, 3ch, 5tr] into next arch, 1ch, 1dc into next arch; rep from * 3 times, omitting 1dc at end of last rep, sl st to first dc. Fasten off.

1 — A   2 — B   3 — A   4 — B

## Daisy Wheel Square

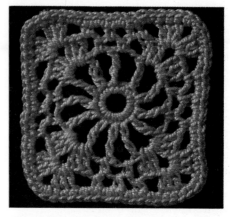

Base ring: 8ch, join with sl st.

**1st round:** 1ch, 12dc into ring, sl st to first dc. (12 sts).

**2nd round:** 6ch (count as 1dtr and 2ch), miss 1 st, [1dtr into next st, 2ch] 11 times, sl st to 4th of 6ch.

**3rd round:** 5ch (counts as 1tr and 2ch), *[1dc into next sp, 2ch] twice, [3tr, 2ch, 3tr] into next sp, 2ch; rep from * 3 times, omitting 1tr and 2ch at end of last rep, sl st to 3rd of 5ch.

**4th round:** 1ch, *[1dc into next sp, 2ch] 3 times, [3tr, 2ch, 3tr] into corner sp, 2ch; rep from * 3 times, sl st to first dc.

**5th round:** 1ch, work 2dc into each sp and 1dc into each st all round, but working 3dc into each corner sp, sl st to first dc.

Fasten off.

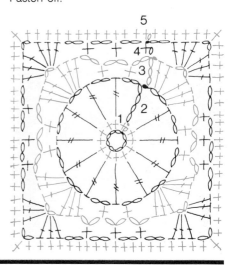

# Motifs

## Puff Stitch Square

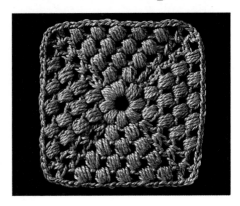

Base ring: 8ch, join with sl st.
**Special Abbreviation**
**Puff st** = htr5tog,

**1st round:** 2ch, htr4tog into ring (counts as 1 Puff st), 2ch, work [puff st, 2ch] 7 times into ring, sl st to first Puff st.

**2nd round:** 5ch (count as 1tr and 2ch), 1tr into same Puff st, *2ch, [Puff st into next sp, 2ch] twice**, work a V st of [1tr, 2ch, 1tr] into next Puff st; rep from * twice and from * to ** again, sl st to 3rd of 5ch.

**3rd round:** Sl st into next ch, 5ch (count as 1tr and 2ch), 1tr into same sp, *2ch, [Puff st into next sp, 2ch] 3 times**, V st into next sp at corner; rep from * twice and from * to ** again, sl st to 3rd of 5ch.

**4th round:** As for 3rd round, but work 4 Puff sts along each side of square.

**5th round:** As for 3rd round, but work 5 Puff sts along each side of square.
Fasten off.

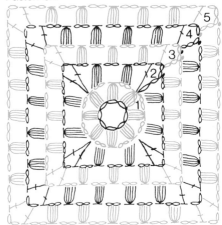

## Spanish Square

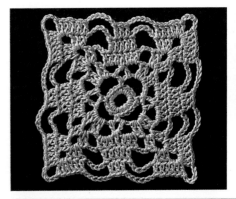

Base ring: 8ch, join with sl st.

**1st round:** 1ch, 16dc into ring, sl st to first dc. (16 sts).

**2nd round:** 1ch, 1dc into same place as 1ch, 1dc into next st] 3 times, 7ch, miss 3 sts, sl st to first dc.

**3rd round:** Sl st across to 3rd ch of next arch, 3ch (count as 1tr), 1tr into same place, *[3ch, 2tr] into same arch, 3ch, tr2tog inserting hook into same arch for first leg and into next arch for 2nd leg, 3ch, 2tr into same arch; rep from * 3 times, omitting 2tr at end of last rep, sl st to top of 3ch.

**4th round:** Sl st into next tr and next ch, 3ch (count as 1tr), 1tr into same place, *[3ch, 2tr] into same arch, 3ch, miss 2tr, 3tr into next 3ch, 1tr into next cluster, 3tr into next 3ch, 3ch, miss 2tr, 2tr into next arch; rep from * 3 times, omitting 2tr at end of last rep, sl st to top of 3ch.

**5th round:** Sl st into next tr and next ch, 3ch, 2tr into same place, *[3ch, 3tr] into same arch, 6ch, miss [2tr, 3ch, 1tr], 1tr into each of next 5tr, 6ch, miss [1tr, 3ch, 2tr], 3tr into next 3ch arch; rep from * 3 times, omitting 3tr at end of last rep, sl st to top of 3ch.

**6th round:** 3ch (count as 1tr), 1tr into each of next 2tr, *[3tr, 5ch, 3tr] into next 3ch arch, 1tr into each of next 3tr, 6ch, miss [6ch and 1tr], 1tr into each of next 3tr, 6ch, miss [1tr and 6ch], 1tr into each of next 3tr; rep from * 3 times, omitting 3tr at end of last rep, sl st to top of 3ch.
Fasten off.

## Crystal Square

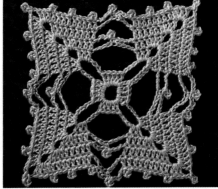

Base ring: 10ch, join with sl st.
**1st round:** 14ch, [5tr into ring, 11ch] 3 times, 4tr into ring, sl st to 3rd of 14ch.

**2nd round:** Sl st into each of next 5ch, 3ch (count as 1tr), [2tr, 3ch, 3tr] into same ch arch, *9ch, [3tr, 3ch, 3tr] into next arch; rep from * twice, 9ch, sl st to top of 3ch.

**3rd round:** 3ch (count as 1tr), 1tr into each of next 2tr, *[3tr, 3ch, 3tr] into 3ch sp, 1tr into each of next 3tr, 4ch, miss 4ch, 1 dc into next ch, make a picot of [3ch, sl st down through top of last st], 4ch, miss 4ch**, 1tr into each of next 3tr; rep from * twice and from * to ** again, sl st to top of 3ch.

**4th round:** 3ch (count as 1tr), 1tr into each of next 5tr, *[3tr, 3ch, 3tr] into 3ch sp, 1tr into each of next 6tr, 9ch**, 1tr into each of next 6tr; rep from * twice and from * to ** again, sl st to top of 3ch.

**5th round:** 6ch, sl st to 4th ch from hook (counts as 1tr and picot), *[1tr into each of next 4tr, picot] twice, work [3tr, 5ch, sl st to 4th ch from hook, 1ch, 3tr] into 3ch sp, 1tr into next tr, picot, [1tr into each of next 4tr, picot] twice, 4ch, miss 4ch, 1dc into next ch, picot, 4ch, miss 4ch**, 1tr into next tr, picot; rep from * twice and from * to ** again, sl st to top of 3ch.
Fasten off.

## Moorish Medallion

Base Ring: 6ch, join with sl st.
**Special Abbreviation**
**Sdc (Spike double crochet)** = insert hook 2 rounds below as indicated, i.e. into top of 1st round, yo, draw loop through and up to height of current round, yo, draw through both loops on hook

**1st round:** 1ch, 16dc into ring, sl st to first dc. (16 sts).

**2nd round:** 1ch, 1dc into same place as 1ch, 1dc into next dc, *[1dc, 9ch, 1dc] into

Stitch Variations, Abbreviations and Symbols on pages 7 to 15.

next dc**, 1dc into each of next 3dc; rep from * twice and from * to ** again, 1dc into next dc, sl st to first dc.

**3rd round:** 1ch, 1dc into same place as 1ch, *miss next 2dc, work [2htr, 17tr, 2htr] into next 9ch arch, miss next 2dc, 1dc into next dc; rep from * 3 more times omitting 1dc at end of last rep and ending sl st to first dc.

**4th round:** 1ch, 1Sdc over first st, *5ch, miss 5 sts, 1dc into next st, 3ch, sl st into 3rd ch from hook, [5ch, miss 4 sts, 1dc into next st, 3ch, sl st into 3rd ch from hook] twice, 5ch, miss 5 sts, 1Sdc over next st; rep from * 3 times omitting Sdc at end of last rep and ending sl st to first Sdc.

Fasten off.

## Russian Square

Base ring: Using A, 8ch, join with sl st.

**1st round:** 6ch (count as 1tr and 3ch), [3tr into ring, 3ch] 3 times, 2tr into ring, sl st to 3rd of 6 ch. Fasten off.

**2nd round:** Using B join into a different corner sp, 3ch (count as 1tr), 2tr into same corner sp, *1tr/rf round each of next 3 sts**, [3tr, 3ch, 3tr] into next corner sp; rep from * twice more and from * to ** again, [3tr, 3ch] into last corner sp, sl st to top of 3 ch. Fasten off.

**3rd round:** Using C join into a different corner sp, 6ch (count as 1tr and 3ch), 3tr into same corner sp, *1tr/rf round each of next 3 sts, 1tr/rb round each of next 3 sts, 1tr/rf round each of next 3 sts**, [3tr, 3ch, 3tr] into next corner sp; rep from * twice more and from * to ** again, 2tr into last corner sp, sl st to 3rd of 6ch. Fasten off.

**4th round:** Using D join into a different corner sp, 3ch (count as 1tr), 2tr into same corner sp, *[1tr/rf round each of next 3 sts, 1tr/rb round each of next 3 sts] twice, 1tr/rf round each of next 3 sts**, [3tr, 3ch, 3tr] into next corner sp; rep from * twice more and from * to ** again, [3tr, 3ch] into last corner sp, sl st to top of 3ch.

Fasten off.

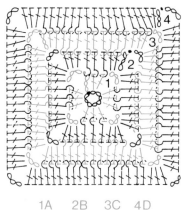

1A    2B    3C    4D

## Frozen Star

Base ring: 12ch, join with sl st.

**1st round:** 1ch, 24dc into ring, sl st to first dc. (24 sts).

**2nd round:** 6ch, ttr3tog over next 3 sts (counts as ttr4tog), [7ch, ttr4tog over same st as last leg of previous cluster and next 3 sts] 7 times, 7ch, sl st to top of first cluster.

**3rd round:** 1ch, 1dc into same place as 1ch, *[3ch, miss 1ch, 1dc into next ch] 3 times, 3ch, miss 1ch, 1dc into top of next cluster; rep from * 7 times, omitting dc at end of last rep, sl st to first dc.

**4th round:** Sl st to centre of next 3ch arch, 1ch, 1dc into same arch, *3ch, 1dc into next arch; rep from * to end, omitting dc at end of last rep, sl st to first dc.

**5th round:** As 4th round.

**6th round:** Sl st to centre of next 3ch arch, 1ch, 1dc into same arch, *[3ch, 1dc into next arch] 4 times, 3ch, miss next arch, work [dtr3tog, 5ch, ttr4tog, 4ch, sl st to top of last cluster, 5ch, dtr3tog] into next arch, 3ch, miss next arch, 1dc into next arch; rep from * 3 times, omitting dc at end of last rep, sl st to first dc.

Fasten off.

## Spider Square

Base ring: 6ch, join with sl st.

**1st round:** 1ch, [1dc into ring, 15ch] 12 times, sl st to first dc.

**2nd round:** Sl st along to centre of next 15ch arch, 3ch, tr2tog into same arch (counts as tr3tog), *4ch, tr3tog into same arch, [4ch, 1dc into next arch] twice, 4ch, tr3tog into same arch; rep from * 3 times, omitting tr3tog at end of last rep, sl st to first cluster.

**3rd round:** Sl st into next arch, 3ch, tr2tog into same arch (counts as tr3tog), *4ch, tr3tog into same arch, [4ch, 1dc into next 4ch arch, 4ch, tr3tog into next 4ch arch] twice; rep from * 3 times, omitting tr3tog at end of last rep, sl st to first cluster.

Fasten off.

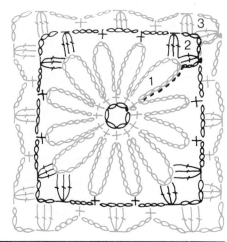

# Motifs

## Spiral Pentagram

Base ring: 5ch, join with sl st.

**1st round:** [6ch, 1dc into ring] 5 times. (Hint: mark last dc of each round with contrasting thread.

**2nd round:** [6ch, 3dc into next 6ch arch] 5 times.

**3rd round:** [6ch, 3dc into next 6ch arch, 1dc into each of next 2dc] 5 times. (5 blocks of 5 dc each).

**4th round:** [6ch, 3dc into next 6ch arch, 1dc into each dc of next block except miss last dc] 5 times. (5 blocks of 7 dc each).

Continue as given on 4th round for 3 more rounds finishing with 5 blocks of 13 dc each.

**8th round:** *5ch, 1dc into centre of next 6ch arch, 5ch, miss 1dc, 1dc into each dc of next block except last; rep from * 4 more times.

**9th round:** *[5ch, 1dc into next arch] twice, 5ch, miss 1dc, 1dc into each dc of next block except last dc; rep from * 4 more times.

Continue as given on 9th round for 3 more rounds, but work 1 more 5ch arch in each segment on each round at same time as number of dc in each block reduces, finishing with 6 arches and 3dc in each of 5 segments.

**13th round:** 5ch, 1dc into next arch, *[3ch, 1dc into next arch] 5 times, 3ch, 1tr into 2nd of next 3dc, 3ch, 1dc into next arch; rep from * 4 more times omitting dc at end of last rep, sl st to first dc.

Fasten off.

## 2-Colour Star

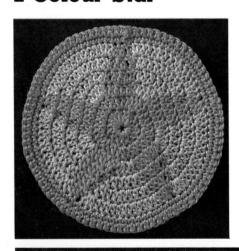

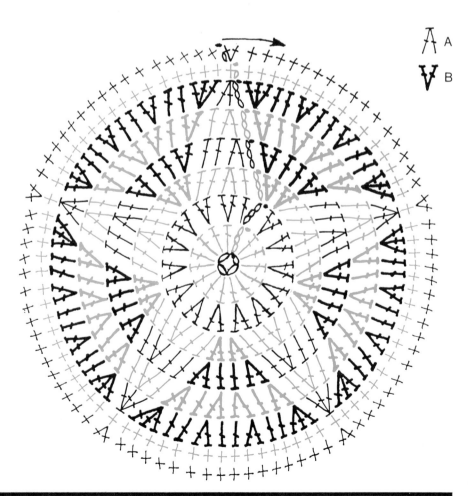

Stitch Variations, Abbreviations and Symbols on pages 7 to 15.

Base ring: Using A, 4ch, join with sl st.

**1st round:** 3ch (count as 1tr), 14tr into ring, sl st to top of 3ch. (15 sts).

**2nd round:** 3ch (count as 1tr), 1tr into same place as 3ch, 2tr into next and each tr all round, sl st to top of 3ch. (30 sts).

**3rd round:** 3ch (count as 1tr), *1tr into next st, tr2tog over next 2 sts, 1tr into each of next 2 sts, change to B, 2tr into same place as last tr with A, 2tr into next st, change to A**, 1tr into same place as last tr with B; rep from * 3 more times and from * to ** again, sl st to top of 3ch.

**4th round:** 3ch (count as 1tr), *tr2tog over next 2 sts, 1tr into each of next 2 sts, change to B, 2tr into next st, 1tr into each of next 2 sts, 2tr into next st, change to A**, 1tr into next st; rep from * 3 more times and from * to ** again, sl st to top of 3ch.

**5th round:** 3ch (count as 1tr), *tr2tog over next 2 sts, 1tr into next st, change to B, 2tr into next st, 1tr into next st, 2tr into each of next 2 sts, 1tr into next st, 2tr into next st, change to A**, 1tr into next st; rep from * 3 more times and from * to ** again, sl st to top of 3ch.

**6th round:** 3ch, *tr2tog over next 2 sts (counts as tr3tog), change to B, 3tr into next st, [1tr into each of next 2 sts, 2tr into next st] twice, 1tr into each of next 2 sts, 3tr into next st, change to A**, tr3tog over next 3 sts; rep from * 3 more times and from * to ** again, sl st to top of first cluster.

**7th round:** Continue using A only 1ch, 1dc into same place as 1ch, 1dc into next and each st all round, sl st to first dc, turn.

**8th round** (wrong side): 1ch, 2dc into same place as 1ch, 1dc into next and each st all round, except 2dc into each of 4 sts corresponding to remaining points of Star, ending sl st to first dc.

Fasten off.

# Ridged Hexagon I

Base ring: 4ch, join with sl st.

**1st round:** 3ch (count as 1tr), 1tr into ring, [1ch, 2tr into ring] 5 times, 1ch, sl st to top of 3ch. (6 spaces).

**2nd round:** Sl st into next tr and into next ch, 3ch (count as 1tr), *1tr/rb round each of next 2tr**, work a V st of [1tr, 1ch, 1tr] into next sp; rep from * 4 more times and from

* to ** again, 1tr into last sp, 1ch, sl st to top of 3ch.

**3rd round:** 3ch (count as 1tr), 1tr/rb round each tr and 1 V st into each sp all round, ending with a sl st to top of 3ch. (6 groups of 6tr).

**4th round:** As 3rd round. (6 groups of 8tr).

**5th round:** As 3rd round. (6 groups of 10tr Fasten off.

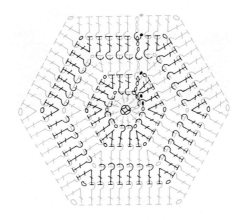

# Ridged Hexagon II

Worked as Ridged Hexagon I.
Work 1 round each in colours A, B, C, D and E.

# Traditional Hexagon I

Base ring: 6ch, join with sl st.

**1st round:** 3ch tr2tog into ring (counts as tr3tog), [3ch, tr3tog into ring] 5 times, 1ch, 1htr into top of first cluster.

**2nd round:** 3ch, tr2tog into arch formed by htr (counts as tr3tog), *3ch, work [tr3tog, 3ch, tr3tog] into next sp: rep from * 4 more times, 3ch, tr3tog into last sp, 1ch, 1htr into top of first cluster.

**3rd round:** 3ch, tr2tog into arch formed by htr (counts as tr3tog), *3ch, work [tr3tog, 3ch, tr3tog] into next sp**, 3ch, tr3tog into next sp; rep from * 4 more times and from * to ** again, 1ch, 1htr into top of first cluster.

**4th round:** 3ch (counts as 1tr), 1tr into arch formed by htr, *3tr into next sp, [3tr, 2ch, 3tr] into next sp**, 3tr into next sp; rep from * 4 more times and from * to ** again, 1tr into next sp, sl st to top of 3ch.

**5th round:** 1ch, 1dc into same place, 1dc into each tr and each ch all round, ending sl st to first dc.
Fasten off.

# Traditional Hexagon II

Worked as Traditional Hexagon I.
Work 1 round each in colours A, B, C, D and E.

# Motifs

## 2-Colour Popcorn Hexagon

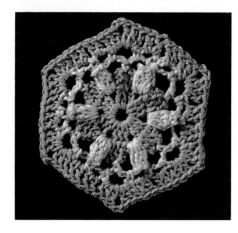

Base ring: Using A, 6ch, join with sl st.

**1st round:** 3ch (count as 1tr), 2tr into ring, [2ch, 3tr into ring] 5 times, 2ch, sl st to top of 3ch. (6 spaces).

**2nd round:** 1ch, 1dc into same place, *2ch, 1tr into next tr, 2ch, 1dc into next tr, 1ch, sl st into each of next 2 ch, 1ch, 1dc into next tr; rep from * 5 more times omitting last dc and ending sl st to first dc. Fasten off.

**3rd round:** Using B, join into 2ch sp, 3ch, 4tr Popcorn into same sp (counts as 5tr Popcorn), *4ch, miss 1dc and 2ch, 1dc into next tr, 4ch, miss 2ch and 1dc, 5tr Popcorn into next sp; rep from * 5 more times omitting last Popcorn and ending sl st to top of first Popcorn.

**4th round:** 1ch, 1dc into same place, *3ch, 1dc into next arch] twice, 3ch, 1dc into next Popcorn; rep from * 5 more times omitting last dc and ending sl st to first dc. Fasten off.

**5th round:** Using A, join into next ch, 3ch (count as 1tr), 1tr into same sp, *[3tr, 2ch, 3tr] into next sp**, 2tr into each of next 2 sps; rep from * 4 more times and from * to ** again, 2tr into next sp, sl st to top of 3ch. Fasten off.

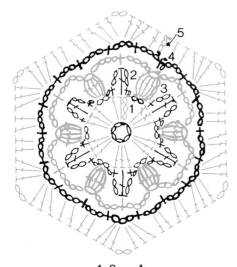

1, 2 — A

3, 4 — B

5 — A

## Eastern Star

Base ring: 6ch, join with sl st.

**1st round:** 1ch, [1dc into ring, 3ch] 12 times, sl st to first dc.

**2nd round:** Sl st into each of next 2ch, 1ch, 1dc into same 3ch arch, [3ch, 1dc into next 3ch arch] 11 times, 1ch, 1htr into top of first dc.

**3rd round:** *6ch, 1dc into next 3ch arch**, 3ch, 1dc into next 3ch arch; rep from * 4 more times and from * to ** again, 1ch, 1tr into htr which closed previous round.

**4th round:** *[5tr, 2ch, 5tr] into next 6ch arch, 1dc into next 3ch arch; rep from * 5 more times ending last rep in tr which closed previous round, sl st into next st. Fasten off.

## Water Wheel

Base ring: 4ch, join with sl st.

**1st round:** 3ch (count as 1tr), 1tr into ring, [2ch, 2tr into ring] 5 times, 2ch, sl st to top of 3ch.

**2nd round:** 3ch (count as 1tr), 2tr into same place as 3ch, 1tr into next tr, *3ch, miss 2ch, 3tr into next tr, 1tr into next tr; rep from * 4 more times, 3ch, miss 2ch, sl st to top of 3ch. (6 segments of 4tr and 3ch).

**3rd round:** 3ch (count as 1tr), 2tr into same place as 3ch, 1tr into next tr, tr2tog over next 2tr, *4ch, miss 3ch, 3tr into next tr, 1tr into next tr, tr2tog over next 2tr; rep from * 4 more times, 4ch, miss 3ch, sl st to top of 3ch.

**4th round:** 3ch (count as 1tr), 2tr into same place as 3ch, [1tr into next tr] twice, tr2tog over next 2tr, *5ch, miss 4ch, 3tr into next tr, [1tr into next tr] twice, tr2tog over next 2tr; rep from * 4 more times, 5ch, miss 4ch, sl st to top of 3ch.

**5th round:** 3ch (count as 1tr), 2tr into same place as 3ch, [1tr into next tr] 3 times, tr2tog over next 2tr, *6ch, miss 5ch, 3tr into next tr, [1tr into next tr] 3 times, tr2tog over next 2tr; rep from * 4 more times, 6ch, miss 5ch, sl st to top of 3ch.

**6th, 7th and 8th rounds:** As 5th round, but adding 1 more single tr in each tr block and 1 more ch in each ch arch on each round. Fasten off.

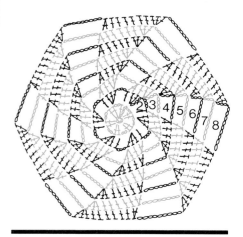

## Little Gem

Base ring: Using A. 5ch, join with sl st.

**1st round:** 4ch (count as 1dtr), 2tr into 4th ch from hook, *3ch, 1dtr into ring, 2tr into

Stitch Variations, Abbreviations and Symbols on pages 7 to 15.

# Motifs

base of stem of dtr just made; rep from * 4 more times, 3ch, sl st to top of 4ch.

**2nd round:** 3ch, tr2tog over next 2tr (counts as tr3tog), *6ch, miss 3ch, tr3tog over next 3 sts; rep from * 5 more times omitting last tr3tog and ending sl st to top of first cluster. Fasten off.

**3rd round:** Using B join in to centre of 3ch arch of 1st round, then so as to enclose 6ch arch of 2nd round work 1ch, 1dc into same place as 1ch, *5ch, 1tr into top of next cluster, 5ch, 1dc into 3ch arch of 1st round at same time enclosing 6ch arch of 2nd round; rep from * 5 more times omitting last dc and ending sl st into first dc. Fasten off.

**4th round:** Using C join in to same place, 1ch, 1dc into same place as 1ch, *5ch, miss 5ch, 3dc into next tr, 5ch, miss 5ch, 1dc into next dc; rep from * 5 more times omitting last dc and ending sl st into first dc.

Fasten off.

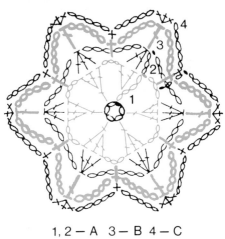

1, 2 – A  3 – B  4 – C

## Snowflake

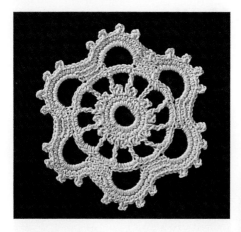

Base ring: 12ch, join with sl st.

**1st round:** 1ch, 24dc into ring, sl st to first dc. (24 sts).

**2nd round:** 1ch, 1dc into same place as 1ch, *1dc into next st, work a picot of [3ch, insert hook down through top of dc just made and work sl st]**, 1dc into next st; rep from * 10 times and from * to ** again, sl st to first dc.

**3rd round:** 8ch (count as 1dtr and 4ch), miss Picot, [1dtr into next dc between Picots, 4ch] 11 times, sl st to 4th of 8ch.

**4th round:** 1ch, [5dc into next 4ch arch] 12 times, sl st to first dc.

**5th round:** 1ch, *1dc into back loop only of each of next 5dc, 15ch, miss 5dc; rep from * 5 more times, sl st to first dc.

**6th round:** 1ch, *1dc into back loop only of each of next 5dc, 15dc into next 15ch arch; rep from * 5 more times, sl st to first dc.

**7th round:** Sl st into back loop only of next

st, 1ch, 1dc into same place as 1ch, 1dc into back loop only of each of next 2dc, *miss 1dc, [1dc into each of next 3dc, Picot] 4 times, 1dc into each of next 3dc, miss 1dc**, 1dc into back loop only of each of next 3dc; rep from * 4 more times and from * to ** again, sl st to first dc.

Fasten off.

## Scallop Flower

Base ring: Using A, 6ch, join with sl st.

**1st round:** 3ch (count as 1tr), 17tr into ring, sl st to top of 3ch. (18 sts).

**2nd round:** 1ch, 1dc into same place as 1ch, *3ch, miss 2 sts, 1dc into next st; rep from * 5 more times omitting last dc and ending sl st to first dc. Fasten off.

**3rd round:** Using B join in to next ch, 1ch, *work a Petal of [1dc, 1htr, 3tr, 1htr, 1dc] into 3ch arch, sl st into next dc; rep from * 5 more times.

**4th round:** Sl st into each of next 4 sts to centre tr of next Petal, 1ch, 1dc into same place as 1ch, *8ch, 1dc into centre tr of next Petal; rep from * 5 more times omitting last dc and ending sl st to first dc. Fasten off.

**5th round:** Using A join in to next ch, 1ch, *work [1dc, 3htr, 5tr, 3htr, 1dc] into next arch; rep from * 5 more times, ending sl st into first dc.

Fasten off.

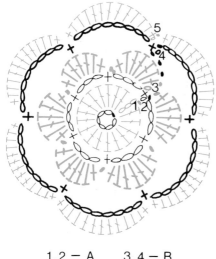

1, 2 – A    3, 4 – B
5 – A

113

# Motifs

## Ice Crystal

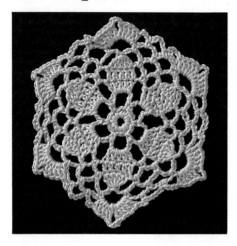

## Rainbow Petal Motif

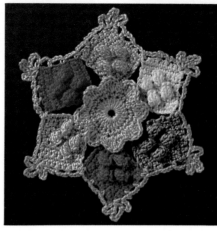

**Base ring:** 6ch, join with sl st.

**1st round:** 1ch, 12dc into ring, sl st to first dc. (12 sts).

**2nd round:** 1ch, 1dc into same place as 1ch, [7ch, miss 1dc, 1dc into next dc] 5 times, 3ch, miss 1dc, 1dtr into top of first dc.

**3rd round:** 3ch (count as 1tr), 4tr into arch formed by dtr, [3ch, 5tr into next 7ch arch] 5 times, 3ch, sl st to top of 3ch.

**4th round:** 3ch (counts as 1tr), 1tr into each of next 4tr, *3ch, 1dc into next 3ch arch, 3ch**, 1tr into each of next 5trs; rep from * 4 more times and from * to ** again, sl st to top of 3ch.

**5th round:** 3ch, tr4tog over next 4trs (counts as tr5tog), *[5ch, 1dc into next 3ch arch] twice, 5ch**, tr5tog over next 5trs; rep from * 4 more times and from * to ** again, sl st to first cluster.

**6th round:** Sl st into each of next 3ch, 1ch, 1dc into same place, *5ch, 1dc into next 5ch arch; rep from * all round omitting last dc and ending sl st to first dc.

**7th round:** Sl st into each of next 3ch, 1ch, 1dc into same place, *5ch, 1dc into next 5ch arch, 3ch, [5tr, 3ch, 5tr] into next arch, 3ch, 1dc into next arch; rep from * 5 more times omitting last dc and ending sl st to first dc. Fasten off.

### Centre

Base ring: Using A (Blue), 6ch, join with sl st.

**1st round:** 3ch (count as 1tr), 23tr into ring, sl st to top of 3ch. (24 sts).

**2nd round:** 1ch, 1dc into same place as 1ch, 1dc into front loop only of next and each st all round, sl st to first dc.

**3rd round:** 1ch, 1dc into same place as 1ch, *work [1htr, 1tr, 1dtr] into next st, [1dtr, 1tr, 1htr] into next st, 1dc into next st; rep from * 7 more times, omitting dc at end of last rep, sl st to first st. Fasten off.

### Star Blocks

Make 6 Star Blocks alike, 1 each in B (Red), C (Orange), D (Yellow), E (Green), F (Indigo) and G (Violet) as follows:

### 1st Block

Join yarn to back loop of any st in 1st round of Centre and make 10ch, turn.

**1st row** (right side): Miss 2ch (count as 1dc), 1dc into next and each ch to end, turn. (9 dc).

**2nd and every alt row:** 1ch (counts as 1dc), miss first st, 1dc into next and each st to end working last st into tch, turn.

**3rd row:** Work as 2nd row but make a 5tr popcorn (to stand out on right side of fabric) on 5th st.

**5th row:** As 2nd row but making 5tr popcorns on the 3rd and 7th sts.

**7th row:** As 3rd row.

Work 2 more rows as 2nd row. (10 rows in all). Fasten off.

### Remaining Blocks

Miss 3 sts of 1st round of Centre and join new yarn into back loop of next st, then work as for 1st Block.

### Edging

Making sure all parts of fabric are right side facing, join A at left corner of 1st Block, 1ch,

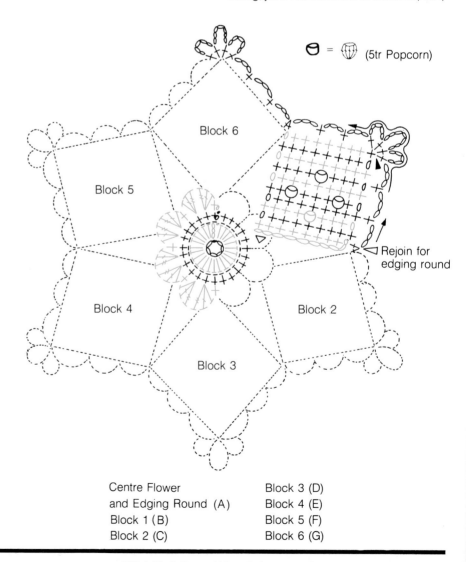

⊖ = ⬡ (5tr Popcorn)

Block 6

Block 5

Block 4

Block 2

Block 3

▷ Rejoin for edging round

Centre Flower
and Edging Round (A)
Block 1 (B)
Block 2 (C)

Block 3 (D)
Block 4 (E)
Block 5 (F)
Block 6 (G)

Stitch Variations, Abbreviations and Symbols on pages 7 to 15.

dc2tog over same place as 1ch and right corner of 2nd Block, *make 3 arches evenly spaced along edge of Block ending at top corner as follows: [3ch, 1dc into edge] 3 times, work [5ch, 1dc, 7ch, 1dc, 5ch, 1dc] into same corner, work 3 arches evenly spaced as before along next edge of same Block as follows: [3ch, 1dc into edge] twice, 3ch**, dc2tog over left corner of same Block and right corner of next Block; rep from * 4 more times and from * to ** again, sl st to first dc.

Fasten off.

## Crystal Motif

Base ring: Using A make 12ch, join with sl st.

**1st round:** 1ch, 1dc into ring, *work [7ch, 1dc, 4ch, 1ttr, 4ch, 1dc] into ring; rep from * 5 more times omitting dc at end of last rep, sl st to first dc. Fasten off.

**2nd round:** Join B into top of any ttr, 1ch, 1dc into same place as 1ch, *13ch, miss 7ch arch, 1dc into top of next ttr; rep from * 5 more times omitting dc at end of last rep, sl st to first dc.

**3rd round:** 1ch, 1dc into each of next 6ch, *3dc into next ch, 1dc into each of next 5ch**, dc3tog over [next ch, next dc and next ch], 1dc into each of next 5ch; rep from * 4 more times and from * to ** again, 1dc into next st, sl st to first dc.

**4th round:** 1ch, miss first st, 1dc into next st, *1dc into each of next 5 sts, 3dc into next st, 1dc into each of next 5dc**, dc3tog over next 3 sts; rep from * 4 more times and from * to ** again, 1dc into next st, sl st to first dc.

**5th round:** As 4th round. Fasten off.

**6th round:** Join C into same place, 1ch, 1dc into same place, *7ch, miss 6dc, work 1ttr, [5ch, 1ttr] 4 times into next dc at tip of star, 7ch, miss 6dc, 1dc into next dc cluster; rep from * 5 more times omitting dc at end of last rep, sl st to first dc.

Fasten off.

## Mica Motif

Base ring: 6ch, join with sl st.

**1st round:** 5ch (count as 1tr and 2ch), [1tr into ring, 2ch] 7 times, sl st to 3rd of 5ch. (8 spaces).

**2nd round:** 3ch (count as 1tr), [4tr into next sp, 1tr into next tr] 7 times, 4tr into next sp, sl st to top of 3ch.

**3rd round:** Sl st into next st, 3ch (count as 1tr), *1dc into each of next 2 sts, 1tr into next st, 5ch, miss 1 st**, 1tr into next st; rep from * 6 more times and from * to ** again, sl st to top of 3ch.

**4th round:** 3ch, tr3tog over next 3 sts (counts as tr4tog), *5ch, 1dc into next 5ch arch, 5ch**, tr4tog over next 4 sts; rep from * 6 more times and from * to ** again, sl st to top of first cluster.

**5th round:** 8ch (count as 1tr and 5ch), *1dc into next 5ch arch, 1dc into next dc, 1dc into next arch, 5ch**, 1tr into next cluster, 5ch; rep from * 6 more times and from * to ** again, sl st to 3rd of 8ch.

**6th round:** 10ch (count as 1tr and 7ch), miss 5ch, *1dc into 2nd of next 3dc, 7ch, miss 5ch**, 1tr into next tr, 7ch, miss 5ch; rep from * 6 more times and from * to ** again, sl st to 3rd of 10ch.

**7th round:** 6ch (count as 1tr and 3ch), 1tr into same place as 6ch, *[2ch, 1tr] 3 times into next 7ch arch, 1tr into next dc, [1tr, 2ch] 3 times into next 7ch arch**, work [1tr, 3ch, 1tr] into next tr; rep from * 6 more times and from * to ** again, sl st to 3rd of 6ch.

Fasten off.

1 — A

2, 3, 4, 5 — B

6 — C

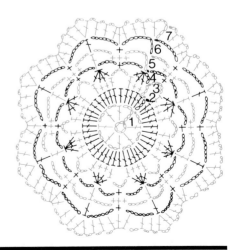

# Motifs

## Astrolabe Motif

Base ring: 4ch, join with sl st.

**1st round:** 4ch (count as 1tr and 1ch), [1tr into ring, 1ch] 7 times, sl st to 3rd of 4ch. (8 spaces).

**2nd round:** 1ch, 1dc into same place as 1ch, [3ch, miss 1ch, 1dc into next tr] 8 times omitting dc at end of last rep, sl st to first dc.

**3rd round:** Sl st into each of next 2ch, 1ch, 1dc into same place as 1ch, [6ch, 1dc into next 3ch arch] 8 times omitting dc at end of last rep, sl st to first dc.

**4th round:** Sl st into each of next 3ch, 1ch, 1dc into same place as 1ch, [6ch, 1dc into next arch] 8 times omitting dc at end of last rep, sl st to first dc.

**5th round:** 1ch, 1dc into same place as 1ch, *work [2tr, 4ch, 2tr] into next arch, 1dc into next dc; rep from * 7 more times omitting dc at end of last rep, sl st to first dc.

**6th round:** Sl st into each of next 2tr and next 2ch, 1ch, 1dc into same place as 1ch, [8ch, 1dc into next arch] 8 times omitting dc at end of last rep, sl st to first dc.

**7th round:** 1ch, *work a Wave of [1dc, 1htr, 2tr, 1dtr, 2tr, 1htr, 1dc] into next arch; rep from * 7 more times, sl st to first dc.

**8th round:** Sl st into each of next 4 sts to dtr, 1ch, 1dc into same place as 1ch, [11ch, 1dc into dtr at centre of next Wave] 8 times omitting dc at end of last rep, sl st to first dc.

**9th round:** 1ch, work [2dc, 2htr, 2tr, 4dtr, 2tr, 2htr, 2dc] into next 11ch arch 8 times, sl st to first dc.

Fasten off.

## Halley's Comet Motif

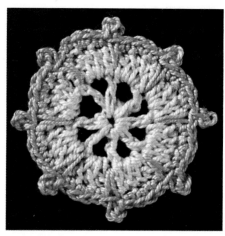

### Special Abbreviation

**Sdc (Spike double crochet)** = insert hook below st indicated 1 row down, i.e. into top of 1st round, yo, draw loop through and up to height of current round, yo, draw through both loops on hook

Base ring: Using A, 4ch, sl st to join.

**1st round:** 5ch (count as 1tr and 2ch), [1tr into ring, 2ch] 7 times, sl st to 3rd of 5ch. (8 spaces).

**2nd round:** 3ch (count as 1tr), 3tr into next sp, [1tr into next tr, 3tr into next sp] 7 times, sl st to top of 3ch. (32 sts). Fasten off.

**3rd round:** Join B into same place, 1ch, 1Sdc over first st, work a picot of [3ch, insert hook down through top of dc just made and work sl st to close], *1dc into next st, 2dc into next st**, 1Sdc over next st, picot; rep from * 6 more times and from * to ** again, sl st to first sdc.

Fasten off.

1, 2 — A
3 — B

## Briar Rose

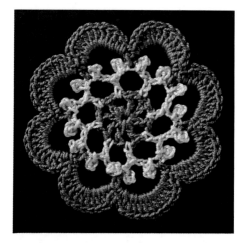

Base ring: Using A, 3ch, join with sl st.

**1st round:** 5ch (count as 1tr and 2ch), [1tr into ring, 2ch] 7 times, sl st to 3rd of 5ch. Fasten off. (8 spaces).

**2nd round:** Join B into a sp, 9ch, sl st into 4th ch from hook, 5ch, sl st into 4th ch from hook, 1ch, *1tr into next sp, work a picot of [5ch, sl st into 4th ch from hook] twice, 1ch; rep from * 6 more times, sl st to 3rd ch of starting ch. Fasten off.

**3rd round:** Join C into 1ch between 2 Picots, 1ch, 1dc into same place as 1ch, *7ch, miss [1 picot, 1tr and 1 picot], 1dc into next ch between picots; rep from * 7 more

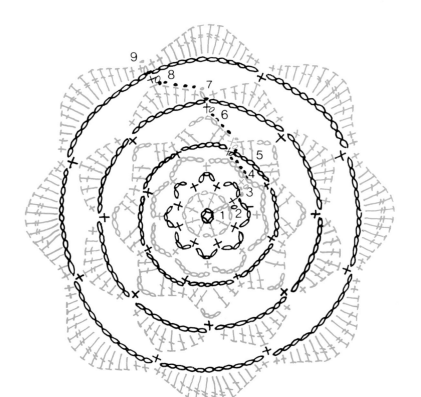

Stitch Variations, Abbreviations and Symbols on pages 7 to 15.

times omitting dc at end of last rep, sl st to first dc.

**4th round:** Sl st into next ch, 1ch, *work [1dc, 1htr, 9tr, 1htr, 1dc] into next arch; rep from * 7 more times, sl st to first dc. Fasten off.

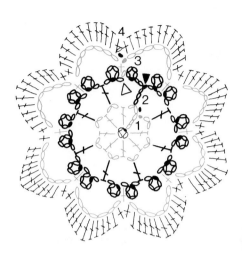

1 – A  2 – B
3, 4 – C

## Galaxy Motif

## Sylvan Circles

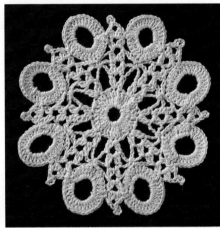

Base ring: 8ch, join with sl st.

**1st round:** 3ch (count as 1tr), 31tr into ring, sl st to top of 3ch. (32 sts).

**2nd round:** 3ch, 1tr into same place as 3ch (counts as tr2tog), 3ch, work tr2tog into same place as last cluster, *7ch, miss 3 sts, work [tr2tog, 3ch, tr2tog] into next st; rep from * 6 more times, 7ch, miss 3 sts, sl st to top of first cluster.

**3rd round:** Sl st into next ch, 3ch, 1tr into same place as 3ch (counts as tr2tog), 3ch, work tr2tog into same 3ch sp, *7ch, miss 7ch, work [tr2tog, 3ch, tr2tog] into next 3ch sp; rep from * 6 more times, 7ch, miss 7ch, sl st to top of first cluster.

**4th round:** Sl st into next ch, 3ch, 1tr into same place as 3ch (counts as tr2tog), 3ch, work tr2tog into same 3ch sp, *4ch, 1dc under 7ch arch of 2nd round so as to enclose 7ch arch of 3rd round, 4ch**, work [tr2tog, 3ch, tr2tog] into next 3ch sp; rep from * 6 more times and from * to ** again, sl st to top of first cluster.

**5th round:** Sl st into next ch, 3ch, 1tr into same place as 3ch (counts as tr2tog), 3ch, work tr2tog into same 3ch sp, *15ch, sl st into 12th ch from hook, 3ch, sl st to top of previous cluster, 6tr into 12ch ring, miss 4ch, sl st to next dc, 8tr into ring, miss 4ch, (inner half of Sylvan Circle completed)**, work [tr2tog, 3ch, tr2tog] into next 3ch sp; rep from * 6 more times and from * to ** again, sl st to top of first cluster.

**6th round:** *1ch, work [tr2tog, 6ch, sl st to 5th ch from hook, 1ch, tr2tog] into next 3ch sp, 1ch, sl st to top of next cluster, 16tr into 12ch ring (outer half of Sylvan Circle completed), sl st to top of next cluster; rep from * 7 times. Fasten off.

Base ring: 6ch, join with sl st.

**1st round:** 6ch (count as 1dtr and 2ch), [1dtr into ring, 2ch] 7 times, sl st to 4th of 6ch. (8 spaces).

**2nd round:** 2ch, work htr4tog into next sp (counts as htr5tog), work [7ch, htr5tog into next sp] 7 times, 7ch, sl st to first cluster.

**3rd round:** Sl st into each of next 3ch, 1ch, 3dc into same arch, [9ch, 3dc into next arch] 7 times, 8ch, 1dc into first dc.

**4th round:** 3ch, tr2tog over next 1dc and next ch missing dc between (counts as tr3tog), *2ch, miss 1ch, 1tr into next ch, 2ch, miss 1ch, work [1tr, 3ch, 1tr] into next ch, 2ch, miss 1ch, 1tr into next ch, 2ch, miss 1ch**, work tr3tog over [next ch, 2nd of next 3dc and next ch]; rep from * 6 more times and from * to ** again, sl st to top of first cluster. Fasten off.

# Motifs

## Flemish Motif

Base ring: 8ch, join with sl st.

**1st round:** 1ch, 16dc into ring, sl st to first dc. (16 sts).

**2nd round:** 12ch (count as 1dtr and 8ch), miss first 2dc, [1dtr into next dc, 8ch, miss 1dc] 7 times, sl st to 4th of 12 ch.

**3rd round:** 1ch, *into next 8 ch arch work [1dc, 1htr, 1tr, 3dtr, 4ch, insert hook down through top of dtr just made and work a sl st to close, 2dtr, 1tr, 1htr, 1dc]; rep from * 7 more times, sl st to first dc.

Fasten off.

## Barnacle Motif

Base ring: 8ch, join with sl st.

**1st round:** 1ch, [1dc into ring, 3ch, 1dtr into ring, 3ch] 8 times, sl st to first dc.

**2nd round:** Sl st into each of next 3ch and into dtr, [12ch, 1tr into 9th ch from hook, 3ch, sl st to top of next dtr] 8 times.

**3rd round:** Sl st into each of next 4ch, 3ch (count as 1tr), *work [1htr, 7dc, 1htr] into next 8ch arch, 1tr into next tr, miss last 3ch of same segment and first 3ch of next segment**, 1tr into next ch, (i.e. opposite side of same ch as tr of 2nd round); rep from * 6 more times and from * to ** again, sl st to top of 3ch.

**4th round:** 1ch, 1dc inserting hook under sl st which joined 3rd round, *3ch, miss [1htr and 1dc], 1dc into next dc, 3ch, miss 1dc, work [1dc, 4ch, 1dc] into next dc, 3ch, miss 1dc, 1dc into next dc, 3ch, miss [1dc, 1htr and 1tr]**, work 1dc between 2tr, miss 1tr; rep from * 6 more times and from * to ** again, sl st to first dc.

Fasten off.

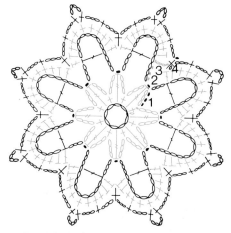

## Pulsar Motif

Base ring: 8ch, join with sl st.

**1st round:** 8ch, sl st into 6th ch from hook (counts as 1tr and picot), *4tr into ring, work a picot of [5ch, insert hook down through top of last tr made and work sl st to close]; rep from * 6 more times, 3tr into ring, sl st to 3rd of 8ch at beg of round. (8 picots).

**2nd round:** Sl st into each of next 2ch, 3ch (count as 1tr), work [1tr, 2ch, 2tr] into same picot, *4ch, work a DV st of [2tr, 2ch, 2tr] into next picot; rep from * 6 more times, 4ch, sl st to top of 3ch.

**3rd round:** Sl st into next tr and next ch, 3ch (count as 1tr), work [1tr, 2ch, 2tr] into same sp, *6ch, miss 4ch, DV st into next sp; rep from * 6 more times, 6ch, miss 4ch, sl st to top of 3ch.

**4th round:** Sl st into next tr and next ch, 3ch (count as 1tr), work [1tr, 2ch, 2tr] into same sp, *8ch, miss 6ch, DV st into next sp; rep from * 6 more times, 8ch, miss 6ch, sl st to top of 3ch.

**5th round:** Sl st into next tr and next ch, 3ch (count as 1tr), 4tr into same sp, *1dc into each of next 8ch, 5tr into next sp; rep from * 6 more times, 1dc into each of next 8ch, sl st to top of 3ch.

Fasten off.

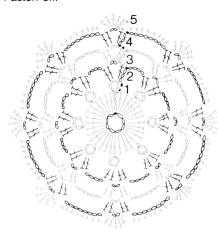

## Amanda Whorl

**Note:** Segments are worked in 4 colours A, B, C and D used successively.

**1st Segment**

Base ring: Using A 12ch, join with sl st.

**1st row** (right side): 4ch (count as 1dtr), [1dtr into ring, 6ch, 1tr into top of dtr just made, 1dtr into ring] 3 times, 1dtr into ring, 2ch, 10dtr into ring, turn.

**2nd row:** Work a picot of [5ch, sl st to 5th ch from hook], ★miss first dtr, 1dc into each of next 9dtr, change to next colour, turn.

**2nd Segment**

1ch, 1dc into same place as 1ch, 3ch, miss 3dc, 1dc into next dc, 9ch, sl st to first dc to complete joined base ring.

**1st row:** As given for 1st Segment.

**2nd row:** 2ch, 1dc into Picot of previous Segment, 3ch, sl st to first ch of row to complete Picot, continue as for 1st Segment from ★.

Work 5 more Segments as 2nd Segment using C, D, A, B and C.

**8th Segment**

Using D work as for previous Segments,

Stitch Variations, Abbreviations and Symbols on pages 7 to 15.

except also join to 1st Segment during 2nd row as follows: 2ch, 1dc into picot of 7th Segment, 1ch, 1dc into picot of 1st Segment, 2ch, sl st to first ch of row to complete picot, miss first dtr, 1dc into each of next 5dtr, sl st to 1st Segment, 1dc into each of next 4dtr, sl st to 1st Segment. Fasten off.

**Centre Ring**

Using A work inwards round centre to make edging as follows: join into any dc, 1ch, 1dc into same place as 1ch, [1dc into next picot, 1dc into side of next dc] 7 times, 1dc into next picot, sl st to first dc.

Fasten off.

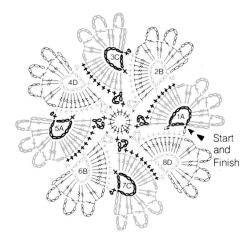

**6th round:** 1ch, 1dc into same place as 1ch, 1dc into each of next 4tr, *into next 2ch sp work [1dc, 3ch, insert hook down through top of dc just made and work sl st to close, 1dc] **, 1dc into each of next 5tr; rep from * 6 more times and from * to ** again, sl st to first dc.

Fasten off.

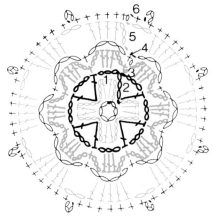

1 — A

2,3 — B

4,5,6 — C

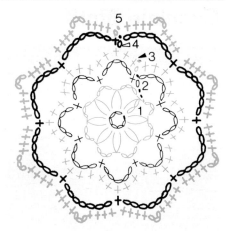

1,2,3 — A

4,5 — B

## Starfish

**Base ring:** 5ch, join with sl st.

**1st round:** 7ch (count as 1dtr and 3ch), [1dtr into ring, 3ch] 7 times, sl st to 4th of 7ch. (8 spaces).

**2nd round:** 3ch (count as 1tr), [4tr into next sp, 1tr into next dtr] 7 times, 4tr into next sp, sl st to top of 3ch. (40 sts).

**3rd round:** 1ch, 1dc into same place as 1ch, *6ch, 1dc into 2nd ch from hook, 1htr into next ch, 1tr into next ch, 1dtr into next ch, 1ttr into next ch, miss 4 sts, 1dc into next st; rep from * 7 more times omitting dc at end of last rep, sl st to first dc.

Fasten off.

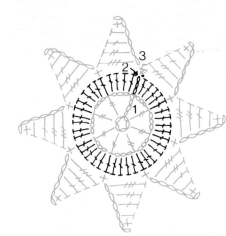

## Celtic Motif

**Base ring:** Using A, 6ch, join with sl st.

**1st round:** Work a Leaf of [3ch, 2tr into ring, 3ch, sl st into ring] 4 times. Fasten off.

**2nd round:** Join B into same place, 6ch (count as 1tr and 3ch), miss next Leaf, *[1tr, 3ch, 1tr] into sl st, 3ch, miss next Leaf; rep from * twice more, 1tr into next sl st, 3ch, sl st to 3rd of 6ch.

**3rd round:** 1ch, 1dc into same place as 1ch, *work a Leaf of [3ch, 3tr into next 3ch sp, 3ch, 1dc into next tr]; rep from * 7 more times omitting dc at end of last rep, sl st to first dc. Fasten off.

**4th round:** Join C into same place, 1ch, 1dc into same place as 1ch, *4ch, miss next Leaf, 1dc into next dc; rep from * 7 more times omitting dc at end of last rep, sl st to first dc.

**5th round:** 3ch (count as 1tr), 4tr into next 4ch arch, [2ch, 5tr into next arch] 7 times, 2ch, sl st to top of 3ch.

## Druid Motif

**Base ring:** Using A, 6ch, join with sl st.

**1st round:** 2ch, 1htr into ring (counts as htr2tog), [3ch, htr2tog into ring] 7 times, 3ch, sl st to first cluster.

**2nd round:** Sl st into each of next 2ch, 1ch, 1dc into same place as 1ch, [5ch, 1dc into next 3ch arch] 7 times, 5ch, sl st to first dc.

**3rd round:** 1ch, [5dc into next 5ch arch] 8 times, sl st to first dc. Fasten off.

**4th round:** Join B to 3rd of next 5dc, 1ch, 1dc into same place as 1ch, *7ch, miss 4dc, 1dc into next dc; rep from * 7 more times omitting dc at end of last rep, sl st to first dc.

**5th round:** 1ch, *[4dc, 3ch, 4dc] all into next 7ch arch; rep from * 7 more times, sl st to first dc.

Fasten off.

# Motifs

## Curlicue Motif

Base ring: 6ch, join with sl st.

**1st round:** 1ch, 12dc into ring, sl st to first dc. (12 sts).

**2nd round:** *work a Curlicue of [12ch, 5tr into 4th ch from hook, 5tr into next and each ch ending sl st into same place as 12ch], sl st into each of next 2dc; rep from * 5 more times omitting 1 sl st at end of last rep.

**3rd round:** 14ch, *1dc into tip of next Curlicue, 8ch**, 1 quad tr into dc of 1st round between Curlicues, 8ch; rep from * 4 more times and from * to ** again, sl st to 6th ch of 14ch.

**4th round:** 8ch (count as 1 quad tr and 2ch), [1 quad tr, 2ch] 4 times into same place as 8ch, *miss 8ch, 1dc into next dc, 2ch, miss 8ch**, [1 quad tr, 2ch] 5 times into next quad tr; rep from * 4 more times, and from * to ** again, sl st to 6th ch of 8ch.

**5th round:** 1ch, *3dc into next 2ch sp, 3ch, insert hook down through top of dc just made and work sl st to close; rep from * into each 2ch sp all round, sl st to first dc. Fasten off.

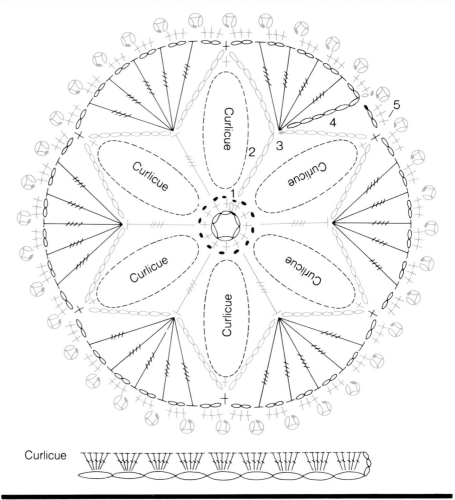

Curlicue

## Lazy Wheel

### 1st Segment
Make 17ch, sl st into 8th ch from hook, 1dc into next ch, 1htr into next ch, 1tr into next ch, 2tr into next ch, 1tr into next ch, 2dtr into next ch, 1dtr into next ch, 2ttr into next ch, 1ttr into last ch. Do not turn, but work corded dc back from left to right inserting hook under front loop only of each st, ending sl st into ring.

### 2nd Segment
Working behind corded dc row into back loop only of next 9 sts of previous Segment work 1dc into first st, 1htr into next st, 1tr into next st, 2tr into next st, 1tr into next st, 2dtr into next st, 1dtr into next st, 2ttr into next st, 1ttr into next st. Do not turn, but complete as for 1st Segment.

### 3rd to 10th Segments
Work as given for 2nd Segment. Fasten off leaving enough yarn to sew 10th Segment to 1st Segment on wrong side.

### Edging
**1st row** (right side): Rejoin yarn at tip of any Segment in corded edge row, 1ch, 1dc into same place as 1ch, [7ch, 1dc into tip of next Segment] 9 times, 7ch, sl st to first dc.

**2nd row:** 1ch, 2dc into same place as 1ch, *7dc into next arch**, 2dc into next dc; rep from * 8 more times and from * to ** again, sl st to first dc.
Fasten off.

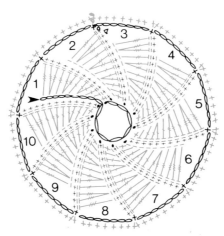

## Granite Wheel

Base ring: 7ch, join with sl st.

**1st round:** 1ch, 12dc into ring sl st to first dc. (12 sts).

**2nd round:** 3ch (count as 1tr), 1tr into next dc, *3ch, 1tr into each of next 2 sts; rep from * 4 more times, 3ch, sl st to top of 3ch.

**3rd round:** Sl st into next tr and next ch, 3ch, htr2tog into same arch (counts as htr3tog), 4ch, work htr3tog into same arch, *4ch, work [htr3tog, 4ch, htr3tog] into next arch; rep from * 4 more times, 4ch, sl st to top of first cluster. (12 clusters).

**4th round:** 1ch, *work [2dc, 3ch, 2dc] into next arch; rep from * 11 more times, sl st to first dc.
Fasten off.

Stitch Variations, Abbreviations and Symbols on pages 7 to 15.

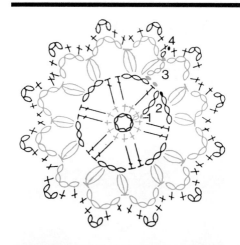

Base ring: Using A, 4ch, join with sl st.

**1st round:** 1ch, 1dc into ring, [4ch, 1ttr into ring, 4ch, 1dc into ring] 4 times omitting dc at end of last rep, sl st to first dc. Fasten off.

**2nd round:** Join B into same place, 11ch, miss 4ch, 1dc into next ttr, *7ch, miss 4ch**, 1dtr into next dc, 7ch, miss 4ch, 1dc into next ttr; rep from * twice more and from * to ** again, sl st to 4th ch of 11ch. Fasten off.

**3rd round:** Join C into same place, 4ch (count as 1dtr), 2dtr into same place as 4ch, *1ch, 1dc into next arch, 1ch, work [2ttr, 2ch, 2ttr] into next dc, 1ch, 1dc into next arch, 1ch**, 3dtr into next dtr; rep from * twice more and from * to ** again, sl st to top of 4ch. Fasten off.

**4th round:** Rejoin B into same place, 1ch, 1dc into same place as 1ch, 1dc into next and each ch and each st all round, except 3dc into each 2ch sp at corners, ending sl st to first dc. Fasten off.

**5th round:** Rejoin A into next dc, 6ch (count as 1dtr and 2ch), miss first 2dc, *1dtr into next dc, 2ch, miss 1dc, 1tr into next dc, 2ch, miss 1dc, 1htr into next dc, 2ch, miss 1dc, 1dc into next dc, 2ch, miss 1dc, 1htr into next dc, 2ch, miss 1dc, 1tr into next dc, 2ch, miss 1dc, 1dtr into next dc, 2ch, miss 1dc**, 1dtr into next dc, 2ch, miss 1dc; rep from * twice more and from * to ** again, sl st to 4th ch of 6ch.

**6th round:** 1ch, into first st work a trefoil of [1dc, 5ch, 1dc, 7ch, 1dc, 5ch, 1dc], *[2dc into next 2ch sp, 1dc into next st] twice, work a picot of [3ch, insert hook down through top of dc just made and work sl st to close], [2dc into next 2ch sp, 1dc into next st] 4 times, picot, 2dc into next 2ch sp, 1dc into

next st, 2dc into next 2ch sp**, trefoil into next st; rep from * twice more and from * to ** again, sl st to first dc.
Fasten off.

## Spandrell Motif

## Sunflower Motif

Base ring: Using A, 8ch, join with sl st.

**1st round:** 1ch, 12dc into ring, sl st to first dc. (12 sts)

**2nd round:** 3ch, 1tr into same place as 3ch (counts as tr2tog), [3ch, tr2tog into next st] 11 times, 3ch, sl st to first cluster.

**3rd round:** Sl st into each of next 2ch, 1ch, 1dc into same place as 1ch, [4ch, 1dc into next 3ch arch] 11 times, 4ch, sl st to first dc.

**4th round:** 1ch, *[2dc, 3ch, 2dc] all into next 4ch arch; rep from * 11 more times, sl st to first dc. Fasten off.

**5th round:** Join B into next 3ch arch, 3ch, tr2tog into same arch (counts as tr3tog), 4ch, tr3tog all into same arch, *[tr3tog, 4ch, tr3tog] all into next 3ch arch; rep from * 10 more times, sl st to first cluster.

**6th round:** 1ch, 1dc into same place as 1ch, *[2dc, 3ch, 2dc] all into next 4ch arch, miss next cluster**, 1dc into next cluster; rep from * 10 more times and from * to ** again, sl st to first dc.

Fasten off.

1 — A
2 — B
3 — C
4 — B
5 — A

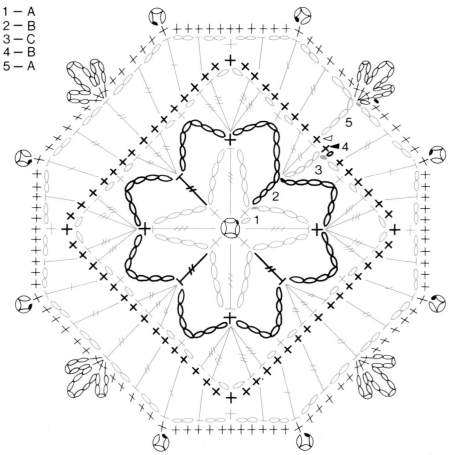

1, 2, 3, 4 — A

5, 6 — B

# Motifs

## Birds Nest I

### Special Abbreviation

**Popcorn** = work 5tr into next st, drop loop off hook, insert hook into first of these tr, pick up dropped loop and draw through.

Make 5ch, sl st into first ch to form a ring.

**1st round:** 4ch (count as 1tr, 1ch), work [1tr, 1ch] 11 times into ring, sl st into 3rd of 4ch at beg of round.

**2nd round:** 6ch (count as 1tr, 3ch), 1 popcorn into next tr, 3ch, [1tr into next tr, 3ch, 1 popcorn into next tr, 3ch] 5 times, sl st into 3rd of 6ch at beg of round.

**3rd round:** 1ch, 1dc into same st as last sl st, 4ch, 1dc into top of next popcorn, 4ch, [1dc into next tr, 4ch, 1dc into top of next popcorn, 4ch] 5 times, sl st into first dc.

**4th round:** Sl st into first 4ch arch, 2ch (count as 1htr), into same arch work [1tr, 1dtr, 1ttr, 1dtr, 1tr, 1htr], into each of next 11 4ch arches work [1htr, 1tr, 1dtr, 1ttr, 1dtr, 1tr, 1htr], sl st into 2nd of 2ch at beg of round. Fasten off.

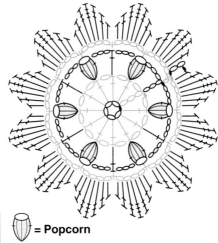

 = Popcorn

## Birds Nest II

Work as given for Birds Nest I **but** working 1st and 2nd rounds in A and 3rd and 4th rounds in B.

**3rd round:** 3ch, into top of first bobble work [first bobble as at beg of previous round, 2ch, 1 bobble], 1ch, 1tr into next dc, 1ch, into same dc as last tr work [1tr, 1ch, 1tr], 1ch, *into top of next bobble work [1 bobble, 2ch, 1 bobble], 1ch, 1tr into next dc, 1ch, into same dc as last tr work [1tr, 1ch, 1tr], 1ch; rep from * 4 times more, sl st into top of first bobble.

**4th round:** 3ch, 1 bobble into first bobble as at beg of 2nd round, 2ch, 1 bobble into next 2ch sp, 2ch, 1 bobble into top of next bobble, 1ch, [1tr into next tr, 1ch] 3 times, *1 bobble into next bobble, 2ch, 1 bobble into next 2ch sp, 2ch, 1 bobble into next bobble, 1ch, [1tr into next tr, 1ch] 3 times; rep from * 4 times more, sl st into top of first bobble.

**5th round:** 3ch, 1 bobble into first bobble as at beg of 2nd round, 2ch, 1 bobble into next 2ch sp, 3ch, 1 bobble into next 2ch sp, 2ch, 1 bobble into next bobble, 1ch, [1tr into next tr, 1ch] 3 times, *1 bobble into next bobble, 2ch, 1 bobble into next 2ch sp, 3ch, 1 bobble into next 2ch sp, 2ch, 1 bobble into next bobble, 1ch, [1tr into next tr, 1ch] 3 times; rep from * 4 times more, sl st into first bobble. Fasten off.

## Six Pack

### Special Abbreviation

**Bobble** = work 5tr into next dc until 1 loop of each remains on hook, yo and through all 6 loops on hook.

Make 6ch, sl st into first ch to form a ring.

**1st round:** 1ch, work 12dc into ring, sl st into first dc.

**2nd round:** 3ch, work 4tr into same st as last sl st until 1 loop of each tr remains on hook, yo and through all 5 loops on hook (1 bobble made at beg of round), *5ch, miss 1dc, 1 bobble into next dc; rep from * 4 times more, 5ch, sl st into top of first bobble. Fasten off.

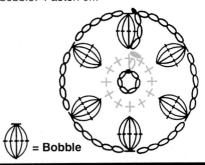

= Bobble

## Flat Disc

### Special Abbreviation

**Bobble** = work 3tr into next st until 1 loop of each remains on hook, yo and through all 4 loops on hook.

Make 12ch, sl st into first ch to form a ring.

**1st round:** 4ch (count as 1tr, 1ch), into ring work [2tr, 1ch] 11 times, 1tr into ring, sl st into 3rd of 4ch at beg of round.

**2nd round:** Sl st into first ch sp, 3ch, into same sp work 2tr until 1 loop of each remains on hook, yo and through all 3 loops on hook (1 bobble made at beg of round), 3ch, 1dc into next ch sp, 3ch, [1 bobble into next ch sp, 3ch, 1dc into next ch sp, 3ch] 5 times, sl st into top of first bobble.

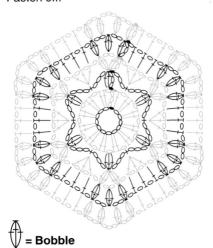

= Bobble

Stitch Variations, Abbreviations and Symbols on pages 7 to 15

## Blue Corner

**Special Abbreviations**

**4tr cluster** = work 1tr into each of next 4tr until 1 loop of each remains on hook, yo and through all 5 loops on hook.

**4tr bobble or 5tr bobble** = work 4tr (or 5tr) into next ch until 1 loop of each remains on hook, yo and through all 5 (or 6) loops on hook.

Make 6ch, sl st into first ch to form a ring.

**1st round:** 3ch (count as 1tr), work 15tr into ring, sl st into 3rd of 3ch at beg of round.

**2nd round:** 3ch, 1tr into each of next 3tr, [7ch, 1tr into each of next 4tr] 3 times, 7ch, sl st into 3rd of 3ch at beg of round.

## Bermuda Triangle

**Special Abbreviations**

**Popcorn** = work 5dtr into next ch, drop loop from hook, insert hook from the front into first of these dtr, pick up dropped loop and draw through, 1ch to secure.

**Picot** = make 5ch, sl st into top of tr just worked.

Make 6ch, sl st into first ch to form a ring.

**1st round:** 6ch (count as 1tr, 3ch), into ring work [1tr, 3ch] 11 times, sl st into 3rd of 6ch at beg of round.

**3rd round:** 3ch, work 1tr into each of next 3tr until 1 loop of each remains on hook, yo and through all 4 loops on hook (1 cluster made at beg of round), 5ch, miss 3ch, into next ch work [1tr, 5ch, 1tr], 5ch, *4tr cluster over next 4tr, 5ch, miss 3ch, into next ch work [1tr, 5ch, 1tr], 5ch; rep from * twice more, sl st into top of first cluster.

**4th round:** 1ch, *1dc into top of cluster, 1dc into each of next 5ch, 1dc into next tr, 2ch, 4tr bobble into next ch, 5ch, miss 1ch, 5tr bobble into next ch, 5ch, miss 1ch, 4tr bobble into next ch, 2ch, 1dc into next tr, 1dc into each of next 5ch; rep from * 3 times more, sl st into first dc. Fasten off.

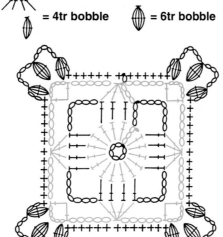

↑ = 4tr cluster

⬮ = 4tr bobble   ⬯ = 6tr bobble

**2nd round:** 1 sl st into each of first 2ch of first arch, 4ch (count as 1dtr), work 4dtr into same ch as last sl st, drop loop from hook, insert hook from the front into 4th of 4ch, pick up dropped loop and draw through, 1ch to secure (popcorn made at beg of round), 5ch, 1dc into next 3ch arch, [5ch, miss 1ch of next 3ch arch, 1 popcorn into next ch, 5ch, 1dc into next 3ch arch] 5 times, 5ch, sl st into top of first popcorn.

**3rd round:** 4ch, into top of first popcorn work [3dtr, 5ch, 4dtr], 3ch, 1tr into next dc, 1 picot, 3ch, 1dc into top of next popcorn, 3ch, 1tr into next dc, 1 picot, 3ch, *into top of next popcorn work [4dtr, 5ch, 4dtr], 3ch, 1tr into next dc, 1 picot, 3ch, 1dc into top of next popcorn, 3ch, 1tr into next dc, 1 picot, 3ch; rep from * once more, sl st into 4th of 4ch at beg of round. Fasten off.

⬮ = **Popcorn**

## Star Web

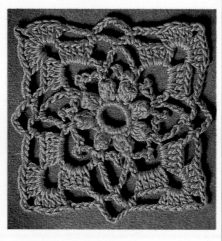

**Special Abbreviations**

**Popcorn** = work 5htr into next dc, drop loop from hook, insert hook from the front into top of first of these htr, pick up dropped loop and draw through, 1ch to secure popcorn.

**Picot** = make 3ch, work 1dc into first of these ch.

Make 10ch, sl st into first ch to form a ring.

**1st round:** 1ch, work 16dc into ring, sl st into first dc.

**2nd round:** 2ch, work 4htr into first dc, drop loop from hook, insert hook from the front into 2nd of 2ch, pick up dropped loop and draw through, 1ch to secure (1 popcorn made at beg of round), 2ch, 1 picot, 2ch, [miss 1dc, 1 popcorn into next dc, 2ch, 1 picot, 2ch] 7 times, sl st into top of first popcorn.

**3rd round:** 1ch, 1dc into same st as last sl st, [9ch, 1dc into top of next popcorn] 7 times, 4ch, 1ttr into first dc.

**4th round:** Sl st into arch just formed, 3ch (count as 1tr), work 4tr into same arch as last sl st, 4ch, 1dc into next 9ch arch, 4ch, *work [5tr, 5ch, 5tr] into next 9ch arch, 4ch, 1dc into next 9ch arch, 4ch; rep from * twice more, 5tr into same arch as first 5tr, 5ch, sl st into 3rd of 3ch at beg of round.

**5th round:** 7ch (count as 1tr, 4ch), *1dc into next 4ch arch, 6ch, 1dc into next 4ch arch, 4ch, work [5tr, 3ch, 5tr] into next 5ch arch, 4ch; rep from * 3 times more omitting 1tr and 4ch at end of last rep, sl st into 3rd of 7ch at beg of round. Fasten off.

⬮ = **Popcorn**   ⊛ = **Picot**

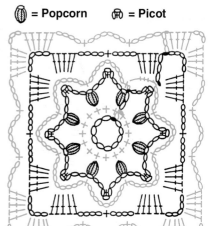

# Motifs

## Eighty Eight

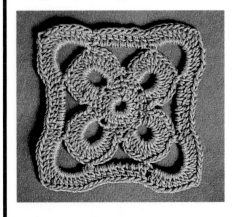

Make 6ch, sl st into first ch to form a ring.

**1st round:** 3ch (count as 1tr), work 15tr into ring, sl st into 3rd of 3ch at beg of round.

**2nd round:** 1ch, 1dc into same st as last sl st, 1dc into next tr, *[1dc, 7ch, 1dc] into next tr, 1dc into each of next 3tr; rep from * 3 times more omitting 2dc at end of last rep, sl st into first dc.

**3rd round:** 1ch, 1dc into same st as last sl st, *into next 7ch arch work [2htr, 17tr, 2htr] (1 shell made), miss 2dc, 1dc into next dc; rep from * 3 times more omitting 1dc at end of last rep, sl st into first dc.

**4th round:** Sl st into each of first 2htr and 6tr of first shell, 1ch, 1dc into same st as last sl st, 9ch, miss 5tr, 1dc into next tr, *7ch, miss first 2htr and 5tr on next shell, 1dc into next tr, 9ch, miss 5tr, 1dc into next tr; rep from * twice more, 7ch, sl st into first dc.

**5th round:** 3ch, *into next 9ch arch work [8tr, 1dtr, 8tr], 1tr into next dc, 7tr into next 7ch sp, 1tr into next dc; rep from * 3 times

more omitting 1tr at end of last rep, sl st into 3rd of 3ch at beg of round. Fasten off.

## Crystal Web

**Special Abbreviation**

**Cluster** = work 2ttr into next arch until 1 loop of each remains on hook, yo and through all 3 loops on hook.

**1st round:** Make 5ch, work 19dtr into first ch, sl st into top of 5ch.

**2nd round:** 8ch (count as 1ttr, 3ch), [1ttr into next dtr, 3ch] 19 times, sl st into 5th of 8ch at beg of round. 20 sps.

**3rd round:** Sl st into first arch, 5ch (count as 1ttr), work 1ttr into same arch as sl st, 6ch, [1 cluster into next arch, 6ch] 19 times, sl st into top of first ttr.

**4th round:** Work 1 sl st into each of first 3ch of first arch, 1ch, 1dc into same arch as sl sts, [8ch, 1dc into next 6ch arch] 19 times, 4ch, 1dtr into first dc.

**5th round:** 1ch, 1dc into arch just formed, 9ch, [1dc into next 8ch arch, 9ch] 19 times, sl st into first dc. Fasten off.

 = Cluster

## Overture

**Special Abbreviation**

**Bobble** = work 3ttr into ch until 1 loop of each remains on hook, yo and through all 4 loops on hook.

**1st round:** Make 6ch, work 2ttr into first ch until 1 loop of each remains on hook, yo and through all 3 loops on hook (bobble made at beg of round), into same ch work [5ch, 1 bobble] 7 times, 2ch, 1tr into top of first bobble.

**2nd round:** 1ch, work 1dc into arch just formed, 6ch, [1dc into next 5ch arch, 6ch] 7 times, sl st into first dc.

**3rd round:** Sl st into first 6ch arch, 3ch (count as 1tr), work 5tr into same arch, 3ch, [6tr into next 6ch arch, 3ch] 7 times, sl st into 3rd of 3ch at beg of round. Fasten off.

= Bobble

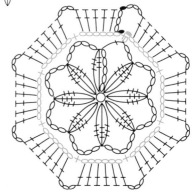

Stitch Variations, Abbreviations and Symbols on pages 7 to 15

## Wavy Line

Make 10ch, sl st into first ch to form a ring.

**1st round:** 3ch (count as 1tr), work 23tr into ring, sl st into 3rd of 3ch at beg of round.

**2nd round:** 3ch (count as 1tr), 1tr into next tr, 2tr into next tr, [1tr into each of next 2tr, 2tr into next tr] 7 times, sl st into 3rd of 3ch at beg of round.

**3rd round:** 3ch, 2tr into next tr, 2ch, [1tr into each of next 3tr, 2tr into next tr, 2ch] 7 times, 1tr into each of last 2tr, sl st into 3rd of 3ch at beg of round.

**4th round:** 3ch, 1tr into each of next 2tr, 2ch, 1tr into next 2ch sp, 2ch, [1tr into each of next 5tr, 2ch, 1tr into next 2ch sp, 2ch] 7 times, 1tr into each of last 2tr, sl st into 3rd of 3ch at beg of round.

**5th round:** 3ch, 1tr into next tr, 5ch, miss 1tr, 1tr into next tr, [5ch, miss 1tr, 1tr into each of next 3tr, 5ch, miss 1tr, 1tr into next tr] 7 times, 5ch, miss 1tr, 1tr into last tr, sl st into 3rd of 3ch at beg of round.

## Red Revolver

Make 12ch, sl st into first ch to form a ring.

**1st round:** 1ch, work 24dc into ring, sl st into first dc.

**2nd round:** 12ch, miss next dc, 1dc into next dc, turn, *3ch (count as 1tr), 1tr into each of first 7ch of arch, turn, 3ch, miss first tr, 1tr into each of next 6tr, 1tr into top of 3ch**, (first block made). ★Miss next dc on ring, work 1dtr into next dc, 8ch, miss 1dc, 1dc into next dc, turn and work from * to ** for next block. Rep from ★ 4 times more, sl st into 4th of 12ch at beg of round.

**3rd round:** Sl st to top of 3ch at corner of first block, 1ch, 1dc into top of 3ch, 13ch, [1dc into 3rd of 3ch at top of next block, 13ch] 5 times, sl st into first dc.

**6th round:** 11ch (count as 1tr, 8ch), miss next tr, 1tr into next tr, [8ch, miss 1tr, 1tr into next tr] 14 times, 8ch, sl st into 3rd of 11ch at beg of round. Fasten off.

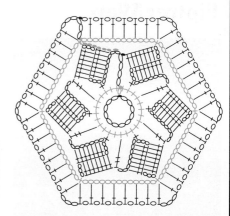

**4th round:** 6ch (count as 1tr, 3ch), 1tr into same st as last sl st, [1ch, miss 1ch, 1tr into next ch] 6 times, 1ch, *into next dc work [1tr, 3ch, 1tr], [1ch, miss 1ch, 1tr into next ch] 6 times, 1ch; rep from * 4 times more, sl st into 3rd of 6ch. Fasten off.

## Low Tide

Make 9ch, sl st into first ch to form a ring.

**1st round:** 1ch, work 18dc into ring, sl st into first dc.

**2nd round:** 9ch, work 1dc into 4th ch from hook, 1htr into each of next 2ch, 1tr into each of next 3ch, miss first 3dc on ring, sl st into next dc, *9ch, work 1dc into 4th ch from hook, 1htr into each of next 2ch, 1tr into each of next 3ch, miss next 2dc on ring, sl st into next dc; rep from *4 times more placing last sl st into same st as sl st of previous round. Fasten off.

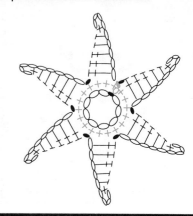

# Motifs

## Flower Web

### Special Abbreviation

**Cluster** = work 1dtr into each of next 5dtr until 1 loop of each remains on hook, yo and through all 6 loops on hook.

Make 8ch, sl st into first ch to form a ring.

**1st round:** 9ch (count as 1dtr, 5ch), into ring work [1dtr, 5ch] 7 times, sl st into 4th of 9ch at beg of round.

**2nd round:** Sl st into first 5ch arch, 4ch (count as 1dtr), work 6dtr into same arch, work 7dtr into each of next 7 arches, sl st into 4th of 4ch at beg of round.

**3rd round:** 4ch (count as 1dtr), work 1dtr into each of next 6dtr, 5ch, [1dtr into each of next 7dtr, 5ch] 7 times, sl st into 4th of 4ch at beg of round.

**4th round:** Sl st into next dtr, 4ch, 1dtr into each of next 4dtr until 1 loop of each remains on hook, yo and through all 5 loops on hook (1 cluster made at beg of round), 6ch, 1dc into next 5ch arch, [6ch, miss 1dtr, work 1 cluster across next 5dtr, 6ch, 1dc into next 5ch arch] 7 times, 3ch, 1tr into top of first cluster.

**5th round:** 1ch, 1dc into arch just formed, [8ch, 1dc into next 6ch arch] 15 times, 4ch, 1dtr into first dc.

**6th round:** 1ch, 1dc into arch just formed, 9ch, [1dc into next 8ch arch, 9ch] 15 times, sl st into first dc. Fasten off.

$\overline{\phantom{xxxx}}$ = **Cluster**

Make 6ch, sl st into first ch to form a ring.

**1st round:** 3ch (count as 1tr), work 15tr into ring, sl st into 3rd of 3ch at beg of round.

**2nd round:** 5ch (count as 1tr, 2ch), 1tr into same st as last sl st, *1ch, miss 1tr, into next tr work [1tr, 2ch, 1tr]; rep from * 6 times more, 1ch, sl st into 3rd of 5ch at beg of round.

**3rd round:** Sl st into first 2ch sp, 3ch (count as 1tr), into same sp work [1tr, 2ch, 2tr], *1ch, into next 2ch sp work [2tr, 2ch, 2tr]; rep from * 6 times more, 1ch, sl st into 3rd of 3ch at beg of round.

**4th round:** Sl st into next tr and first 2ch sp, 3ch, work 6tr into same sp as last sl st, 1dc into next ch sp, [7tr into next 2ch sp, 1dc into next ch sp] 7 times, sl st into 3rd of 3ch at beg of round. Fasten off.

## Teardrops

Make 8ch, sl st into first ch to form a ring.

**1st round:** 3ch (count as 1tr), into ring work 1tr, [6ch, 3tr] 5 times, 6ch, 1tr, sl st into 3rd of 3ch at beg of round.

**2nd round:** *1ch, into next 6ch arch work [1dc, 1htr, 7tr, 1htr, 1dc], 1ch, miss 1tr, 1 sl st into next tr; rep from * 5 times more placing last sl st into 3rd of 3ch at beg of previous round. Fasten off.

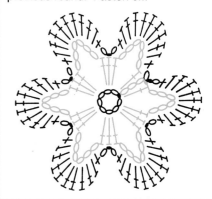

## Watermark

Stitch Variations, Abbreviations and Symbols on pages 7 to 15

## Cloister Window I

Make 8ch, sl st into first ch to form a ring.

**1st round:** 3ch (count as 1tr), work 19tr into ring, sl st into 3rd of 3ch at beg of round.

**2nd round:** [11ch, miss next tr, sl st into next tr] 9 times, 6ch, 1quadtr into sl st of previous round.

**3rd round:** Sl st into loop just formed, 3ch, into same loop work [2tr, 3ch, 3tr], work [3tr, 3ch, 3tr] into each of next 9 loops, sl st into 3rd of 3ch at beg of round. Fasten off.

**Note:** After working 3rd round it may be necessary to ease the shells of [3tr, 3ch, 3tr] to centre of loop formed in previous round.

## Gear Wheel

### Special Abbreviations

**Petal** = 1ch, 1dtr into next dc, 2ch, work 1dtr into stem of last dtr two thirds of the way down, 2ch, into stem of last dtr (two thirds of the way down as before) work [1tr, 2ch] twice, work 1tr two thirds of the way down stem of first dtr, 1ch, 1dc into next tr.

**3tr bobble** = work 3tr into next dc until 1 loop of each remains on hook, yo and through all 4 loops on hook.

Make 8ch, sl st into first ch to form a ring.

**1st round:** 1ch, work 16dc into ring, sl st into first dc.

**2nd round:** 3ch, work 2tr into same st as last sl st until 1 loop of each tr remains on hook, yo and through all 3 loops, (1 bobble made at beg of round), [3ch, miss next dc, 1 bobble into next dc] 7 times, 3ch, sl st into 3rd of 3ch at beg of round.

**3rd round:** 6ch (count as 1tr, 3ch), 1dc into first 3ch arch, 3ch, [1tr into next bobble, 3ch, 1dc into next 3ch arch, 3ch] 7 times, sl st into 3rd of 6ch at beg of round.

**4th round:** 1ch, work 1dc into same st as last sl st, work 8 petals omitting dc at end of last petal, sl st into first dc. Fasten off.

 = Petal      = 3tr bobble

## Cloister Window II

Work as given for Cloister Window I working 1 round each in colours A, B and C.

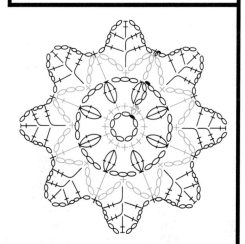

## Open Slice

### Special Abbreviations

**Dtr2tog** = work 2dtr into ring until 1 loop of each remains on hook, yo and through all 3 loops on hook.

**Cluster** = work 3tr into sp until 1 loop of each remains on hook, yo and through all 4 loops on hook.

Make 10ch, sl st into first ch to form a ring.

**1st round:** 4ch, 1dtr into ring, 2ch, into ring work [dtr2tog, 2ch] 11 times, sl st into first dtr.

**2nd round:** Sl st into 2ch sp, 3ch, into same 2ch sp as sl st, work 2tr until 1 loop of each remains on hook, yo and through all 3 loops on hook (first cluster made), 3ch, [1 cluster into next 2ch sp, 3ch] 11 times, sl st into top of first cluster.

**3rd round:** 5ch (count as 1htr, 3ch), miss first 3ch arch, into next 3ch arch work [1 cluster, 2ch, 1 cluster, 4ch, 1 cluster, 2ch, 1 cluster], 3ch, *miss next 3ch arch, 1htr into top of next cluster, 3ch, miss next 3ch arch, into next 3ch arch work [1 cluster, 2ch, 1 cluster, 4ch, 1 cluster, 2ch, 1 cluster], 3ch; rep from * twice more, sl st into 2nd of 5ch at beg of round.

**4th round:** 1ch, work 1dc into same st as last sl st, *3dc into next 3ch sp, 1dc into top of next cluster, 2dc into next 2ch sp, 1dc into next cluster, 5dc into next 4ch arch, 1dc into next cluster, 2dc into next 2ch sp, 1dc into next cluster, 3dc into next 3ch sp, 1dc into next htr; rep from * 3 times more omitting 1dc at end of last rep, sl st into first dc. Fasten off.

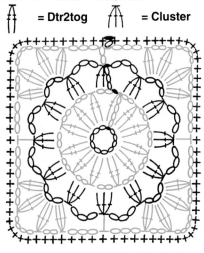

= Dtr2tog     = Cluster

# Motifs

## Venetian Star I

### Special Abbreviations

**Bobble** = work 3tr into next st until 1 loop of each remains on hook, yo and through all 4 loops on hook.

**Picot** = make 3ch, sl st into first of these ch.

**1st round:** Make 2ch, work 12dc into first ch, sl st into first dc.

**2nd round:** 3ch (count as 1tr), miss first dc, 1tr into next dc, 3ch, [1tr into each of next 2dc, 3ch] 5 times, sl st into 3rd of 3ch at beg of round.

**3rd round:** Sl st into next tr and 3ch sp, 3ch (count as 1tr), into same 3ch sp work [2tr until 1 loop of each remains on hook, yo and through all 3 loops on hook (bobble made at beg of round), 3ch, 1 bobble], 7ch, *into next 3ch sp work [1 bobble, 3ch, 1 bobble], 7 ch; rep from * 4 times more, sl st into top of first bobble.

**4th round:** Work 2 sl sts into first 3ch arch, 1ch, 1dc into same arch, *into next 7ch arch work [6tr, 1 picot, 6tr], 1dc into next 3ch arch; rep from * 5 times more omitting dc at end of last rep, sl st into first dc. Fasten off.

 = Bobble

 = Picot

## Venetian Star II

Work as given for Venetian Star I **but** working 1st and 2nd rounds in A, 3rd round in B and 4th round in C.

## Speedy Spiral

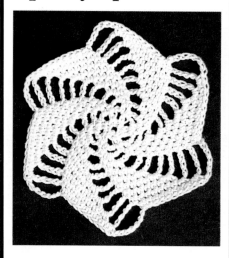

**Note:** This motif is worked as a continuous spiral, the size can therefore be increased or decreased as required.

**1st round:** Make 2ch, work 6dc into 2nd ch from hook, sl st into first dc.

Continue in a spiral as follows:
1ch, work 1dc into same st as last sl st, 3ch, [1dc into next dc, 3ch] 5 times, [1dc into next dc, 1dc into next sp, 3ch] 6 times, [miss 1dc, 1dc into next dc, 2dc into next sp, 3ch] 6 times, [miss 1dc, 1dc into each of next 2dc, 2dc into next sp, 4ch] 6 times, [miss 1dc, 1dc into each of next 3dc, 2dc into next 4ch sp, 4ch] 6 times, [miss 1dc, 1dc into each of next 4dc, 2dc into next 4ch sp, 5ch] 6 times, [miss 1dc, 1dc into each of next 5dc, 2dc into next 5ch sp, 5ch] 6 times, [miss 1dc, 1dc into each of next 6dc, 2dc into next 5ch sp, 6ch] 6 times, [miss 1dc, 1dc into each of next 7dc, 2dc into next 6ch sp, 6ch] 6 times, [miss 1dc, 1dc into each of next 8dc, 2dc into next 6ch sp, 7ch] 6 times, miss 1dc, sl st into next dc. Fasten off.

## Four Blade

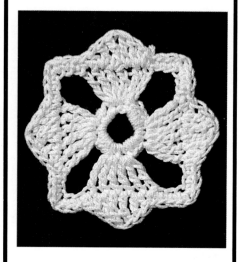

Make 8ch, sl st into first ch to form a ring.

**1st round:** 1ch, work 16dc into ring, sl st into first dc.

**2nd round:** 4ch (count as 1dtr), work 2dtr into first dc, 3dtr into next dc, 5ch, [miss 2dc, 3dtr into each of next 2dc, 5ch] 3 times, sl st into 4th of 4ch at beg of round.

**3rd round:** 1ch, 1dc into same st as last sl st, *[1htr, 1tr] into next dtr, 2dtr into each of next 2dtr, [1tr, 1htr] into next dtr, 1dc into next dtr, 1dc into each of next 2dc, 3dc into next ch, 1dc into each of next 2dc, 1dc into next dtr; rep from * 3 times more omitting 1dc at end of last rep, sl st into first dc. Fasten off.

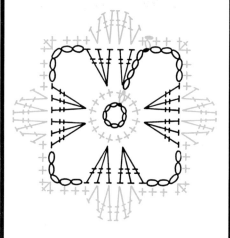

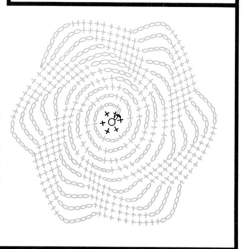

Stitch Variations, Abbreviations and Symbols on pages 7 to 15

## Garland I

### Special Abbreviation

**Tr2tog** = work 1tr into next tr until 2 loops remain on hook, miss 2tr, work 1tr into next tr until 3 loops remain on hook, yo and through all 3 loops on hook.

Make 10ch, sl st into first ch to form a ring.

**1st round:** 3ch (count as 1tr), work 31tr into ring, sl st into 3rd of 3ch at beg of round.

**2nd round:** [7ch, miss 3tr, sl st into next tr] 7 times, 3ch, 1dtr into same st as last sl st of previous round.

**3rd round:** 3ch, work 6tr into top of dtr, [7tr into 4th ch of next 7ch arch] 7 times, sl st into 3rd of 3ch at beg of round.

**4th round:** Sl st into next tr, 6ch (count as 1tr, 3ch), *miss 1tr, into next tr work [1dtr, 5ch, 1dtr], 3ch, miss 1tr, tr2tog, 3ch, miss 1tr, 1dc into next tr, 3ch, miss 1tr, tr2tog, 3ch; rep from * 3 times more omitting 1tr2tog and 3ch at end of last rep, miss 1tr, 1tr into next tr, sl st into 3rd of 6ch at beg of round.

**5th round:** 1ch, 1dc into same st as last sl st, *3dc into next 3ch sp, 1dc into next dtr, 6dc into 5ch arch, 1dc into next dtr, 3dc into next 3ch sp, 1dc into top of next tr2tog, 3dc into next 3ch sp, 1dc into next dc, 3dc into next 3ch sp, 1dc into top of next tr2tog; rep from * 3 times more omitting 1dc at end of last rep, sl st into first dc. Fasten off.

 = Tr2tog

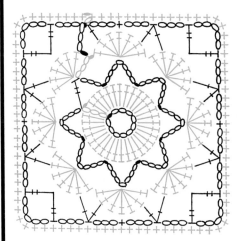

## King of Siam I

### Special Abbreviation

**3-Picot Cluster** = work 4ch, sl st into first ch, [3ch, sl st into same ch as first sl st] twice.

Make 6ch, sl st into first ch to form a ring.

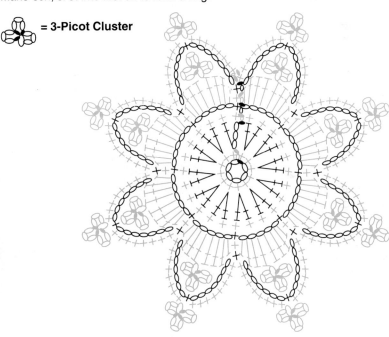 = 3-Picot Cluster

**1st round:** 1ch, work 12dc into ring, sl st into first dc.

**2nd round:** 3ch (count as 1tr), 1tr into same st as last sl st, work 2tr into each of next 11dc, sl st into 3rd of 3ch at beg of round.

**3rd round:** 1ch, 1dc into same st as last sl st, 1dc into each of next 23tr, sl st into first dc.

**4th round:** 1ch, 1dc into same dc as last sl st, 5ch, miss 2dc, [1dc into next dc, 5ch, miss 2dc] 7 times, sl st into first dc.

**5th round:** 1ch, 1dc into same st as last sl st, *into next 5ch arch work [1htr, 3tr, 3-picot cluster, 3tr, 1htr], 1dc into next dc; rep from * 7 times more omitting 1dc at end of last rep, sl st into first dc.

**6th round:** 1ch, 1dc into same st as last sl st, *7ch, 1dc into centre picot of 3-picot cluster, 7ch, 1dc into next dc; rep from * 7 times more omitting 1dc at end of last rep, sl st into first dc.

**7th round:** Sl st into first 7ch arch, 1ch, [work 8dc into next 7ch arch, 3-picot cluster, 8dc into same 7ch arch] 8 times, sl st into first dc. Fasten off.

## Garland II

Work as given for Garland I **but** working 1 round in each of colours A, B and C, then work 4th and 5th rounds in A.

## King of Siam II

Work as given for King of Siam I **but** working 1st, 2nd and 3rd rounds in A, 4th and 5th rounds in B and 6th, 7th rounds in C.

# Motifs

## Easy Rider

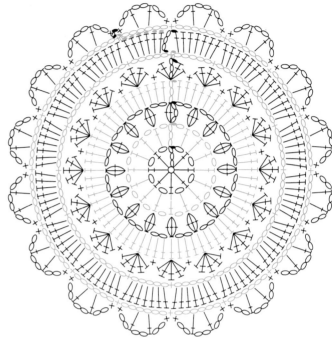

### Special Abbreviations

**Bobble** = work 3tr into next st until 1 loop of each remains on hook, yo and through all 4 loops on hook.

**Fan** = into next tr work [1htr, 3tr, 1htr].

**1st round:** Make 5ch, work [1tr, 1ch] 7 times into first ch, sl st into 4th of 5ch.

**2nd round:** 4ch (count as 1tr, 1ch), work 1tr into first ch sp, 1ch, [1tr into next tr, 1ch, 1tr into next ch sp, 1ch] 7 times, sl st into 3rd of 4ch at beg of round.

**3rd round:** 3ch (count as 1tr), work 2tr into same st as last sl st until 1 loop of each remains on hook, yo and through all 3 loops on hook (1 bobble made at beg of round), 2ch, [1 bobble into next tr, 2ch] 15 times, sl st into top of first bobble.

**4th round:** 3ch, work 3tr into first 2ch sp, [1tr into next bobble, 3tr into next 2ch sp] 15 times, sl st into 3rd of 3ch at beg of round.

**5th round:** 3ch, work [1tr, 1htr] into same st as last sl st, miss 1tr, 1dc into next tr, [miss 1tr, 1 fan into next tr, miss 1tr, 1dc into next tr] 15 times, miss last tr, work [1htr, 1tr] into same st as sl st at end of previous round, sl st into 3rd of 3ch at beg of round.

**6th round:** 1ch, 1dc into same st as last sl st, 5ch, [1dc into centre tr of next fan, 5ch] 15 times, sl st into first dc.

**7th round:** Sl st into first 5ch arch, 3ch, work 6tr into same arch as sl st, work 7tr into each of next 15 5ch arches, sl st into 3rd of 3ch at beg of round.

**8th round:** Sl st into each of first 6tr, 1ch, 1dc between last tr worked into and next tr, 6ch, [miss 7tr, 1dc between last tr missed and next tr, 6ch] 14 times, miss 7tr, 1dc between last tr missed and 3ch at beg of previous round, 6ch, sl st into first dc.

**9th round:** Sl st into first 6ch arch, 1ch, into each of next 16 6ch arches work [1dc, 2ch, 1tr, 2ch, 1tr, 2ch, 1dc], sl st into first dc. Fasten off.

 = Bobble    = Fan

## Watercolour

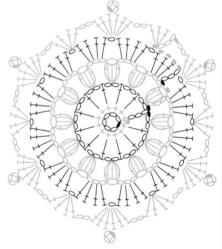

### Special Abbreviations

**Popcorn** = work 5tr into next st, drop loop from hook, insert hook into top of first of these tr, pick up dropped loop and draw through, 1ch to secure popcorn.

**Picot** = 3ch, sl st into first of these ch.

Make 6ch, sl st into first ch to form a ring.

**1st round:** 1ch, work 12dc into ring, sl st into first dc.

**2nd round:** 5ch (count as 1tr, 2ch), miss first dc, [1tr into next dc, 2ch] 11 times, sl st into 3rd of 5ch at beg of round.

**3rd round:** Sl st into first 2ch sp, 3ch, 4tr into same sp as sl st, drop loop from hook, insert hook into top of 3ch, pick up dropped loop and draw through, 1ch to secure (1 popcorn made at beg of round), 3ch, [1 popcorn into next 2ch sp, 3ch] 11 times, sl st into top of first popcorn.

**4th round:** Sl st into first 3ch sp, 3ch (count as 1tr), 3tr into same sp as sl st, 1ch, [4tr into next 3ch sp, 1ch] 11 times, sl st into 3rd of 3ch at beg of round.

**5th round:** Sl st into each of next 3tr and into ch sp, 3ch, 3tr into same sp as last sl st, 2ch, into next ch sp work [3tr, 1 picot, 3tr], *2ch, work 4tr into next ch sp, 2ch, into next ch sp work [3tr, 1 picot, 3tr]; rep from * 4 times more, 2ch, sl st into 3rd of 3ch at beg of round. Fasten off.

 = Popcorn     = Picot

Stitch Variations, Abbreviations and Symbols on pages 7 to 15

## Octagon Star

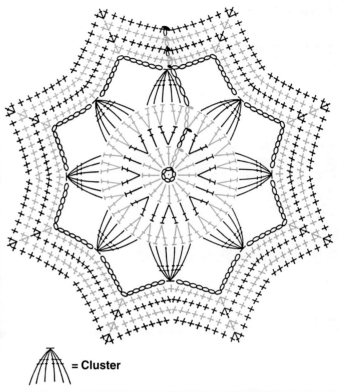

 = Cluster

### Special Abbreviation

**Cluster** = work 1dtr into each of next 6tr until 1 loop of each remains on hook, yo and through all 7 loops on hook.

Make 6ch, sl st into first ch to form a ring.

**1st round:** 3ch (count as 1tr), work 15tr into ring, sl st into 3rd of 3ch at beg of round.

**2nd round:** 3ch, 2tr into next tr, [1tr into next tr, 2tr into next tr] 7 times, sl st into 3rd of 3ch at beg of round.

**3rd round:** 3ch, work 2tr into each of next 23tr, 1tr into same st as sl st at end of previous round, sl st into 3rd of 3ch at beg of round.

**4th round:** 4ch, work 1dtr into each of next 5tr until 1 loop of each remains on hook, yo and through all 6 loops on hook (1 cluster made at beg of round), 13ch, [1 cluster over next 6tr, 13ch] 7 times, sl st into top of first cluster.

**5th round:** 1ch, 1dc into same st as last sl st, *1dc into each of next 6ch, 3dc into next ch, 1dc into each of next 6ch, 1dc into top of next cluster; rep from * 7 times more omitting 1dc at end of last rep, sl st into first dc.

**6th round:** 1ch, miss first dc, 1dc into each of next 7dc, 3dc into next dc, 1dc into each of next 7dc, [miss 1dc, 1dc into each of next 7dc, 3dc into next dc, 1dc into each of next 7dc] 7 times, sl st into first dc at beg of round.

**7th round:** 1ch, miss first dc, 1dc into each of next 7dc, 3dc into next dc, 1dc into each of next 7dc, [miss 2dc, 1dc into each of next 7dc, 3dc into next dc, 1dc into each of next 7dc] 7 times, miss next dc, sl st into first dc.

**8th round:** As 7th round. Fasten off.

## Evening Light

### Special Abbreviation

**3tr bobble or 4tr bobble** = work 3 (or 4) tr into next st until 1 loop of each remains on hook, yo and through all 4 (or 5) loops on hook.

**1st round:** Make 4ch, work 11tr into first of these ch, sl st into 4th of 4ch at beg of round.

**2nd round:** 3ch, work 2tr into same st as last sl st until 1 loop of each remains on hook, yo and through all 3 loops on hook (3tr bobble made at beg of round), [1ch, 3tr bobble into next tr] twice, 5ch, *3tr bobble into next tr, [1ch, 3tr bobble into next tr] twice, 5ch; rep from * twice more, sl st into top of first bobble.

**3rd round:** Sl st into first ch sp, 3ch, into same ch sp as last sl st work 3tr until 1 loop of each remains on hook, yo and through all 4 loops on hook (4tr bobble made at beg of round), *1ch, 4tr bobble into next ch sp, 2ch, 5tr into 5ch arch, 2ch, work 4tr bobble into next ch sp; rep from

* 3 times more omitting bobble at end of last rep, sl st into top of first bobble.

**4th round:** Sl st into first ch sp, 3ch then complete first 4tr bobble as on 3rd round, *2ch, 1tr into 2ch sp, 1tr into each of next 2tr, 5tr into next tr, 1tr into each of next 2tr, 1tr into next 2ch sp, 2ch, 4tr bobble into next ch sp; rep from * 3 times more omitting bobble at end of last rep, sl st into top of first bobble.

**5th round:** 3ch, *2tr into next 2ch sp, 1tr into each of next 4tr, 3ch, miss 1tr, 4tr bobble into next tr, 3ch, miss 1tr, 1tr into each of next 4tr, 2tr into next 2ch sp, 1tr into top of next bobble; rep from * 3 times more omitting 1tr at end of last rep, sl st into 3rd of 3ch at beg of round.

**6th round:** 3ch, 1tr into each of next 6tr, *2ch, miss 2ch, 4tr bobble into next ch, 5ch, 4tr bobble into next ch, 2ch, 1tr into each of next 13tr; rep from * 3 times more omitting 7tr at end of last rep, sl st into 3rd of 3ch at beg of round. Fasten off.

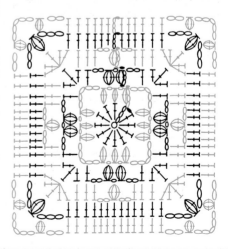

= 3tr bobble

= 4tr bobble

# Motifs

## Timelock

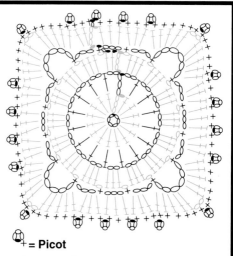

**= Picot**

### Special Abbreviation

**Picot** = 3ch, sl st into side of last dc worked.

Make 6ch, sl st into first ch to form a ring.

**1st round:** 3ch (count as 1tr), work 15tr into ring, sl st into 3rd of 3ch at beg of round.

**2nd round:** 5ch (count as 1tr, 2ch), [1tr into next tr, 2ch] 15 times, sl st into 3rd of 5ch at beg of round.

**3rd round:** Sl st into first 2ch sp, 3ch (count as 1tr), work 2tr into first 2ch sp, 1ch, [3tr into next 2ch sp, 1ch] 15 times, sl st into 3rd of 3ch at beg of round.

**4th round:** Sl st into each of next 2tr, 1ch, 1dc into first ch sp, 3ch, 1dc into next ch sp, 6ch, *1dc into next ch sp, [3ch, 1dc into next ch sp] 3 times, 6ch; rep from * twice more, [1dc into next ch sp, 3ch] twice, sl st into first dc.

**5th round:** Sl st into first 3ch sp, 3ch, work 2tr into first 3ch sp, into next 6ch arch work [5tr, 2ch, 5tr], *3tr into each of next 3 3ch sps, into next 6ch arch work [5tr, 2ch, 5tr]; rep from * twice more, 3tr into each of last 2 3ch sps, sl st into 3rd of 3ch at beg of round.

**6th round:** 1ch, 1dc into same st as last sl st, 1dc into each of next 2tr, 1 picot, 1dc into each of next 5tr, into next 2ch sp work [1dc, 1 picot, 1dc], 1dc into each of next 5tr, *1 picot, [1dc into each of next 3tr, 1 picot] 3 times, 1dc into each of next 5tr, into next 2ch sp work [1dc, 1 picot, 1dc], 1dc into each of next 5tr; rep from * twice more, 1 picot, [1dc into each of next 3tr, 1 picot] twice, sl st into first dc. Fasten off.

## Fourways

Make 6ch, sl st into first ch to form a ring.

**1st round:** 3ch (count as 1tr), work 15tr into ring, sl st into 3rd of 3ch at beg of round.

**2nd round:** 3ch (count as 1tr), 2tr into same st as last sl st, 2ch, miss 1tr, 1tr into next tr, 2ch, miss 1tr, *3tr into next tr, 2ch, miss 1tr, 1tr into next tr, 2ch, miss 1tr; rep from * twice more, sl st into 3rd of 3ch at beg of round.

**3rd round:** 3ch, 5tr into next tr, *1tr into next tr, [2ch, 1tr into next tr] twice, 5tr into next tr; rep from * twice more, [1tr into next tr, 2ch] twice, sl st into 3rd of 3ch at beg of round.

**4th round:** 3ch, 1tr into each of next 2tr, 5tr into next tr, *1tr into each of next 3tr, 2ch, 1tr into next tr, 2ch, 1tr into each of next 3tr, 5tr into next tr; rep from * twice more, 1tr into each of next 3tr, 2ch, 1tr into next tr, 2ch, sl st into 3rd of 3ch at beg of round.

**5th round:** 3ch, 1tr into each of next 4tr, 5tr into next tr, *1tr into each of next 5tr, 2tr into next 2ch sp, 1tr into next tr, 2tr into next 2ch sp, 1tr into each of next 5tr, 5tr into next tr; rep from * twice more, 1tr into each of next 5tr, 2tr into next 2ch sp, 1tr into next tr, 2tr into last 2ch sp, sl st into 3rd of 3ch at beg of round. Fasten off.

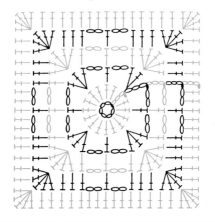

## Ship Shape

### Special Abbreviation

**Bobble** = work 5tr into next st until 1 loop of each remains on hook, yo and through all 6 loops on hook.

**1st round:** Make 6ch and working into first of these ch work [1tr, 2ch] 7 times, sl st into 4th of 6ch at beg of round.

**2nd round:** 3ch (count as 1tr), work 2tr into same st as last sl st, 2ch, [3tr into next tr, 2ch] 7 times, sl st into 3rd of 3ch at beg of round.

**3rd round:** 3ch, 1tr into same st as last sl st, 1tr into next tr, 2tr into next tr, 2ch, [2tr into next tr, 1tr into next tr, 2tr into next tr, 2ch] 7 times, sl st into 3rd of 3ch at beg of round.

**4th round:** 5ch (count as 1tr, 2ch), miss next tr, 1 bobble into next tr, 2ch, miss 1tr, 1tr into next tr, 2ch, [1tr into next tr, 2ch, miss 1tr, 1 bobble into next tr, 2ch, miss 1tr, 1tr into next tr, 2ch] 7 times, sl st into 3rd of 5ch at beg of round.

**5th round:** 3ch, 1tr into same st as last sl st, 2tr into first 2ch sp, 1tr into top of next bobble, 2tr into next 2ch sp, 2tr into next tr, 2ch, [2tr into next tr, 2tr into next 2ch sp, 1tr into top of next bobble, 2tr into next 2ch sp, 2tr into next tr, 2ch] 7 times, sl st into 3rd of 3ch at beg of round. Fasten off.

 **= Bobble**

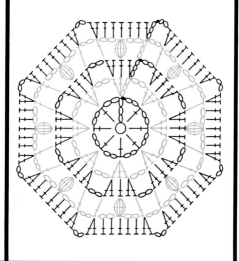

Stitch Variations, Abbreviations and Symbols on pages 7 to 15

## Viola

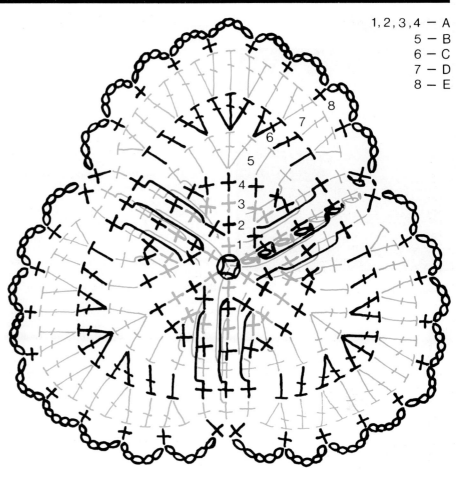

| | |
|---|---|
| 1, 2, 3, 4 | — A |
| 5 | — B |
| 6 | — C |
| 7 | — D |
| 8 | — E |

**Base ring:** Using A, 4ch, join with sl st.

**Special Abbreviation**

**Sdc (Spike double crochet)** = insert hook lower than usual (as indicated), yo, draw loop through and up to height of current row, yo, draw through both loops on hook

**1st round:** 1ch, 6dc into ring, sl st to first dc. (6 sts).

**2nd round:** 1ch, 2dc into each dc, sl st to first dc. (12 sts).

**3rd round:** 1ch, 1dc into first st, [2dc into next st, 1dc into next st] 5 times, 2dc into last st, sl st to first dc. (18 sts).

**4th round:** 1ch, 1dc into first st, [2dc into next st, 1dc into each of next 2 sts] 5 times, 2dc into next st, 1dc into last st, sl st to first dc. (24 sts). Fasten off.

**5th round:** Using B join into same place, 1ch, then starting in same st as 1ch work *1Sdc inserting hook into base ring, [1Sdc over next st inserting hook to left of last dc, but 1 round higher] twice, 1htr into next st, 3tr into next st, 1htr into next st, 1Sdc over next st inserting hook through top of 2nd round, 1Sdc over next st inserting hook through top of 1st round; rep from * twice, sl st to first Sdc. Fasten off.

**6th round:** Using C join into same place, 1ch, then starting in same st as 1ch work *1Sdc inserting hook between threads of previous Sdc and through top of 1st round, 1Sdc over next st inserting hook between threads of previous Sdc and through top of 2nd round, 1htr into next st, 1tr into next st, 2tr into next st, 3tr into next st, 2tr into next st, 1tr into next st, 1htr into next st, 1Sdc over next st inserting hook between threads of 2nd of 5 previous Sdcs and 1 round higher; rep from * twice, sl st to first Sdc. Fasten off.

**7th round:** Using D join into same place, 1ch, starting in same st as 1ch *1Sdc inserting hook between threads of previous Sdcs and through top of 2nd round, 1dc into next st, [1htr, 1tr] into next st, [1tr, 1htr] into next st, 2tr into next st] 4 times, 1tr into next st, [1tr, 1htr] into next st, 1dc into next st; rep from * twice, sl st to first Sdc. Fasten off.

**8th round:** Using E join into next st, 1ch, 1dc into same st as 1ch, *[5ch, miss next st, 1dc into next st] 9 times, miss next st**, 1dc into next st; rep from * and from * to ** again, sl st to first dc. Fasten off.

## Popcorn Trefoil

**Base ring:** Using A, 5ch, join with sl st.

**1st round:** 1ch, 6dc into ring, sl st to first dc. Fasten off.

**2nd round:** Using B, 1ch, 1dc into same place as 1ch, *3ch, 5tr Popcorn into next st, 3ch**, 1dc into next st; rep from * and from * to ** again, sl st into first dc.

**3rd round:** 1ch, 1dc into same place as 1ch, *4ch, 2tr into next 3ch arch, tr2tog inserting hook into same ch arch for first leg and into next ch arch for 2nd leg, 2tr into same ch arch, 4ch**, 1dc into next dc; rep from * and from * to ** again, sl st to first dc. Fasten off.

**4th round:** Using C join into corner cluster, 1ch, 1dc into same place as 1ch, *2ch, miss 2tr, going behind ch arches of 3rd round work [3tr into next ch arch of 2nd round] twice, 2ch, miss 2tr**, 1dc into corner cluster; rep from * and from * to ** again, sl st to first dc. Fasten off.

**5th round:** Using B join into last 2ch arch of 4th round, 1ch, *[1dc, 1htr, 1tr] into 2ch arch, 1ch, 1tr into next dc, 1ch, [1tr, 1htr, 1dc] into next 2ch arch, 1dc into each of next 6tr; rep from * twice, sl st to first dc. Fasten off.

**6th round:** Using A join into same place, 1ch, 1dc into same place as 1ch, 3ch, 1dc into each of next 2sts, 3ch, *2dc into next ch sp, 3ch, 3dc into tr at corner, 3ch, 2dc into next ch sp, 3ch**, [1dc into each of next 2 sts, 3ch] 6 times; rep from * and from * to ** again, [1dc into each of next 2 sts, 3ch] 4 times, 1dc into next st, sl st to first dc. Fasten off.

| | |
|---|---|
| 1 — A | 4 — C |
| 2, 3 — B | 5 — B |
| | 6 — A |

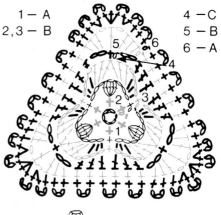

⬡ = 5dc Popcorn

# Motifs

## Royal Square

Base ring: 16ch, join with sl st.

**1st round:** 1ch, 24dc into ring, sl st to first dc, (24sts).

**2nd round:** 1ch, 1dc into same place as 1ch, *4ch, ttr2tog over next 2 sts, into top of cluster just made work set of 3 leaves as follows: [8ch, 1 quin tr, 7ch, 1dc, 8ch, 1 sext tr, 8ch, 1dc, 7ch, 1 quin tr, 7ch, sl st] 4ch, 1dc into next st of 1st round, 7ch, miss 2 sts, 1dc into next st; rep from * 3 more times, omitting dc at end of last rep, sl st to first dc. Fasten off.

**3rd round:** Rejoin yarn at tip of 2nd Leaf of next set, in top of 8ch before sext tr work 1ch, 1dc into same place, *2ch, miss sext tr, 1dc into next ch, 5ch, into tip of 3rd Leaf

of same set work in same way 1dc just before and 1dc just after quin tr, 7ch, into tip of 1st Leaf of next set work 1dc just before and 1dc just after quin tr, 5ch, into tip of 2nd Leaf of same set work 1dc just before sext tr; rep from * 3 more times, omitting dc at end of last rep, sl st to first dc.

**4th round:** 1ch, 1dc in same place as 1ch, *3dc into next 2ch sp, 1dc into next dc, 1dc into each of next 5ch, 1dc into each of next 2dc, 1dc into each of next 7ch, 1dc into each of next 2dc, 1dc into each of next 5ch, 1dc into next dc; rep from * 3 more times, omitting dc at end of last rep, sl st to first dc.

**5th round:** Sl st into each of next 2dc to corner, 4ch (count as 1tr and 1ch), 1tr into same place as 4ch, *[1ch, miss 1 st, 1tr into next st] 13 times to next corner**, [1ch, 1tr] twice all into same place as last tr; rep from * twice more and from * to ** again, ending 1ch, sl st to 3rd of 4ch.

**6th round:** 4ch (count as 1tr and 1ch), 1tr into same place as 4ch, *[1ch, 1tr into next ch sp] 15 times, 1ch**, [1tr, 1ch, 1tr, 1ch, 1tr] all into next corner st; rep from * twice and from * to ** again, ending 1tr into corner st, 1ch, sl st to 3rd of 4ch.

**7th round:** 3ch (count as 1tr), 1tr into same place as 3ch, *1ch, [1tr into next ch sp, 1tr into next tr, 1ch, miss 1ch, 1tr into next tr, 1tr into next ch sp, 1ch, miss 1tr] 5 times, 1tr into next ch sp, 1tr into next tr, 1ch, miss 1ch, 1tr into next tr, 1tr into next ch sp, 1ch**, 3tr into corner st; rep from * twice and from * to ** again, ending 1tr into corner st, sl st to top of 3ch.

**8th round:** 4ch (count as 1tr and 1ch), 1tr into same place as 4ch, *1tr into next tr, [1ch, miss 1ch, 1tr into each of next 2 sts] 13 times to next corner, 1ch**, [1tr, 1ch, 1tr] into same place as last tr; rep from * twice

and from * to ** again, ending sl st to 3rd of 4ch.

**9th round:** 1ch, 2dc into same place as 1ch, 1dc into each ch sp and each tr all round, except 3dc into st at each of next 3 corners and ending 1dc into first corner, sl st to first dc.

**10th round:** 5ch, ttr2tog all into same place as 5ch (counts as ttr3tog), 2ch, ttr3tog all into same place as last cluster, *5ch, miss 4 sts, ttr3tog all into next st, [5ch, miss 5 sts, ttr3tog all into next st] 6 times, 5ch, miss 4 sts**, [ttr3tog, 2ch, ttr3tog] all into next corner st; rep from * twice and from * to ** again, ending sl st to top of first cluster.

**11th round:** Sl st to next ch, 8ch, 1dc into 5th ch from hook, 1tr into same 2ch sp, work a picot of [5ch, 1dc into 5th ch from hook] *1tr into next cluster, [picot, miss 2ch, 1tr into next ch, picot, miss 2ch, 1tr into next cluster] 8 times, picot**, [1tr, picot] twice into 2ch sp at corner; rep from * twice more and from * to ** again, ending sl st to 3rd of 8ch. Fasten off.

## Pineapple Square

Base ring: 4ch, join with sl st.

**1st round:** 4ch (count as 1tr and 1ch), [1tr into ring, 1ch] 7 times, sl st to 3rd of 4ch.

**2nd round:** 5ch (count as 1tr and 2ch), *3tr into next ch sp, 1ch**, 3tr into next sp, 2ch; rep from * twice more and from * to ** again, 2tr into next sp, sl st to 3rd of 5ch.

**3rd round:** Sl st into next ch, 5ch (count as 1tr and 2ch), 3tr into next sp, *1ch, 1dc into next sp, 1ch**, work a V st of [3tr, 2ch, 3tr] into next 2ch sp; rep from * twice more and from * to ** again, 2tr into next sp, sl st to 3rd of 5ch.

**4th round:** Sl st into next ch, 5ch (count as 1tr and 2ch), 3tr into next ch sp, *1ch, miss 1ch, work [1tr, 2ch, 1tr] into next dc, 1ch, miss 1ch**, V st into next 2ch sp; rep from * twice more and from * to ** again, 2tr into next sp, sl st to 3rd of 5ch.

**5th round:** Sl st into next ch, 5ch (count as 1tr and 2ch), 3tr into next sp, *2ch, miss 1ch, 10tr into next 2ch sp, 2ch, miss 1ch**, V st into next sp; rep from * twice more and from * to ** again, 2tr into next sp, sl st to 3rd of 5ch.

**6th round:** Sl st into next ch, 5ch (count as 1tr and 2ch), 3tr into next sp, *2ch, miss 2ch, 1tr into next tr, [1ch, 1tr into next tr] 9 times, 2ch, miss 2ch**, V st into next sp; rep from

Stitch Variations, Abbreviations and Symbols on pages 7 to 15.

**17th round:** Sl st into each of next 2ch, 5ch (count as 1tr and 2ch), miss 3tr, *V st into next sp, [2ch, miss 2ch, V st into next sp] 3 times, V st into next sp, [2ch, miss 2ch, V st into next sp] 3 times**, 2ch; rep from * twice more and from ' to ** again omitting 1tr at end of last rep and ending sl st to 3rd of 5ch.

Fasten off.

## Trefoil Motif

**Leaf** (make 3 alike)

**Base chain:** 17ch.

**1st row** (right side): Miss 2ch (count as 1dc), 1dc into each ch to last ch, work 3dc into last ch for point, then work back along underside of base chain with 1dc into each ch to end, turn.

**2nd row:** 1ch (counts as 1dc), miss 1 st, 1dc into each st up to st at centre of point, work 3dc into centre st, 1dc into each st to last 3 sts and tch, turn.

**3rd, 4th, 5th, 6th and 7th rows:** As 2nd row.

Fasten off.

### Stem

Make 22ch (or as required), sl st to centre Leaf (2nd) as diagram, work back along base chain in dc and at same time join in side Leaves (1st and 3rd) at, say, 6th and 7th sts as follows: *insert hook through 1st Leaf and base chain, make 1dc, sl st to 3rd Leaf to match; rep from * once more. Continue to end of base chain in dc.

Fasten off.

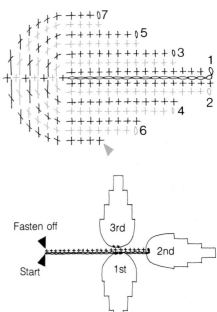

* twice more and from * to ** again, 2tr into next sp, sl st to 3rd of 5ch.

**7th round:** Sl st into next ch, 5ch (count as 1tr and 2ch), V st into next sp, *2ch, miss 2ch, 1dc into next sp, [3ch, 1dc into next sp] 8 times, 2ch, miss 2ch**, work [V st, 2ch, 3tr] into next sp; rep from * twice more and from * to ** again, 2tr into next sp, sl st to 3rd of 5ch.

**8th round:** Sl st into each of next 2ch, 5ch (count as 1tr and 2ch), miss 3tr, *V st into next sp, 2ch, miss 2ch, 1dc into next 3ch arch, [3ch, 1dc into next sp] 7 times, 2ch, miss 2ch**, V st into next sp, 2ch; rep from * twice more and from * to ** again, work [3tr, 2ch, 2tr] into next sp, sl st to 3rd of 5ch.

**9th round:** Sl st into next ch, 5ch (count as 1tr and 2ch), 3tr into next sp, *V st into next sp, 2ch, miss 2ch, 1dc into next 3ch arch, [3ch, 1dc into next 3ch arch] 6 times, 2ch, miss 2ch, V st into next sp**, V st into next sp; rep from * twice more and from * to ** again, 2tr into next sp, sl st to 3rd of 5ch.

**10th round:** Sl st into next ch, 5ch (count as 1tr and 2ch), V st into next sp, *2ch, V st into next sp, 2ch, miss 2ch, 1dc into next 3ch arch, [3ch, 1dc into next 3ch arch] 5 times, 2ch, miss 2ch, V st into next sp, 2ch**, work [V st, 2ch, 3tr] into next sp; rep from * twice more and from * to ** again, 2tr into next sp, sl st to 3rd of 5ch.

**11th round:** Sl st into each of next 2ch, 5ch (count as 1tr and 2ch), miss 3tr, *[V st into next sp, 2ch, miss 2ch] twice, 1dc into next 3ch arch, [3ch, 1dc into next 3ch arch] 4 times, [2ch, miss 2ch, V st into next sp] twice**, 2ch; rep from * twice more and from * to ** again omitting 1tr at end of last rep and ending sl st to 3rd of 5ch.

**12th round:** Sl st into next ch, 5ch (count

as 1tr and 2ch), 3tr into next sp, *[V st into next sp, 2ch, miss 2ch] twice, 1dc into next 3ch arch, [3ch, 1dc into next 3ch arch] 3 times, [2ch, miss 2ch, V st into next sp] twice**, V st into next sp; rep from * twice more and from * to ** again, 2tr into next sp, sl st to 3rd of 5ch.

**13th round:** Sl st into next ch, 5ch (count as 1tr and 2ch), V st into next sp, *2ch, [V st into next sp, 2ch, miss 2ch] twice, 1dc into next 3ch arch, [3ch, 1dc into next 3ch arch] twice, [2ch, miss 2ch, V st into next sp] twice, 2ch**, work [V st, 2ch, 3tr] into next sp; rep from * twice more and from * to ** again, 2tr into next sp, sl st to 3rd of 5ch.

**14th round:** Sl st into each of next 2ch, 5ch (count as 1tr and 2ch), miss 3tr, *[V st into next sp, 2ch, miss 2ch] 3 times, 1dc into next 3ch arch, 3ch, 1dc into next 3ch arch, [2ch, miss 2ch, V st into next sp] 3 times**, 2ch; rep from * twice more and from * to ** again omitting 1tr at end of last rep and ending sl st to 3rd of 5ch.

**15th round:** Sl st into next ch, 5ch (count as 1tr and 2ch), 3tr into next sp, *[V st into next sp, 2ch, miss 2ch] twice, V st into next sp, 3ch, miss 2ch, 1dc into next 3ch arch, 3ch, miss 2ch, V st into next sp, [2ch, miss 2ch, V st into next sp] twice**, V st into next sp; rep from * twice more and from * to ** again, 2tr into next sp, sl st to 3rd of 5ch.

**16th round:** Sl st into next ch, 5ch (count as 1tr and 2ch), V st into next sp, *2ch, [V st into next sp, 2ch, miss 2ch] twice, V st into next sp, 2ch, miss 3ch, 1dc and 3ch, [V st into next 2ch sp, 2ch, miss 2ch] twice, V st into next sp, 2ch**, work [V st, 2ch, 3tr] into next sp, rep from * twice more and from * to ** again, 2tr into next sp, sl st to 3rd of 5ch.

# Motifs

## Bachelor's Buttonhole

Base ring: Using A, 4ch, join with sl st.
**Special Abbreviations**
**Ltr (Linked Treble)** = insert hook down through horizontal loop round stem of last st made, yo, draw loop through; insert hook as indicated to make st and complete normally.

**Note:** at beginning of round to make first Ltr treat 2nd ch of starting ch as horizontal loop.

**Lttr (Linked Triple Treble)** = insert hook down through uppermost of 3 horizontal loops round stem of last st made, yo, draw loop through, [insert hook down through next lower horizontal loop , yo, draw loop through] twice; insert hook as indicated to make st and complete normally.

**Note:** at beginning of round to make first Lttr treat 2nd, 3rd and 4th chs of starting ch as horizontal loops.

**1st round:** 3ch (count as 1tr), 5Ltr into ring, sl st to top of 3ch. (6 sts).

**2nd round:** 5ch (count as 1ttr), 1Lttr into first st, (2Lttr into next st) 5 times, sl st to top of 5ch. (12 sts). Fasten off A.

**3rd round:** Using B, 1ch, 1dc into each st all round, sl st to first dc.

**4th round:** As 3rd round.

**5th round:** 1ch, 2dc into first st, 3dc into each st all round, 1dc into same place as first 2dc, sl st to first dc. (36 sts)

**6th round:** 3ch (count as 1tr), 2tr into first st, 3tr into each st all round, sl st to top of 3ch, 108 sts. Turn.

**7th round** (wrong side): 1ch, 1dc into first st, 5ch, *1dc into next st, 5ch; rep from * all round, ending sl st to first dc. (108 arches). Fasten off.

**Stem:** Rejoin A at underside of flower head into base ring, make 20ch (or as required), 1dc into 2nd ch from hook, 1dc into next and each ch, sl st to opposite side of base ring; now work back down stem in sl st, twisting stem as you go to create interest.
Fasten off.

## Lace Triangle

Base ring: Wrap yarn round finger.

**1st round:** 1ch, 12dc into ring, sl st to first dc.

**2nd round:** 10ch (count as 1tr and 7ch arch), miss first 2dc, *1tr into next dc, 3ch, miss 1dc, 1tr into next dc, 7ch, miss 1dc; rep from * once, 1tr into next dc, 3ch, miss last dc, sl st to 3rd of 10ch.

**3rd round:** 3ch (count as 1tr), into next ch arch work [3tr, 7ch, 4tr], *3tr into next ch arch, [4tr, 7ch, 4tr] into next ch arch; rep from * once, 3tr into last ch arch, sl st to top of 3ch.

**4th round:** 6ch (count as 1tr and 3ch arch), *[4tr, 5ch, 4tr] into next 7ch arch, 3ch, miss 2tr, 1tr into next tr, 3ch, miss 2tr, 1dc into next tr, 3ch**, miss 2tr, 1tr into next tr, 3ch; rep from * once and from * to ** again, sl st to 3rd of 6ch.

Fasten off.

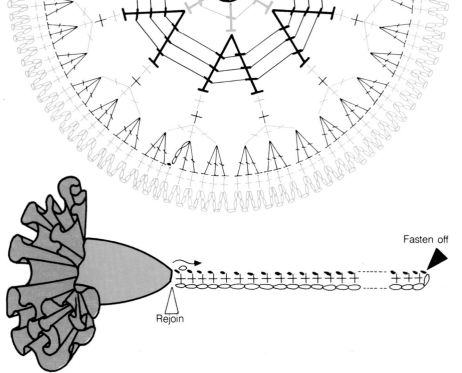

Stitch Variations, Abbreviations and Symbols on pages 7 to 15.

## Irish Crochet

True Irish crochet is made by first working motifs and then creating a net or mesh background incorporating the motifs and forming the fabric which holds them in position. This is done by placing the motifs in the required position face down on paper or a scrap of fabric and temporarily securing them. The background or filling, is then worked progressively joining in the motifs, after the work is completed the paper or fabric is carefully removed.

Historically crochet is believed to have been introduced into Ireland in the early part of the 19th century by nuns, probably from Italy or France. It was evolved by them and convent-educated girls into an art-form in itself, reaching levels of complexity and delicacy not seen in other styles of crochet work.

Stitches and techniques were developed which are particular to Irish crochet. The use of padding threads which are held at the edge of the work, so that subsequent rows or rounds are worked over them to give a three-dimensional effect is one example, another is the Clones Knot, and both of these are described below.

Because of the difficulty of giving general instructions for the construction of true Irish crochet, and particularly since the various motifs can each be incorporated into almost any crocheted net background, we have simplified the following selection to give you a taste of Irish style crochet.

## Padding Threads

Padding threads are used to give a three-dimensional appearance to some Irish crochet motifs. The thread used is usually the same as the thread used for the motif and the number of threads worked over determines the amount of padding. In this book we have usually worked over three thicknesses of thread.

The example below is for padding threads at the beginning of a motif, but they can also be used in other areas of motifs (see Tristar on page141).

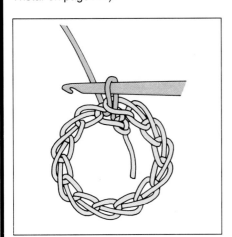

1. Make the required number of chain and join with a slip stitch.

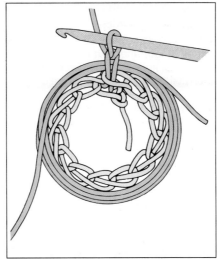

2. Wind a length of thread three or four times around the end of a pencil or finger and hold against the chain.

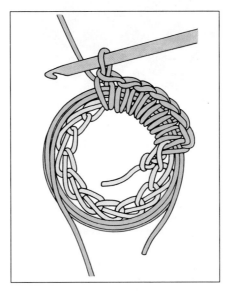

3. The stitches are then worked over the chain and 'padding' threads.

When the motif is complete the ends of the padding thread are pulled through several stitches and cut.

The instructions and diagrams of individual patterns indicate where it is appropriate to use padding threads. On the diagrams the padding thread is indicated with a thicker line.

## Working into Base of Stitch

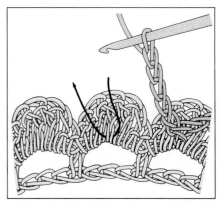

Insert the hook under two strands at the base of the stitch (this is indicated on the diagrams by red arrows see Tea Rose I on page 144). The diagram above shows work viewed from the back.

## Clones Knot

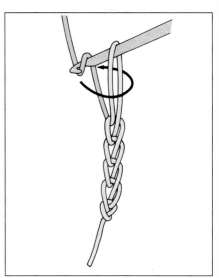

1. Draw up a chain. The length of the chain dictates the size of the Clones Knot.

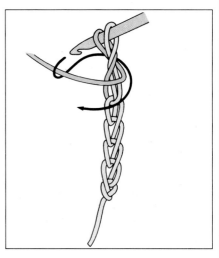

2. Holding chain in place, yarn over. Twist the hook over then under the loop.

# Irish Style Crochet

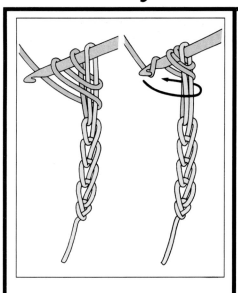

3. Pull the yarn back under the loop with the hook.

4. Repeat steps 2 and 3 until loop is completely covered.

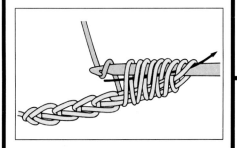

5. Yarn over, draw hook through all the loops.

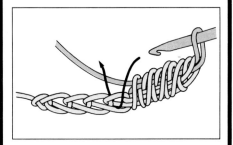

6. Secure knot by working a double crochet into the last chain worked before Clones Knot.

The Clones Knot can be secured in different ways, see individual pattern for instructions.

## Filament

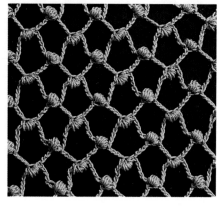

Starting chain: Multiple of 8 sts + 2.

### Special Abbreviation

**Clones Knot** = draw up a chain to required length and hold it in place, *yarn over, twist hook over then under the loop, then pull the yarn back under the loop with the hook; rep from * until the loop is completely covered. Yo, draw hook through all loops on hook. To secure knot work 1dc into last ch before Clones Knot.

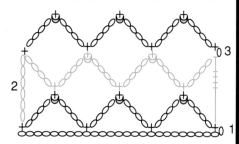

⊕ = **Clones Knot**

**1st row** (right side): Work 1dc into 2nd ch from hook, *4ch, 1 Clones Knot, 4ch, miss 7ch, 1dc into next ch; rep from * to end, turn.

**2nd row:** 10ch (count as 1quadtr, 4ch), working behind first Clones Knot work 1dc into dc securing knot, *4ch, 1 Clones Knot, 4ch, 1dc into dc securing next Clones Knot as before; rep from * ending with 4ch, 1quadtr into last dc, turn.

**3rd row:** 1ch, 1dc into quadtr, *4ch, 1 Clones Knot, 4ch, working behind next Clones Knot work 1dc into dc securing knot; rep from * to end placing last dc into 6th of 10ch at beg of previous row, turn.

Rep 2nd and 3rd rows.

## Chainlink

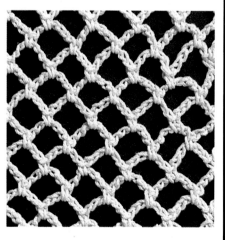

Starting chain: Multiple of 4 sts + 2.

**1st row** (right side): Work 1dc into 2nd ch from hook, *6ch, miss 3ch, 1dc into next ch; rep from * to end, turn.

**2nd row:** 8ch (count as 1ttr, 3ch), 1dc into first 6ch arch, *6ch, 1dc into next 6ch arch; rep from * to end, 3ch, 1ttr into last dc, turn.

**3rd row:** 1ch, 1dc into first ttr, *6ch, 1dc into next 6ch arch; rep from * to end placing last dc into 5th of 8ch at beg of previous row, turn.

Rep 2nd and 3rd rows.

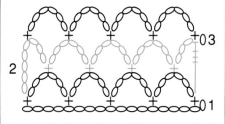

## Coathanger

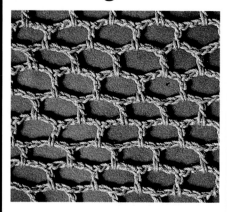

Starting chain: Multiple of 5 sts + 7.

**1st row** (right side): Work 1tr into 12th ch from hook, *4ch, miss 4ch, 1tr into next ch; rep from * to end, turn.

**2nd row:** 6ch (count as 1dtr, 2ch), 1tr into next 4ch sp, *4ch, 1tr into next 4ch sp; rep from * to end, 2ch, 1dtr into 5th ch, turn.

**3rd row:** 7ch (count as 1tr, 4ch), *1tr into next 4ch sp, 4ch; rep from * to last sp, 1tr into 4th of 6ch at beg of previous row, turn.

Rep 2nd and 3rd rows.

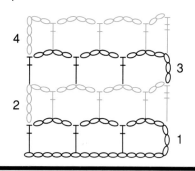

Stitch Variations, Abbreviations and Symbols on pages 7 to 15

## Open Diamond

Starting chain: Multiple of 7 sts + 6.

**1st row** (right side): Work 1dc into 6th ch from hook, 10ch, miss 6ch, *into next ch work [1dc, 4ch, 1dc], 10ch, miss 6ch; rep from * to last ch, into last ch work [1dc, 2ch, 1tr], turn.

**2nd row:** 11ch (count as 1quadtr, 5ch), into next 10ch arch work [1dc, 4ch, 1dc], *10ch, into next 10ch arch work [1dc, 4ch, 1dc]; rep from * to end, 5ch, 1quadtr into 3rd of 5ch at beg of previous row, turn.

**3rd row:** 5ch (count as 1tr, 2ch), 1dc into first arch, 10ch, *into next 10ch arch work [1dc, 4ch, 1dc], 10ch; rep from * to last arch, into last arch work [1dc, 2ch, 1tr], turn.

Rep 2nd and 3rd rows.

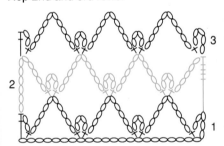

## Daisy Time

**Special Abbreviation**

**Tr2tog** = work 1tr into each of next 2dc until 1 loop of each remains on hook, yo and through all 3 loops on hook.

Make 6ch, sl st into first ch to form a ring.

**1st round:** 1ch, work 15dc into ring, sl st into first dc.

**2nd round:** [3ch, tr2tog over next 2dc, 3ch, sl st into next dc] 5 times placing last sl st into first dc of previous round.

Fasten off.

## Time Warp

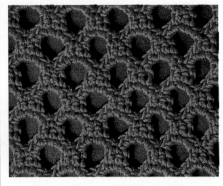

Starting chain: Multiple of 5 sts + 2.

**1st row** (right side): Work 1dc into 2nd ch from hook, 1dc into each ch to end, turn.

**2nd row:** 1ch, 1dc into each of first 2dc, *5ch, miss 2dc, 1dc into each of next 3dc; rep from * to end omitting 1dc at end of last rep, turn.

**3rd row:** 1ch, 1dc into first dc, *5dc into next 5ch arch, miss 1dc, 1dc into next dc; rep from * to end, turn.

## Four Petal

**Special Abbreviation**

**Bobble** = work 3dtr into next dc until 1 loop of each remains on hook, yo and through all 4 loops on hook.

Make 5ch, sl st into first ch to form a ring.

**1st round:** 1ch, work 12dc into ring, sl st into first dc.

**2nd round:** *4ch, work 1 bobble into next dc, 4ch, sl st into each of next 2dc; rep from * 3 times more omitting 1 sl st at end of last rep, 7ch, work 1dc into 2nd ch from hook, 1dc into each of next 5ch, sl st into first dc on first round. Fasten off.

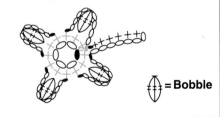

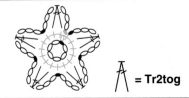

= Bobble

= Tr2tog

## 4th row, 5th row, 6th row

**4th row:** 6ch (count as 1dtr, 2ch), miss first 2dc, 1dc into each of next 3dc, *5ch, miss 3dc, 1dc into each of next 3dc; rep from * to last 2dc, 2ch, 1dtr into last dc, turn.

**5th row:** 1ch, 1dc into first dtr, 2dc into 2ch sp, miss 1dc, 1dc into next dc, *5dc into next 5ch arch, miss 1dc, 1dc into next dc; rep from * to last 2ch sp, 2dc into last sp, 1dc into 4th of 4ch at beg of previous row, turn.

**6th row:** 1ch, 1dc into each of first 2dc, *5ch, miss 3dc, 1dc into each of next 3dc; rep from * to end omitting 1dc at end of last rep, turn.

Rep 3rd to 6th rows.

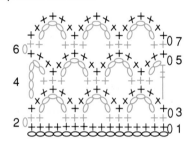

## Trellis Stitch

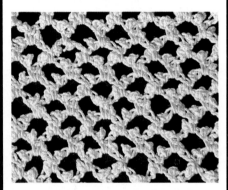

Starting Chain: Multiple of 5 sts + 2.

**1st row** (right side): Work 1dc into 2nd ch from hook, *[4ch, 1dc into 3rd ch from hook] twice, 1ch, miss 4ch, 1dc into next ch; rep from * to end, turn.

**2nd row:** 9ch (count as 1ttr, 4ch), 1dc into 3rd ch from hook, 1ch, 1dc into centre of first arch, *[4ch, 1dc into 3rd ch from hook] twice, 1ch, 1dc into centre of next arch; rep from * to end, 4ch, 1dc into 3rd ch from hook, 1ch, 1ttr into last dc, turn.

**3rd row:** 1ch, 1dc into first ttr, *[4ch, 1dc into 3rd ch from hook] twice, 1ch, 1dc into centre of next arch; rep from * to end placing last dc into 5th of 9ch at beg of previous row, turn.

Rep 2nd and 3rd rows.

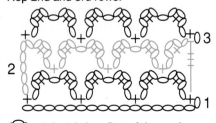

= 3ch, 1dc into first of these ch.

# Irish Style Crochet

## Diamond Cluster

3 0 + — 4 — 2 — 1

Line shows the direction of work for first two rows.

= sl st into next st, [7ch, sl st into same st as last sl st] 3 times.

The starting chain for this pattern forms part of the first row, and continues to form part of the second row.

**1st row** (right side): Make 16ch, sl st into 8th ch from hook, [7ch, sl st into same ch as last sl st] twice, *23ch, sl st into 8th ch from hook, [7ch, sl st into same ch as last sl st] twice; rep from * the number of times required, (diagram shows one repeat), make 8ch and turn work ready for **2nd row:** make 7 more ch, sl st into 8th ch from hook, 7ch, sl st into same ch as last sl st, 7ch, miss next 7ch loop, 1dc into next 7ch loop, *7ch, miss 7ch on previous row, sl st into next ch, [7ch, sl st into same ch as last sl st] 3 times, 7ch, miss next 7ch loop, 1dc into next 7ch loop; rep from * to last 8ch, 7ch, miss 7ch, into last ch work [1 sl st, 7ch, 1 sl st, 4ch, 1dtr], turn.

**3rd row:** 1ch, 1dc into dtr, *7ch, 1 sl st into next dc, [7ch, 1 sl st into same dc as last sl st] 3 times, 7ch, 1dc into 2nd 7ch loop; rep from * to end, turn.

**4th row:** [7ch, sl st into first dc] twice, 7ch, miss next 7ch loop, 1dc into next 7ch loop, *7ch, sl st into next dc, [7ch, sl st into same dc as last sl st] 3 times, 7ch, miss next 7ch loop, 1dc into next 7ch loop; rep from * to last dc, 7ch, into last dc work [1 sl st, 7ch, 1 sl st, 4ch, 1dtr], turn.

Rep 3rd and 4th rows.

## Roulette Wheel

= 3 loop cluster

___ = Padding thread

### Special Abbreviation

**3 loop cluster** = 7ch, sl st into first of these ch, [6ch, sl st into same ch as last sl st] twice.

Make 8ch, sl st into first ch to form a ring.

**1st round:** 1ch, working into ring and over padding threads, work 18dc, sl st into first dc.

**2nd round:** 6ch (count as 1htr, 4ch), miss first 3dc, 1htr into next dc, [4ch, miss 2dc, 1htr into next dc] 4 times, 4ch, sl st into 2nd of 6ch at beg of round.

**3rd round:** 1ch, work [1dc, 1htr, 3tr, 1htr, 1dc] into each of the 6 4ch arches, sl st into first dc. (6 petals).

**4th round:** Working behind each petal, sl st into base of each of first 4 sts, [5ch, miss next 6 sts, sl st into base of next tr] 6 times, working last sl st into base of same tr as sl st at beg of round.

**5th round:** 1ch, work [1dc, 1htr, 1tr, 5dtr, 1tr, 1htr, 1dc] into each of the 6 5ch arches, sl st into first dc.

**6th round:** Working behind each petal, sl st into base of each of first 6 sts, [6ch, miss next 10 sts, sl st into base of next dtr] 5 times, 3ch, miss next 10 sts, 1dtr into base of next dtr.

**7th round:** Sl st into arch just formed, into same arch work [1dc, 6ch, 1dc], 6ch, *into next arch work [1dc, 6ch, 1dc], 6ch; rep from * 4 times more, sl st into first dc.

**8th round:** Sl st into each of first 3ch of 6ch loop, into same loop work [1dc, 6ch, 1dc], 6ch, 1dc into next 6ch arch, 6ch, *into next 6ch loop work [1dc, 6ch, 1dc], 6ch, 1dc into next 6ch arch, 6ch; rep from * 4 times more, sl st into first dc.

**9th round:** Sl st into each of first 3ch of 6ch loop, into same loop work [1dc, 6ch, 1dc], 6ch, [1dc into next 6ch arch, 6ch] twice, *into next 6ch loop work [1dc, 6ch, 1dc], 6ch, [1dc into next 6ch arch, 6ch] twice; rep from * 4 times more, sl st into first dc.

**10th round:** Sl st into each of first 3ch of first 6ch loop, into same loop work [1dc, 3 loop cluster, 1dc], 6ch, [1dc into next 6ch arch, 6ch] 3 times, *into next 6ch loop work [1dc, 3 loop cluster, 1dc], 6ch, [1dc into next 6ch arch, 6ch] 3 times; rep from * 4 times more, sl st into first dc. Fasten off.

Stitch Variations, Abbreviations and Symbols on pages 7 to 15

## Tristar

**2nd round:** *1ch, working into next 9ch loop and over **padding threads** work [2dc, 1htr, 11tr, 1htr, 2dc], 1ch, sl st into same ch as sl sts of first round; rep from * twice more.

**3rd round:** Sl st into each of first 9 sts of first loop, [16ch, miss first 8 sts on next loop, sl st into next tr] twice, 16ch, sl st into same tr as last sl st at beg of round.

**4th round:** 1ch, working over **padding threads**, work 1dc into same tr as last sl st of previous round, 19dc into first 16ch arch, [1dc into same tr as next sl st of previous round, 19dc into next 16ch arch] twice, sl st into first dc. 60dc.

**5th round:** 8ch (count as 1tr, 5ch), miss next 3dc, [1tr into next dc, 5ch, miss 3dc] 14 times, sl st into 3rd of 8ch at beg of round.

**6th round:** Sl st into first 3ch of first arch, 1ch, working over **padding threads** work 4dc into first arch, 7dc into each of next 14 arches, 3dc into same arch as first 4dc, sl st into first dc.

**7th round:** 6ch, [miss next 6dc, sl st into next dc] 14 times, 6ch, sl st into same dc as last sl st of previous round.

**8th round:** 1ch, into each 6ch arch and over **padding threads** work 2dc, [1 picot, 2dc] 3 times. Sl st into first dc and fasten off.

**Special Abbreviation**

**Picot** = make 3ch, sl st into first of these ch.

**1st round:** Make 10ch, sl st into first ch, [9ch, sl st into same ch as last sl st] twice (3 loops formed).

## Pin Wheel

Make 6ch, sl st into first ch to form a ring and continue as follows:

1ch, work [1dc, 12ch] 12 times into ring, sl st into first dc. Fasten off.

 = Picot          —— = Padding thread

# Irish Style Crochet

## Magic Cirle

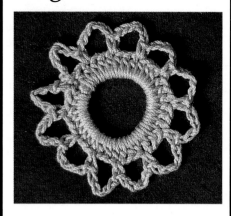

Make 16ch, sl st into first ch to form a ring.

**1st round:** 2ch (count as 1htr), work 35htr into ring and over **padding threads,** sl st into 2nd of 2ch at beg of round.

**2nd round:** 1ch, work 1dc into same st as last sl st, [5ch, miss 2htr, 1dc into next htr] 11 times, 5ch, sl st into first dc. Fasten off.

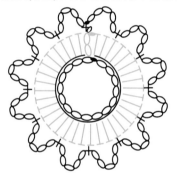

—— = Padding thread

## Green Leaf

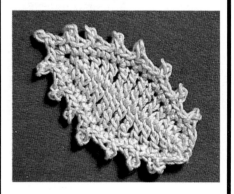

**Special Abbreviation**

**Picot** = make 3ch, sl st into first of these ch.

Make 15ch and work in a spiral as follows:
1dc into 2nd ch from hook, working 1 st into each ch work 1htr, 3tr, 4dtr, 3tr, 1htr and 1dc, 3ch, then working 1 st into each ch on other side of starting chain work 1dc, 1htr, 3tr, 4dtr, 3tr, 1htr, 1dc, 3ch, 1dc into first dc at beg of spiral, 1dc into next htr, 1 picot, [1dc into each of next 2 sts, 1 picot] 6 times, into 3ch sp at point of leaf work [1dc, 4ch, sl st into 3rd ch from hook, 1ch, 1dc], [1 picot, 1dc into each of next 2 sts] 7 times, sl st into 3ch sp. Fasten off.

## Fine Branches

## Spring Time

Make 5ch, sl st into first ch to form a ring.
**1st round:** 1ch, work 10dc into ring, sl st into first dc.

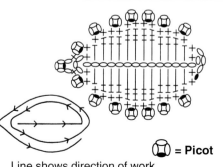

= Picot

Line shows direction of work.

**2nd round:** 1ch, work 1dc into each dc, sl st into first dc.

**3rd round:** 2ch (count as 1htr), miss first dc, work 2htr into each of next 9dc, 1htr into first dc, sl st into 2nd of 2ch.

**4th round:** *2ch, **working into front loop only** of each htr work 2tr into each of next 3htr, 2ch, sl st into next htr; rep from * 4 times more placing last sl st into 2nd of 2ch at beg of previous round. (5 petals made).

**5th round:** Working behind each petal of previous round and **into back loop** of each htr on 3rd round, sl st into first 2htr, *4ch, work 2ttr into each of next 3htr, 4ch, sl st into next htr; rep from * 3 times more, 4ch, 2ttr into next htr, 2ttr into 2nd of 2ch at beg of 3rd round, 2ttr into next htr, 4ch, sl st into next htr. Fasten off.

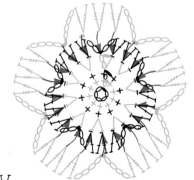

$\bigvee$ = 2tr into **front loop only** of next st. On final round work into **back loop only** of htr on 3rd round.

Stitch Variations, Abbreviations and Symbols on pages 7 to 15

# Irish Style Crochet

Make 7ch, sl st into first ch to form a ring.

**1st round:** 1ch, work 16dc into ring, sl st into first dc.

**2nd round:** 1ch, 1dc into first dc, [5ch, miss 1dc, 1dc into next dc] 7 times, 5ch, sl st into first dc.

**3rd round:** Sl st into first 5ch arch, 1ch, work [1dc, 5htr, 1dc] into each 5ch arch to end, sl st into first dc. (8 petals).

**4th round:** 1ch, working behind each petal work 1dc into first dc on 2nd round, [6ch, 1dc into next dc on 2nd round] 7 times, 6ch, sl st into first dc.

**5th round:** Sl st into first 6ch arch, 1ch, work [1dc, 6htr, 1dc] into each 6ch arch to end, sl st into first dc.

**6th round:** 1ch, working behind each pet-al work 1dc into first dc on 4th round, [7ch, 1dc into next dc on 4th round] 7 times, 7ch, sl st into first dc.

**7th round:** Sl st into first 7ch arch, 1ch, work [1dc, 7htr, 1dc] into each 7ch arch to end, sl st into first dc.

**8th round:** 1ch, working behind each pet-al work 1dc into first dc on 6th round, *[9ch, sl st into 6th ch from hook (1 picot made)] twice, 4ch, 1dc into next dc on 6th round, [13ch, sl st into 6th ch from hook (1 picot made)] twice, 8ch, 1dc into same dc as last dc, [9ch, sl st into 6th ch from hook] twice, 4ch, 1dc into next dc on 6th round; rep from * 3 times more omitting 1dc at end of last rep, sl st into first dc.

**9th round:** Sl st into each of first 3ch, behind first picot and into next ch of arch between picots, 1ch, 1dc into same arch as sl st, **[10ch, sl st into 6th ch from hook] twice, 5ch, 1dc into corner loop between 2 picots, *[10ch, sl st into 6th ch from hook] twice, 5ch, 1dc into arch be-tween 2 picots; rep from * once more; rep from ** 3 times more omitting 1dc at end of last rep, sl st into first dc.

**10th round:** Sl st into each of first 4ch, behind first picot and into next 2ch of arch between 2 picots, 1ch, 1dc into same arch between 2 picots, **[10ch, sl st into 6th ch from hook] twice, 5ch, 1dc into next dc at top of loop, *[10ch, sl st into 6th ch from hook] twice, 5ch, 1dc into next arch be-tween 2 picots; rep from * twice more; rep from ** 3 times more omitting 1dc at end of last rep, sl st into first dc. Fasten off.

# Irish Style Crochet

## Tea Rose I

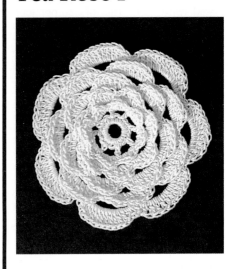

Make 8ch, sl st into first ch to form a ring.

**1st round:** 1ch, work 16dc into ring, sl st into first dc.

**2nd round:** 5ch (count as 1tr, 2ch), miss next dc, [1tr into next dc, 2ch, miss 1dc] 7 times, sl st into 3rd of 5ch at beg of round.

**3rd round:** Sl st into 2ch sp, 1ch, work [1dc, 1htr, 1tr, 1htr, 1dc] into each of the 8 2ch sps, sl st into first dc. (8 petals).

**4th round:** Working behind each petal, sl st into base of each of next 2 sts, 1ch, 1dc into base of same tr as last sl st, [3ch, miss 4 sts, 1dc into base of next tr] 7 times, 3ch, sl st into first dc.

**5th round:** Sl st into 3ch arch, 1ch, work [1dc, 1htr, 3tr, 1htr, 1dc] into each of the 8 3ch arches, sl st into first dc.

**6th round:** Working behind each petal, sl st into base of each of next 3 sts, 1ch, 1dc into base of same tr as last sl st, [5ch, miss 6 sts, 1dc into base of next tr] 7 times, 5ch, sl st into first dc.

**7th round:** Sl st into 5ch arch, 1ch, work [1dc, 1htr, 5tr, 1htr, 1dc] into each of the 8 5ch arches, sl st into first dc.

**8th round:** Working behind each petal, sl st into base of each of next 4 sts, 1ch, 1dc into base of same tr as last sl st, [7ch, miss 8 sts, 1dc into base of next tr] 7 times, 7ch, sl st into first dc.

**9th round:** Sl st into 7ch arch, 1ch, work [1dc, 1htr, 7tr, 1htr, 1dc] into each of the 8 7ch arches, sl st into first dc.

**10th round:** Working behind each petal, sl st into base of each of next 5 sts, 1ch, 1dc into base of same tr as last sl st, [9ch, miss 10 sts, 1dc into base of next tr] 7 times, 9ch, sl st into first dc.

**11th round:** Sl st into 9ch arch, 1ch, work [1dc, 1htr, 9tr, 1htr, 1dc] into each of the 8 9ch arches, sl st into first dc. Fasten off.

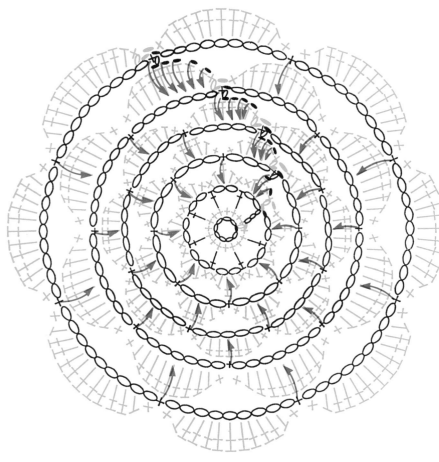

## Tea Rose II

Work as given for 1st to 7th round of Tea Rose I. Fasten off.

## Twisting

Starting chain: Any number of sts, plus 3.

**Note:** Sample photographed has starting chain of 31 sts.

Work 2tr into 4th ch from hook, 3tr into each ch to end. Fasten off.

Stitch Variations, Abbreviations and Symbols on pages 7 to 15

## Windmills

Make 6ch, sl st into first ch to form a ring.

**1st round:** 3ch (count as 1tr), work 17tr into ring and over **padding threads**, sl st into 3rd of 3ch at beg of round.

**2nd round:** 8ch (count as 1tr, 5ch), [1tr into next tr, 5ch] 17 times, sl st into 3rd of 8ch at beg of round.

**3rd round:** Sl st into each of next 3ch of first arch, 1ch, into same ch as last sl st work [1dc, 1ch, 1dc], *2dc into 2nd part of arch and 2dc into first part of next arch, into centre ch of arch work [1dc, 1ch, 1dc]; rep from * 16 times more, 2dc into 2nd part of last arch, 2dc into first part of first arch, sl st into first dc.

**4th round:** Sl st into first ch sp, 1ch, into same sp as last sl st work [1dc, 1ch, 1dc], 1dc into each of next 6dc, *into next ch sp work [1dc, 1ch, 1dc], 1dc into each of next 6dc; rep from * 16 times more, sl st into first dc.

**5th round:** Sl st into first ch sp, 1ch, into same sp as last sl st work [1dc, 1ch, 1dc], 1dc into each of next 8dc, *into next ch sp work [1dc, 1ch, 1dc], 1dc into each of next 8dc; rep from * 16 times more, sl st into first dc.

**6th round:** Sl st into first ch sp, 1ch, into same sp as last sl st work [1dc, 1ch, 1dc], 1dc into each of next 10dc, *into next ch sp work [1dc, 1ch, 1dc], 1dc into each of next 10dc; rep from * 16 times more, sl st into first dc.

**7th round:** Sl st into first ch sp, 1ch, work 1dc into same sp as last sl st, 5ch, [1dc into next ch sp, 5ch] 17 times, sl st into first dc.

**8th round:** 1ch, 1dc into first dc of previous round, 3ch, 1dc into next 5ch arch, [3ch, 1dc into next dc, 3ch, 1dc into next 5ch arch] 17 times, 3ch, sl st into first dc.

**9th round:** Sl st into first ch of first 3ch arch, 1ch, 1dc into same arch as last sl st, *4ch, 1dc into next 3ch arch; rep from * to end, 4ch, sl st into first dc.

**10th round:** Sl st into each of first 2ch of first 4ch arch, 1ch, 1dc into same arch as last sl sts, *5ch, 1dc into next 4ch arch; rep from * to end, 5ch, sl st into first dc. Fasten off.

—— = Padding thread

An enlargement of the area within the red frame showing in detail the stitches represented by the dotted lines on the main diagram.

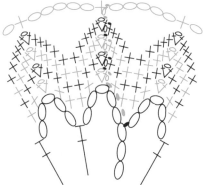

# Irish Style Crochet

## Solar System

## Showtime

**Special Abbreviation**

**Picot** = make 3ch, sl st into first of these ch.

Make 10ch, sl st into first ch to form a ring.

**1st round:** 1ch, into ring work 5dc, 1 picot, [8dc, 1 picot] twice, 3dc, sl st into first dc.

**2nd round:** 1ch, 1dc into same st as last sl st, *12ch, miss [4dc, 1 picot, 3dc], 1dc into next dc; rep from * once more, 12ch, sl st into first dc.

**3rd round:** Sl st into first 12ch arch, 1ch, into each of the 3 arches work [1dc, 1htr, 2tr, 9dtr, 2tr, 1htr, 1dc], sl st into first dc.

**4th round:** *1ch, 1dc into next htr, 1ch, [1tr into next st, 1ch] 13 times, 1dc into next htr, 1ch, sl st into each of next 2dc; rep from * twice more omitting 1 sl st at end of last rep.

**5th round:** Sl st into each of first [sl st, ch sp, dc and ch sp], 1ch, into same ch sp as last sl st work [1dc, 4ch, 1dc], into each of next 13 ch sps work [1dc, 4ch, 1dc], *1ch, sl st into each of next [dc, ch sp, 2 sl sts, ch sp, dc and ch sp], 1ch, into same sp as last sl st work [1dc, 4ch, 1dc], into each of next 13 ch sps work [1dc, 4ch, 1dc]; rep from * once more, 1ch, sl st into each of last [dc, ch sp and sl st]. Fasten off.

Make 8ch, sl st into first ch to form a ring.

**1st round:** 1ch, work 15dc into ring, sl st into first dc.

**2nd round:** 5ch, miss first 3dc, [sl st into next dc, 5ch, miss 2dc] 4 times, sl st into sl st at end of previous round.

**3rd round:** Sl st into first 5ch arch, 1ch, into same arch and each of next 4 arches work [1dc, 1htr, 5tr, 1htr, 1dc], sl st into first dc. (5 petals).

**4th round:** 1ch, working behind each petal of previous round, work 1 sl st into last sl st on 2nd round, 8ch, [1 sl st into next sl st on 2nd round, 8ch] 4 times, sl st into same st as first sl st at beg of round.

**5th round:** Sl st into first 8ch arch, 1ch, into same arch and each of next 4 arches work [1dc, 1htr, 8tr, 1htr, 1dc], sl st into first dc.

**6th round:** 2ch, working behind each petal of previous round work 1 sl st into last sl st on 2nd round, 10ch, [1 sl st into next sl st on 2nd round, 10ch] 4 times, sl st into same st as first sl st at beg of round.

**7th round:** Sl st into first 10ch arch, 1ch, work 15dc into same arch and into each of next 4 arches, sl st into first dc.

**8th round:** Sl st into next dc, *[4ch, miss 1dc, sl st into next dc] 6 times, turn, work 2 sl sts into first 4ch arch, [4ch, sl st into next 4ch arch] 5 times, turn, work 2 sl sts into first 4ch arch, [4ch, sl st into next 4ch arch] 4 times, turn, work 2 sl sts into first 4ch arch, [4ch, sl st into next 4ch arch] 3 times, turn, work 2 sl sts into first 4ch arch, [4ch, sl st into next 4ch arch] twice, turn, work 2 sl sts into first 4ch arch, 4ch, sl st into next arch and fasten off*. [Turn, miss next 2dc on 7th round, rejoin yarn to next dc and rep from * to *] 4 times.

⬚ = Picot

Stitch Variations, Abbreviations and Symbols on pages 7 to 15

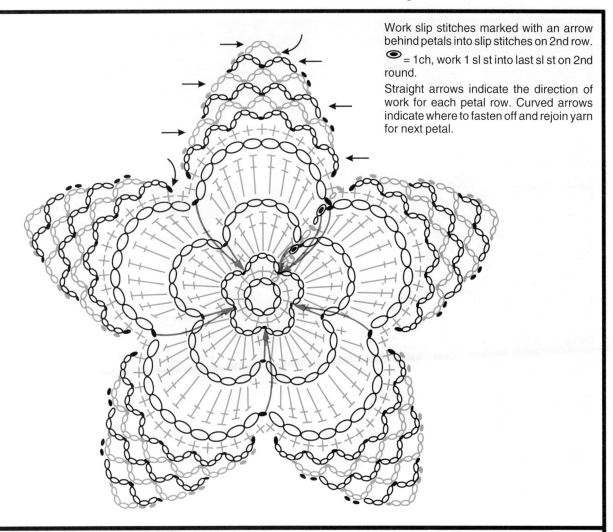

Work slip stitches marked with an arrow behind petals into slip stitches on 2nd row.

⬬ = 1ch, work 1 sl st into last sl st on 2nd round.

Straight arrows indicate the direction of work for each petal row. Curved arrows indicate where to fasten off and rejoin yarn for next petal.

## Traffic Lights

Make 6ch, sl st into first ch to form a ring.

**1st round:** 1ch, work 2dc into ring, *13ch, sl st into 6th ch from hook, 3ch, miss 3ch, sl st into next ch, 3ch, sl st into side of last dc worked, work 4dc into ring; rep from * 3 times more omitting 2dc at end of last rep, sl st into first dc. (4 points made).

**2nd round:** *Into each of first 2 sps on next point work [1dc, 3tr, 1dc], 1dc into top sp of same point, into same top sp work [3tr, 1dc] twice, then working on other side of loop work [1dc, 3tr, 1dc] into each of next 2 sps, 1 sl st into each of next 3dc on first round; rep from * 3 times more omitting 1 sl st at end of last rep.

**3rd round:** 1ch, work 1dc into same dc as last sl st, *16ch, 1dc into centre dc at top of point, 16ch, 1dc into centre dc between 2 points on first round; rep from * 3 times more omitting 1dc at end of last rep, sl st into first dc.

**4th round:** 1ch, *work 1dc into each of next 16ch, 1dc into next dc, 1dc into each of next 16ch, miss 1dc; rep from * 3 times more, sl st into first dc. Fasten off.

# Irish Style Crochet

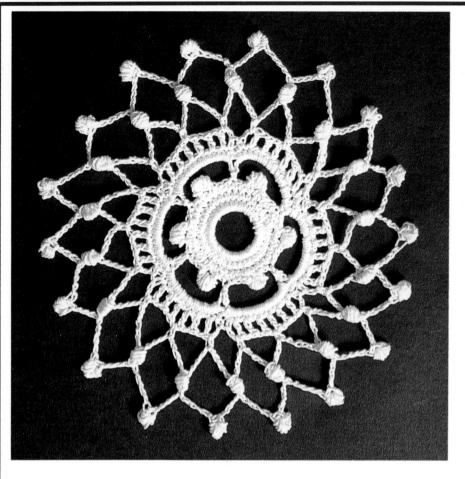

## Irish Eyes

### Special Abbreviations

**Clones Knot** = ★draw up a chain to required length and hold it in place, *yarn over, twist hook over then under the loop, then pull the yarn back under the loop with the hook; rep from * until the loop is completely covered. Yo, draw hook through all loops on hook★. To secure knot work 1dc into last ch before Clones Knot.

**Dc-Clones Knot** = work as given for Clones Knot from ★ to ★. To secure knot work 1dc into last dc before Clones Knot.

Make 18ch, sl st into first ch to form a ring.

**1st round:** 1ch, working into ring and over **padding threads**, work 36dc, sl st into first dc.

**2nd round:** 1ch, work 1dc into same st as last sl st, 1dc into each of next 35dc, sl st into first dc.

**3rd round:** 1ch, work 1dc into same st as last sl st, 1dc into each of next 2dc, *into next dc work [1dc, 1Dc-Clones Knot], 1dc into each of next 5dc; rep from * 5 times more omitting 3dc at end of last rep, sl st into first dc.

**4th round:** 11ch, miss [first 3dc, 1Dc-Clones Knot, 2dc], sl st into next dc, *11ch, miss [2dc, 1Dc-Clones Knot, 2dc], sl st into next dc; rep from * 4 times more placing last sl st into first dc of previous round.

**5th round:** 1ch, work 15dc into each of the 6 arches and over **padding threads**, sl st into first dc.

**6th round:** 1ch, 1dc into next dc, 2ch, 1tr into next dc, [1ch, miss 1dc, 1tr into next dc] 5 times, 2ch, 1dc into next dc, *miss 2dc, 1dc into next dc, 2ch, 1tr into next dc, [1ch, miss 1dc, 1tr into next dc] 5 times, 2ch, 1dc into next dc; rep from * 4 times more, sl st into first dc.

**7th round:** Sl st into first ch, 1ch, 1dc into 2ch sp, *4ch, 1 Clones Knot, 4ch, miss 3tr, 1dc into next ch sp, [4ch, 1 Clones Knot, 4ch, 1dc into next 2ch sp] twice; rep from * 5 times more omitting 1dc at end of last rep, sl st into first dc.

**8th round:** Sl st into each ch to first Clones Knot, 1ch, [working behind Clones Knot work 1dc into dc securing Clones Knot, 4ch, 1 Clones Knot, 4ch] 18 times, sl st into first dc. Fasten off.

= Dc-Clones Knot

= Clones Knot

―――― = Padding thread

Stitch Variations, Abbreviations and Symbols on pages 7 to 15

# Irish Style Crochet

## Anemone

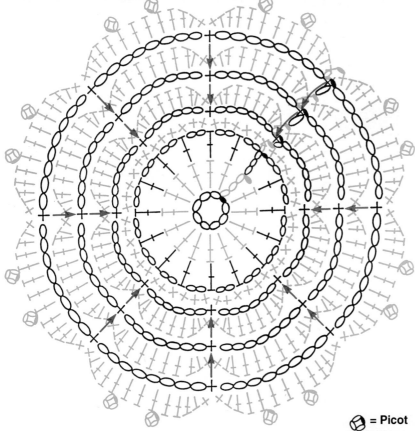

⊕ = Picot

### Special Abbreviation

**Picot** = make 3ch, sl st into first of these ch.

Make 8ch, sl st into first ch to form a ring.

**1st round:** 3ch (count as 1tr), work 15tr into ring, sl st into 3rd of 3ch at beg of round.

**2nd round:** 5ch (count as 1tr, 2ch), [1tr into next tr, 2ch] 15 times, sl st into 3rd of 5ch at beg of round.

**3rd round:** 1ch, work 3dc into each of the 16 2ch sps, sl st into first dc.

**4th round:** 1ch, work 1dc into same dc as last sl st, *6ch, miss 5dc, 1dc into next dc; rep from * 6 times more, 6ch, sl st into first dc.

**5th round:** Sl st into first 6ch arch, 1ch, work [1dc, 1htr, 6tr, 1htr, 1dc] into each of the 8 6ch arches, sl st into first dc. (8 petals worked).

## Trefoil Design

**1st round:** Make 16ch, sl st into first ch (first loop formed), [15ch, sl st into same ch as last sl st] twice.

**2nd round:** 1ch, working over **padding threads** work [28dc into next loop, 1 sl st into same ch as sl sts of first round] 3 times.

**3rd round:** Sl st into each of first 3dc, 1ch, 1dc into same st as last sl st, 1dc into each of next 23dc, [miss 4dc, 1dc into each of next 24dc] twice, 17ch, working over **padding threads** work 1dc into 2nd ch from hook, 1dc into each of next 15ch, sl st into first dc. Fasten off.

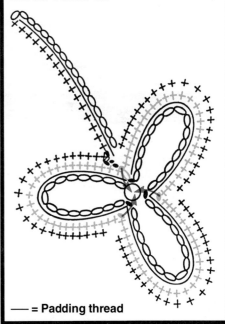

—— = Padding thread

**6th round:** 1ch, working behind each petal of previous round, work 1dc into first dc on 4th round, *7ch, 1dc into next dc on 4th round; rep from * 6 times more, 7ch, sl st into first dc.

**7th round:** Sl st into first 7ch arch, 1ch, work [1dc, 1htr, 7tr, 1htr, 1dc] into each of the 8 7ch arches, sl st into first dc.

**8th round:** 1ch, working behind each petal of previous round, work 1dc into first dc on 6th round, *8ch, 1dc into next dc on 6th round; rep from * 6 times more, 8ch, sl st into first dc.

**9th round:** Sl st into first 8ch arch, 1ch, work [1dc, 1htr, 3tr, 1 picot, 3tr, 1 picot, 3tr, 1htr, 1dc] into each of the 8 8ch arches, sl st into first dc. Fasten off.

# Edgings and Trimmings

## Using Edgings

Edgings are self evidently an addition to something which already exists. Household items such as table mats or cloths, handkerchiefs, towels and pillowcases are all enhanced when trimmed with a matching or toning crochet border.

All the written and diagramatic instructions in this section include the starting chain. If you are going to sew the border on to material you need this chain to work into. However in many cases it is preferable to omit the starting chain and work a row of double crochet directly into the folded edge of the fabric (see illustration of Big Top II which has been worked in this way). If the first row of the design is a double crochet row the instructions as given do not need amending. If however this base is not included in the pattern it is recommended that you work a row of firm double crochet on to the folded edge of the material using the same multiple as given for the starting chain.

We have included a few examples of curved versions of some of the edgings (see Crown Edge II). These can be used as collar or neck edgings, or if worked or sewn on to a straight edge they will flute or form a frill.

The direction in which the edging is made can also vary. If a particularly long piece is required, as for example the border for a large table cloth, it may be advisable to choose one which is worked sideways like Flower Group on page 160. The advantage of this is that you can pin or tack the border in position before it is finished, to ensure that the length you have worked is correct.

## Loop Line

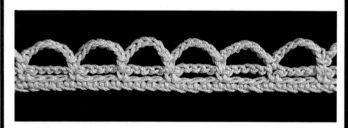

Starting chain: Multiple of 4 sts + 2.

**1st row** (right side): Work 1dc into 2nd ch from hook, 1dc into each ch to end, turn.

**2nd row:** 1ch, 1dc into first dc, *5ch, miss 3dc, 1dc into next dc; rep from * to end, turn.

**3rd row:** 1ch, 1dc into first dc, *7ch, 1dc into next dc; rep from * to end.

Fasten off.

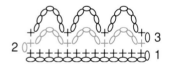

## Big Top I

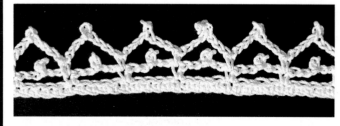

Starting chain: Multiple of 5 sts + 2.

**1st row** (right side): Work 1dc into 2nd ch from hook, 1dc into each ch to end, turn.

## Big Top II

To make edging in rounds, make a starting chain of a multiple of 5 sts + 1 for each side + 1 for each of the 4 corners. Place a marker in last ch (4th corner ch) and in each of the other 3 corner ch. Sl st into first ch to form a ring.

**1st round** (right side): 1ch, work 1dc into same ch as last sl st, 1dc into each ch to first corner ch, [3dc into corner ch, 1dc into each ch to next corner ch] 3 times, 3dc into last corner ch, sl st into first dc.

**2nd round:** 1ch, work 1dc into same st as last sl st, *5ch, sl st into 3rd ch from hook, 3ch, miss 4dc, 1dc into next dc; rep from * to next corner, 6ch, sl st into 3rd ch from hook, 4ch, miss 3dc (corner dcs), 1dc into next dc**; rep from * to ** 3 times more omitting 1dc at end of last rep, sl st into first dc.

**3rd round:** 1ch, work 1dc into same st as last sl st, *6ch, sl st into 3rd ch from hook, 4ch, 1dc into next dc; rep from * to next corner, 8ch, sl st into 3rd ch from hook, 6ch, 1dc into next dc**; rep from * to ** 3 times more omitting 1dc at end of last rep, sl st into first dc. Fasten off.

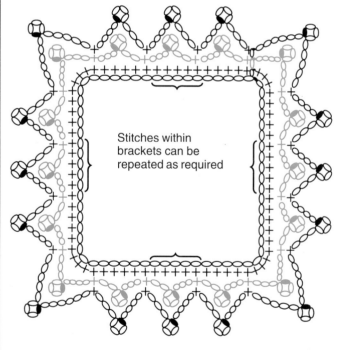

Stitches within brackets can be repeated as required

**2nd row:** 1ch, 1dc into first dc, *5ch, sl st into 3rd ch from hook, 3ch, miss next 4dc, 1dc into next dc; rep from * to end, turn.

**3rd row:** 1ch, 1dc into first dc, *6ch, sl st into 3rd ch from hook, 4ch, 1dc into next dc; rep from * to end. Fasten off.

Stitch Variations, Abbreviations and Symbols on pages 7 to 15

## Crown Edge I

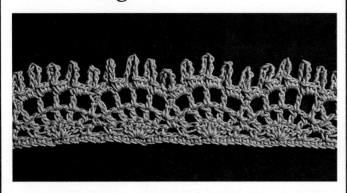

Starting chain: Multiple of 9 sts + 5.

**Special Abbreviation**

**Tr2tog** = work1tr into each of next 2tr until 1 loop of each remains on hook, yo and through all 3 loops on hook.

**1st row** (right side): Work 1dc into 2nd ch from hook, 1dc into each ch to end, turn.

**2nd row:** 1ch, 1dc into first dc, 2ch, miss 2dc, 1dc into next dc, *miss 2dc, 5tr into next dc, miss 2dc, 1dc into next dc, 2ch, miss 2dc, 1dc into next dc; rep from * to end, turn.

**3rd row:** 1ch, 1dc into first dc, 2ch, *1tr into next tr, [1ch, 1tr into next tr] 4 times, 1dc into next 2ch sp; rep from * to end omitting 1dc at end of last rep, 2ch, 1dc into last dc, turn.

**4th row:** 3ch (count as 1tr), [1tr into next tr, 2ch] 4 times, *tr2tog, 2ch, [1tr into next tr, 2ch] 3 times; rep from * to last tr, work 1tr into next tr until 2 loops remain on hook, 1tr into last dc until 3 loops remain on hook, yo and through all 3 loops, turn.

**5th row:** 1ch, 1dc into first st, 3dc into first 2ch sp, *7ch, 3dc into next 2ch sp; rep from * to end, 1dc into 3rd of 3ch at beg of previous row. Fasten off.

$\stackrel{}{\text{A}}$ = **Tr2tog**

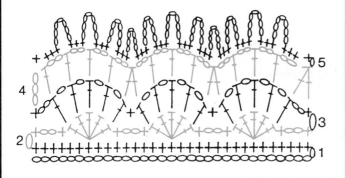

## Crown Edge II

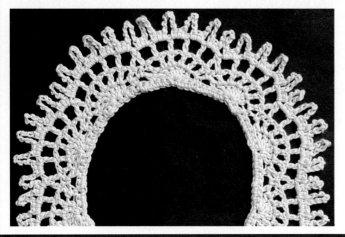

## Driftwood

Starting chain: Multiple of 10 sts + 8.

**1st row** (wrong side): Work 1dc into 2nd ch from hook, 1dc into next ch, 6ch, miss 3ch, *1dc into each of next 7ch, 6ch, miss 3ch; rep from * to last 2ch, 1dc into each of last 2ch, turn.

**2nd row:** 1ch, 1dc into first dc, *into next 6ch arch work [1dc, 1htr, 5tr, 1htr, 1dc], 7ch; rep from * omitting 7ch at end of last rep, work 1dc into last dc, turn.

**3rd row:** 5ch, miss first 5 sts, work 1dc into next tr, [3ch, 1dc] 3 times into same st as last dc, *3ch, [1dc, 3ch, 1dc] into next 7ch arch, 3ch, miss next 4 sts, 1dc into next tr, [3ch, 1dc] 3 times into same st as last dc; rep from * to last 5 sts, 5ch, sl st into last dc. Fasten off.

Starting chain: Multiple of 9 sts + 5.

**Special Abbreviation**

**Tr2tog** = work1tr into each of next 2tr until 1 loop of each remains on hook, yo and through all 3 loops on hook.

**1st row** (right side): Work 1dc into 2nd ch from hook, 1dc into each ch to end, turn.

**2nd row:** 1ch, 1dc into first dc, 2ch, miss 2dc, 1dc into next dc, *miss 2dc, 6tr into next dc, miss 2dc, 1dc into next dc, 2ch, miss 2dc, 1dc into next dc; rep from * to end, turn.

**3rd row:** 1ch, 1dc into first dc, 2ch, *1tr into next tr, [1ch, 1tr into next tr] 5 times, 1dc into next 2ch sp; rep from * to last 2dc, omitting 1dc at end of last rep, 2ch, 1dc into last dc, turn.

**4th row:** 3ch (count as 1tr), [1tr into next tr, 2ch] 5 times, *tr2tog, 2ch, [1tr into next tr, 2ch] 4 times; rep from * to last tr, work 1tr into next tr until 2 loops remain on hook, 1tr into last dc until 3 loops remain on hook, yo and through all 3 loops, turn.

**5th row:** 1ch, 1dc into first st, 3dc into first 2ch sp, *7ch, 3dc into next 2ch sp; rep from * to last 2tr, 1dc into 3rd of 3ch at beg of previous row. Fasten off.

$\stackrel{}{\text{A}}$ = **Tr2tog**

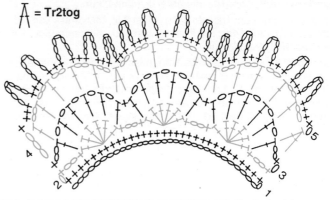

# Edgings and Trimmings

## Tightrope

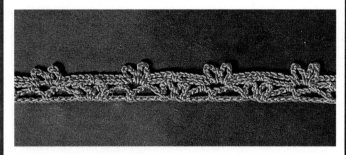

Starting chain: Multiple of 12 sts.

**1st row** (right side): Work 1dc into 2nd ch from hook, [5ch, miss 4ch, 1dc into next ch] twice, *[5ch, 1dc into next ch] twice, [5ch, miss 4ch, 1dc into next ch] twice; rep from * to end.

**2nd row:** 6ch (count as 1tr, 3ch), 1dc into first 5ch arch, *3ch, 1dc into next 5ch arch; rep from * to end, 3ch, 1tr into last dc, turn.

**3rd row:** 1ch, 1dc into first tr, *5ch, miss 1 arch, 1dc into next 3ch arch, into same arch as last dc work [5ch, 1dc] twice, 5ch, miss 1 arch, 1dc into next 3ch arch; rep from * to end working last dc into 3rd of 6ch at beg of previous row. Fasten off.

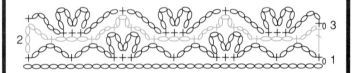

## Wide Variety

Starting chain: Multiple of 17 sts + 3.

**Special Abbreviation**

**Bobble** = work 3tr into next space until 1 loop of each remains on hook, yo and through all 4 loops on hook.

**1st row** (right side): Work 1dc into 2nd ch from hook, 1dc into each ch to end, turn.

**2nd row:** 1ch, work 1dc into each dc to end, turn.

**3rd row:** 1ch, work 1dc into each of first 8dc, *4ch, miss 3dc, 1dc into each of next 14dc; rep from * to last 11dc, 4ch, miss 3dc, 1dc into each of last 8dc, turn.

**4th row:** 3ch (count as 1htr, 1ch), miss first 2dc, 1dc into each of next 3dc, 1ch, into next 4ch sp work [1tr, 1ch] 6 times, miss 3dc, 1dc into each of next 3dc, *3ch, miss 2dc, 1dc into each of next 3dc, 1ch, into next 4ch sp work [1tr, 1ch] 6 times, miss 3dc, 1dc into each of next 3dc; rep from * to last 2dc, 1ch, 1htr into last dc, turn.

**5th row:** 1ch, 1dc into first htr, 2ch, [1 bobble into next ch sp, 2ch] 7 times, *1dc into next 3ch arch, 2ch, [1 bobble into next ch sp, 2ch] 7 times; rep from * to last 3ch, miss 1ch, 1dc into next ch, turn.

## Minstrel Gallery

Starting chain: Multiple of 10 sts + 2.

**Special Abbreviation**

**Bobble** = work 3tr into next space until 1 loop of each remains on hook, yo and through all 4 loops on hook.

**1st row** (wrong side): Work 1dc into 2nd ch from hook, 1dc into each ch to end, turn.

**2nd row:** 5ch (count as 1dtr, 1ch), work [1dtr, 1ch] twice into first dc, miss 4dc, 1dc into next dc, *1ch, miss 4dc, into next dc work [1dtr, 1ch] 5 times, miss 4dc, 1dc into next dc; rep from * to last 5dc, 1ch, work 1dtr into last dc, 1ch, into same st as last dtr work [1dtr, 1ch, 1dtr], turn.

**3rd row:** 1ch, 1dc into first dtr, *2ch, into next dc work [1ttr, 2ch] 4 times, miss 2dtr, 1dc into next dtr; rep from * to end placing last dc into 4th of 5ch at beg of previous row, turn.

**4th row:** 1ch, 1dc into first dc, *4ch, miss next sp, 1 bobble into next 2ch sp, [3ch, 1 bobble into next 2ch sp] twice, 4ch, 1dc into next dc; rep from * to end. Fasten off.

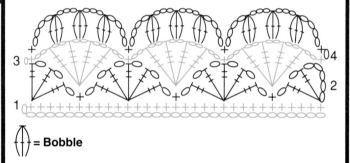

| = Bobble

**6th row:** 1ch, 1dc into first dc, 2dc into first 2ch sp, 1dc into top of first bobble, 2dc into next 2ch sp, [3ch, 2dc into next sp] twice, 5ch, [2dc into next sp, 3ch] twice, 2dc into next sp, 1dc into top of next bobble, 2dc into next sp, *miss 1dc, 2dc into next sp, 1dc into top of next bobble, 2dc into next sp, [3ch, 2dc into next sp] twice, 5ch, [2dc into next sp, 3ch] twice, 2dc into next sp, 1dc into top of next bobble, 2dc into next sp; rep from * to last dc, 1dc into last dc. Fasten off.

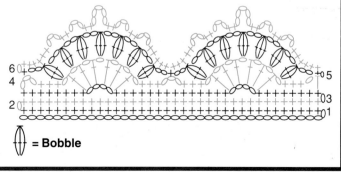

| = Bobble

Stitch Variations, Abbreviations and Symbols on pages 7 to 15

## Square Dance

Starting chain: Multiple of 6 sts + 3.

**1st row** (wrong side): Work 1dc into 2nd ch from hook, 1dc into each ch to end, turn.

**2nd row:** 3ch (count as 1tr), miss first dc, 1tr into next dc, *1ch, miss 1dc, 1tr into each of next 2dc; rep from * to end, turn.

**3rd row:** 5ch (count as 1tr, 2ch), 1dc into next ch sp, *4ch, 1dc into next ch sp; rep from * to last 2 sts, 2ch, 1tr into 3rd of 3ch at beg of previous row, turn.

**4th row:** 1ch, 1dc into first tr, *work 5tr into next 4ch sp, 1dc into next 4ch sp; rep from * to end placing last dc into 3rd of 5ch at beg of previous row. Fasten off.

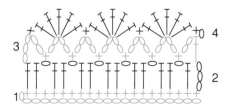

## Horizon

Starting chain: Multiple of 6 sts + 3.

**Special Abbreviation**

**Picot** = make 3ch, sl st into 3rd ch from hook.

**1st row** (wrong side): Work 1dc into 2nd ch from hook, 1dc into each ch to end, turn.

**2nd row:** 5ch (count as 1tr, 2ch), miss first 3dc, 1dc into next dc, work 3 picots, 1dc into next dc, *5ch, miss 4dc, 1dc into next dc, work 3 picots, 1dc into next dc; rep from * to last 3dc, 2ch, 1tr into last dc, turn.

**3rd row:** 1ch, 1dc into first tr, *8ch, 1dc into next 5ch arch; rep from * to end placing last dc into 3rd of 5ch at beg of previous row, turn.

**4th row:** 1ch, 1dc into first dc, *11dc into next 8ch arch, 1dc into next dc; rep from * to end. Fasten off.

 = Picot

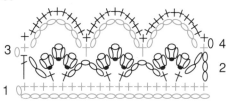

## High Rise

Starting chain: Multiple of 16 sts + 2.

**Special Abbreviation**

**Bobble** = work 4dtr into arch until 1 loop of each remains on hook, yo and through all 5 loops on hook.

**1st row** (wrong side): Work 1dc into 2nd ch from hook, 1dc into each ch to end, turn.

**2nd row:** 1ch, 1dc into first dc, *3ch, miss 3dc, 1dc into next dc; rep from * to end, turn.

**3rd row:** 1ch, 1dc into first dc, 1ch, 1dc into first sp, *3ch, 1dc into next sp; rep from * to last dc, 1ch, 1dc into last dc, turn.

**4th row:** 6ch (count as 1tr, 3ch), miss first dc, 1dc into next dc, 3dc into next 3ch sp, 1dc into next dc, *6ch, 1dc into next dc, 3dc into next 3ch sp, 1dc into next dc; rep from * to last dc, 3ch, 1tr into last dc, turn.

**5th row:** 1ch, 1dc into first tr, *4ch, work 1 bobble into next 6ch arch, into same arch as last bobble work [3ch, 1 bobble] twice, 4ch, 1dc into next 6ch arch; rep from * to end placing last dc into 3rd of 6ch at beg of previous row, turn.

**6th row:** 7ch (count as 1dtr, 3ch), *work 1 bobble into next 4ch arch, 3ch, [1 bobble into next 3ch arch, 3ch] twice, 1 bobble into next 4ch arch, 3ch, 1dtr into next dc, 3ch; rep from * to end omitting 3ch at end of last rep, turn.

**7th row:** 1ch, 1dc into first dtr, 1ch, [1dc into next arch, 3ch] twice, 4tr into next arch, *3ch, [1dc into next arch, 3ch] 4 times, 4tr into next arch; rep from * to last 2 arches, [3ch, 1dc into next arch] twice, 1ch, 1dc into 4th of 7ch at beg of previous row, turn.

**8th row:** 1ch, 1dc into first dc, 3ch, [1dc into next 3ch arch, 3ch] twice, miss 1tr, 1tr into each of next 2tr, *3ch, [1dc into next arch, 3ch] 5 times, miss 1tr, 1tr into each of next 2tr; rep from * to last 2 3ch arches, 3ch, [1dc into next arch, 3ch] twice, 1dc into last dc, turn.

**9th row:** 1ch, 1dc into first dc, work 3dc into each of next 3 arches, 1dc into next tr, 3ch, 1dc into next tr, *3dc into each of next 6 arches, 1dc into next tr, 3ch, 1dc into next tr; rep from * to last 3 arches, 3dc into each of last 3 arches, 1dc into last dc. Fasten off.

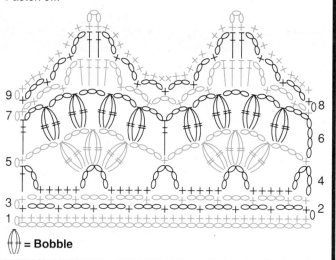

= Bobble

# Edgings and Trimmings

## Duette

Starting chain: Multiple of 4 sts + 4.

**1st row** (right side): Work 1tr into 6th ch from hook, *1ch, miss 1ch, 1tr into next ch; rep from * to end, turn.

**2nd row:** 1ch, 1dc into first tr, *5ch, miss 1tr, 1dc into next tr; rep from * to last tr, 5ch, miss 1tr and 1ch, 1dc into next ch, turn.

**3rd row:** 1ch, 1dc into first dc, work 7dc into each 5ch arch to end, 1dc into last dc, turn.

**4th row:** 5ch (count as 1tr, 2ch), miss first 4dc, 1dc into next dc, *3ch, miss 6dc, 1dc into next dc; rep from * to last 4dc, 2ch, 1tr into last dc, turn.

**5th row:** 1ch, 1dc into first tr, 5ch, 1dc into 2ch sp, into each sp work [1dc, 5ch, 1dc] to end placing last dc into 3rd of 5ch at beg of previous row. Fasten off.

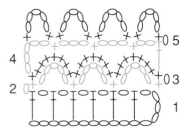

## Scissors

Starting chain: Multiple of 9 sts + 4.

**1st row** (right side): Work 1tr into 4th ch from hook, 1tr into each ch to end, turn.

**2nd row:** 1ch, 1dc into first tr, 1ch, 1dc into next tr, 9ch, miss 7tr, 1dc into next tr, *3ch, 1dc into next tr, 9ch, miss 7tr, 1dc into next tr; rep from * to end, 1ch, 1dc into top of 3ch, turn.

**3rd row:** 1ch, 1dc into first dc, 1dc into first ch sp, *5tr into next 9ch arch, 2ch, into same arch as last 5tr work [1dc, 2ch, 5tr], 1dc into next 3ch arch; rep from * to end placing last dc into last ch sp, 1dc into last dc, turn.

**4th row:** 9ch (count as 1ttr, 4ch), 1dc into next 2ch sp, 3ch, 1dc into next 2ch sp, *9ch, 1dc into next 2ch sp, 3ch, 1dc into next 2ch sp; rep from * to last 5tr, 4ch, 1ttr into last dc, turn.

## Half Token

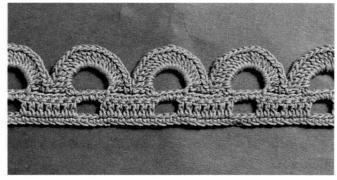

Starting chain: Multiple of 10 sts + 2.

**1st row** (right side): Work 1dc into 2nd ch from hook, 1dc into each ch to end, turn.

**2nd row:** 3ch (count as 1tr), miss first dc, 1tr into each of next 3dc, *3ch, miss 3dc, 1tr into each of next 7dc; rep from * to end omitting 3tr at end of last rep, turn.

**3rd row:** 1ch, 1dc into each of first 4tr, 3dc into next 3ch sp, *1dc into each of next 7tr, 3dc into next 3ch sp; rep from * to last 4tr, 1dc into each of next 3tr, 1dc into 3rd of 3ch at beg of previous row, turn.

**4th row:** 1ch, 1dc into first dc, 2ch, miss 2dc, 1dc into next dc, 8ch, miss 3dc, 1dc into next dc, *5ch, miss 5dc, 1dc into next dc, 8ch, miss 3dc, 1dc into next dc; rep from * to last 3dc, 2ch, 1dc into last dc, turn.

**5th row:** 1ch, 1dc into first dc, 19tr into 8ch arch, *1dc into next 5ch sp, 19tr into next 8ch arch; rep from * to last 2ch sp, 1dc into last dc. Fasten off.

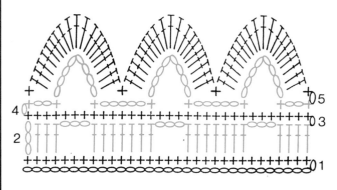

**5th row:** 3ch (count as 1tr), 5tr into 4ch arch, 1dc into next 3ch arch, *5tr into next 9ch arch, 2ch, into same arch as last 5tr work [1dc, 2ch, 5tr], 1dc into next 3ch arch; rep from * to last arch, 5tr into last arch, 1tr into 5th of 9ch at beg of previous row. Fasten off.

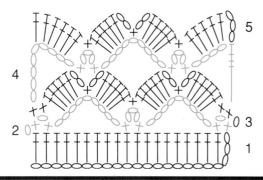

Stitch Variations, Abbreviations and Symbols on pages 7 to 15

## Shoreline

**5th row:** 1ch, 1dc into dtr, 3dc into first arch, 1dc into each of next 3dc, *7dc into next 7ch arch, 1dc into each of next 3dc; rep from * to last arch, 3dc into last arch, 1dc into 4th of 7ch at beg of previous row. Fasten off.

Starting chain: Multiple of 7 sts + 3.

**1st row** (right side): Work 1tr into 4th ch from hook, 1tr into each ch to end, turn.

**2nd row:** 1ch, 1dc into each of first 2tr, *7ch, miss 4tr, 1dc into each of next 3tr, rep from * to end omitting 1dc at end of last rep and placing last dc into top of 3ch, turn.

**3rd row:** 1ch, 1dc into each of first 2dc, *7dc into 7ch arch, 1dc into each of next 3dc, rep from * to end omitting 1dc at end of last rep, turn.

**4th row:** 7ch (count as 1dtr, 3ch), miss 4dc, 1dc into each of next 3dc, *7ch, miss 7dc, 1dc into each of next 3dc; rep from * to last 4dc, 3ch, 1dtr into last dc, turn.

## New Dimension

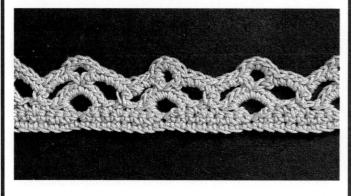

Starting chain: Multiple of 8 sts + 2.

**1st row** (right side): Work 1dc into 2nd ch from hook, 1dc into each ch to end, turn.

**2nd row:** 1ch, 1dc into each of first 4dc, into next dc work [1dc, 7ch, 1dc], *1dc into each of next 7dc, into next dc work [1dc, 7ch, 1dc]; rep from * to last 4dc, 1dc into each of last 4dc, turn.

**3rd row:** 3ch (count as 1tr), miss first dc, *1dc into next dc, 9dc into next arch, miss 3dc, 1dc into next dc, 1tr into next dc; rep from * to end, turn.

**4th row:** 1ch, 1dc into first tr, *4ch, miss 5dc, into next dc work [1dc, 5ch, 1dc], 4ch, miss 5dc, 1dc into next tr; rep from * to end placing last dc into 3rd of 3ch at beg of previous row, turn.

**5th row:** 1ch, 1dc into first dc, *3dc into next 4ch arch, 5dc into next 5ch arch, 3dc into next 4ch arch, 1dc into next dc; rep from * to end. Fasten off.

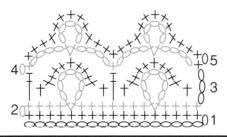

## Quintet

Starting chain: Multiple of 16 sts + 3.

**Special Abbreviation**

**Cluster** = work 2ttr into next st until 1 loop of each remains on hook, yo and through all 3 loops on hook.

**1st row** (right side): Work 1tr into 4th ch from hook, *1ch, miss 1ch, 1tr into next ch; rep from * to last ch, 1tr into last ch, turn.

**2nd row:** 3ch (count as 1tr), miss first tr, 1tr into each of next tr, ch sp and tr, 5ch, miss 2 sps, 1dtr into next sp, 5ch, miss 2tr, 1tr into next tr, *[1tr into next sp, 1tr into next tr] 3 times, 5ch, miss 2 sps, 1dtr into next sp, 5ch, miss 2tr, 1tr into next tr; rep from * to last 3 sts, 1tr into next sp, 1tr into next tr, 1tr into top of 3ch, turn.

**3rd row:** 3ch, miss first tr, 1tr into each of next 2tr, 7ch, 1dc into next dtr, 7ch, *miss 1tr, 1tr into each of next 5tr, 7ch, 1dc into next dtr, 7ch; rep from * to last 4 sts, miss 1tr, 1tr into each of next 2tr, 1tr into 3rd of 3ch at beg of previous row, turn.

**4th row:** 3ch, miss first tr, 1tr into next tr, 7ch, into next dc work [1dc, 5ch, 1dc], 7ch, *miss 1tr, 1tr into each of next 3tr, 7ch, into next dc work [ 1dc, 5ch, 1dc], 7ch; rep from * to last 3 sts, miss 1tr, 1tr into next tr, 1tr into 3rd of 3ch at beg of previous row, turn.

**5th row:** 6ch (count as 1tr, 3ch), *miss 7ch arch, work 1 cluster into 5ch arch then [1ch, 1 cluster] 4 times into same arch, 3ch, miss 1tr, 1tr into next tr, 3ch; rep from * to end omitting 3ch at end of last rep and placing last tr into 3rd of 3ch. Fasten off.

〉 = Cluster

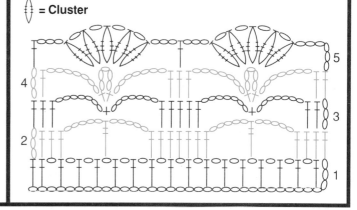

# Edgings and Trimmings

## Loose Leaf

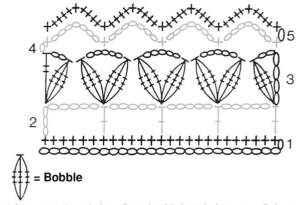

**Starting chain:** Multiple of 6 sts + 2.

**Special Abbreviation**

**Bobble** = work 3ttr into next st until 1 loop of each remains on hook, yo and through all 4 loops on hook.

**1st row** (right side): Work 1dc into 2nd ch from hook, 1dc into each ch to end, turn.

**2nd row:** 8ch (count as 1tr, 5ch), miss first 6dc, 1tr into next dc, *5ch, miss 5dc, 1tr into next dc; rep from * to end, turn.

**3rd row:** 6ch (count as 1dtr, 2ch), work 1 bobble into first tr, *into next tr work [1 bobble, 5ch, 1 bobble]; rep from * to last tr, into 3rd of 3ch at beg of previous row work [1 bobble, 2ch, 1dtr], turn.

= Bobble

**4th row:** 1ch, 1dc into first dtr, *7ch, 1dc into next 5ch arch; rep from * to end placing last dc into 4th of 6ch at beg of previous row, turn.

**5th row:** 1ch, 1dc into first dc, *9dc into next 7ch arch, 1dc into next dc; rep from * to end. Fasten off.

## Far Eastern

**Starting chain:** Multiple of 9 sts + 5.

**Special Abbreviation**

**Bobble** = work 3ttr into sp until one loop of each remains on hook, yo and through all 4 loops on hook.

**1st row** (wrong side): Work 1tr into 8th ch from hook, *2ch, miss 2ch, 1tr into next ch; rep from * to end, turn.

**2nd row:** 3ch (count as 1tr), miss next sp, work 1 bobble into next sp, [6ch, 1tr into first of these ch] 3 times, 1 bobble into same sp as last bobble, *miss 2 sps, work 1 bobble into next sp, [6ch, 1tr into first of these ch] 3 times, 1 bobble into same sp as last bobble; rep from * to last sp, miss 2ch, 1tr into next ch. Fasten off.

= Bobble

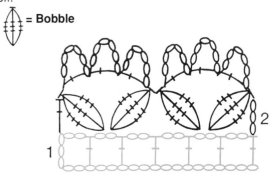

## Plough Share

**Starting chain:** Multiple of 18 sts + 18.

**1st row** (right side): Work 1dc into 2nd ch from hook, 1dc into each ch to end, turn.

**2nd row:** 4ch (count as 1dtr), *miss next 2dc, work [1dtr, 2ch, 1dtr] into next dc; rep from * to last 2dc, 1dtr into last dc, turn.

**3rd row:** 3ch (count as 1tr), work 4tr into first 2ch sp, *3ch, miss 1 sp, 4tr into next sp; rep from * to end, 1tr into 4th of 4ch at beg of previous row, turn.

**4th row:** 6ch (count as 1tr, 3ch), 2dc into first 3ch sp, 7ch, 2dc into next sp, *3ch, into next sp work [1tr, 2ch, 1tr], 3ch, 2dc into next sp, 7ch, 2dc into next sp; rep from * to last 5 sts, 3ch, 1tr into 3rd of 3ch at beg of previous row, turn.

**5th row:** 1ch, 1dc into first tr, 2ch, into 7ch arch work 4dtr and [5ch, sl st into first of these ch, 4dtr] 3 times, 2ch, *miss 1 sp, into next 2ch sp work [1dc, 3ch, 1dc], 2ch, into 7ch arch work 4dtr and [5ch, sl st into first of these ch, 4dtr] 3 times; rep from * to last sp, 2ch, 1dc into 3rd of 6ch at beg of previous row. Fasten off.

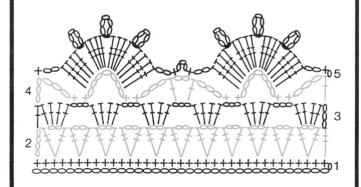

Stitch Variations, Abbreviations and Symbols on pages 7 to 15

## White Knight I

Starting chain: Multiple of 10 sts + 3.

**1st row** (right side): Work 1tr into 4th ch from hook, 1tr into each ch to end, turn.

**2nd row:** 1ch, 1dc into each of first 3tr, *2ch, miss 2tr, into next tr work [2tr, 2ch] twice, miss 2tr, 1dc into each of next 5tr; rep from * to end omitting 2dc at end of last rep and placing last dc into top of 3ch at beg of previous row, turn.

**3rd row:** 1ch, 1dc into each of first 2dc, *3ch, miss next 2ch sp, into next 2ch sp work [3tr, 2ch, 3tr], 3ch, miss 1dc, 1dc into each of next 3dc; rep from * to end omitting 1dc at end of last rep, turn.

**4th row:** 1ch, 1dc into first dc, *4ch, miss next 3ch sp, into next 2ch sp work [4tr, 2ch, 4tr], 4ch, miss 1dc, 1dc into next dc; rep from * to end, turn.

**5th row:** 1ch, 1dc into first dc, *5ch, miss next 4ch sp, into next 2ch sp work [4tr, 2ch, 4tr], 5ch, 1dc into next dc; rep from * to end. Fasten off.

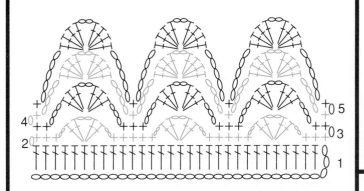

## White Knight II

Starting chain: Multiple of 8 sts + 3.

**1st row** (right side): Work 1tr into 4th ch from hook, 1tr into each ch to end, turn.

**2nd row:** 1ch, 1dc into each of first 3tr, *2ch, miss 1tr, into next tr work [2tr, 2ch] twice, miss 1tr, 1dc into each of next 5tr; rep from * to end omitting 2dc at end of last rep and placing last dc into top of 3ch at beg of previous row, turn.

## Sand Castle

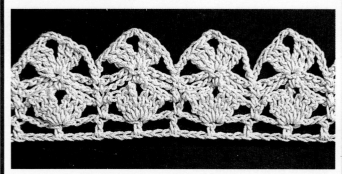

Starting chain: Multiple of 8 sts + 6.

**1st row** (right side): Work 1tr into 10th ch from hook, *3ch, miss 3ch, 1tr into next ch; rep from * to end, turn.

**2nd row:** 1ch, 1dc into first tr, *2ch, into next tr work [3dtr, 3ch, 3dtr], 2ch, 1dc into next tr; rep from * to end placing last dc into 4th ch, turn.

**3rd row:** 1ch, 1dc into first dc, *5ch, 1dc into next 3ch sp, 5ch, 1dc into next dc; rep from * to end, turn.

**4th row:** 1ch, 1dc into first dc, *4ch, 1dc into next dc; rep from * to end, turn.

**5th row:** 1ch, 1dc into first dc, *3ch, into next dc work [3dtr, 3ch, 3dtr], 3ch, 1dc into next dc; rep from * to end. Fasten off.

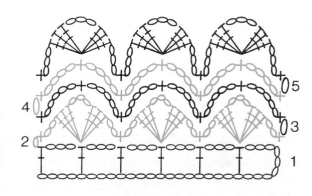

**3rd row:** 1ch, 1dc into each of first 2dc, *3ch, miss next 2ch sp, into next 2ch sp work [3tr, 2ch, 3tr], 3ch, miss 1dc, 1dc into each of next 3dc; rep from * to end omitting 1dc at end of last rep, turn.

**4th row:** 1ch, 1dc into first dc, *4ch, miss next 3ch sp, into next 2ch sp work [4tr, 2ch, 4tr], 4ch, miss 1dc, 1dc into next dc; rep from * to end, turn.

**5th row:** 1ch, 1dc into first dc, *6ch, miss next 4ch sp, into next 2ch sp work [4tr, 2ch, 4tr], 6ch, 1dc into next dc; rep from * to end. Fasten off.

# Edgings and Trimmings

## Mirabelle

Starting chain: Multiple of 6 sts + 6.

**Special Abbreviation**

**Bobble** = work 4ttr into ch until 1 loop of each remains on hook, yo and through all 5 loops on hook.

**1st row** (right side): Work 1dc into 2nd ch from hook, 1dc into each ch to end, turn.

**2nd row:** 6ch (count as 1tr, 3ch), miss 4dc, 1tr into next dc, *1ch, miss 1dc, 1tr into next dc, 3ch, miss 3dc, 1tr into next dc; rep from * to end, turn.

**3rd row:** 1ch, 1dc into first tr, *4ch, miss 1ch, 1 bobble into next ch, 4ch, 1dc into next tr, 1ch, 1dc into next tr; rep from * to end, omitting last ch and dc and working final dc into 3rd of 6ch at beg of previous row. Fasten off.

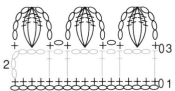

 = Bobble

## Springtime

Starting chain: Multiple of 11 sts + 3.

**Special Abbreviation**

**Bobble** = Work 3ttr into 3ch loop until 1 loop of each remains on hook, yo and through all 4 loops on hook.

**1st row** (right side): Work 1tr into 4th ch from hook, 1tr into each ch to end, turn.

**2nd row:** 1ch, 1dc into first tr, *9ch, sl st into 3rd ch from hook, 7ch, miss 10tr, 1dc into next tr; rep from * to end placing last dc into top of 3ch, turn.

**3rd row:** 5ch, *work 1 bobble into next 3ch loop, 5ch, into same loop as last bobble work [1 bobble, 5ch, 1 bobble], 1ttr into next dc; rep from * to end. Fasten off.

 = Bobble

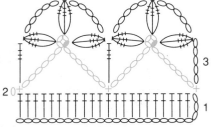

## Long Bows

Starting chain: Multiple of 8 sts + 2.

**Special Abbreviation**

**Triple loop** = sl st into next dc, [7ch, 1 sl st] 3 times into same dc.

**1st row** (wrong side): Work 1dc into 2nd ch from hook, 1dc into each ch to end, turn.

**2nd row:** 1ch, work 1dc into each dc to end, turn.

**3rd row:** 1ch, 1dc into each of first 3dc, *9ch, miss 3dc, 1dc into each of next 5dc; rep from * to end omitting 2dc at end of last rep, turn.

**4th row:** 1ch, 1dc into each of first 2dc, *5ch, 1dc into next 9ch arch, 5ch, miss 1dc, 1dc into each of next 3dc; rep from * to end omitting 1dc at end of last rep, turn.

**5th row:** 1ch, 1dc into first dc, *5ch, miss 1dc, 1dc into next dc; rep from * to end, turn.

**6th row:** 1ch, 1dc into first dc, *5ch, work 1 triple loop into next dc, 5ch, 1dc into next dc; rep from * to end. Fasten off.

 = Triple loop

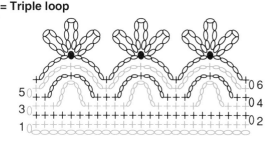

## Quadrille

Starting chain: Multiple of 5 sts + 1.

**Special Abbreviation**

**Popcorn** = work 4tr into next dc, drop loop from hook, insert hook from the front into top of first of these tr, pick up dropped loop and draw through tr, 1ch to secure popcorn.

**1st row** (right side): Work 1dc into 2nd ch from hook, 1dc into each ch to end, turn.

**2nd row:** 4ch (count as 1htr, 2ch), miss first 2dc, 1dc into next dc, *5ch, miss 4dc, 1dc into next dc; rep from * to last 2dc, 2ch, 1htr into last dc, turn.

**3rd row:** 1ch, 1dc into first htr, 3ch, 1 popcorn into next dc, 3ch, *1dc into next 5ch arch, 3ch, 1 popcorn into next dc, 3ch; rep from * to last sp, 1dc into 2nd of 4ch at beg of previous row. Fasten off.

 = Popcorn

Stitch Variations, Abbreviations and Symbols on pages 7 to 15

## Medal Ribbon

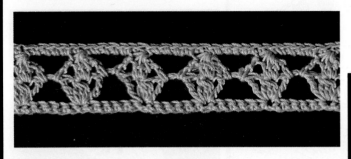

Starting chain: Multiple of 6 sts + 4.

**Special Abbreviations**

**Bobble** = work 3tr into next st until 1 loop of each remains on hook, yo and through all 4 loops on hook.

**Cluster** = work 1dtr into next ch sp until 2 loops remain on hook, 3tr into top of next bobble until 1 loop of each remains on hook (5 loops on hook), miss 1ch sp, 1dtr into next ch sp until 6 loops remain on hook, yo and through all 6 loops on hook

**1st row** (wrong side): Work 1dc into 2nd ch from hook, 1dc into each ch to end, turn.

**2nd row:** 4ch (count as 1tr, 1ch), miss first 4dc, 1dtr into next dc, work [1ch, 1 bobble, 1ch, 1dtr] into same st as last dtr, 1ch, *miss 5dc, 1dtr into next dc, work [1ch, 1 bobble, 1ch, 1dtr] into same st as last dtr, 1ch; rep from * to last 4dc, 1tr into last dc, turn.

**3rd row:** 6ch (count as 1tr, 3ch), *1 cluster, 5ch; rep from * to end working first dtr of each cluster into same ch sp as last dtr of previous cluster and omitting 2ch at end of last rep, 1tr into 3rd of 4ch at beg of previous row, turn.

**4th row:** 1ch, 1dc into first tr, 3dc into first 3ch sp, 1dc into top of first cluster, *5dc into next 5ch sp, 1dc into top of next cluster; rep from * to last sp, 3dc into last sp, 1dc into 3rd of 6ch at beg of previous row. Fasten off.

## Keyline

Starting chain: Multiple of 4 sts + 2.

**1st row** (right side): Work 1dc into 2nd ch from hook, 1dc into each ch to end, turn.

**2nd row:** 6ch (count as 1tr, 3ch), miss first 4dc, 1tr into next dc, *3ch, miss 3dc, 1tr into next dc; rep from * to end.

**3rd row:** 1ch, 1dc into first tr, *3ch, 1tr into next sp, 3ch, work 7tr over stem of tr just worked, 1dc into next tr; rep from * to end placing last dc into 3rd of 6ch at beg of previous row. Fasten off.

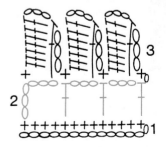

**⬯ = Bobble**

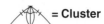  **= Cluster**

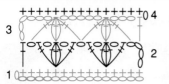

## Plant Life

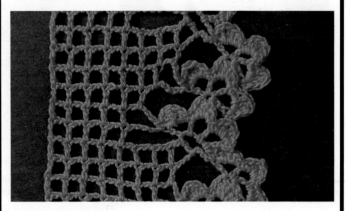

Worked lengthways.

**1st row** (right side): Make 31ch, work 1tr into 7th ch from hook, [2ch, miss 2ch, 1tr into next ch] 8 times, turn. (9 sps).

**2nd row:** 5ch (count as 1tr, 2ch), miss first tr, 1tr into next tr, [2ch, 1tr into next tr] 3 times, 5ch, miss next 4 sps, 1tr into next sp, work [3ch, 1tr] 3 times into same sp as last tr, turn.

**3rd row:** 1ch, 1dc into first tr, into first 3ch sp work [1htr, 1tr, 1dtr, 1tr, 1htr, 1dc], into next 3ch sp work [1dc, 1htr, 1tr, 1dtr, 1tr, 1htr, 1dc], into next 3ch sp work [1dc, 1htr, 1tr, 1dtr, 1tr, 1htr], 1dc into next tr, 5ch, 1tr into next tr, [2ch, 1tr into next tr] 4 times placing last tr into 3rd of 5ch at beg of previous row, turn.

**4th row:** 5ch (count as 1tr, 2ch), miss first tr, [1tr into next tr, 2ch] 4 times, 1tr into 5ch sp, 7ch, miss first group of 7 sts, work 1tr into dtr at centre of next group of 7 sts, [3ch, 1tr] 3 times into same st as last tr, turn.

**5th row:** 1ch, 1dc into first tr, into first 3ch sp work [1htr, 1tr, 1dtr, 1tr, 1htr, 1dc], into next 3ch sp work [1dc, 1htr, 1tr, 1dtr, 1tr, 1htr, 1dc], into next 3ch sp work [1dc, 1htr, 1tr, 1dtr, 1tr, 1htr], 1dc into next tr, 5ch, 1tr into 7ch sp, [2ch, 1tr into next tr] 6 times placing last tr into 3rd of 5ch at beg of previous row, turn.

**6th row:** 5ch (count as 1tr, 2ch), miss first tr, [1tr into next tr, 2ch] 6 times, 1tr into 5ch sp, 7ch, miss first group of 7 sts, work 1tr into dtr at centre of next group of 7 sts, [3ch, 1tr] 3 times into same st as last tr, turn.

**7th row:** 1ch, 1dc into first tr, into first 3ch sp work [1htr, 1tr, 1dtr, 1tr, 1htr, 1dc], into next 3ch sp work [1dc, 1htr, 1tr, 1dtr, 1tr, 1htr, 1dc], into next 3ch sp work [1dc, 1htr, 1tr, 1dtr, 1tr, 1htr], 1dc into next tr, 5ch, 1tr into 7ch sp, [2ch, 1tr into next tr] 8 times placing last tr into 3rd of 5ch at beg of previous row, turn.

Rep 2nd to 7th rows ending with a 7th row.

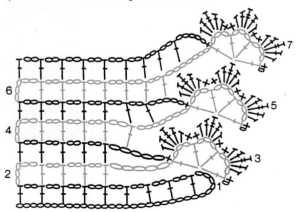

# Edgings and Trimmings

## Flower Group

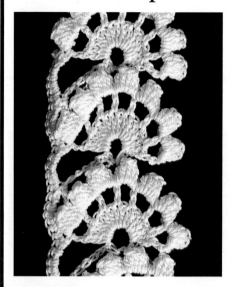

Worked lengthways.

**Special Abbreviations**

**Popcorn at beg of row** = 3ch, work 6tr into first sp, drop loop from hook, insert hook from the front into top of 3ch, pick up dropped loop and draw through, 1ch to secure.

**7tr-Popcorn** = work 7tr into next sp, then complete as for popcorn at beg of row inserting hook into top of first of these tr.

## Bandoleer

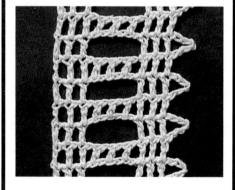

Worked lengthways.

**1st row** (wrong side): Make 20ch, work 1tr into 6th ch from hook, *1ch, miss 1ch, 1tr into next ch; rep from * to end, turn.

**2nd row:** 7ch, 1tr into first tr, [1ch, 1tr into next tr] twice, 7ch, miss 3tr, [1tr into next tr, 1ch] twice, miss 1ch, 1tr into next ch, turn.

**3rd row:** 4ch (count as 1tr, 1ch), miss first tr, 1tr into next tr, 1ch, 1tr into next tr, [1ch, miss 1ch, 1tr into next ch] 3 times, [1ch, 1tr into next tr] 3 times.

Rep 2nd and 3rd rows.

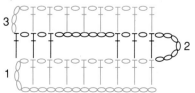

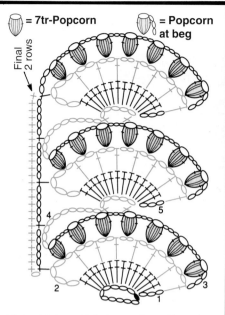

= 7tr-Popcorn

= Popcorn at beg

Make 10ch and join into a ring with a sl st.

**1st row** (right side): 3ch (count as 1tr), work 14tr into ring, turn.

**2nd row:** 5ch (count as 1tr, 2ch), miss first 2tr, 1tr into next tr, [2ch, miss 1tr, 1tr into next tr] 6 times placing last tr into 3rd of 3ch at beg of previous row, turn.

**3rd row:** Work 1 popcorn at beg of row, [3ch, 1 7tr-popcorn into next 2ch sp] 6 times, turn.

**4th row:** 10ch, miss first 2 sps, work [1dc, 5ch, 1dc] into next 3ch sp, turn.

**5th row:** 3ch (count as 1tr), work 14tr into 5ch sp, turn.

Rep 2nd to 5th rows until edging is required length ending with a 3rd row. Do not turn work but continue along side edge as follows:

**1st Final row:** 3ch, 1dc into sp formed at beg of 2nd row of pattern, *5ch, 1dc into sp formed at beg of 4th row of pattern, 5ch, 1dc into sp formed at beg of 2nd row of pattern; rep from * to end, turn.

**2nd Final row:** 1ch, 1dc into first dc, *5dc into 5ch sp, 1dc into next dc; rep from * to end. Fasten off.

## Daisy Chain

Worked lengthways.

**1st row** (wrong side): Make 4ch (count as 1tr, 1ch), work 2tr into first of these ch, 2ch, 3tr into same ch as last 2tr, turn.

## Saw Tooth

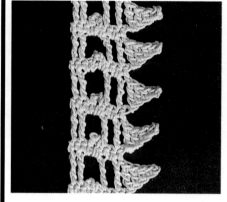

Worked lengthways.

**1st row** (right side): Make 14ch, work 1dc into 3rd ch from hook, 1htr into next ch, 1tr into next ch, 1dtr into next ch, [1ch, miss 1ch, 1dtr into next ch] twice, 2ch, miss 2ch, 1dtr into each of last 2ch, turn.

**2nd row:** 1ch, 1dc into each of first 2dtr, 1dc into 2ch sp, 4ch, 1dc into same sp as last dc, 1dc into next dtr, 1dc into ch sp, 1dc into next dtr, turn.

**3rd row:** 7ch, work 1dc into 3rd ch from hook, 1htr into next ch, 1tr into next ch, 1dtr into next ch, 1ch, 1dtr into next dc, 1ch, miss 1dc, 1dtr into next dc, 2ch, miss 2dc, 1dtr into each of last 2dc, turn.

Rep 2nd and 3rd rows.

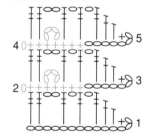

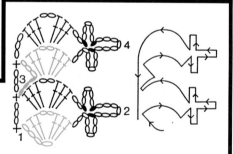

**2nd row:** 8ch, sl st into 6th ch from hook, 7ch, sl st into same ch as last sl st, 5ch, sl st into same ch as last 2 sl sts, 2ch, 3tr into 2ch sp, 2ch, 3tr into same sp as last 3tr, turn.

**3rd row:** Sl st into each of first 3tr, 3ch (count as 1tr), 2tr into 2ch sp, 2ch, 3tr into same sp as last 2tr, turn.

Rep 2nd and 3rd rows until edging is required length ending with a 2nd row. Do not turn work but continue along side edge as follows:

**Final row:** *3ch, 1dc into top of 3ch at beg of next fan, 3ch, 1dc into first sl st at beg of next fan; rep from * to last fan, 1dc into top of 4ch at beg of 1st row. Fasten off.

Stitch Variations, Abbreviations and Symbols on pages 7 to 15

## Tunisian Crochet

Tunisian or Afghan crochet is worked with a long hook available in the same range of thicknesses as traditional crochet hooks. The hooks are longer than crochet hooks as they are required to hold the loops created on the first (Forward) half of the row before working them off on the return half.

The fabric produced by this technique can be dense and thick. It is important to use a suitable size of hook in relation to the yarn. This is usually at least two sizes larger than would be used when working ordinary crochet with the same yarn.

Each row is worked in two parts. The first or 'Forward' part of the row involves working from right to left and pulling up loops or stitches on to the hook. On the second or 'Return' part of the row these loops are worked off again as the hook travels back from left to right. Tunisian crochet is nearly always made without turning, therefore the right side is always facing.

## Holding the Hook

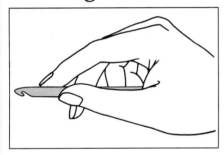

The hook should be held in the centre with the hand as shown in the diagram.

## Starting Chain

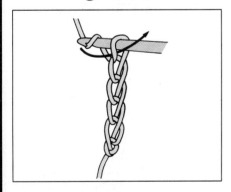

Make the number of chains needed to correspond with the number of stitches required in the first row.

### Tip

When working a large piece it is sensible to start with more chains than necessary as it is simple to undo the extra chains if you have miscounted.

Although there are exceptions, Tunisian stitch patterns usually begin with the same initial forward and return row - referred to as: **Basic Forward and Return row.**

## Forward

1. Working into back loop only of each chain, insert hook into second chain from hook, yarn over, draw loop through and leave on hook.
2. Insert hook into next chain, yarn over, draw loop through and leave on hook.

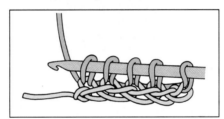

Repeat this in each chain to end. Do not turn.

The number of loops on hook should equal the number of stitches required for first row.

**Note:** Because the fabric produced in Tunisian crochet is usually firmer than in ordinary crochet we recommend that the hook is inserted into the back loop only of the starting chain as this produces a firmer edge.

## Return

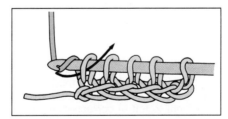

1. Yarn over, draw through one loop. (This chain forms the edge stitch).

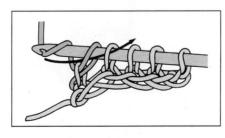

2. Yarn over, and draw through two loops.

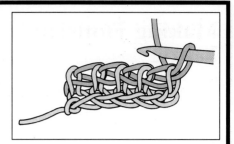

3. Repeat step 2 until one loop remains on hook. Do not turn. The loop remaining on the hook becomes the first stitch of the following row.

## The Basic Stitches

These are produced by varying the technique of picking up loops on the Forward row.

### Tunisian Simple Stitch (Tss ⃗ )

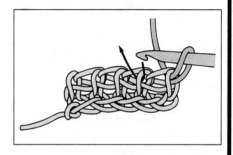

1. Insert hook from right to left behind single vertical thread.

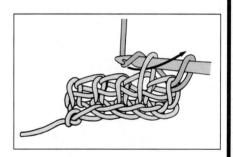

2. Yarn over hook.

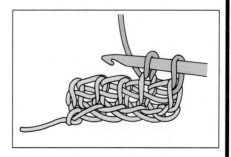

3. Draw loop through and leave on hook. Unless otherwise stated, the hook is always inserted in this way. For example, Tunisian half trebles, trebles etc. are usually worked from this position.

# Tunisian Crochet

## Making Tunisian Fabric

Make chain as required and work a Basic Forward and Return row. Generally the single loop on the hook at the end of each Return row counts as the first stitch in the next Forward row and so the first stitch is missed. (As shown in first diagram for Tunisian simple stitch).

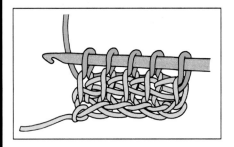

**Next row:** Pick up loop in each stitch (Tss or as required) including edge stitch.

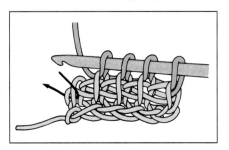

If you require a firmer edge at this end of the row you can work through two loops of the last stitch.

Return as Basic Return row.

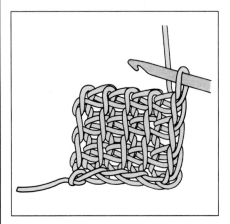

Repeat Forward and Return row as required. It is important to understand how to produce basic Tunisian fabric before attempting pattern stitches.

## Finishing Off

It is possible simply to finish with a Return row, cutting yarn and threading it through the remaining stitch to secure. However the following method leaves a neater edge and is useful where the Tunisian fabric is complete in itself - as for a mat or rug for example.

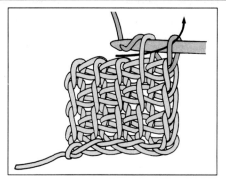

1. Finish with Return row. Insert hook into next stitch, yarn over.

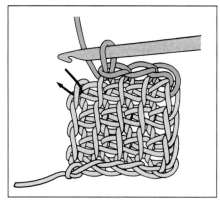

2. Draw through two loops.
Repeat steps 1 and 2 to end. Fasten off remaining loop.

**Note:** The hook can be inserted as if working Tunisian simple, Tunisian knit or Tunisian purl stitches so that stitches can be finished off in pattern.

## Tunisian Knit Stitch (Tks ⧄ )

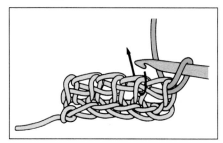

1. Insert hook from front to back through fabric and below chains formed by previous Return row, to right of front vertical thread but to left of corresponding back thread.

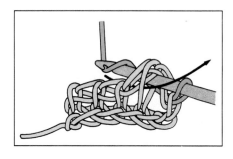

2. Yarn over, draw loop through and leave on hook.

3. Repeat steps 1 and 2 into each stitch to end. At the last stitch of each Forward row work under two loops, return as Basic Return row.

## Tunisian Purl Stitch (Tps ⧂ )

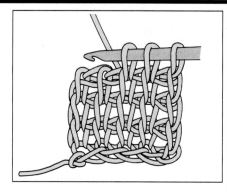

1. Bring yarn to front, insert hook as for Tunisian simple stitch.

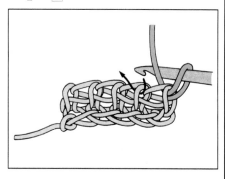

2. Take yarn to back of work and over hook (yo). Draw loop through and leave on hook.

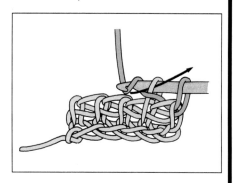

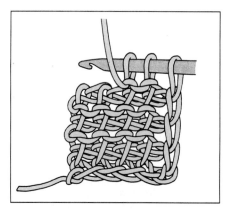

Repeat steps 1 and 2 in each stitch to end, return as Basic Return row.

## Increasing

### Inc 1Tss

1. To increase one stitch on a Forward row, insert hook under the back loop between two stitches, yarn over and draw loop through.

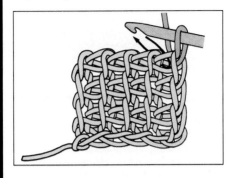

2. Work next stitch in the normal way.

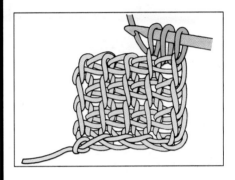

Two loops are to be worked off on Return row.

## Decreasing

### Tss2tog

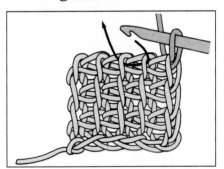

1. To decrease one stitch on a Forward row, insert hook through two stitches.
2. Yarn over and draw through loops. One loop to be worked off on Return row.

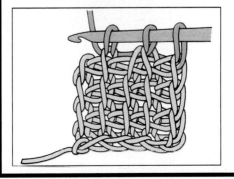

**Note:** Tss2tog is often worked in conjunction with a yarn over to create a lacy effect. For example:

**Yo, Tss2tog**

**Tss2tog, yo**

Two loops are then worked off on the Return row.

### Tss3tog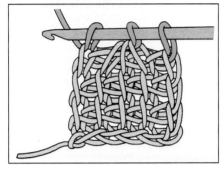

To decrease two stitches on a Forward row work as Tss2tog but insert hook through next three stitches.

## Changing Colour

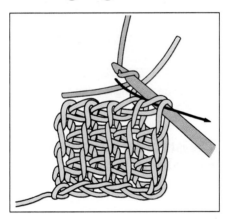

1. When a colour change is required at the beginning of a Forward row, yarn over in the new colour when two loops remain on the hook at the end of previous Return row.

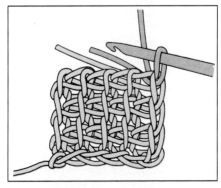

2. Draw through both loops.

To change colour at the beginning of a Return row change yarn and continue to work as normal.

## Stitch Variations

### Tunisian Treble (Ttr 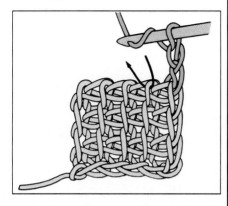 )

1. Make two chain for the first stitch at beginning of the row. Yarn over and insert hook into the next stitch as if working a Tunisian simple stitch.

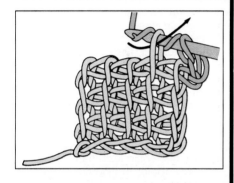

2. Yarn over and draw loop through.

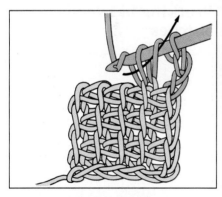

3. Yarn over and draw through two loops on hook.

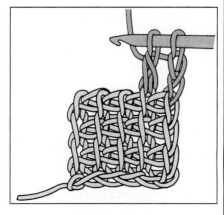

4. Leave remaining loop on hook.

163

# Tunisian Crochet

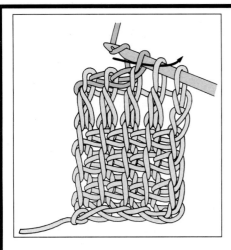

5. Treble is completed when Return row is worked.

**Tunisian half treble (Thtr), Tunisian double treble (Tdtr), Tunisian triple treble (Tttr) etc.** are also used frequently within Tunisian patterns. As with Tunisian trebles these stitches are worked in the same way as for crochet. Refer to introduction on pages 5 and 6 for detailed instructions of how to work these stitches. When working Tunisian fabric, unless otherwise stated, the hook should be inserted as if working a Tunisian simple stitch and the stitch then worked as for crochet until one loop remains on the hook. Stitches are completed on the Return row. Turning chains are made at the beginning of Forward rows and are usually one chain less than for ordinary crochet. (Refer to individual pattern instructions).

## Working between stitches

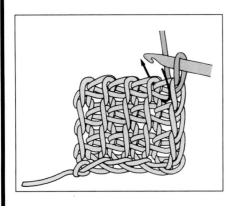

1. Insert hook between vertical loops that form stitches.
2. Yarn over and draw loop through.

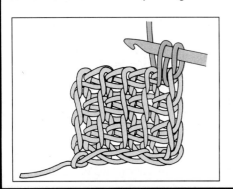

Thtr, Ttr, Tdtr etc. can also be worked between stitches.

## Tunisian Slipped Stitch (Tsl st $\tilde{v}$ )

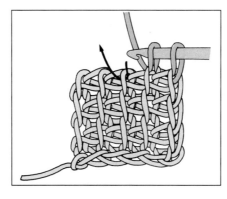

1. Insert hook into stitch as if working Tunisian simple stitch but do not pull yarn through.

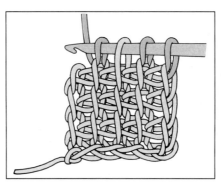

2. Continue working leaving slipped stitch on hook.

## Twisted Tunisian Simple Stitch (TwTss $\tilde{s}$ )

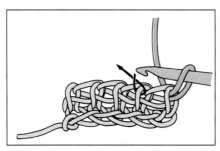

1. Insert hook into stitch from left to right.

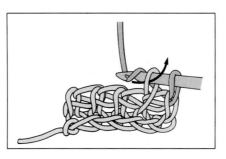

2. Yarn over and draw loop through.

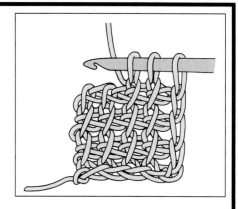

3. Finish stitch with Basic Return row.

## Tunisian Bobbles

The following instructions are for a frequently used bobble. However individual pattern instructions should be followed.

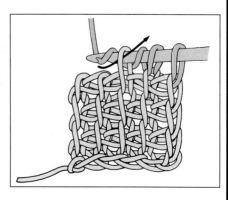

1. Yarn over and insert hook into next stitch as if working Tunisian simple stitch, yarn over and draw loop through.

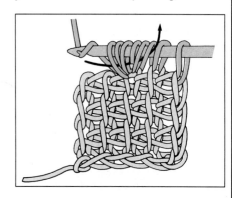

2. Repeat step 1 twice more into same stitch as before.

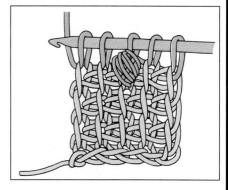

3. Yarn over and draw through all six loops. Remaining loop is worked off on Return row.

## Surface Decoration

The evenness of Tunisian simple stitch makes it ideal to add surface decoration. The fabric in the photograph above has been embroidered using cross stitch. The diagram below indicates where to position the crosses in relation to the threads of the fabric.

It is also possible to use many other embroidery stitches in a similar way.

## Following Tunisian Pattern Instructions

All Tunisian patterns are given in the form of written instructions and stitch diagrams. Much of the information about following pattern instructions, pattern repeats, tension etc. given on pages 13 to 15 apply equally to Tunisian crochet. The stitch diagrams however are given on a grid where one rectangle represents one stitch

worked over a Forward and Return row. Stitches within dark lines form the pattern repeat. Compare stitch diagrams with written instructions if you have difficulty following the pattern.

# Abbreviations and Symbols
## Abbreviations

**beg** = beginning, **ch** = chain, **dec** = decrease, **inc** = increase, **rep** = repeat, **sp** = space, **st(s)** = stitch(es), **tog** = together, **Tdtr** = Tunisian double treble, **Thtr** = Tunisian half treble, **Tks** = Tunisian knit stitch, **Tps** = Tunisian purl stitch, **Tsl st** = Tunisian slipped stitch, **Tss** = Tunisian simple stitch, **Ttr** = Tunisian treble, **Tttr** = Tunisian triple treble, **TwTss** = Twisted Tunisian simple stitch, **yo** = yarn over, **yf** = yarn forward, **yb** = yarn back.

## Common Symbols

**Note:** All symbols represent a completed stitch; the lower part of the symbol is worked on the Forward row where the loops are held on the hook, the upper part (or swash ⁓ ) is worked on the Return row when the loops are worked off.

| | |
|---|---|
| | = Tunisian simple stitch (Tss) |
| | = Tunisian purl stitch (Tps) |
| | = Tunisian knit stitch (Tks) |
| | = Tunisian slipped stitch (Tsl st) |
| | = Twisted Tunisian simple stitch (TwTss) |
| | = Tss worked under chain loop and between two vertical loops of previous row |
| | = Tss worked into back loop only of stitch in previous row |
| | = Tunisian half treble (Thtr) |
| | = Tunisian treble (Ttr) |
| | = Tunisian treble worked between stitches |
| | = Increase one Tunisian simple stitch (Inc 1Tss) |
| | = Tunisian simple stitch two together (Tss2tog) |
| | = Tunisian simple stitch three together (Tss3tog) |
| | = Make Bobble (MB) |
| | = Yo, Tss2tog |
| | = Tss2tog, yo |
| | = Yo, tss3tog, yo |

## Tunisian Web

**Note:** Because this pattern incorporates a slipped stitch it should be worked on a hook which is at least 2 sizes (1mm) larger than usual.

Multiple of 2 sts + 3.

**1st row:** Using A, as Basic Forward and Return row, changing to B when 2 loops remain at end of return.

**2nd row:** Using B, with 1 loop on hook, *1Tss into next st, 1Tsl st into next st; rep from * to last 2 sts, 1Tss into each of next 2 sts. Return, changing to A when 2 loops remain.

**3rd row:** Using A, with 1 loop on hook, *1Tsl st into next st, 1Tss into next st; rep from * to end. Return, changing to B when 2 loops remain.

Rep 2nd and 3rd rows.

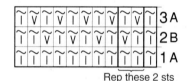

Rep these 2 sts

## Close Weave

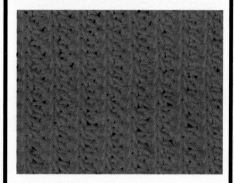

Multiple of 2 sts + 1.

**1st row:** As Basic Forward and Return row.

**2nd row:** With 1 loop on hook, *1TwTss into next st, 1Tss into next st; rep from * to end. Return.

Rep 2nd row.

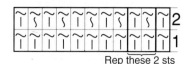

Rep these 2 sts

# Tunisian Crochet

## Mesh Stitch

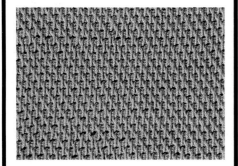

Any number of sts.

**Note:** Check the number of sts after each Forward row. It will be easier to keep the number of sts correct and the edges of the material straight if you take care to alternate the placing of the first Tss, as given on 2nd and 3rd rows.

**1st row:** As Basic Forward and Return row.

**2nd row:** With 1 loop on hook, work 1Tss into space between 2nd and 3rd sts, 1Tss into each sp to end, 1Tss into last st. Return.

**3rd row:** With 1 loop on hook, work 1Tss into sp between first and 2nd sts, 1Tss into each sp to last sp, miss last sp, work 1Tss into last st. Return.

Rep 2nd and 3rd rows.

Rep this stitch

## Cover Pattern

Multiple of 2 sts + 3.

**1st row:** As Basic Forward and Return row.

**2nd row:** With 1 loop on hook, *1Tps into next st, 1Tss into next st; rep from * to end. Return.

**3rd row:** With 1 loop on hook, *1Tss into next st, 1Tps into next st; rep from * to last 2 sts, 1Tss into each of last 2 sts. Return.

Rep 2nd and 3rd rows.

Rep these 2 sts

## Masonry Stitch

Multiple of 4 sts + 3.

**1st row:** Using A, as Basic Forward and Return row, changing to B when 2 loops remain.

**2nd row:** Using B, with 1 loop on hook, *1Tsl st into next st, work 1Tss into each of next 3 sts; rep from * to last 2 sts, 1Tsl st into next st, work 1Tss into last st. Return, changing to A when 2 loops remain.

**3rd row:** Using A with 1 loop on hook work 1Tss into each st to end. Return, changing to B when 2 loops remain.

**4th row:** Using B, with 1 loop on hook, work 1Tss into each of next 2 sts, *1Tsl st into next st, 1Tss into each of next 3 sts; rep from * to end. Return, changing to A when 2 loops remain.

**5th row:** As 3rd row.

Rep 2nd to 5th rows.

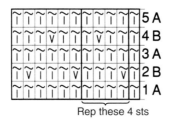

Rep these 4 sts

## Buckle Pattern

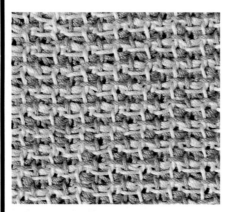

**Note:** It is recommended that this stitch is worked using a hook 1 or 2 sizes (0.5mm or 1mm) larger than usual.

Multiple of 2 sts + 3.

## Sparkle Stitch

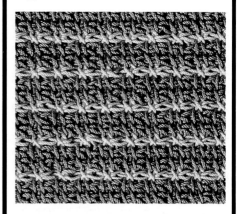

Multiple of 2 sts + 2.

**Special Abbreviation**

**Cross 2** = miss next st, 1Tss into next st, 1Tss into missed st.

**Note:** The crossed stitches appear 1 row below the row on which the cross 2 is worked.

**1st row:** Using A, as Basic Forward and Return row.

**2nd row:** Using A, with 1 loop on hook, 1Tss into each st to end. Return.

**3rd row:** Using B, as 2nd row.

**4th row:** Using A, with 1 loop on hook, *cross 2; rep from * to last st, 1Tss into last st. Return.

Rep 2nd to 4th rows.

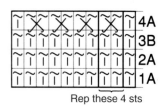

Rep these 4 sts

**Special Abbreviation**

**Sl 1 fwd** = yf, insert hook into next st without working it, yb.

**1st row:** Using A, as Basic Forward and Return row.

**2nd row:** Using B, with 1 loop on hook, *sl 1 fwd, 1Tss into next st; rep from * to end. Return, changing to A when 2 loops remain.

**3rd row:** Using A, with 1 loop on hook, *1Tss into next st, sl 1 fwd; rep from * to last 2 sts, 1Tss into each of last 2 sts. Return, changing to B when 2 loops remain.

Rep 2nd and 3rd rows.

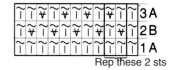

Rep these 2 sts

## Platform Stitch

Multiple of 14 sts + 7.

**1st row:** As Basic Forward and Return row.

**2nd row:** With 1 loop on hook, work 1Tss into each of next 6 sts, *work 1Tps into each of next 7 sts, work 1Tss into each of next 7 sts; rep from * to end. Return.

**3rd to 7th rows:** Rep 2nd row 5 times more.

**8th row:** With 1 loop on hook, work 1Tps into each of next 6 sts, *work 1Tss into each of next 7 sts, work 1Tps into each of next 7 sts; rep from * to end. Return.

**9th to 13th rows:** Rep 8th row 5 times more.

Rep 2nd to 13th rows.

## Roulette

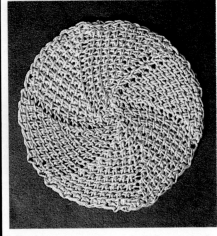

Using A make 12ch.

**1st row:** With 1 loop on hook, work 1Tss into next ch. Return.

**2nd row:** With 1 loop on hook, work 1Tss into next st, then work 1Tss into next ch (3 loops on hook). Return.

**3rd row:** With 1 loop on hook, work 1Tss into each of next 2 sts, then work 1Tss into next ch (4 loops on hook). Return.

Continue working in this manner until all 12ch have been picked up (12 loops on hook). Return, changing colour when 2 loops remain.

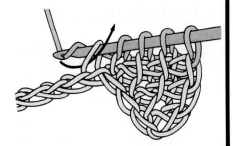

Using B, rep these 11 rows but working into sts of previous colour instead of ch. Continue working segments in alternate colours until **6** segments in all have been worked. Fasten off last st.

Join seam.

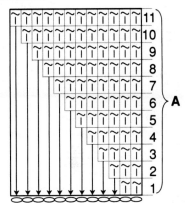

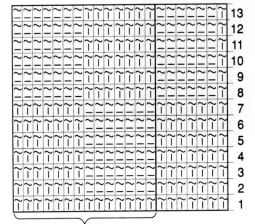

Rep these 14 sts

## Cutter Edging II

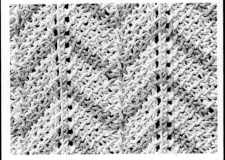

Work as Cutter Edging I **but** working 3 rows in A and 1 row in B throughout **or** using random colours as illustrated below.

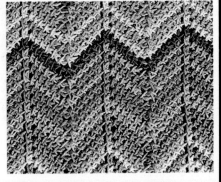

## Cutter Edging I

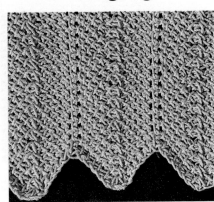

Multiple of 14 sts + 1.

**1st row:** As Basic Forward and Return row.

**2nd row:** With 1 loop on hook, *inc 1Tss, work 1Tss into each of next 4 sts, Tss3tog, work 1Tss into each of next 5 sts, inc 1Tss; rep from * to end. Return.

Rep 2nd row.

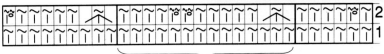

Rep these 14 sts

# Tunisian Crochet

## Opera Pattern I

Multiple of 2 sts + 3.

**Special Abbreviation**

**Long Ttr** (worked on Forward rows) = loosely work 1 Ttr into next st 2 rows below.

**1st row:** As Basic Forward and Return row.

**2nd row:** With 1 loop on hook, work 1Tss into each st to end. Return.

**3rd row:** With 1 loop on hook, *1 long Ttr, 1Tss into next st; rep from * to end. Return.

**4th row:** With 1 loop on hook, *1Tss into next st, 1 long Ttr; rep from * to last 2 sts, 1Tss into each of last 2 sts. Return.

Rep 3rd and 4th rows.

Rep these 2 sts

## Opera Pattern II

Work as Opera Pattern I **but** working 1 row each in colours A and B throughout.

## Strand Pattern

Multiple of 8 sts + 4.

**1st row:** As Basic Forward and Return row.

**2nd row:** With 1 loop on hook, work 1Tss into each of next 3 sts, *work 1Tps into each of next 4 sts, work 1Tss into each next 4 sts; rep from * to end. Return.

Rep 2nd row.

## Duel Band

Multiple of 10 sts + 11.

**1st row:** As Basic Forward and Return row.

**2nd row:** With 1 loop on hook, 1Tps into next st, 1Tss into each of next 2 sts, *1TwTss into next st, 1Tss into next st, 1TwTss into next st, 1Tps into next st, [1Tss into next st, 1Tps into next st] twice, 1Tss into each of next 2 sts; rep from * to last 7 sts, 1TwTss into next st, 1Tss into next st, 1TwTss into next st, [1Tps into next st, 1Tss into next st] twice. Return.

**3rd row:** With 1 loop on hook, 1Tss into next st, 1Tps into next st, 1Tss into next st, *[1TwTss into next st, 1Tss into next st] twice, [1Tps into next st, 1Tss into next st] 3 times; rep from * to last 7 sts, [1TwTss into next st, 1Tss into next st] twice, 1Tps into next st, 1Tss into next st, 1Tps into last st. Return.

Rep 2nd and 3rd rows.

Rep these 10 sts

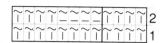

Rep these 8 sts

## Kiln Stitch I

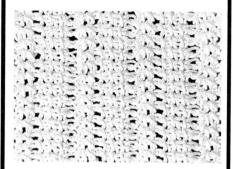

Multiple of 6 sts + 3.

**Special Abbreviations**

**Basic Group 3** = first part worked as Basic Forward row, on return row work 1ch, yo, draw hook through 4 loops, 1ch.

**Group 3** = on Forward row insert hook under next ch, yo, draw loop through, insert hook into loop over the group 3 on previous row, yo, draw loop through, insert hook under next ch, yo, draw loop through. On return row work 1ch, yo, draw hook through 4 loops, 1ch.

**1st row:** As Basic Forward row. Return as follows: Yo, draw hook through 1 loop, [yo, draw hook through 2 loops] twice, *basic group 3, [yo, draw through 2 loops] 3 times; rep from * to end.

**2nd row:** With 1 loop on hook, work 1Tss into each of next 2 sts, *group 3, work 1Tss into each of next 3 sts; rep from * to end. Return as follows: Yo, draw hook through 1 loop, [yo, draw hook through 2 loops] twice, *group 3, [yo, draw through 2 loops] 3 times; rep from * to end.

Rep 2nd row.

Rep these 6 sts

## Kiln Stitch II

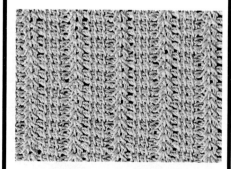

Work as given for Kiln Stitch I **but** working 1 row in A and 1 row in B throughout.

Stitch Variations, Abbreviations and Symbols on pages 161 to 165

## Tunisian Pearls I

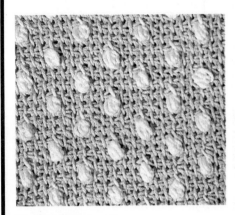

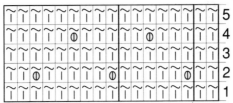

Rep these 6 sts

**Multiple of 6 sts + 5.**

### Special Abbreviation

 **MB (Make Bobble)** = using colour B [yo, insert hook into next st, yo and draw loop through] 3 times into same st, yo and draw through 6 loops, see Note.

**Note:** Pattern is worked in colour A on every row. Colour B is used for bobbles only and is carried **loosely** across back of work on 2nd and 4th rows. Cut and rejoin colour B at beginning of each bobble row.

**1st row:** As Basic Forward and Return row.

**2nd row:** With 1 loop on hook, work 1Tss into next st, MB into next st, *1Tss into each of next 5 sts, MB into next st; rep from * to last 2 sts, Tss into each of last 2 sts. Return using A only.

**3rd row:** With 1 loop on hook, 1Tss into each st to end. Return.

**4th row:** With 1 loop on hook, 1Tss into each of next 4 sts, *MB into next st, 1Tss into each of next 5 sts; rep from * to end. Return using A only.

**5th row:** As 3rd row.

Rep 2nd to 5th rows.

## Tunisian Pearls II

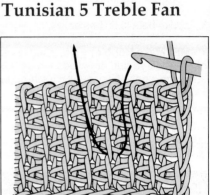

Work as given for Tunisian Pearls I, working 1 row of bobbles each in B, C and D.

## Tunisian 5 Treble Fan

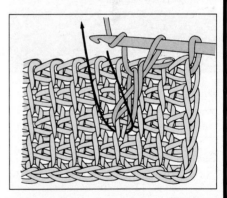

1. Miss two stitches. Loosely work a Tunisian treble into the next stitch three rows below (inserting hook as indicated).

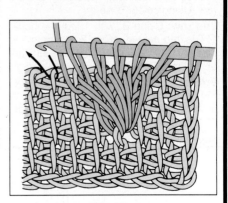

2. Loosely work four more Tunisian trebles into the same stitch.

3. Miss two stitches and continue working.

## Bushel Pattern

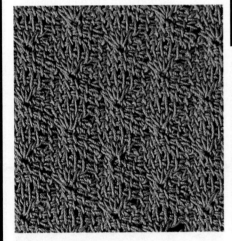

**Multiple of 10 sts + 7.**

### Special Abbreviation

**5Ttr fan** = miss next 2 sts, work 5 **loose** Ttr round stem of next st 3 rows below, miss next 2 sts (see diagrams).

**1st row:** As Basic Forward and Return row.

**2nd row:** With 1 loop on hook, 1Tss into each st to end. Return.

**3rd and 4th rows:** Rep 2nd row twice.

**5th row:** With 1 loop on hook, work 5Ttr fan, *1Tss into each of next 5 sts, work 5Ttr fan; rep from * to last st, 1Tss into last st. Return.

**6th and 7th rows:** Rep 2nd row twice.

**8th row:** With 1 loop on hook, *1Tss into each of next 5 sts, work 5Ttr fan; rep from * to last 6 sts, 1Tss into each of last 6 sts. Return.

Rep 3rd to 8th rows.

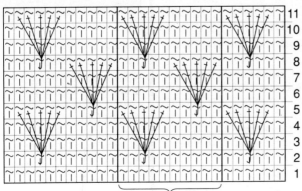

Rep these 10 sts

= 5Ttr fan

# Tunisian Crochet

## Studio Pattern

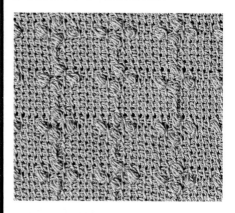

Multiple of 8 sts + 7.

### Special Abbreviations

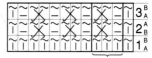 **Long Ttr** (worked on Forward rows) = loosely work 1Ttr into vertical loop above bobble 3 rows below.

**MB (Make Bobble)** = [yo, insert hook into next st, yo and draw loop through] 3 times into same st, yo, draw yarn through 6 loops.

**1st row:** As Basic Forward and Return row.

**2nd row:** With 1 loop on hook, work 1Tss into each of next 2 sts, *MB into next st, 1Tss into each of next 7 sts; rep from * to last 4 sts, MB, 1Tss into each of last 3 sts. Return.

**3rd row:** With 1 loop on hook, *MB into next st, 1Tss into each of next 3 sts; rep from * to last 2 sts, MB, 1Tss into last st. Return.

**4th row:** As 2nd row.

**5th row:** With 1 loop on hook work 1Tss into each st to end. Return.

**6th row:** As 5th row.

**7th row:** With 1 loop on hook, work 1Tss into each of next 2 sts, *work long Ttr, 1Tss into each of next 7 sts; rep from * to last 4 sts, work long Ttr, 1Tss into each of last 3 sts. Return.

Rep 2nd to 7th rows.

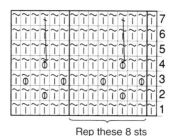

Rep these 8 sts

## Twist Stitch

Multiple of 3 sts + 3.

**Note:** Colour is changed after each **Forward** row. Work first ch of each Return row in new colour.

### Special Abbreviation

**Cross 2** = miss next st, 1Tss into next st, 1Tss into missed st.

Make chain in colour A.

**1st row:** Using colour A as Basic Forward row. Using colour B Return.

**2nd row:** Using B, with 1 loop on hook, *1Tps into next st, cross 2; rep from * to last 2 sts, 1Tps into next st, 1Tss into last st. Using A Return.

**3rd row:** Using A, with 1 loop on hook, *1Tps into next st, cross 2; rep from * to last 2 sts, 1Tps into next st, 1Tss into last st. Using B Return.

Rep 2nd and 3rd rows.

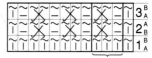

Rep these 2 sts

## Cone Pattern

Multiple of 2 sts + 3.

### Special Abbreviation

**MB (Make Bobble)** = work [yo, insert hook into next st, yo and draw loop through] 3 times into same st, yo, draw yarn through 6 loops.

**1st row:** As Basic Forward and Return row.

**2nd row:** With 1 loop on hook, work 1Tss into next st, *MB into next st, 1Tss into next st; rep from * to last st, 1Tss into last st. Return.

**3rd row:** With 1 loop on hook, *MB into next st, 1Tss into next st; rep from * to end. Return.

Rep 2nd and 3rd rows.

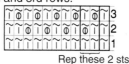

Rep these 2 sts

## Spectrum Stitch

Multiple of 3 sts + 2.

### Special Abbreviation

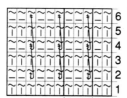 **Long Tdtr** (worked on Forward rows) = loosely work 1 Tdtr into vertical loop of next st 2 rows below.

**1st row:** As Basic Forward and Return row.

**2nd row:** With 1 loop on hook, 1Tps into next st, *1Ttr into next st, 1Tps into each of next 2 sts; rep from * to end. Return.

**3rd row:** With 1 loop on hook, work 1Tss into each st to end. Return.

**4th row:** With 1 loop on hook, 1Tps into next st, *work 1 long Tdtr, 1Tps into each of next 2 sts; rep from * to end. Return.

Rep 3rd and 4th rows.

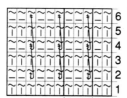

Rep these 3 sts

## Mill Pattern

Multiple of 2 sts + 1.

**1st row:** As Basic Forward and Return row.

**2nd row:** With 1 loop on hook, *1Ttr into next st, 1Tps into next st; rep from * to end. Return.

**3rd row:** With 1 loop on hook, *work 1Tps into next st, 1Ttr into next st; rep from * to end. Return.

Rep 2nd and 3rd rows.

Rep these 2 sts

Stitch Variations, Abbreviations and symbols on pages 161 to 165

## Tunisian Windows

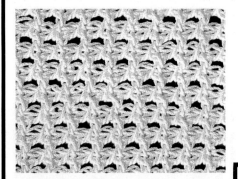

Multiple of 2 sts + 3.

**1st row:** As Basic Forward and Return row.

**2nd row:** With 1 loop on hook, *Tss2tog, yo; rep from * to last 2 sts, 1Tss into each of last 2 sts. Return.

**3rd row:** With 1 loop on hook, *1Tss into next vertical loop, 1Tss under ch loop of next st; rep from * to last 2 sts, 1Tss into each of last 2 sts. Return.

Rep 2nd and 3rd rows.

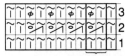

Rep these 2 sts

## Candle Pattern

Multiple of 7 sts + 7.

**Special Abbreviation**

**T3st cable** = miss next 2 sts, work 1Tks into 3rd st, work 1Tks into 2nd st, work 1Tks into first st.

**1st row:** As Basic Forward and Return row.

**2nd row:** With 1 loop on hook 1Tps into next st, *1Tks into each of next 3 sts, 1Tps into each of next 4 sts; rep from * to last 5 sts, 1Tks into each of next 3 sts, 1Tps into next st, 1Tss into last st. Return.

**3rd and 4th rows:** Rep 2nd row twice.

**5th row:** With 1 loop on hook 1Tps into next st, *T3st cable, 1Tps into each of next 4 sts; rep from * to last 5 sts, T3st cable, 1Tps into next st, 1Tss into last st. Return.

**6th to 11th rows:** Rep 2nd row 6 times.

Rep 5th to 11th rows.

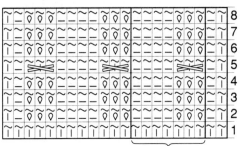

Rep these 7 sts

**Diagram only:** Rep 2nd to 8th rows.

## Tunisian Warp

Multiple of 11 sts + 2.

**Note:** When working Tss2tog work through diagonal loop of yo of previous row where applicable.

**1st row:** As Basic Forward and Return row.

**2nd row:** With 1 loop on hook, 1Tss into each of next 3 sts, [yo, Tss2tog] twice, *1Tss into each of next 7 sts, [yo, Tss2tog] twice; rep from * to last 5 sts, 1Tss into each of last 5 sts. Return.

**3rd row:** With 1 loop on hook, 1Tss into each of next 3 sts, 1Tss under ch loop of next st, [yo, Tss2tog] twice, *1Tss into each of next 6 sts, 1Tss under ch loop of next st, [yo, Tss2tog] twice; rep from * to last 4 sts, 1Tss into each of last 4 sts. Return.

**4th row:** With 1 loop on hook, 1Tss into each of next 4 sts, 1Tss under ch loop of next st, [yo, Tss2tog] twice, *1Tss into each of next 6 sts, 1Tss under ch loop of next st, [yo, Tss2tog] twice; rep from * to last 3 sts, 1Tss into each of last 3 sts. Return.

**5th row:** With 1 loop on hook, 1Tss into each of next 5 sts, 1Tss under ch loop of next st, [yo, Tss2tog] twice, *1Tss into each of next 6 sts, 1Tss under ch loop of next st, [yo, Tss2tog] twice; rep from * to last 2 sts, 1Tss into each of last 2 sts. Return.

**6th row:** With 1 loop on hook, *1Tss into each of next 6 sts, 1Tss under ch loop of next st, [yo, Tss2tog] twice; rep from * to last st, 1Tss into last st. Return.

**7th row:** With 1 loop on hook, 1Tss into each of next 7 sts, 1Tss under ch loop of next st, *[yo, Tss2tog] twice, 1Tss into each of next 6 sts, 1Tss under ch loop of next st; rep from * to last 4 sts, yo, Tss2tog, 1Tss into each of last 2 sts. Return.

**8th row:** With 1 loop on hook, yo, Tss2tog, 1Tss into each of next 6 sts, 1Tss under ch loop of next st, *[yo, Tss2tog] twice, 1Tss into each of next 6 sts, 1Tss under ch loop of next st; rep from * to last 3 sts, yo, Tss2tog, 1Tss into last st. Return.

**9th row:** With 1 loop on hook, 1Tss under ch loop of next st, yo, Tss2tog, 1Tss into each of next 6 sts, 1Tss under ch loop of next st, *[yo, Tss2tog] twice, 1Tss into each of next 6 sts, 1Tss under ch loop of next st; rep from * to last 2 sts, 1Tss into each of last 2 sts. Return.

**10th row:** With 1 loop on hook, [yo, Tss2tog] twice, *1Tss into each of next 6 sts, 1Tss under ch loop of next st, [yo, Tss2tog] twice; rep from * to last 8 sts, 1Tss into each of last 8 sts. Return.

**11th row:** With 1 loop on hook, *1Tss under ch loop of next st, [yo, Tss2tog] twice, 1Tss into each of next 6 sts; rep from * to last st, 1Tss into last st. Return.

**12th row:** With 1 loop on hook, 1Tss into next st, *1Tss under ch loop of next st, [yo, Tss2tog] twice, 1Tss into each of next 6 sts; rep from * to end. Return.

**13th row:** With 1 loop on hook, 1Tss into each of next 2 sts, 1Tss under ch loop of next st, [yo, Tss2tog] twice, *1Tss into each of next 6 sts, 1Tss under ch loop of next st, [yo, Tss2tog] twice; rep from * to last 5 sts, 1Tss into each of last 5 sts. Return.

Rep 3rd to 13th rows.

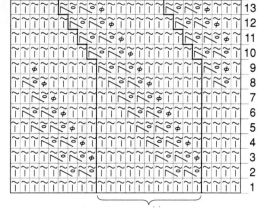

Rep these 11 sts

# Tunisian Crochet

## Bell Pattern

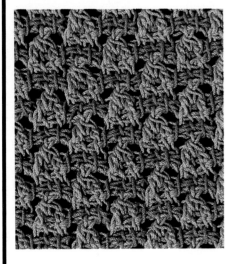

Multiple of 6 sts + 7.

### Special Abbreviation

**3 st triangle** = on Forward row work 1Ttr into previous st 2 rows below, work 1Tss into next st, work 1Ttr into next st 2 rows below, yo, draw through 3 loops. Return as follows: Yo, draw through 2 loops.

**1st row:** Using A, as Basic Forward and Return row.

**2nd row:** Using B, with 1 loop on hook, work 1Tss into next st, *miss 1 st, work 1Tss into next st, miss 1 st, work 1Tss into each of next 3 sts; rep from * to last 5 sts, miss next st, work 1Tss into next st, miss next st, work 1Tss into each of last 2 sts. Return as follows: Yo, draw hook through 1 loop, yo, draw hook through 2 loops, *1ch, yo, draw hook through 2 loops, 1ch, [yo, draw hook through 2 loops] 3 times; rep from * until 4 loops remain on hook, 1ch, yo, draw hook through 2 loops, 1ch, [yo, draw hook through 2 loops] twice.

**3rd row:** Using A, with 1 loop on hook, work 1Tss into next st, miss next sp, work 3 st triangle, miss next sp,* work 1Tss into each of next 3 sts, miss next sp, work 3 st triangle, miss next sp; rep from * to last 2 sts, work 1Tss into each of last 2 sts. Return as follows: Yo, draw hook through 1 loop, yo, draw hook through 2 loops, *1ch, yo, draw hook through 2 loops, 1ch, [yo, draw hook through 2 loops] 3 times; rep from * until 4 loops remain on hook, 1ch, yo, draw hook through 2 loops, 1ch, [yo, draw hook through 2 loops] twice.

**4th row:** Using B, with 1 loop on hook, *miss next st, 1Tss under ch loop of next st, 1Tss into next st, 1Tss under ch loop of next st, miss 1 st, 1Tss into next st; rep from * to end. Return as follows: Yo, draw hook through 1 loop, *1ch, [yo, draw hook through 2 loops] 3 times, 1ch, yo, draw hook through 2 loops; rep from * to end.

**5th row:** Using A, with 1 loop on hook, work 1Ttr into next vertical loop 2 rows below, yo, draw hook through 2 loops, miss next sp, 1Tss into each of next 3 sts, miss next sp, *work 3 st triangle, miss next sp, 1Tss into each of next 3 sts, miss next sp; rep from * to last st, work 1Ttr into previous st 2 rows below, 1Tss into last st, yo and through 2 loops. Return as follows: Yo, draw hook through 1 loop, *1ch, [yo, draw hook through 2 loops] 3 times, 1ch, yo, draw hook through 2 loops; rep from * to end.

**6th row:** Using B, with 1 loop on hook, *work 1Tss under ch loop of next st, miss next st, 1Tss into next st, miss next st, 1Tss under ch loop of next st, 1Tss into next st; rep from * to end. Return as follows: Yo, draw hook through 1 loop, yo, draw hook through 2 loops, *1ch, yo, draw hook through 2 loops, 1ch, [yo, draw hook through 2 loops] 3 times; rep from * until 4 loops remain on hook, 1ch, yo, draw hook through 2 loops, 1ch, [yo, draw hook through 2 loops] twice.

Rep 3rd to 6th rows always working Ttr into sts 2 rows below.

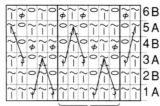

Rep these 6 sts

 = On Forward rows miss 1 st or space, on Return rows work 1ch.

 = With 1 loop on hook on Forward row work 1Tss and 1Ttr of 3 st triangle, return as normal.

= On Forward row work 1Ttr of 3 st triangle and 1Tss, Return as normal.

## Tunisian Weave

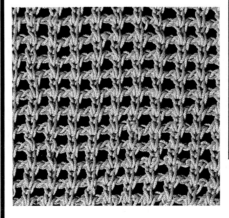

Multiple of 2 sts + 1.

**1st row:** As Basic Forward and Return row.

**2nd row:** With 1 loop on hook, 2ch, *miss next st, yo, 1Tks into next st, 2ch; rep from * to end. Return.

**3rd row:** With 1 loop on hook, 2ch, *miss next sp, yo, 1Tks into upper of 2ch of previous Forward row, 2ch; rep from * to end. Return.

Rep 3rd row.

## Spray Pattern

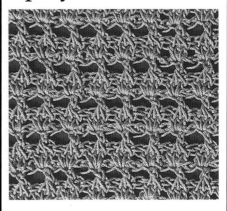

Multiple of 3 sts + 2.

### Special Abbreviations

 **Fan** = work 3Ttr into centre of upper of 2ch in previous Forward row.

**Lace 3tog** = insert hook through next 3 vertical loops, yo, draw loop through, 2ch (on Return row 1ch, yo, draw hook through 2 loops, 1ch).

**Note:** Only count sts after 3rd row.

**1st row:** As Basic Forward and Return row.

**2nd row:** With 1 loop on hook, 2ch, *Lace 3tog; rep from * to last st, 1Tss into last st, 2ch. Return as follows: Yo, draw hook through 1 loop, 1ch, *yo, draw hook through 2 loops, 2ch; rep from * until 3 loops remain on hook, yo draw hook through 2 loops, 1ch, yo, draw hook through 2 loops.

**3rd row:** With 1 loop on hook, 2ch, *work 1 Fan; rep from * to last st, 1Ttr into upper ch of last st. Return.

Rep 2nd and 3rd rows.

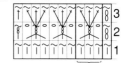

Rep these 3 sts

= With 1 loop on hook at beginning of Forward row work 2ch. 1 loop to be worked off on Return row.

= Into last st of Forward row work 1Tss, 2ch. On Return row work yo and through 1 loop.

Rep these 2 sts

= With 1 loop on hook at beginning of Forward row work 2ch.

= Miss next st, yo on Forward row, (1 loop to be worked off on Return row).

= 1Tks, 2ch on Forward row, (1 loop to be worked off on Return row). **Note:** On 3rd and every following Forward row work 1Tks into the upper of 2ch of previous Forward row.

Stitch Variations, Abbreviations and symbols on pages 161 to 165

# Index